# The Subjective Eye

# Princeton Theological Monograph Series

K. C. Hanson, Series Editor

*Recent volumes in the series*

Stephen Finlan and Vladimir Kharlamov, editors
*Theosis: Deification in Christian Theology*

David Ackerman
*Lo, I Tell You a Mystery:*
*Cross, Resurrection, and Paraenesis in the Rhetoric of 1 Corinthians*

John A. Vissers
*The Neo-Orthodox Theology of W. W. Bryden*

Sam Hamstra, editor
*The Reformed Pastor:*
*Lectures on Pastoral Theology by John Williamson Nevin*

Byron C. Bangert
*Consenting to God and Nature:*
*Toward a Theocentric, Naturalistic, Theological Ethics*

Caryn Riswold
*Coram Deo: Human Life in the Vision of God*

Paul O. Ingram, editor
*Constructing a Relational Cosmology*

Mark A. Ellis, editor and translator
*The Arminian Confession of 1621*

Michael G. Cartwright
*Practices, Politics, and Performance:*
*Toward a Communal Hermeneutic for Christian Ethics*

# *Across the Miles*

Words by Victoria Sirota (20 Sept. 2003)
Tune: *Miles* by Robert Sirota (28 Sept. 2003)

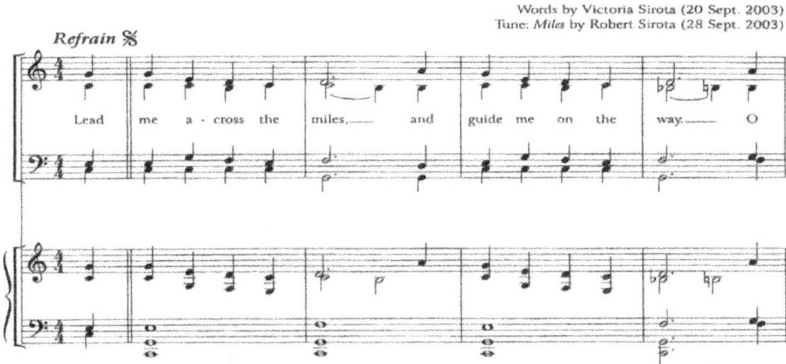


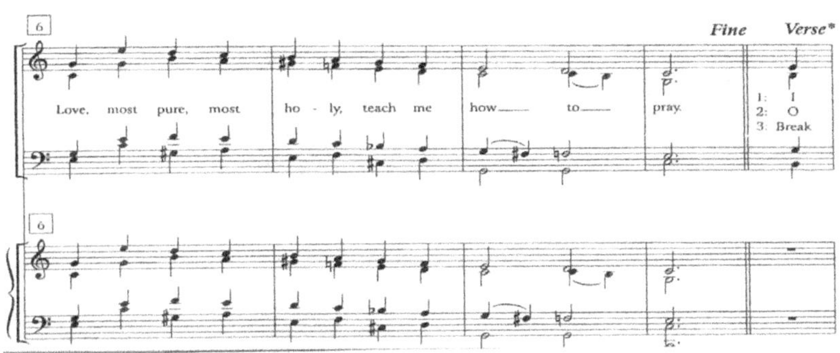


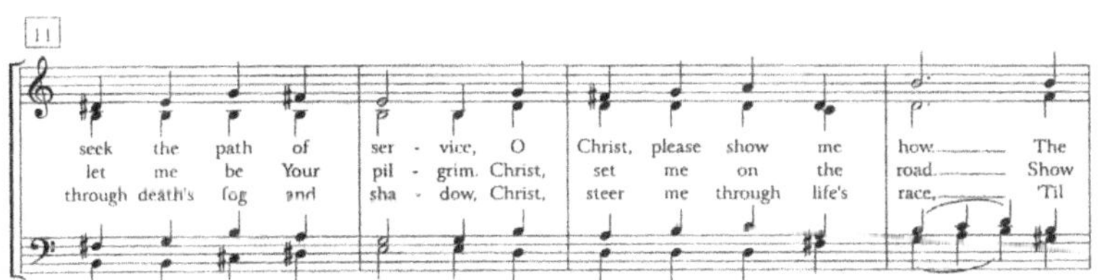


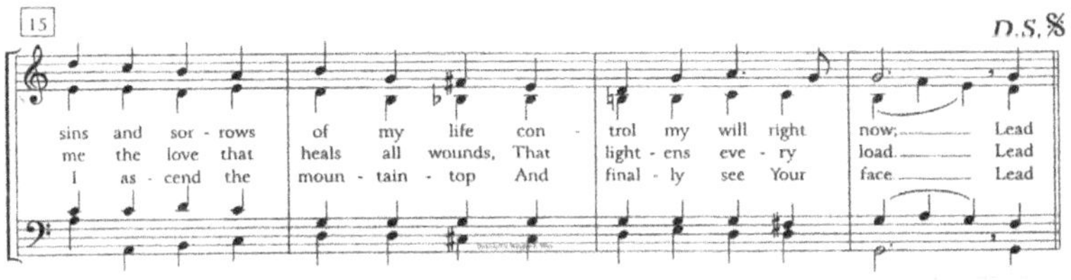


* Verses may be *a capella* or accompanied (duplicating vocal lines), as desired.



*Dedicated to Margaret R. Miles*

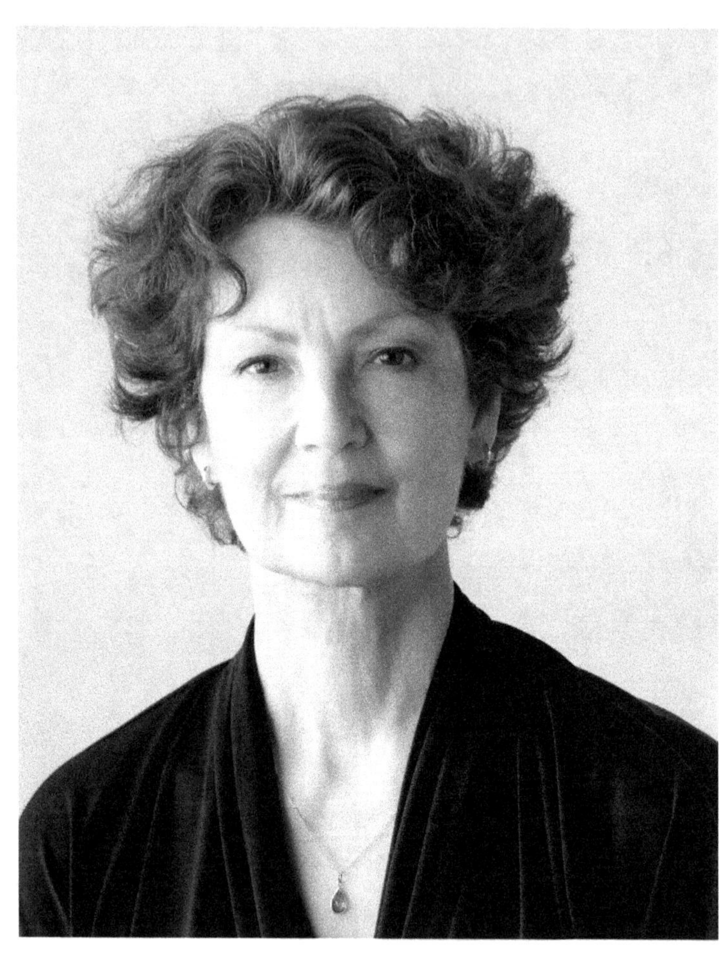

Photograph by Katie Parquet; used by permission.

# The Subjective Eye

## *Essays in Culture, Religion, and Gender in Honor of Margaret R. Miles*

edited by
Richard Valantasis

in collaboration with
Deborah J. Haynes
James D. Smith III
Janet F. Carlson

Pickwick *Publications*
An imprint of *Wipf and Stock Publishers*
199 West 8th Avenue • Eugene OR 97401

THE SUBJECTIVE EYE
Essays in Culture, Religion, and Gender in Honor of Margaret R. Miles
Princeton Theological Monograph Series 59



ISBN: 1-59752-519-7

*Cataloging-in-Publication data:*

---

The subjective eye : essays in culture, religion, and gender in honor of Margaret R. Miles / edited by Richard Valantasis, in collaboration with Deborah J. Haynes, James D. Smith III, and Janet F. Carlson.

Eugene, Ore.: Pickwick Publications, 2006
Princeton Theological Monograph Series 59

xxx + 356 p.; 23 cm.

ISBN 1-59752-519-7

1. Church history—primitive and early church, 30-600. 2. Mediterranean region—Church history. 3. Christian art and symbolism. 4. Christian martyrs. 5. Women—religious aspects. 6. Women and religion. 7. Aesthetics. I. Miles, Margaret R. (Margaret Ruth), 1937. II. Valantasis, Richard. III. Haynes, Deborah J. IV. Smith, James D. III. V. Carlson, Janet. VI. Title. VII. Series.

BV150 S78 2006

---

Manufactured in the U.S.A.

Dedicated to
Margaret R. Miles

*Make us truly alive.*
—Serapion of Thmuis

## Studebat

*for Margaret*

Love snipped the knots that tied your tongue,
the tangled and congested vines
and muddled weedy garden,
cracked parapets, split and spoilt fruit.

Yours is no starving mind to lick
shadows. For the new pupil
of Torah, rabbis dab the first
scroll with honey. Your finger, too,
finds words sweet: *accipe*
*comedite.* Beauty beckons
at the gates, *Come love, come run.*

All from whom you caught
delight, you praise– a fiery assembly.
Refined by friendship you again
enlarge your too-small house,
run naked to follow
the naked one, carrying along
as many as you can,  so ordered
by delight, with life, mettle,
vigor from such a past,

boiling with life–until rest
with the settled dove an interval;
caroling *id quod est,* the discipline
of joy, the rushing lovely
bright brief lifefulness
of creatures. Yes. All.
—Jennifer M. Phillips

# Contents

## Interlude



## Religion and Culture



## Interlude

## Religion and Gender



## Interlude



## Religion and the Visual Arts

# Contributors

Douglas G. Adams
*Professor of Christianity and the Arts*
Pacific School of Religion and the Graduate Theological Union

Kari Elisabeth Børresen
*Senior Professor, Department of Church History*
University of Oslo

Stephen B. Boyd
*J. Allen Easley Professor of Religion*
Wake Forest University

Frank Burch Brown
*Frederick Doyle Kershner Professor of Religion and the Arts*
Christian Theological Seminary

Paula M. Cooey
*Harmon Professor of Religion*
Macalester College

Jane Daggett Dillenberger
*Professor Emerita*
Graduate Theological Union

Georgia Frank
*Associate Professor of Philosophy and Religion*
Colgate University

Deborah J. Haynes
*Professor of Art and Art History*
University of Colorado at Boulder

Arthur G. Holder
*Dean and Vice President for Academic Affairs; Professor of Christian Spirituality*
Graduate Theological Union

Robin M. Jensen
*Luce Chancellor's Professor of the History of Art and Worship*
Vanderbilt Divinity School

Kimerer L. LaMothe
*Formerly Fortieth-Anniversary Fellow*
Center for the Study of World Religions, Harvard Divinity School
Currently an independent scholar

Michelle M. Lelwica
*Assistant Professor in Religion and Chair of Women's Studies*
Concordia College

Peter Manchester
*Associate Professor of Philosophy*
Stony Brook University

Julie B. Miller
*Assistant Professor, Department of Religious Studies*
University of the Incarnate Word

Jennifer M. Phillips
*Vicar, St. Augustine's Church*
Kingston, Rhode Island

Anthony B. Pinn
*Agnes Cullen Arnold Professor of Humanities and Professor of Religious Studies*
Rice University

S. Brent Plate
*Assistant Professor of Religion and the Visual Arts*
Texas Christian University

Lynn Randolph
*Artist*

Robert Sirota
*President*
Manhattan School of Music

Victoria Sirota
*Priest and musician*

James D. Smith III
*Associate Professor of Church History,* Bethel Seminary
*Lecturer in Theology and Religious Studies,* University of San Diego
*Associate Pastor,* College Avenue Baptist Church

Martha Ellen Stortz
*Professor of Historical Theology and Ethics*
Pacific Lutheran Theological Seminary and the Graduate Theological Union

Gail Corrington Streete
*Associate Professor of Religious Studies*
Rhodes College

Owen C. Thomas
*Frances Lathrop Fiske Professor Emeritus of Systematic Theology*
Episcopal Divinity School

Richard Valantasis
*Professor of Ascetical Theology and Christian Practice*
Candler School of Theology, Emory University

Kimberly Vrudny
*Assistant Professor of Systematic Theology*
University of St. Thomas

# Abbreviations

| | |
|---|---|
| ACW | Ancient Christian Writers |
| *ATR* | *Anglican Theological Review* |
| *BMGS* | *Byzantine and Modern Greek Studies* |
| CCSL | Corpus Christianorum: Series latina. Turnhout: Brepols, 1953– |
| *CH* | *Church History* |
| *CisSt* | *Cistercian Studies* (journal) |
| CisSt | Cistercian Studies (series) |
| *ClAnt* | *Classical Antiquity* |
| ET | English translation |
| FC | Fathers of the Church |
| GCS | Die griechische christliche Schriftsteller der ersten Jahrhunderte |
| *HDB* | *Harvard Divinity Bulletin* |
| HDS | Harvard Divinity School |
| *HTR* | *Harvard Theological Review* |
| *JAAR* | *Journal of American Academy of Religion* |
| *JAC* | *Jahrbuch für Antike und Christentum* |
| *JECS* | *Journal of Early Christian Studies* |
| *JFSR* | *Journal of Feminist Studies in Religion* |
| *JR* | *Journal of Religion* |
| *JTS* | *Journal of Theological Studies* |
| *JTTRS* | *Journal for Teaching Theology and Religious Studies* |
| LCL | Loeb Classical Library |
| NPNF | Nicene and Post-Nicene Fathers |
| PG | Patrologia graeca |
| *PGL* | *Patristic Greek Lexicon*. Edited by G. W. H. Lampe. Oxford: Clarendon, 1961 |
| PO | Patrologia orientalis |
| PTS | Patristische Texte und Studien |
| SC | Sources chrétiennes. Paris: Cerf, 1942– |
| SJLA | Studies in Judaism in Late Antiquity |
| *StPatr* | *Studia Patristica* |
| *STR* | *Sewanee Theological Review* |
| *ThEd* | *Theological Education* |
| *ThTo* | *Theology Today* |
| TT | Texts and Translations |

| | |
|---|---|
| *USQR* | *Union Seminary Quarterly Review* |
| *VC* | *Vigiliae christianae* |

# Foreword

## *The Eye of the Beholder*

Margaret R. Miles

SCHOLARS are only as good as the conversations in which they participate. The traditional (gendered) picture of scholarship in which a solitary scholar sits alone at his desk, constructing brilliant ideas and emerging only to drop these ideas on the heads of grateful audiences is inadequate and misleading. Books can be good conversation partners, of course, but they do not encourage the give and take, the back and forth, by which ideas are refined and strengthened. The essays in this volume represent many stimulating conversations among colleagues—teachers and students (who were, in these conversations, always *both* teachers and learners)—at Harvard Divinity School and the Graduate Theological Union, Berkeley. The quality and diversity of their conversations is evident in the essays.

I am profoundly grateful for the immense privilege of conversing with the authors throughout my professional life in classrooms, halls, my office, and conferences—sometimes even on warm sand. This rich experience has convinced me that the delight in learning by which the best scholarship is motivated is contagious; one catches it from warm bodies in a room. In such encounters we begin with the *speculum in aenigmate* of Augustine's favorite scripture verse (1 Corinthians 13:12) and sometimes, when there is skillful articulation and generous listening, just barely glimpse the promised *facie ad faciem.*

Plotinus taught that no one can adequately understand the universe who has not been startled and instructed by its beauty. Artworks—poems, music, paintings, and architecture—tutor the eye in perceiving the beauty that reveals the intimate interconnectedness of the universe. To see accurately is to see *as beautiful*; "beauty is reality" (*Ennead* I.6.6). As one who seeks to train and exercise the eye that sees the great beauty (Augustine's "beauty so old and so new"; *Confessions* 10.27) refracted in the beauties of the natural world and in the artworks people make, I am especially delighted by the inclusion in this volume of Jennifer Phillips' richly evocative poems and Victoria and Robert Sirota's wonderful hymn. The poems feature longing; Augustine taught that longing stretches the heart, making it deep, capacious, and generous. The hymn repeats the refrain, "Teach me how to pray." Surely a lifetime could be spent in learning how to pray, from the me-me-me prayers of childhood and youth to learning to "get over oneself" in prayer. These themes form and inform my life and scholarship.

The essays in this volume are divided into four sections that match shared research interests on which the authors and I worked together: historical theology and religion and culture, gender, and the visual arts. In the last thirty years—the period of my academic engagement—in each of these fields new methods have produced startling new insights. As our authors exemplify, old texts, both literary and visual, are being read with new eyes and in new ways. They have both learned from and contributed to these new readings. They also propose directions for future scholarship. In what follows, I will comment on the proposals advanced in each section.

## Historical Theology

Two essays in this section discuss Plotinus, the third-century Platonic philosopher Augustine found "good to think with" (Arthur Holder). Plotinus is one of the most influential, but misunderstood and misrepresented, philosophers of the Western philosophical tradition; thus, a more accurate grasp of concepts central to his philosophy promises to revise some fundamental assumptions. Frank Burch Brown addresses one of Plotinus's most influential silences, namely a failure to specify connections between sensible and intelligible beauty. Plotinus's strong distinction between sensible and intelligible worlds, drawn for the purpose of inciting his students to pursuit of intelligible realities, has led modern readers to accuse him of dualism. I agree with Burch Brown that more emphatic articulation of the fundamental consanguinity of intelligible and sensible could have prevented these accusations. Nevertheless, I suspect that Plotinus thought that his description of the sensible world as a perfect reflection and imitation of the intelligible world *did* articulate that connection (*Ennead* 2.9.17).

It is exceedingly difficult for modern readers to catch the nuances of words like "reflection" and "imitation." To make matters worse, translations often reflect the translator's assumptions about an historical author rather than the actual sense of the passage. For example, Plotinus's best modern translator, A. H. Armstrong (for Loeb) translates "only a reflection," although Plotinus has actually said that the sensible world is a *perfect* reflection of the intelligible world. The word "only" is not in the Greek. In many passages Plotinus makes it clear that sensible and intelligible worlds "oppose" one another in the sense that the thumb opposes the fingers; each requires the other. Plotinus spoke of "a unity produced from opposites" (*Ennead* 3.3.1).

Plotinus's interest lay in seeing "the one thing"—the One thing. His ladder metaphor has not served his thought well as a description of the universe, for attention to the ladder's *rungs* invites charges of hierarchical disparagement of the sensible world. But *Plotinus's* attention was on the sides or uprights that hold the whole together. In brief, Plotinus was not interested in what we call aesthetics, the study of what makes objects beautiful. Certainly objects are beautiful; beauty is a property of the world that was/is informed and supported by the "great beauty" (*mega kalos; Ennead* 1.6.9). But he wanted to incite students to develop the eye that sees the great beauty in sensible beauty. For Plotinus, beauty is, quite literally, in the eye of the beholder; it is a way of *perceiving*, not a rational judgment.

Peter Manchester's essay on Augustine's notion of time and eternity makes a similar point about the unity of opposites. For Augustine, who was heavily influenced by Plotinus, eternity and time are, in Manchester's words, "one topic, not two." Time is eternity mediated, "in reach." Like numbers, time is *both* sensible and intelligible, linking—or better—exhibiting the unity of sensible and intelligible. Why make these distinctions in the first place, if they are only to be collapsed into unity? In order to be able to grasp, not undifferentiated chaos, but *how the universe works*. Although Western educated readers tend to think of distinctions as separations, Manchester's essay demonstrates that, in Augustine's philosophy, time and eternity are one.

Misconceptions about the Platonic tradition affect interpretations of Christianity. For example, many historical theologians have ascribed to "Neoplatonism" habits of mind they considered problematic, such as "dualism" and disparagement of body and the sensible world. A closer reading of Plotinus does not authorize this stategy. Rather, it suggests that Augustine and other Christian authors shared Plotinus's *project* of articulating distinctions without implying separations. Strangely, the Platonic problem of describing the consanguinity of intelligible and sensible was not solved by the Christian doctrines of creation, Incarnation, and the resurrection of body. Like Plotinus, Christian authors wrote scornfully about the sensible world when they were intent on prompting students to grasp a reality inherent in, but also transcending, the sensible. Like Plotinus, Christian authors wrote euphorically about the beauty and goodness of the sensible world when writing in a metaphysical context. Proof texts mislead unless they are examined in the context of a particular passage's agenda.

Arthur Holder's suggestion that Christian authors like Bede often used secular philosophers as critical conversation partners offers a promising *via media* between demonstrating the influence of secular authors and assuming their rejection by Christians. Holder's proposal that "abstract" theology often has practical urgency also points to the necessity of paying more attention to the social and institutional pressures on theological construction.

Georgia Frank reads a familiar Platonic theme in fourth-century Christian authors. She demonstrates the existence of continuity between ancient admonitions to intentional self-crafting and those of patristic authors. Her research on the actual methods of production of ancient workshops illuminates textual admonitions to paint the self as if it were a work of art.

In sum, the essays in the historical theology section make several methodological proposals that can serve to refine a field that has often focused on texts rather than on examining a text as one voice in a larger cultural conversation. First, the essays model close attention to cultural practices and practical pressures. Second, careful consideration of agenda *within* texts is necessary if an historical author's inconsistent or even contradictory statements are to be understood. In short, these essays model a discipline of historical theology that combines historians' interest in cultural practices with theologians' interest in close textual readings. In short, they demonstrate the fruitfulness of responsible interdisciplinary work and its capacity for refreshing the field.

## Religion and Culture

The essays grouped under Religion and Culture problematize the role of religion in American societies. In a culture in which hedonism, consumer goods, and entertainment are considered central to the good life, Cooey's suggestion that "sustained dissent requires the willingness to put one's own self-fulfillment on the back burner," is profoundly countercultural. Her historical example of sixteenth-century Anabaptists provides a comparative context for her consideration of twenty-first-century dissent in the United States, allowing the strengths and temptations of dissent in both situations to be identified. Cooey demonstrates that responsible historical scholarship is not necessarily incompatible with presentist concerns. Indeed, historical scholarship that refuses to entertain the possibility of insight for the present may be an unaffordable luxury in our desperate world.

Kimerer LaMothe's essay on dance in relation to a feminist philosophy of religion discusses an art that has been largely excluded from religious practice in the dominantly Christian West; neither liturgy nor devotional exercises include dance. For the religion of "the Word made flesh," this is a startling omission. Following Isadora Duncan, LaMothe describes dance as a kind of "incarnating activity—a practice in which a self becomes sensible by transcending her sense of opposition to her own embodiment," a way of "seeing with her body." The ambiguous use of "seeing" to indicate understanding as well as physical vision suggests that dancing can enhance both spatial awareness and understanding of oneself as body. It is, perhaps, no coincidence that both dance and the implications of incarnation are underdeveloped within Christianity.

In media societies in which images are used primarily to sell consumer products or for entertainment, training is required to overcome the socialized eye. Images that confront, challenge, disturb settled stereotypes, and comfort must be deliberately sought. Brent Plate's essay on Goya's dog demonstrates the patience required for looking at an image long past its entertainment value, allowing oneself to be changed by committed engagement with the image. James Smith describes awakening to the conjunction of spirituality and vision during his doctoral studies at Harvard University. He identifies "passion" as the medium by which a rich spiritual life conveyed by images became accessible to him.

Martha Stortz regards metaphors and stories as a form of revelation in that they illuminate and interpret experience. Her discussion of Weil and Murdock emphasizes the discipline of imagining the real, a meditative practice that replaces instant judgments—"I like this," or "I don't like this" with the simple, "here it is." As people constrained by the limits of our constructed worlds, "unselfing," is a lifelong serious job of detecting and discarding self-interest in the interest of seeing accurately and lovingly.

Owen Thomas urges recognition of the public climate in which contemporary theological construction is practiced. He demonstrates that a new Romantic movement is presently circulating in public media culture. Romanticism influences theological values and discourse in the direction of favoring the individual, chaos, "a confrontation with the abyss," an emphasis on the interior life over public and social life, and "a sharp distinction between religion, which is disparaged, and spirituality, which is honored." These values marginalize rational thought, structure, and commitment. Thomas acknowledges the value of criticism of "the dominance of scientism, technology, industrialization and the resulting overrationalization, bureaucratization and dehumanization of human society and culture." But he urges theologians to recognize and evaluate Romanticism's assumptions, subjecting them to critical analysis.

Richard Valantasis's earlier work, *Asceticism*,[1] was an important contribution to prompting discussion of a phenomenon that has become a major feature of contemporary public life. In his essay in this volume, he distinguishes "asceticism" and "formation" in his examination of several contemporary countercultural movements. Both "define subjectivity in a particular context." Formation "constructs a subject for the dominant society or culture, while asceticism constructs a subject for an alternative or subversive society or culture." His examples, Jean Genet, the Branch Davidians, and the terrorists of September 11, 2001, exemplify the ambiguous power of asceticism by which a self is designed *over against* widely consented social norms. Asceticism is powerful, for good or ill.

Intentional self-shaping is central to a pluralistic society, but it can also produce a Branch Davidian-type tragedy. Historical Christian asceticism was monitored by a discerning community within a particular religious or philosophical tradition. Lacking governing norms for discernment, contemporary ascetics are often subject to the whims of a psychotic leader, literal interpretations of incendiary passages of scripture, or individual efforts to deal with psychic pain. Valantasis's essay demonstrates that it is impossible for interpreters to identify the meaning of asceticism simply by observing its practices.

The essays in this section demonstrate the fruitfulness of exploring religious practices as cultural products. The lens of more than one academic discipline is usually necessary if the complex relationships that constitute religion *as* culture are to be recognized. Although it is difficult to indicate the conjunction of these relationships without appearing to define "religion" and "culture" as distinct entities, the essays included here show that a distinction, and thus a "relationship" between religion and culture, is ultimately specious. Religion *is* culture.

## Religion and Gender

At present, inclusive language and ordination of women are in place in many Jewish and Christian congregations, giving way to subtler questions and problems. Börresen suggests that women can make use of sexist religious traditions by identifying usable suggestions within those traditions. As Vrudny shows in her essay in this volume, this is a time-honored strategy for women desperate for resources that enable them to survive horrendous loss and grief. However, Börresen is more hopeful than I am that detachable conclusions can be identified that are untouched by the assumptions within which they are embedded. For example, Lady Julian of Norwich uses images of Jesus as

[1] Vincent L. Wimbush and Richard Valantasis, editors, *Asceticism* (New York: Oxford University Press, 1995).

loving mother, but her point is the contrast between earthly mothers who bear children for nothing but pain and death, and Jesus, who bears us for eternal life.

Boyd identifies advocacy for gender complementarity as the latest form of sexism. Both liberals and conservatives, he says, suffer from a paralysis, or inability to move past their settled convictions to gender justice. Boyd suggests that nothing short of mutual vulnerability and transformation will enable heterosexual women and men, as well as gay, lesbian, bisexual and transgendered people to work together to overcome the exclusion and potential and actual violence promoted by commitment to gender complementarity. This solution will, of course, require large amounts of generosity, both from women and GLBT people who are harmed and angered by dominant gender practices and by those who are privileged by those practices and will not easily volunteer to lose that privilege. There is, however, little alternative but to assume the existence of the necessary generosity and then find ways to call it forth.

Michelle Lelwica, the first graduate of the doctoral concentration in Religion, Gender, and Culture in the Harvard University Committee on the Study of Religion, demonstrates the conjunction of theoretical analysis and social research the program was designed to expedite. Lelwica contributes to understanding eating disorders among (primarily) girls and women by arguing that a single (inevitably reductive) interpretation of wide range of behaviors and motivations is inadequate. Productive as well as destructive motivations must be considered. Perhaps, Lelwica writes, "women's desire for thinness reflects not just a desire to diminish their bodies, but also a longing to inhabit these bodies, to live fully and deeply in the home of their own flesh." "Thinness," expressed as desire for control of one's body and life, may be a symbolic substitute for a longing for effective provisions for the development of an interior life, subjectivity, or spirituality.

Julie Miller, the second graduate of the concentration in Religion, Gender, and Culture, connects the assumptions behind rape laws to descriptions of ecstatic pain in mystical treatises in order to trace the historical roots of rape in contemporary North American society. Studying religious texts and rape laws in historical societies, Miller finds danger in the medieval mystical rhetoric of ecstatic pain. Such rhetoric, she writes, can easily slip into authorization to inflict pain on oneself or another.

The "Gender and Religion" essays explore "texts"—contemporary popular culture (Boyd, Lelwica), medieval mystical treatises (Börresen, Miller), and early Christian novels (Corrington Streete) in order to understand how gender constructions *work* in different societies and communities. These dissimilar texts, a largely unmined source of sociological information, illuminate the common assumptions of a particular time and place; they also reveal how common assumptions are woven into institutions and practices, continuing to operate in individuals and communities long after their origins have been forgotten. Caution is, of course, always necessary when interpreting information texts do not *intend* to convey. Nevertheless, while historical theologians have obediently focused on author's *intentions*, information that would give us glimpses into historical communities has been ignored. Current interests in understanding the role of gender arrangements in their social, institutional, and religious settings prompt new questions, which in turn, elicit new understandings of past and present communities.

## Religion and the Visual Arts

In the last twenty years, the study of religion and the visual arts has been stimulated by trends in historical study more generally. The postmodern collapse of distinctions between "high" and "popular" art, attention to the visual experience of—for want of a better word—"ordinary" people, interest in gender arrangements, in socialization, and in devotional and liturgical practices, has required a broader repertoire of historical evidence than literature can provide. From the perspective of Religious Studies, artworks offer democratic access to the symbolic religious resources of whole communities. From the side of Art History, there is growing interest in the specifically *religious* content and valence of historical images that had formerly been described only in terms of their formal qualities and as examples of a history of style.

However, until there is broad recognition that religious images represent an alternative *conceptual* access to religious ideas, historical theologians will continue to assume that "art" played the same peripheral role in historical cultures that it does in twenty-first century North America. Contemporary experience of museum art and coffee table reproductions do not give a sense of the religious and social importance of images seen by historical people in churches attended by most members of the society. In addition, in times before mass reproduction, the scarcity of secular images enhanced the power of religious images. Yet the power of images to crystallize and communicate religious ideas and sensibilities is a point that must still be made within religious studies.

Lynn Randolph brings an artist's perspective to considering the conceptual elements in painting. Familiar as most people are with the claim that art provokes emotional response, her consideration of how visual metaphors form and inform values provides a more comprehensive understanding of art. Aware of the power of images, she seeks "images that confirm and challenge as well as confront, images that connect to the consciousness of others, . . .

that intervene . . . that bring suffering to the surface, that distribute pain, that centralize the marginal, that resist commercialism, empower women, and magnify dreams."

The "Religion and the Visual Arts" essays explore the power of visual images. Doug Adams brings a Hebrew Bible prototype to interpretation of a seventeenth-century woman painter's depiction of "Noli Me Tangere," analyzing the painting's force by collating scripture from the two testaments. Jane Dillenberger's description of her own vivid engagement with art gives a sense of that power in shaping a productive life and career. Historian Robin Jensen argues that the often repeated shibboleth that educated elites disdained religious images while the illiterate drew most of their religious information from them lacks textual support. She suggests that it was actually the more educated and sophisticated Christians who defended the use of religious images. Kimberly Vrudny sensitively combines sympathetic and critical interpretation to explore the symbolic repertoire available to medieval women whose children died in plagues. She argues that desperate women overlooked the social messages embedded in images of the Virgin Mary that instructed them in meekness, humility, and obedience in relation to male defined and administered societies. They identified instead with the Mary who, as a woman like themselves, mourned the death of a beloved child.

Translating the power of images into pedagogy based on comparative visual studies, Deborah Haynes describes the theory and method she finds useful in teaching courses that include meditative practice. Students taught in this way often experience changed lives—the goal of pedagogy, after all, but one rarely achieved. Innovative theory and method must produce enhanced teaching practices. Anthony Pinn explores the uses of art for black theology, finding in modernist art an incitement to irreverence that unsettles acquiescence with unjust social arrangements, encouraging "suspicion concerning the current arrangement and structure" of society.

## Postscript

Scholars are inclined to take themselves very seriously. Yet most of us became scholars because, as children, we liked to read. Scholarship is a luxury and a privilege. To get a quick sense of this, imagine a society that had to choose between maintaining its scholars or its garbage collectors. Yes, scholarship is a luxury. I have treasured the following quotation for many years.

> All the genuine deep delight in life is in showing people the mudpies you have made: and life is at its best when we confidingly recommend our mudpies to each other's sympathetic consideration.

J. M. Thornburn is the author; he is otherwise unknown to me. The quotation appears at the end of the Suzanne Langer's Preface to her profoundly serious book, *Philosophy in a New Key*.[2]

Because scholarship is a luxury and a privilege it should be engaged in with delight and responsibility. In this spirit I have wanted to understand as much as I can about how people of the past constructed religious orientations that held them in the exigencies of life and death. Moreover, present interest in rich diversities—diversities of race, ethnicity, gender, class, sexual orientation, and religion, to name only the most obvious—prompts interest in the diversity of communities and societies of the past. As an historian of Christianity in search of evidence of past diversity, I ask the non-judgmental question, How did a particular society or community *work?* In order to approach answers to this question, I need a larger repertoire of evidence than texts provide. So I explore images, music, and architecture, not to *illustrate*, but as historical evidence in its own right of the religious provisions accessible to everyone in the community. Benefiting from the detailed work of many scholars, I sought the history of women, of slaves, and of so-called "heretics," people who had distinctive, rich, and coherent religious sensibilities for which they were willing to suffer.

In sum, I believe that it is necessary and sufficient to be faithful to the "genuine deep delight in life." Augustine, the historical author from whom I have been learning for forty years, put it this way: "Delight is, as it were, the weight of the soul, for delight orders the soul. . . .Where the soul's delight is, there is its treasure" (*De musica* 6. 11. 29). Augustine was well aware that delight is a mysterious and slippery thing. He wrote in *The Spirit and the Letter*:

> Perfect righteousness . . . would come about if there were brought to bear the will sufficient for such an achievement; and that might be, if all the requirements of righteousness were known to us, and if they inspired in the soul such delight as to overcome the obstacle set by any other pleasure or pain. . . . For we are well aware that the extent of a person's knowledge is not in his own power, and that he will not follow what he knows to be worth pursuing unless he delight in it no less than it deserves his love. . . . "For we see now through a glass darkly, but then face to face." (1 Corinthians 13:12)

[2] Suzanne Langer, *Philosophy in a New Key: A Study in the Symbolism of Reason, Rite and Art*, 3d ed. (Cambridge: Harvard University Press, 1970).

Lacking perfect knowledge, delight is our best guide. My life in scholarship has been motivated by delight at every turn, and the people whose work is included in this volume, along with many others, have been the best part of that richness of delight.

# Introduction

Richard Valantasis

One of the great joys of the academic life is to pay homage in a Festschrift to a scholar who has influenced both colleagues and students over years of interaction and friendship both professional and personal. This volume honors a scholar and theologian of historical theology, a theorist and a practitioner of religion and the arts, and a keen analyst of cultural trends both ancient and modern. Her enthusiastically grateful students and colleagues have written these essays, poems, and music as a testament to her influence, her presence, her intellectual vitality, her engagement with many disciplines in the humanities and the arts, and her generous attention to the work of others. These essays express an admiration and gratitude for her as a person whose spirit and character, both in print and in person, have fostered "fullness of life" among us.

Miles's prodigious production as a scholar has legendary qualities. Her dozen-plus books alone explore history, patristics, ancient philosophy, art and art history, spiritual formation and religious practice, critical theory, film, ethics and values, personal growth, gender and women's studies, as well as her true academic loves, Augustine of Hippo and Plotinus. Additionally, she has written over fifty articles or chapters of books. The breadth and depth of her own work and her influence upon others demands an expansive volume, which the editors of this Festschrift unfortunately had to restrict to four categories—Historical Theology, Religion and Culture, Religion and Gender, and Religion and the Visual Arts—in order to capture the heart of our appreciation for her.

After completing her doctorate at the Graduate Theological Union in Berkeley, California in 1977, Miles taught at Harvard University's Divinity School for nearly two decades (1978–96). Her impact was enormous, not only in theology and history, but also in gender studies and the theological interpretation of art and culture. Having been the first woman to be granted tenure at Harvard's Divinity School in 1985, Miles became the Bussey Professor of Historical Theology in 1987. Returning to the Graduate Theological Union in 1996, Miles became its Dean and Vice-President for Academic Affairs and the Dillenberger Professor of Historical Theology until her retirement in 2001. But Miles's influence extended farther than her local institutions: the American Academy of Religion elected her President in 1998–99; she served on the editorial boards of the *Journal of the American Academy of Religion, Augustinian Studies*, and the *Journal of Feminist Studies in Religion*; she participated in such boards as Radcliffe College's Graduate Consortium in Women's Studies and the Church Divinity School of the Pacific; and she lectured extensively in such places as Armenia, Finland, and in the United States at Harvard, Princeton, Yale, Stanford, Syracuse, Vanderbilt, Emory, among many others. This constitutes a legendary career indeed.

Although many of the contributors came to know Miles as a scholar, we were transformed by her presence. In the classroom, or at a conference, in a session of an academic meeting, or at receptions, Miles translated an academic hermeneutic of generosity into a generosity of spirit and mind that not only challenged our thinking, but also our manner of living. Whether in the classroom or at a conference, wrestling with theory or offering thanks, she brings a characteristic grace and graciousness to the moment. A classical scholar as well as a contemporary theorist, Miles's determined pursuit of beauty and moral responsibility has encouraged her companions to value these ideals and seek their embodiment as well. Her presence is both profit and delight. Her books titles themselves have become watchwords in academic discourse and touchstones of personal values: "image as insight," "immaculate and powerful," "seeing and believing," "reading for life," and "carnal knowing." Miles put the issues of body, thinking, truth, goodness, and vision not only on the academic, but also the personal, agenda of her colleagues and friends. So as contributors to this small homage to a very great scholar and colleague, we dedicate this volume with respect and affection to a scholar, teacher, friend, colleague, and companion who made us all truly alive.

# Interlude

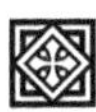

# Christian Spirituality Envisioned

## *A Pastoral Appreciation of Ernst Kitzinger, Margaret Miles, and Henri Nouwen (Harvard, 1976–85)*

James D. Smith III

In June of the year 2000, having concluded his decade of service as President of Harvard University, Dr. Neil Rudenstine offered a personal reflection on the nature of education: "Accessing information is one thing, but there's nothing like talking to someone who is intelligent and imaginative and is likely to know more than you do."[1] While welcoming the indisputable boon of technology, Rudenstine was extolling the relational blessing of shared time and space with gifted teachers as well.

Some twenty-five years earlier, having completed my M.Div. Studies and two years of ministry as a youth pastor in Minnesota, I applied for admission to the Th.M. program at Harvard Divinity School. While prayerfully exploring other options, a key element drawing us toward Boston was the opportunity to study with two professors whose work I greatly admired: Helmut Koester and George Huntston Williams.[2] Working with each of these remarkable scholars, doing both the Th.M. year and subsequent Th.D. studies in Church History, was a lifetime privilege. Their influence, during those Cambridge years, was wonderfully complemented by the contributions of others as well.[3] Three of these professors, in a totally unexpected and life-

[1] David L. Marcus, "A Farewell to Harvard Yard," *U.S. News and World Report* (June 5, 2000) 20.

[2] See James M. Robinson and Helmut Koester, *Trajectories through Early Christianity* (Philadelphia: Fortress, 1971); and George H. Williams, *The Radical Reformation* (Philadelphia: Westminster, 1962).

[3] See James D. Smith III, "Words from the Classroom: An Appreciation of Wisdom for Ministry," *HDB* 19 (Winter, 1990) 15.

giving way, specially opened my eyes to the visual aspects of Christian faith and life: Ernst Kitzinger, Margaret Miles, and Henri Nouwen. As a Christian nurtured in the Free Church (Baptist) tradition, my orientation was for more cerebral and word-centered than aesthetic and informed by the image. Their influence pointed me toward a "Christian spirituality envisioned"—and the challenge of integration has animated me as both pastor and professor over the ensuing years.

Ernst Kitzinger had come to teach at Harvard in 1967.[4] A world-renowned art historian, he had served for a quarter century at Dunbarton Oaks, becoming director of studies and professor of Byzantine art and architecture. Earlier, his 1940 work *Early Medieval Art at the British Museum* had helped transform the discipline of art history in the English-speaking world.[5] Kitzinger, by the mid-1970s, was A. Kingsley Porter University Professor at Harvard.

In the autumn of 1976, my first semester at the University, I knew none of this. What became clear, however, was that by signing up to audit Fine Arts 147, "Early Christian and Early Byzantine Art," I gained a seat in the Fogg Museum and entered the realm of a master.[6] As the slides brought images from the ancient world into our view, the gracious guide with the German accent introduced us to the visual treasures being projected and the rich culture behind the scenes. My notes from that course survive and, in them, cave-drawing quality attempts to pen-sketch the most compelling images. On one occasion, after class, I asked him about the earliest surviving depiction of a Christian whose name is known to us. His response was to invite St. Ambrose into our circle and shed light on the tile mosaic of this bishop's face found in the fifth-century church in Milan. He went on to offer an unforgettable word: in life as in art, always look deeply into the faces.

That word was carried into our new church situation. During that Th.M. year, my wife Linda and I volunteered to work with a group of church youth in the Dorchester section of Boston. The congregation was a century old and had dwindled to about twenty-five adults in attendance, as the neighborhood was changing and the supply of immigrant Swedish Baptists had dried up. Unexpectedly, the Old World cultural resonance between that fellowship's European roots and the professor's experience as a Jewish immigrant from

[4] Tributes include obituaries in *The Guardian* (January 29, 2003), and the *New York Times* (February 9, 2003).

[5] Ernst Kitzinger, *Early Medieval Art in the British Museum* (London: British Museum, 1940. reprint 1969).

[6] As Slade Professor of Fine Art at Cambridge University (1974–75), for example, he had delivered lectures later published as the influential *Byzantine Art in the Making* (Cambridge: Harvard University Press, 1977).

Nazi Germany in the 1930s helped this novice from San Diego to engage more sensitively the faces and lives before me.

Already, approaching retirement, Kitzinger was deeply involved in planning a Fall 1977 exhibition at the Metropolitan Museum of Art in New York City, "The Age of Spirituality." Today, the two published volumes marking that celebration of antiquity (catalogue and symposium) bring the theme to life, while his private papers document the painstaking intellectual and logistical efforts involved.[7] One of his reflections was particularly memorable to me:

> All these factors—let me stress this once more—had played a role in earlier Christian art: what they all had in common was that they involved the divine presence in the here and now. That presence was palpably experienced in relics, tombs and holy sites which literally put the faithful in touch with the persons and the events that had made redemption a reality; it was similarly experienced in the liturgy in which God's redemptive work was reenacted; and it was experienced by sheer intensity of desire in every ardent act of prayer or invocation. To whichever of these experiences the image was related, it ceased to be merely a record, an objective statement, and became a conduit or receptacle of divine power. Quite evidently, visual form was felt to have special properties which enabled it to hold or attract that power.[8]

The following year, Margaret Miles began her teaching at Harvard Divinity School as Assistant Professor of Historical Theology. In retrospect, there were two reasons why her presence did not initially impact my studies. First of all, from 1978–81 I was already enjoying the mentorship of two fine historians, Eleanor McLaughlin (at Andover Newton Theological School) and Clarissa Atkinson at Harvard. With Professors Williams and Koester, they graciously served on my Th.D. General Examinations committee. Secondly, the focus of HDS's Department of Theology seemed typically to be on philosophical theology and contemporary systematics. Only the passing of time removed my departmental myopia and revealed her enduring place at the School as a uniquely gifted faculty member, Bussey Professor of Theology—and the first woman to be tenured at HDS.

In 1981, I welcomed the invitation to serve as Margaret Miles's Teaching Fellow (the first of three occasions) in her History of Christian Thought se-

[7] Kitzinger's papers are archived at the Getty Research Institute. The exhibition's initial volume was *Age of Spirituality: Antique and Early Christian Art Third to Seventh Century*, ed. Kurt Weitzmann (New York: Metropolitan Museum of Art, 1979).

[8] Kurt Weitzmann, editor, *Age of Spirituality: A Symposium* (New York: Metropolitan Museum of Art, 1980) 156.

quence. That same year *Fullness of Life* was published, and throughout her teaching there was interwoven a valuing of physical and visual realities, which seemed at first strange, then wonderfully insightful in a course that many would teach as "intellectual history."[9]

Repeatedly, I was reminded that historical people were (like us), in their own time and cultural milieu, "trying to keep body and soul together." So each text, in word or image, deserved our focused attention and respect in a "hermeneutic of good will." Scholarship should be a matter of shared life, not competing "stags in the clearing." That gracious spirit was warmly demonstrated when Miles timed a lecture of mine to coincide with my parents' visit from the West Coast. I taught, students applauded, my folks were teary-eyed, and Miles was luminous—a day of marvelous blessing.

As I had been encouraged, several years earlier, to look deeply into faces historical and contemporary, so now the emphasis on an embodied spirituality was timely for ministry. I had become (prior to Th.D. studies) pastor of the church in Dorchester. Now, in a congregation beginning to grow again, the aging old-timers were facing physical limitations while the younger newcomers (including our three children) needed spiritual disciplines and integration in their lives. The academic and pastoral dimensions came together in a unique season of our family's life.[10]

Supported by grants and fellowships, Margaret Miles spent the HDS 1982–83 term on sabbatical in Rome. When she returned, and I was privileged to serve as her Teaching Fellow once again, the fruit of her time away was evident. Familiar texts found new depth, and visual resources were being introduced to be "read" through opened eyes. The materials for her *Image as Insight* were coming together, in text and illustrative plates.

> The function of art is to identify and articulate a range of subjective patterns of feeling and to give objective form to feeling. . . . Religion needs art to orient individuals and communities, not only conceptually but also affectively, to the reality that creates and nourishes, in solitude and in community, human life. Religion, as we have seen, is a complex of concepts about the self, the world, and God; it is also an altered perception of the meaning and value of the sensible world, a different way of seeing. . . . Both are skilled operations; for the untrained eye, eyesight is not insight, just as, for the unprepared mind, religious concepts make no sense. Because religion irreducibly involves both concepts and altered perceptions, the training of both

[9] Margaret R. Miles, *Fullness of Life: Historical Foundations for a New Asceticism* (Philadelphia: Westminster, 1981).

[10] See James D. Smith III, "Calvary Remembered, 1975–85," in *Glimpses of Grace*, ed. Marie Hedin-Pereto (forthcoming).

> eye and mind is fundamental to the quickening of religious sensibility. . . . I am urging an analogous juggling of texts and images in the method of historical hermeneutics, a balance based on a respect for an interest in not only historical language users but also historical image users.[11]

One image that particularly stirred me with its beauty was Correggio's *The Virgin Adoring the Child Jesus,* painted sometime before 1534, a copy of which I continue to enjoy today.

During those years in Cambridge, before we both returned (via different paths) to West Coast roots, I discovered that we shared early denominational roots as well. Because her experience of a more fundamentalist Protestant upbringing was not always pleasant and her father a Baptist minister, I confess to being concerned that by transference our relationship might suffer. There was no need to be apprehensive. As she had long read her books, Miles brought both "generosity and critical questions" to the reading of me, academically and personally.[12] And, as she noted recently in a lecture series, one lifelong gift Miles has kept from her conservative upbringing is that of passion, a vital and redemptive engagement with life.[13]

I first met Henri Nouwen, in the late summer of 1975, at Yale Divinity School. Approaching the close of my M.Div. program, our family then visited both Harvard and Yale campuses, prayerfully weighing pastoral possibilities as well. During our day in New Haven, Nouwen was one of the faculty members I met on campus and he cordially welcomed me into his office. Though primarily focused academically on church history, I already had been enriched by his early writings.[14] Ultimately, as we felt led to Harvard, there was a twinge of regret that declining Yale's invitation seemingly made our conversation a one-time thing. Almost a decade later, however, we would cross paths again. Following his years on the Yale faculty, and a deeply moving period in Latin America, which crystallized his convictions on "reverse mission," Nouwen began teaching at Harvard Divinity School early in 1983. He came as Professor of Divinity and Horace DeY. Lentz Lecturer, accepting

[11] Miles, *Image as Insight: Visual Understanding in Western Christianity and Secular Culture* (Boston: Beacon, 1985) 4, 38. Her dedication of this volume to husband Owen Thomas honors a relationship of beauty.

[12] Miles, *Reading for Life: Beauty, Pluralism and Responsibility* (New York: Continuum, 1997).

[13] Miles, "Short Beds and Narrow Sheets: Religion and the Common Good," Eugene M. Burke Lectureship, University of California at San Diego, April 25, 2002.

[14] Three of Henri Nouwen's books with particular impact were *Creative Ministry* (Garden City, N.Y.: Doubleday, 1971), *The Wounded Healer* (Garden City, N.Y.: Doubleday, 1972), and *Reaching Out* (Garden City, N.Y.: Doubleday, 1975).

a Spring-only appointment, which would allow extended time for continued engagement in the Americas and in his native Europe.

In the autumn of that year, during a visit to Jean Vanier's L'Arche community in Trosly, France, Nouwen's eyes fell upon a large poster reproduction of Rembrandt's *Prodigal Son*. Exhausted from a six-week lecture trip through the United States calling Christian communities to help prevent violence and war in Central America, the tender gospel embrace of father and son deeply spoke immediately—and in a lifelong way—to Nouwen's spiritual needs and identity:

> Much happened in the months and years that followed. Even though the extreme fatigue left me, and I returned to the life of teaching and traveling, Rembrandt's embrace remained imprinted on my soul . . . While busy with many people, involved in many issues and quite visible in many places, the homecoming of the prodigal son stayed with me and took on even greater significance in my spiritual life. The yearning for a lasting home, brought to consciousness by Rembrandt's painting, grew deeper and stronger, somehow making the painter himself into a faithful companion and guide.[15]

Returning to the Boston area only weeks after his initial experience, Nouwen was interviewing me to serve as a Teaching Fellow for his first large Harvard lecture course, "Introduction to the Spiritual Life." The opportunity to follow through on studies in historic Christian spirituality begun with Eleanor McLaughlin, and to gain insights on community-building transferable to my pastoral ministry, was exciting. The vision of biblical reconciliation offered in Rembrandt's *Prodigal Son* would provide recurrent inspiration.

As biographer Michael Ford has noted, Nouwen's Spring 1984–85 lecture courses provided a remarkable arena for spiritual development.[16] What was particularly prophetic to me was the manner in which Nouwen himself, both in the classroom and in more personal settings, became the tangible visible expression of his message. Etched in my mind's eye is his incarnation of "passion"—less the contemporary variety of what "turns you on" as a personal agenda to push and more the historic willingness to suffer for a cause of surpassing value. He honored the realities of a pluralistic culture less ideologically than in recognizing the varieties of God's beloved peoples (embattled Sandinistas, the mentally handicapped, Haitian children, et al.) and offering authentic Christian witness, particularly in his 1985 course.

[15] Nouwen, *The Return of the Prodigal Son: A Meditation on Fathers, Brothers, and Sons* (New York: Doubleday, 1992) 5.

[16] Michael Ford, *Wounded Prophet* (New York: Doubleday, 1999) 133–39.

> The task I have, therefore, in this course is not simply to teach Spirituality, but to teach Spirituality in a Spiritual way, that is, a way that opens us to the working of the Holy Spirit. This is especially hard since the Holy Spirit might lead us where we rather would not go. . . . I should allow my teaching to have a quality of witness. Concretely, therefore, I want to be for you what John was for his listeners and readers: a living witness of the Risen Christ. I see this as a sort of spiritual hospitality. I want to invite you into my space, without taking the pictures from the walls or the books from the shelves. But I also want to leave enough room for you to walk in and out and around freely so that you can respond from your own place in life. Part of my struggle will be to find when and how my space becomes too crowded, or too empty, to be truly hospitable. Only you can help me in discovering the right space. It is probably going to require much flexibility. I am aware of the many pitfalls: proselytizing, manipulation, and even oppression. But acknowledging these pitfalls, I still feel strongly that "teaching spiritual things spiritually" also means to move from informing the mind to forming the heart, and that it is not a neutral event but an event that involves us all in a very deep personal way. . .This is also the way to a deep respect for the great variety of experiences, histories, religious and cultural backgrounds among us. Just as the most personal often proves to be the most universal, so too what is most binding can prove to be most liberating. I hope and pray that what binds me most, my faith in the risen Christ, can free you to make your own spiritual affirmations.[17]

Following Spring term 1985, Nouwen left Harvard to continue the search for home, which would lead him to join Daybreak, the L'Arche community in Toronto, as pastor. In that same time frame, our family was leaving the area for a kind of homecoming: I was invited to become Senior Pastor at the church in Minneapolis where we'd worked with youth nine years earlier. Subsequently, within a year of our 1991 return to our hometown, San Diego (for ministry as a pastor and teacher, and to care for our aging parents), *The Return of the Prodigal Son* appeared in print. That biblical imagery has now been a vital part of my ministry for twenty years. In 1995, during my last meeting with Nouwen—and a year before his ultimate, heavenly homecoming—I had the opportunity to thank him once more.

The theme pursued here, "Christian spirituality envisioned," brings to mind a fourth person, one whose service as professor and dean at Harvard Divinity School and lifelong ecumenical Christian ministry uniquely merits him the last word here: Krister Stendahl. Reflecting on the contributions of

[17] Nouwen, "Introduction" [Handout #3] to HDS 2543 (January 31, 1985) 2–5.

Ernst Kitzinger, Margaret Miles, and Henri Nouwen, he offers characteristic grace, precision and insight:

> Those three are so drastically different in their teaching style and life experiences and spirituality. But a common denominator is that, at various levels, they were each deeply in touch with the essential, classical Christian tradition. Kitzinger was taciturn about his faith, but through his marvelous scholarship he related to the spiritual realities, keeping a distance out of respect and humility. At the other extreme was Henri: enormously involved, he lived with, by, and in religious experience and was it. Here was a diver's relationship to the sea, a total immersion. In Margaret there is a wonderful mixture of those two modes of being. You see it already in her thesis on Augustine. I treasured her critical love and understanding of the Christian tradition, so badly needed at HDS at the time, and at all times. We miss her in Cambridge.[18]

[18] Telephone conversation with Krister Stendahl (July 27, 2004) and printed with his permission.

## Antigone (Can a woman be a hero?)

No noble road
over collateral bones
for me, no blaming
fate nor edict.

Derelict parents,
tepid sister, tardy
would-be husband,
none stood with me

heaping even a
fist of dust,
tipping a scant
libation. None.

But it is not, in the
end, my story. Fool
dead Eteocles and
Polyneices slew

each other. Old Creon
has all the lines, the
hubris, I only the
flesh-bred fault

according to my kind.
Whatever death–
waste. I had it
coming. A man's

first duty: serve
himself. Self-serving
citizens of Thebes,
who knows

if this world's
virtues are
in heaven
crimes?

—Jennifer M. Phillips

# Historical Theology

# On Being Beautiful and Religious at the Same Time

## *Plotinus's Aesthetics for the Present*

Frank Burch Brown

## Beautifully Religious

To what extent are beauty and spirituality compatible? Under what conditions is a beautiful person, or a beautiful work of art, to be perceived as religious? Can being beautiful ever contribute to being religious? The third-century pagan philosopher Plotinus offered a whole system of thought that connected beauty with spirituality (or what we might call religion) in ways that—especially as transmitted through Augustine—were to have a profound influence on Christian theology. But the legacy of Plotinus is mixed, having played into a dualism that he only partly embraced. And the more positive spiritual sense of beauty and art that Plotinus describes is, unfortunately, difficult to retrieve, both because of the quite different assumptions that are predominant in modern aesthetics and because of tensions and inconsistencies within Plotinus's own metaphysical thought.

Margaret Miles, in her book *Plotinus: On Body and Beauty*, seeks in part to recover Plotinus for the present.[1] One way in which she tries to accomplish that is by showing how, from Plotinus's point of view, "the beautiful life is made beautiful by light from its [spiritual] source."[2] Life is not the only thing, however, that Plotinus thinks is spiritually enlightened through beauty. The

[1] Margaret R.. Miles, *Plotinus on Body and Beauty: Society, Philosophy, and Religion in Third-Century Rome* (Malden, Mass.: Blackwell, 1999). The quotation is Miles's paraphrase of Plotinus.

[2] Ibid., 158.

same is true of art and, to some extent, of anything that so much as exists. That is because, from the perspective offered by Plotinus, beauty is intrinsic to existence, goodness, and spirituality. Viewed in terms of what we might anachronistically call "aesthetics" (a term coined in the eighteenth century), the goal of everything is to attain its proper level of beauty and to contribute its beauty to the greater whole.

But if that is so, and if Miles is right in thinking that we can learn from such thinking in the present day, what are we supposed to mean by beauty? Does beauty come in degrees? Is there more than one kind of beauty? What are we to make of bodily beauty, or the beauty of art? How do we learn to discern beauty at all and to discriminate higher forms of beauty from lower? Furthermore, if beauty is an integral part of the highest vision of the spiritual life, what kind of beauty best serves that purpose?

Such questions have an ethical dimension (in the Greek sense of being germane to a good life). Here, however, I will mainly treat them from the standpoint of theological aesthetics, although in relation to ethics. My goal, in the end, is not to analyze all the finer points of Plotinus's thought but to use Miles's treatment of Plotinus as a way of grappling with one central issue: imagining how physical beings or works of art can be beautiful and religious at the same time. This essay could be described, therefore, as extending and complicating the discussion begun by Miles in her concluding chapter, "Plotinus for the Present."[3]

## Beauty: An Overview

Before we look more closely at features of Plotinus's view of beauty that Margaret Miles finds especially salient, we would do well to step back and consider briefly how beauty has figured in Western theology and spirituality.[4] Rarely the primary focus of theology and spirituality, beauty nonetheless plays a part in both. From Clement of Alexandria (ca. 150–ca. 215) and Augustine (354–430), through Bonaventure (ca. 1217–74) and Thomas Aquinas (ca. 1225–74), to Hans Urs von Balthasar (1905–88) and Paul Evdokimov (1901–70), theologians of various kinds have held that beauty finds its perfection in God. All created beauty, they have said, reflects and participates to some degree, at least by analogy, in beauty that is divine. The higher forms of beauty, moreover, can attune the soul spiritually and morally.

[3] Ibid., 162–82.

[4] In what follows, I have borrowed and paraphrased brief passages from my article "Beauty," in *Dictionary of Christian Spirituality*, ed. Philip Sheldrake (Philadelphia: Westminster John Knox, 2005).

The main inspiration for such views in antiquity was the philosophy of Plato (ca. 428–ca. 348 B.C.E.) as reinterpreted through the Neoplatonism of Plotinus (ca. 205–270) and the Christian mysticism of Dionysius the Pseudo-Areopagite (ca. 500). Medieval scholastics also drew on Aristotle (384–322 B.C.E.) when they framed the idea that beauty—along with goodness, truth, and unity—is a "transcendental" property of being, so that, to the extent that something exists, it is in some measure beautiful.

In all of this, the idea of beauty itself was never extremely precise or entirely stable. For the ancient Greeks, beauty (*kalon*) had to do not only with aesthetics in our sense but also with goodness. It is that which lures our desire and admiration and which, it was generally agreed, pleases through proportion and symmetry. Since proportion can be expressed numerically, beauty also has a distinctly mathematical and rational dimension.

Medieval ideas of beauty (*formositas*) retained an intellectual and spiritual tenor while placing particular emphasis on delight. In the eyes of scholastic philosophers, culminating in Thomas Aquinas, beauty consists in harmonious proportion, integrity, and radiance or "splendor" of form. At the same time, beauty gives delight in the very act of its being perceived. In approaching the Bible, which says little about beauty as such, theologians paid particular attention to Wisdom 11:21, which stresses the rational aspect of creativity by declaring that God made all things according to "measure and number and weight."

Both the Neoplatonic and scholastic traditions had a less rational side as well—one that, far from hurrying past sensible beauty, sought to glory in it appropriately. This sometimes led to a broadly sacramental approach to such arts as church architecture, stained glass, and manuscript illumination.

By the eighteenth century, however, when the idea of the "fine arts" took hold in Europe, beauty was increasingly understood in subjective terms. While Immanuel Kant (1724–1804) could still regard beauty as a symbol of the morally good, beauty was essentially set free from any necessary grounding in reality and was divorced from any inherent connection to morality.

Much of the resulting ambiguity concerning the ethical and religious meaning of artistry and beauty remains to this day. Art, for instance, is widely seen as essentially autonomous and self-expressive, free of moral obligations, and yet it is also frequently understood as engaging at least indirectly in social critique or even as profoundly prophetic and quite often as revelatory of insights that cannot be expressed in ordinary words. That kind of tension in thinking about the character and purpose of art has affected the whole enterprise of theological aesthetics. Thus, even though recently there has been a major revival of theological interest in aesthetics, the arts are often marginalized in such work—perhaps out of habits formed centuries earlier when art's very association with the senses, excessive emotion, and unfettered imagination aroused theological suspicions.[5] In any case, it remains unclear what place beauty—and artistic beauty in particular—can and should play in theology and religion and in the morally good life.

## What Would Plotinus Say?

In the chapter that concludes *Plotinus on Body and Beauty*, Margaret Miles ventures to present us with "Plotinus for the Present." Along with expressing certain reservations and criticisms, she commends aspects of what Plotinus (205–270 C.E.) has to say about body and its relationship to soul and likewise his ideas of the sensible world and its relation to what Plotinus called "intellect" (akin to Plato's realm of ideas, but not a separate sphere of reality as in Plato). Miles then goes on to talk about Plotinus's thought in relation to questions of moral engagement and the concerns of feminism. Beauty is hardly mentioned in any of this. But in the context of depicting the worldview of Plotinus as a nondogmatic kind of religion (albeit without ritual or a worshiping community), Miles highlights two interrelated "spiritual disciplines" that involve beauty: first, the discipline of contemplating and imagining the real, which includes a receptive (but not passive) perception of beauty and second, the discipline of attentiveness to beauty as the mark "of the presence of the One, the great beauty." Last, Miles connects beauty with mutual communal responsibility, as something implicit in "Plotinus's description of the connectedness of living things in a vast, interdependent, and beautiful universe." This beautifully intimate interconnectedness is not evident, she says, to the "sluggish eye," but comes as a result of "spiritual discipline."[6]

Anyone who has read Miles's discussion leading up to her final chapter will realize that she is selective in choosing what of Plotinus she will recommend as especially pertinent today. Furthermore, throughout her study, Miles is judicious in distilling in a lucid way the bewildering complexity of the *Enneads* (the sole extant work of Plotinus). There is no need in the present context to unpack her discussion in detail. Nor will we want to venture too far, on our own, into the vast complexities of Plotinus and his metaphysics. But I will fill out and modify Miles's picture to some extent as I relate

[5] Hans Urs von Balthasar pays surprisingly little attention to the arts as such in his major work of theological aesthetics, *The Glory of the Lord; A Theological Aesthetics*, 7 vols., various translators (San Francisco: Ignatius, 1982–89). The same is true of Patrick Sherry's *Spirit and Beauty: An Introduction to Theological Aesthetics* (Oxford: Clarendon, 1992) and of Edward Farley's *Faith and Beauty: A Theological Aesthetic* (Aldershot: Ashgate, 2001)—both of which make substantial contributions in other respects.

[6] Miles, *Plotinus on Body and Beauty*, 178, 180, 182.

Plotinus's thought to our central question of how being beautiful is, or can be, related to being religious.

## Body and Soul

Miles knows she faces a challenge in trying to expound the relevance of a philosopher whose life the ancient biographer and former student of Plotinus, Porphyry, chose to introduce by saying: "Plotinus, the philosopher our contemporary, seemed ashamed of being in the body."[7] No matter that Porphyry himself would have regarded his remark as a thinly veiled compliment. No matter that a good many philosophers of that era, in a variety of schools, would have applauded such asceticism. That kind of "praise" would put off most readers today, the majority of whom have tried any number of measures to enhance their body image so as to have no need to be ashamed of being in their particular bodies.

Accordingly, from the very start, Miles emphasizes the complexity of Plotinus's attitudes and she laments the tendency of most philosophers, from Porphyry to the present, to depict Plotinus as more dualistic than he really was. Yes, she admits, Plotinus does sometimes refer to body as something low and "muddy." He can be found saying that a person with self-control will not keep company with bodily pleasures. He is not beyond arguing that greatness of soul entails "despising" the sensible things here on earth.[8] Plotinus, in some of his most memorable and eloquent passages, urges those who seek wisdom and happiness to flee from the sensory and bodily world to the realm of intellect and of potentially disembodied soul–and, ultimately, to the divine One that transcends everything finite and temporal[9] (cf. *Enneads* 6 and 7, which emphatically deny any intrinsic role to be played by bodily vision in the spiritual pursuit of the inner vision of "inaccessible beauty").

Miles observes, moreover, that Plotinus had little reason, personally, to take pleasure and pride in being an embodied soul. He lived in a time of horrid plagues, widespread hunger, and brutal gladiator shows. Eventually he himself fell mortally ill with a foul disease that has since been identified as, in all likelihood, leprosy. One can hardly begrudge Plotinus the comfort of his

7 Porphyry, "On the Life of Plotinus and the Arrangement of His Work," in Stephen MacKenna, trans., *Plotinus: The Enneads*, 4th ed. (New York: Pantheon, 1969), For the most part I will rely on the translations of Plotinus that Miles herself provides, but will turn to MacKenna and Tatarkiewicz (see below) for supplementary material.

8 Miles, *Plotinus on Body and Beauty*, 40.

9 Ibid., 41.

belief that, as Miles puts it, "at body's demise life departs, ready to form and inform other bodies or, ultimately, to retire to union with the universe."[10]

In thinking specifically of Plotinus for today, we may actually find something refreshing about his treating body as dependent on soul for its genuine beauty. Even in a society that caters to bodily pleasures, we can safely surmise that words releasing us from enslavement to our bodies as such could sound especially appealing to the many baby boomers, whose own aging process and bodily vulnerability can no longer be ignored or completely disguised. Be that as it may, aversion to the body as such is not something popular in our time or something Miles herself cares to promote. Accordingly, Miles goes to great lengths to assure her contemporary readers that Plotinus rejects severe asceticism. His is a universe of emanations from the indescribable and invisible One, proceeding to intellect (or Ideas) and, through intellect, to the common soul of all (in which all souls participate and are ultimately unified). Soul in turn creates the plurality of bodies from the forms it receives from intellect. Everything that exists has a share in beauty that derives ultimately from the primal, divine source. Plotinus in this way takes note of the "primary [though not primal] beauty of bodies."[11] He shows us, as well, that the sensible world that is generated by the overflow of the One through intellect is by no means valueless:

> Intellect is, certainly, beautiful, and the most beautiful of all; its place is in pure light and pure radiance and it includes the nature of real beings; this beautiful universe of ours is a shadow and image of it; and it [i.e. intellect] has its place in all glory, because there is nothing unintelligent or dark or unmeasured in it, and it lives a blessed life; so wonder would possess the one who saw this too, and as he should, entered it and became one with it. (*Enneads* 3.8.11, trans. Miles)[12]

So it is that intellect, which derives its supreme beauty from the invisible One, transmits something of that beauty to the sensible world, which in varying degrees bears its imprint, its image—or appears as its shadow. Furthermore, it is not as though there is really a vast distance between the shadowy reality of sensible beauty and the beauty of intellect or even the ineffable unity of the Good—the One. We should not think of the sensible world and intellect as two separate worlds, but as one world apprehended on two different but intimately related levels and in two different ways.[13] Soul mediates between bodily sense and intellect. Because of this intimate relation

[10] Ibid., 25.

[11] Ibid., 41.

[12] Ibid., 140.

[13] Ibid., 148.

or mediation, one need not leave one's body to go beyond the body. One can, instead, delve inward in contemplation in order to attain a "vision" of the higher and more beautiful realities.

Plotinus even avers that there is some spiritual advantage to soul in having communication with body, and in thus comparing, as he says, "things which are, in a way, opposite," which also means "learning, in a way more clearly, the better things. For the experience of evil is a clearer knowledge of the Good for those whose power is too weak to know evil with clear intellectual certainty before experiencing it" (*Enneads* 4.8.7, trans. Miles). Miles declares that this is "Plotinus's most forceful argument for the value of soul's descent." Plotinus, she says, "posits a clear hierarchy, but one that gives their full value to both intellect and the senses."[14]

Here we must pause. One sees the basis for Miles's first assertion, since Plotinus is indeed forceful here and does argue for the value of soul's communication with body. Her second assertion, however, may seem to overstate the case by claiming that Plotinus gives both intellect and senses "full value." What I wish to argue in the remainder of this essay is that, while Plotinus gives some important clues as to how we might give "full value" to both intellect and the senses, he does not entirely achieve that balance, himself. (Nor, we might add, does his admirer Augustine, or many other Christian theologians over the course of history.) Unfortunately, this very failure to attain a balanced appreciation of the senses in relation to soul and intellect (or mind, *nous*) has contributed to an otherwise perplexing theological neglect of what we today think of as the arts and artistry. A less than balanced appraisal of embodied beauty also can make it more difficult to see how beautiful bodies, artworks, and natural objects can be seen as religious by virtue of their beauty–and not merely beautiful by virtue of their religion, which Plotinus emphasizes clearly enough.

Miles, then, does us a service by challenging those who would dismiss Plotinus as a mere dualist who disdains the body and the world of the senses as unworthy of attention. I would suggest, however, that we need to go further. There are ways to be relatively true to Plotinus while paying greater respect than he normally did to the potential of both body and art to engage and illumine soul.

## Being Sensible about Bodily Beauty

Miles is quite right, I think, to insist that, in Plotinus, body and soul are on intimate turns. There is no Manichaean opposition between spirit and body at work here. When on one occasion Plotinus mentions the beauty of Helen

[14] Ibid., 71.

of Troy and of "all those women like in liveliness to Aphrodite," it is not by any means to deprecate their bodily beauty. It is, instead, to say that such beauty truly derives not from "material extension" but from the intellectual creating principle and the ideal form that enters through the eyes—a form apprehended as idea and not as mass with magnitude and measure (*Enneads* 5.8.2). But the very passage that Miles cites above as "Plotinus's most forceful argument for the value of soul's descent" is symptomatic of a pervasive, or at least intermittent, problem in Plotinus's own approach. Here Plotinus comes precariously close to undercutting any genuinely positive attitude toward the "sensible."

To be sure, in the preceding section (*Enneads* 4.8.6) Plotinus sounds remarkably affirmative about the realm of the many sensory things: sensibles. He insists that there must be something besides the sheer unity of the One, because otherwise the whole of reality would be amorphous. A plurality of some sort is needed–not only the plurality of the ideas and thus of intellect but also (in some fashion) a plurality of souls and "varied forms of sense." All this results from the "inexhaustible power" by which the One—the Good—spontaneously overflows and continuously gives "its gift to the universe, no part of which it can endure to see without some share in its being" (*Enneads* 4.8.6., trans. MacKenna). Matter itself can never exist apart from its participation in being, nor can it fall outside the "reach of the principle to whose grace it owes its existence" (*Enneads* 4.8.6). Plotinus goes on to say, "The loveliness that is in the sense-realm is an index of the nobleness of the Intellectual sphere, displaying its power and its goodness alike; and all things are for ever linked" (*Enneads* 4.8.6).

Here we have a warm, almost effusive, embrace of sensible reality. It seems very much in keeping with Plotinus's assertion elsewhere that "if the divine did not exist, the transcendently beautiful, in a beauty beyond all thought, what could be lovelier than the things we see? Certainly no reproach can rightly be brought against this world save only that it is not That" (*Enneads* 5.8.8).

Plotinus, however, does not stop with these passages that are so redolent with the glories of sensible beauty. In the passage to which we referred above, and which Miles quotes at some length (*Enneads* 4.8.7), Plotinus states at once that it would be better for soul to dwell in the realm of intellect. Given its "proper nature," soul is presently under compulsion also to participate in the sense realm. Soul, when it is embodied, need not grieve at not being the highest, through and through, or at occupying a middle rank between pure intellect and sense. Yet, Plotinus says, soul must guard against plunging into the sensory realm with excessive zeal. Soul can put to good use what it sees and suffers here. That, however, is just because soul can compare the highest things with those here, "which are, in a way, opposite," and can attain a better knowledge of the Good by the "experience of evil." In short, the value of the sensible, bodily realm is described, in this passage, as primarily negative, linked more closely with evil than with good. "Here" in everyday reality we encounter what is "in a way, opposite" of higher reality; we encounter in the sensible realm what amounts to evil.

Elsewhere Plotinus sounds simply neutral regarding the sensible realm and bodily existence. He assures us that, finally, nothing bodily can harm the rightly ordered soul–neither disease nor natural calamity nor the loss of a spouse, nor death itself. Whatever happens in the realm of the senses, the rightly disciplined self can attain perfect felicity and can learn to remain calm in the midst of bodily suffering—something many a Stoic or Buddhist of that same era might likewise aver (*Enneads* 1.4.4-8). We are not constituted by our physical life, Plotinus declares (*Enneads* 1.4.9). The act of authentic existence entails activity of intellect that "has no touch whatever with things of sense." Of course we act upon material things, and they act upon our bodies. But the principle of intellect that is active in the life of soul "antedates sensation or any perception" (*Enneads* 1.4.9-10). What body adds is material for imagination; like a mirror, imagination that works with the senses reflects dimly what is good and true. The one who is spiritually adept, however, has no need of life thus "spilled out in sensation" (*Enneads* 1.4.10).

What are we to make of all this? From the perspective offered by Plotinus, whatever beauty is shown forth by body and sense derives from soul. Soul, however, does not learn anything new about beauty from body, though it recognizes bodily beauty and can thereby be reminded of beauty that is invisible. Our souls (ultimately a unity) can, to be sure, benefit in a limited way from embodiment in the sensible realm. We can attain a more vivid sense of the Good from encountering evil in the sensible world. But when Plotinus recommends a method by which to attain a vision of true beauty, he rarely if ever recommends beginning with a close and attentive appreciation of the beauty of bodies and sensible things, as many would say Plato does in the Symposium. The path toward higher spiritual wisdom, in every one of Plotinus's accounts, so far as I can tell, entails turning quickly away from the senses: "How then can you see the sort of beauty a good soul has? Go back into yourself and look; and if you do not yet see yourself beautiful, then, just as someone making a statue which has to be beautiful cuts away here and polishes there, . . . so you too must cut away excess and straighten the crooked and clear the dark and make it bright . . . till the divine glory of virtue shines out on you" (*Enneads* 1.6.9, trans. Miles). The physical act of sculpting in this case is merely an analogy, not an instance of a spiritual exercise. We must develop a spiritual eye that can see what is "beyond all measure and superior to all quantity"; for no one "ever saw the sun without becoming sun-like. . . . You must first become all god-like and all beautiful if you intend to see God and beauty" (*Enneads* 1.6.9). Eternal, unchanging beauty is the goal, perceived through a certain kind of vision, an intellectual vision. We can be certain that the "eye" capable of seeing in a god-like way is not, at this stage, a physical eye. For this eye must see what is beyond all measure and quantity–intellectual beauty and, ultimately, the radiant unity of divine beauty itself. By comparison, the beauty of bodies and natural objects pales almost (never completely) to insignificance.

## Art as a Spiritual Sight

It is now time to examine where art fits into the picture. Plotinus seldom discusses art except by way of analogy with something else. But his statements about art (especially the plastic arts, but also music) are revealing. The ancients had no unified concept of the fine arts (the arts of the beautiful) as that idea came to be developed in eighteenth-century Europe. But much that Plotinus refers to as artistic we would also treat as such. And it is highly pertinent to our topic when Plotinus writes: "I think . . . that those ancient sages, who sought to secure the presence of divine beings by the erection of shrines and statues, showed insight into the nature of the All; they perceived that, though this Soul is everywhere tractable, its presence will be secured all the more readily when an appropriate receptacle is elaborated, a place especially capable of receiving some portion or phase of it, something reproducing it, or representing it and serving like a mirror to catch an image of it" (*Enneads* 1.3.11, trans. MacKenna). Plotinus does not develop this line of thought further, however, leaving only the hint that the temple and possibly its inevitable sculptures are designed to represent and mirror some aspect of the All-Soul especially well and should be valued for that reason. Is it because of their beauty that they attract and manifest divinity, or is it because they somehow produce a semblance of a reality that is itself invisible?

In this passage Plotinus says nothing explicit about the beauty of the temple architecture. Hundreds of years before his time, in fact, the classical Greeks were disinclined to see beauty as a defining or omnipresent trait of art. Plotinus is perhaps the first philosopher to think of all art as beautiful by design and definition. Hellenistic aestheticians, it is true, had increasingly associated art with beauty; but they were inconsistent and they had trouble deciding which was more beautiful: nature or art.[15]

[15] See Wladyslaw Tatarkiewicz, *History of Aesthetics*, 3 vols., vol. 1: *Ancient Aesthetics* (The Hague: Mouton, 1970) 307, 295. The entire volume is an invaluable resource for the study of ancient aesthetics, containing extensive quotations in original languages as well as in English

It is no surprise, therefore, when in another passage Plotinus takes up this very theme, considering the problem of whether art is more excellent than nature and in a way more beautiful. In *Enneads* 5.8.1 Plotinus compares two blocks of stone. One is natural, the other a work of sculpture depicting a human being or a god. The sculpture, which obviously is not a representation of the rock it utilizes, and which in depicting a bodily form is also superior to any particular human body on earth, takes its idea from the artist. "The stone which has been brought to beauty of form by art will appear beautiful not because it is a stone (for then the other [stone] would be just as beautiful), but as a result of the form which art has put into it." Plotinus continues, with a distinctive emphasis of his own: "This beauty was in the art, and it was far better there; for the beauty in the art did not come into the stone: it stays in the art, and another comes from it into the stone which is derived from it and less than it" (*Enneads* 5.8.1, trans. Armstrong).[16]

Plotinus admits that one who is attuned to art will appreciate the beauty of the sculpture, just as a true musician is moved by an audible melody. But the higher beauty is not to be seen in the stone, but in the invisible art of the artist, just as the higher music is actually inaudible. (See *Enneads* 2.9.16 and 4.3.12.) For the adept, "The vision in the temple and the communion are achieved not with the statue, but with the divinity itself. . . . Contemplation is not a spectacle, but another form of vision, namely ecstasy" (*Enneads* 6.9.11, trans. Tatarkiewicz).[17]

Art, then, can be superior to nature. But that is because art has a more direct connection to the invisible form, to intellectual beauty, and possibly to the divine: "If anyone despises the arts because they produce their works by imitating nature, we must tell him, first, that natural things are imitations too: and then he must know that the arts do not simply imitate what they see; they go back to the *logoi* [ideas] from which nature derives; . . . since they possess beauty, they make up what is defective in things" (*Enneads* 5.8.1, trans. Armstrong).[18] In so praising art as in improvement on nature, Plotinus is implicitly distancing himself at this point from his avowed master Plato, who criticized painting as a distant imitation of the real.

But in another respect, Plotinus, in his theory of art, is at least as abstemious as Plato himself. Plotinus acknowledges that "beauty addresses itself chiefly to sight," and that there is also beauty of words and of musical melodies (*Enneads* 1.6.1). But he states repeatedly, and in many different ways,

translation, and offering finely tuned analysis.

16 Tatarkiewcz, *History of Aesthetics*, 329.

17 Ibid., 331.

18 Ibid., 328.

that "minds that lift themselves above the realm of sense to a higher order are aware of beauty in the conduct of life, in actions, in character, in the pursuits of the intellect; and there is the beauty of the virtues" (*Enneads* 1.6.1). Where does all this other beauty come from? It comes, as Plotinus is fond of pointing out, from the One, through the forms of intellect (related to Plato's "ideas") and the activity of embodied soul.

But in what does any or all of this beauty consist? What lures sight and fills the eyes with joy at the sight? (*Enneads* 1.6.1). For centuries, most of the Greek and Roman world would have answered: beauty is beheld in symmetry and in the harmony of parts, or proportion; and secondarily, perhaps, in graceful and colorful representation, or in charming or moving representation (*mimesis*). But Plotinus reminds us that something that is symmetrical or well proportioned must be made of parts. And that, he argues, counts against symmetry as essential to beauty. For if beauty were essentially tied to multiplicity, it would then be seen only in compounds. But in that case the single, individual parts could not be beautiful themselves; nor could individual colors or individual musical tones. Nor, indeed, could someone's character or conduct or a moral virtue (*Enneads* 1.6.1). It is true, he admits, that good proportions are usually beautiful, but what makes them so is not the relation between the many elements but the soul that they manifest together, and thus the unity of the parts (*Enneads* 6.7.22). We therefore have a parallel here to what Plotinus said about the higher beauty as existing in the art that makes the sculpture, not in the sculpture itself. Such an art has no "parts," but it derives from intellect and manifests soul and the quality of unity, which shows up in the sculpture.

Why doesn't Plotinus take a simpler, more obvious approach and conclude that there are various kinds of beauty and correspondingly various ways in which something can be beautiful? That he studiously avoids any such notion suggests that he may have a hidden agenda in defining beauty in such a way–in saying that the essence of beauty is one thing only and that it is never, fundamentally, what one sees or hears, never really dependent on any sensuous perception or imagination, but is instead something alive, soul-ful, imperceptible, but nonetheless unified. Such a unitary but relatively disembodied notion of beauty fits with the larger "religious" aims of Plotinus, because it readily leads us away from sensible beauty toward intellectual beauty, and ultimately from the many to the One. There is never any doubt, in the *Enneads*, that the spiritual discipline of seeing that interests Plotinus most of all is one that ends up as quickly as possible in the image-less realm of pure, intellectual vision, a sense-less though blissful "perception" of invisible, timeless beauty.

Someone familiar with the aesthetics of Augustine, or with Advaita Vedanta in Hindu philosophy, or indeed with many modes of meditation in Buddhism, will recognize their affinity with the ultimately image-less "vision" in which the higher reaches of Plotinus's path culminates. The profundity of such approaches is hardly in doubt. But they may describe only one approach to the heights. What Plotinus and his counterparts typically rule out are alternative and perhaps equally beautiful ways of conceiving a spiritual path, in which art might play a central role. One wonders, in particular, if there is not an alternative that might honor sensory and artistic beauty in a more thoroughgoing manner, which a Christian might call sacramental. Perhaps there is a way to treat with greater love and appreciation the huge diversity of beauties, the individuality of beautiful beings, and the distinctive and different qualities of the many things in which we can find both aesthetic and religious value.

We will return to that possibility. For the moment, we need to round out our discussion of Plotinus's own views of art and beauty with the observation that Plotinus gives no clear indication as to what actually justifies calling both a visible painting of Zeus and an invisible virtue or intellectual pursuit "beautiful." He complains that a notion of beauty that is based on proportion can't account for the beauty of virtuous acts, since such acts are not amenable to measurement and therefore have no proportions. But if, as Plotinus seems to propose, the link between the beauty of a painting and the beauty of a virtue is their unity rather than good proportion, the problem does not disappear. For in what, or by what, is a given virtue "unified"? We can say that it is unified by being the thing it is; that is why it has an identity. But is the mere possession of an identity any reason to be considered beautiful, let alone more beautiful, or less beautiful, than something else? What does the word "beauty" add that the word "unity" lacks? If it adds merely the notion of being desirable, the same could be said of anything that is good, as Plotinus acknowledges. Why add the attribute "beautiful" to a good deed, if it has no specifiable aesthetic features? Moreover, if the beauty of a physical temple is not in some sense greater than—or at least valuable in a different way from—the beauty of the idea of a temple, then it is hard to see what one gains in terms of beauty by building or sculpting anything at all. Indeed, in that case it seems that the temple would be useless for anyone spiritually advanced, which is exactly what Plotinus implies, what various Christians have believed, and what certain Hindu teachers have proclaimed.

But that brings us back to our question: Is there any better way, while drawing on Plotinus, to show or at least glimpse a more integral and reciprocal relationship between being beautifully artistic and being religious?

## Art as Spiritual Embodiment

With sufficient imagination we might be able to go back to bodily beauty itself and see how such beauty contributes something distinctive to the life of the spirit, instead of merely passively mirroring spiritual realities. We could thus try to revise Plotinus for our time by attributing some distinctive spiritual merit to calisthenics and other aesthetic aspects of body training. But finding spiritual meaning in bodily beauty has hazards in a social context in which Halle Berry, in defending Britney Spears against the charge that she is "too sexy," can declare bluntly (if reductively), "That's what [real] women are."[19]

Instead of taking on the whole complex issue of sex, gender, and beauty, it may be easier to revise Plotinus in a different way—by modifying his interpretation of the spiritual value of beautiful art. In the present context I must be content with doing so in terms of a single analogy. Plotinus, in a well-known passage, likens the universe to a musical dance whose choir is under the direction of the great, divine Conductor:

> In the order of its singing the choir keeps round the Conductor but may sometimes turn away, so that he is out of their sight, but when it turns back to him it sings beautifully and is truly with him; so we too are always around him—and if we were not, we should be totally dissolved and no longer exist—but not always turned to him; but when we do look to him, then we are at our goal and at rest and do not sing out of tune as we truly dance our god-inspired dance around him. (*Enneads* 6.9.9, trans. Miles)

In this analogy, which compares the most beautiful existence to the art of singing and dancing (closely related arts in antiquity), it is clear that nothing harmonious would be possible without the divine Conductor. Because this is an analogy, however, the reader must deduce where actual, earthly art as we know it—the art of music or dance or architecture—would fit into the scheme. As we have already seen, Plotinus suggests in many places that there is something special about the beauty of art, which speaks to soul and which brings to mind something of that cosmic dance and inaudible music. What he does not say is that some kind of spiritual discipline might consist in learning to attend to visible art and audible music in such a way that, more and more, one sees the depths of beautiful, sacred reality in the art and increasingly hears the heights of beautiful, sacred reality in the audible music.

Plotinus does not say that; but we could—especially in view of the fact that Plotinus has already prepared us to see with "soul" a kind of beauty in

[19] As reported on "Entertainment Weekly AOL," August 27, 2003.

art and nature that is not strictly physical. Suppose that, contrary to what Plotinus usually says, the embodiment of soul in art's beauty is a creative act that makes for new possibilities not foreseen by soul or intellect—a common testimony of artists and art lovers alike. Then it might turn out that a spiritual attentiveness to sensible forms and to aesthetically embodied imagination would itself be a spiritual discipline capable of great heights.

It is true that one cannot literally see the connection between the beauty we ascribe to sensuous art and the beauty we ascribe, for instance, to moral acts or invisible spiritual realities. But that is already a problem for Plotinus, or for anyone who would apply the term "beauty"—even by way of analogy—to something imperceptible. But the problem is already well known to us in discussing the arts, and it is one we live with all the time. Why do we call a poem beautiful or a story aesthetically engaging? It is only partly because of what we can literally perceive with our senses–the sound of the words, for instance. In larger part it is because the effect of the story or the poem engages our imaginations and senses in a total way that shares a close affinity with aesthetic response to art in its more sensuous and perceptible forms. We thus "perceive" a continuity between beauty as imagined or conceived mentally and beauty as perceived through the senses. Likewise, we "perceive" a continuity or analogy between the less embodied senses of divine presence, for instance, and the sense of the divine induced by a particular work of audible music, the very hearing of which may "sound" ineffably of the spirit.

Spiritual beauty as perceived in a work of music or in the architecture of a temple or Byzantine church could nonetheless be experienced in different ways, depending on different dispositions and the differences in perceptible forms. Subjective and contextual differences need not rule out the reality of some greater beauty or beauties toward which the more subjective responses are likewise attuned, albeit in different ways. There would thus be varieties of beauty and a great good that derives from that very variety.

This would provide multiple ways for beauty to be delightful. Indeed, some beauty could well be a more secular sort that one might enjoy while looking briefly away from the cosmic Conductor, as it were. (Plotinus assures us that the Conductor is always there; why would we need always to be looking directly?) That "looking away" in secular artistry and in relatively autonomous art could be part of the playfulness of art and religion both—not fearing that God jealously requires created beings to give the Conductor exclusive and direct attention, which is impossible for them in any case. We might even discover that looking at other people and objects is how we human beings often "see" best that One who is invisibly among us. That is to say, perhaps we connect with the divine by attending, in part, to the particular delights and moving tensions of the whole varied range of art, and of other beings, including those of nature. As Hildegard of Bingen said she heard in one of her revelations: "I am that living and fiery essence of the divine substance that glows in the beauty of the fields. I shine in the water, I burn in the sun and the moon and the stars."[20]

In modifying Plotinus in the way proposed above, we are recognizing a potential within earthly artistry and beauty that he hinted at, but in other ways questioned or undercut. Above all, we make it plain that we do not always need to turn away from sensible music and visible dance in order to ascend higher, even in a specifically religious sense. That is because Plotinus told a deeper truth than he realized when he said that visible earthly temples (or audible music or bodily dance) can be formed in such a way as to attract divinity (metaphorically speaking) and can enhance the embodied soul's sense of what is spiritual about beauty itself. The soul of us does not know it all, already. It discovers more from actually making and beholding beautiful artistic forms. For the kinds of creatures that we are, that, too, is a way of our becoming "sun-like," and "god-like."

From a Christian point of view, at least, that spiritually disciplined way of making music and of partaking bodily in beauty may be an integral part of our participating in the cosmic dance of a sacramental universe. As John of Damascus wrote in defense of icons: "Perhaps you [iconoclasts] are sublime and able to transcend what is material . . . but I, since I am a human being and bear a body, want to deal with holy things and behold them in a bodily manner."[21] In seeing how art—and not only icons—can participate in that bodily process of dealing with beautiful holy things, we may be able not only to help retrieve Plotinus for the present but also to shape a more vital theological aesthetic for our time.

[20] Hildegard of Bingen, quoted in Umberto Eco, *Art and Beauty in the Middle Ages*, trans. Hugh Bredin (New Haven: Yale University Press, 1986) 47.

[21] John of Damascus quoted in Jaroslav Pelikan, *The Christian Tradition*, vol. 2: *The Spirit of Eastern Christendom (600–1700)* (Chicago: University of Chicago Press, 1974) 122.

# The Image in Tandem

## *Painting Metaphors and Moral Discourse in Late Antique Christianity*

Georgia Frank

ONE key area of Margaret Miles's work has been to examine the metaphors by which men and women in late antiquity crafted religious identity. Just as Plotinus once declared every person a sculptor of the inmost self,[1] Gregory of Nyssa called on every Christian to be "the painter of his own life."[2] Ascetic teachers mined these artistic metaphors to guide their disciples. Basil of Ancyra, for instance, instructed virgins to regard the soul as a canvas on which the mind, like a painter, depicts her thoughts. She should be mindful of her comportment, as she displays that "image of God" from the top of her head down to her feet.[3] Others deferred all picture-making to God or Christ and instructed ascetics to figure themselves as the subject of divine portraits. One homilist exhorted ascetics to face Christ their portraitist and meet his gaze. Looking away would only spoil the savior's work.[4]

1 Plotinus, *Enneads* 1.6.9, trans. A. H. Armstrong, LCL, 7 vols. (1966–88) 1.258, discussed in Margaret R. Miles, *Plotinus on Body and Beauty: Society, Philosophy, and Religion in Third-Century Rome* (Cambridge: Blackwell, 1999) 23–24.

2 Gregory of Nyssa, "On Perfection," in *Ascetical Works,* trans. Virginia Woods Callahan, FC 58 (Washington, D.C.: Catholic University of America Press, 1967) 110, discussed in Margaret R. Miles, *Practicing Christianity: Critical Perspectives for an Embodied Spirituality* (New York: Crossroad, 1988) 22.

3 Teresa Shaw, "*Askesis* and the Appearance of Holiness," *JECS* (1998) 485–99, esp. 492–93.

4 Pseudo-Macarius, *Hom.* 30.4; H. Dörries, E. Klostermann, M. Kroege, eds., *Die 50 Geistlichen Homilien des Makarios,* PTS 6 (Berlin: de Gruyter, 1964) 242; ET: G. A. Maloney, *Pseudo-Macarius: The Fifty Spiritual Homilies and the Great Letter,* Classics of Western Spirituality (New York: Paulist, 1992), 191: "Just as the portrait painter (*eikonographos*) is attentive to the face of the king as he paints, and, when the face of the king is directly opposite,

Such vivid references to the picture-making process were not confined to ascetic writings. Preachers and biographers also called on ordinary men and women to make themselves into pictures as well as to make for themselves pictures.[5] Often, they held up completed images for imitation. John Chrysostom, for instance, regarded the apostles as perfect exemplars of virtue, in whom his audience had "a most excellent portrait. Proportion yourself to it."[6] Yet, preachers and teachers also appealed to the unfinished image. To appropriate or live an image involved many steps: the image had to be copied, sketched, tinted, painted, cleaned, and even redrawn in order to have more lasting effect. These references to techniques and methods of picture-making called on Christians to imitate the painter before they imitated the image produced. This essay focuses on the sermons of John Chrysostom, who reveals the complexities and fruitfulness of painting metaphors. Following a brief discussion of this trope in stories about the saints, I shall examine the use and appeal of these metaphors in sermons he delivered to lay Christians at Antioch, where he preached until he was named bishop of Constantinople in 398. The final part of the essay looks briefly at the decline of the metaphor in the sixth-century sung sermons by Romanos the Melodist. As I shall suggest, the metaphor's displacement coincides with developments in the cult of images during the sixth century.

## Saints' Lives

In the late-antique imagination the creation of the first humans and the creation of saints's biographies were closely intertwined. For while God created humankind in God's likeness (Gen. 1:26), biographers struggled to create a likeness of a human in the image of God. Thus fourth-century theologian Gregory of Nyssa cast God as a patient portraitist, sometimes even a self-portraitist. As the Cappadocian describes the creation of the human person:

> As then painters transfer human forms to their pictures by the means of certain colors, laying on their copy the proper and corresponding tints, so that the beauty of the original may be accurately transferred

face to face, then he paints the portrait (*zôgraphei tên eikona*) easily and well. But when he turns his face away, the painter cannot paint because the face of the subject is not looking at the painter." Here, the homilist combines painter (Christ), paint (light), patron (Spouse), and sitter (ascetic) to call attention to the sitter's responsibility in the art-making process.

5 On the versatility of the trope in the hymns of Ephraem the Syrian (306–73) see Sidney H. Griffith, "The Image of the Image Maker in the Poetry of St. Ephraem the Syrian," *StPatr* 25 (1993) 258–69.

6 *Hom. on Philippians* 12.3; trans. in Margaret M. Mitchell, *The Heavenly Trumpet: John Chrysostom and the Art of Pauline Interpretation* (Louisville: Westminster John Knox, 2002) 50.

> to the likeness, so I would have you understand that our Maker also, painting the portrait to resemble His own beauty.[7]

What Gregory describes is a double creation, such that God establishes a copy and then renders the likeness through the application of color. In his homilies on the Song of Songs, Gregory took that strategy one step further, by outlining a strategy for perception of that image. The viewer may pay exacting attention to each color but will miss the form they constitute. Likewise, readers who pay too much attention to the obvious meanings of scripture's words like mouth, kiss, myrrh, bodily limbs, bed, and so on, risk neglecting the loftier form constituted by these terms: blessedness, detachment, union with God, and so on.[8] For Gregory, then, God made humans in two stages, first the sketch, then the application of colors. Close scrutiny of each color misses the comprehensive view. His preference, then, is for the viewer to step back and take in the completed image rather than the means of production.

Unlike Gregory, however, hagiographers invited their audiences to notice the colors, lines, and brushwork of their word-pictures.[9] Since the Greek verb *graphô* means to write, but also to depict, trace, engrave, or paint, biographers often played on the term's multiple senses.[10] Athanasius, in his *Life of Antony* described the hero of asceticism as a "sufficient picture (*charaktêr*) of the ascetical life."[11] In the fifth century, Theodoret of Cyrrhus's anthology of Syrian saints's lives promised readers "living images and statues" of holy men and women. Unlike pagans, he explains, "we do not portray (*zôgraphoumen*) bodily features nor do we display for those in ignorance representations of them, but we sketch (*skiographoumen*) the forms of invisible souls and display

7 Gregory of Nyssa, *On the Making of the Human*, 5.1 (PG 44.257–98; ET: NPNF II.5.391).

8 *Hom. on the Song of Songs* 1, in Werner Jaeger and Hermann Langerbeck, editors, *Gregorii Nysseni in Canticum Canticorum*, Gregorii Nysseni Opera 6 (Leiden: Brill, 1960) 28; cf. PG 44.776; ET: Casimir McCambley, *Saint Gregory of Nyssa: Commentary on the Song of Songs* (Brookline, Mass.: Hellenic College Press, 1987) 49.

9 The biographer as portraitist was a commonplace in antiquity, see Plutarch, *Lives*. Alexander 1 (LCL 7.224); cf. Eusebius, *Life of Constantine* 1.3.2. F. Winkelmann, editor, *Über das Leben des Kaisers Konstantins*, GCS, Eusebius 1/1 (Berlin, 1975, rev. 1992) 15; ET: Averil Cameron and Stuart G. Hall (Oxford: Clarendon, 1999) 68. On Christian hagiographers, see Derek Krueger, "Hagiography as an Ascetic Practice in the Early Christian East," *JR* 79 (1999) 216–32, developed in Krueger: *Writing and Holiness: The Performance of Authorship in the Early Christian East* (Philadelphia: University of Pennsylvania Press, 2004).

10 On this trope, see Gilbert Dagron, "Mots, Images, Icônes," *Nouvelle revue de psychanalyse* 44 (1991) 151–68, esp 151–52.

11 *Life of Antony*, prol. (SC 400:126). Verbal portrait : 67.4–6; cf. G. J. M. Bartelink, *Athanase d'Alexandrie, Vie d'Antoine*, SC 400 (Paris: Cerf, 1994) 313 n.1.

unseen wars and secret struggles."[12] Fearing that words alone dim the memory, hagiographers expressed hope that their words might generate images and thereby rescue the saint from oblivion for posterity.[13] As the author of the Syriac *Life of Rabbula* declares in the opening, "we are painting before you, by means of writings, an icon of the splendid career of lord Rabbula."[14]

In his conclusion, however, Theodoret abandoned portrait gallery metaphor. He invoked again to "portraits of virtue"; yet, the painter turns out to be the reader rather than Theodoret:

> Just as painters look at their model when imitating eyes, nose, mouth, cheeks, ears, forehead, the very hairs of the head and beard, and in addition the sitting and standing postures, and the very expression of the eyes, whether genial or forbidding, so it is fitting that each of the readers of this work choose to imitate a particular life and order their own life in accordance with the one they choose.[15]

Merging the audience's gaze with the painter's, Theodoret shifted the hearer's identity from beholder to image-maker. His epilogue, then, recast his collection. What began as a public portrait gallery results in a more intimate object, a pattern-book of sorts, from which ordinary Christians might choose a model, gaze upon it, then imitate it.[16]

Another Syrian, Jacob of Sarug (ca. 451–521), was less sanguine about his ability to render a model for imitation. In a sung homily on St. Ephrem,

[12] Theodoret, *History of the Monks of Syria*, prol. 3; ed. Pierre Canivet and Alice Leroy-Molinghen, *Théodoret de Cyr, Histoire des moines de Syrie,* SC 234, 257 (Paris: Cerf, 1977, 1979); ET: R. M. Price, *History of the Monks of Syria,* Cistercian Studies 88 (Kalamazoo, Mich.: Cistercian, 1985) 4 (modified). Cf. "display as in a picture . . . the virtues of the holy men," *Life of Chariton*, prol.; G. Garitte. ed. "La vie prémétaphrastique de s. Chariton." *Bulletin de l'Institut Historique Belge de Rome* 21 (1941) 5–46. ET: Leah di Segni, "The Life of Chariton," in *Ascetic Behavior in Greco-Roman Antiquity: A Sourcebook,* edited by Vincent Wimbush (Minneapolis: Fortress, 1990) 393–421, esp. 396–97.

[13] Cyril of Scythopolis, *Life of Euthymius*, prol. 1. Text: Eduard Schwartz. *Kyrillos von Skythopolis. Texte und Untersuchungen* 49.2 (1939) 8; ET: R. M. Price, *Cyril of Scythopolis, The Lives of the Monks of Palestine,* CisSt 114 (Kalamazoo, Mich.: Cistercian, 1991) 4.

[14] Robert Doran, "The Syriac Life of Rabbula and Syrian Hellenism," in *Greek Biography and Panegyric in Late Antiquity,* edited by Tomas Hägg and Philip Rousseau (Berkeley: University of California Press, 2000) 255–71, esp. 258–59.

[15] Theodoret, *History of the Monks in Syria,* 30.7 (SC 257: 248; ET: Price, 188).

[16] For an example of later pattern-books, see "Ulpius the Roman," M. Chatzidakis, ed. *Epetêris Hetair. Byzant. Spoudôn, 14 (1938),* 393 ff. ET in Cyril Mango, *The Art of the Byzantine Empire, 312–1453* (Englewood Cliffs, N.J.: Prentice Hall, 1972; repr. Medieval Academy Reprints for Teaching; Toronto: University of Toronto Press, 1986) 214–15. On recent debates concerning this text, see John Lowden, *Illuminated Prophet Books: A Study of Byzantine Manuscripts of the Major and Minor Prophets* (University Park: Pennsylvania State University Press, 1988) 61–63.

Jacob takes the conventional appeals to humility in an even more painterly direction. Whereas hagiographers often spoke of the poverty of their words, Jacob lamented the impurity of his paints. He asks,

> How shall I, an ugly man, depict you? The colors of my discourse are too common for your narrative. . . . My paints are dirty because of my foulness, and your image requires colors that are all ablaze. . . . The colors of my discourse are like spattered mud as a result of my faults; if I approach the canvas (lit. board) of your virtues, it would be ruined. These paints of mine are mixed with polluted water; if they were splashed on your narrative, it would be disfigured. My colors are dirty and resemble a dark cloud; your icon requires the brightness of fire for the sake of its beauty. If I, a weak man, come forward to sketch your portrait, the one who depicted you would be reproached by his paints.[17]

Anxious over the sullied paints, he invokes and subverts the painterly process by casting doubt on its promise of rendering likeness. His concern for the incomplete or defective image echoes the writings of the fifth-century theologian, Diadochus of Photice, who compared God's role in baptism to painters who sketch (*diagraphousi*) the image in a single color. Like the painter who colors in the image, grace gradually adds other colors little by little to render the resemblance.[18]

The notion of the several hands required to complete an image also appears in a martyr homily by the fourth-century Bishop Asterius of Amaseia. In his praise of Euphemia, his vivid description (*ekphrasis*) of a mural depicting her gruesome death provided the occasion for graphic details of blood dripping from her wounds, flames surrounding her body, and her executioner's weapons of torture. He presents his excessiveness, however, as a lack, urging his audience to complete (*telein*) the *graphê*, a word that connotes both speech and image.[19] In his homily on the martyr Gordius, composed in 373, Basil of Caesarea likened himself to a painter forced to rely on poor copies

17 Jacob of Sarug, *Homily on Mar Ephrem*, 10–17; J. Amar, ed. PO 47:1 no. 209 (1995) 27–29.

18 Diadochus of Photice, *Capita centum de perfectione spirituali*, 89, Edouard des Places, ed. *Diadoque de Photicé: Oeuvres spirituelles*, SC 5 ter (Paris: Cerf, 1997) 149. On the significance of color as completing the image, see Liz James, "Color and Meaning in Byzantium," *JECS* 11 (2003) 223–33.

19 F. Halkin, editor, *Euphémie de Chalcédoine. Légendes Byzantines*, Subsidia Hagiographica 41 (Brussels: Société des Bollandistes, 1965) 4–8; ET: Elizabeth Castelli, "Asterius of Amasea: *Ekphrasis* on the Holy Martyr Euphemia," in *Religions of Late Antiquity in Practice*, edited by Richard Valantasis (Princeton: Princeton University Press, 2000) 464–68, esp. 468.

for his models.[20] His lament is reminiscent of Jacob of Sarug, for its robust confidence in the model, but anxiety of the materials at hand.

Read through the lens of later iconoclastic debates, one might detect a nascent critique of images and the limits of representing the divine. Yet, it is important to recall how much attention is devoted to the process of production rather than the prototype betrayed. Putting aside the relevance of these images for iconoclasm, we may probe more carefully these analogies to technique and method in their own setting. As these preachers remind us, picture-making was a collaborative enterprise, in which several hands might be involved in the slow and deliberate rendering of likeness. When ancient orators invoke painters, then, they rarely correspond to our image of the solitary artist and creative genius. Rather, they evoke the workshop as a communal space for creating images. Thus, Diadochus will refer to the baptistery as God's *ergastêrion*, or, workshop. This collaboration also invites further reflection on who is responsible for the defective image. The problem is moot for Theodoret, that confident curator of virtue, who assembles and displays his portraits. Yet, for those like Jacob of Sarug, who pointed to gaps between God's firm outline and the hagiographer's sullied colors, the defective image also carried the promise of its perfectibility by some hand other than the hagiographer's.

Such close attention to the process of image-making has not escaped the notice of art historians, who gain insight into ancient artistic techniques from these descriptions.[21] Ancient portraitists painted on wooden boards (panels), starting with preliminary design with hardpoint or white chalk, materials that allowed erasure, redrawing, and correction. This preliminary drawing in a single color was referred to as *skiagraphia*, line drawing or sketch, from *skia*, "shadow," and *graphê*, "writing" or "drawing."[22] When satisfied with the line drawing, the artist would prepare paints, mix colors, and apply them gradually to the image. Thus, the underdrawing defined the image, which would eventually displace or erase it.

[20] Johan Leemans et al., editors, *"Let Us Die That We May Live": Greek Homilies on Christian Martyrs from Asia Minor, Palestine, and Syria (c. AD 350–AD 450)* (London: Routledge, 2003) 59.

[21] My thinking has been shaped by Herbert Kessler, "Configuring the Invisible by Copying the Holy Face," in *Spiritual Seeing: Picturing God's Invisibility in Medieval Art* (Philadelphia: University of Pennsylvania Press, 2000) 64–87. Further technical discussion available in Jonathan J. G. Alexander, *Medieval Illuminators and Their Methods of Work* (New Haven: Yale University Press, 1992) 40–42, 47.

[22] J. J. Pollitt, *The Ancient View of Greek Art: Criticism, History, Terminology* (New Haven: Yale University Press, 1974) 247–54, esp. 251.

As a metaphor, however, *skiagraphia* came to be regarded as antithetical to the finished image (*eikôn*). *Skia* connoted something obscure or sketchy and became synonymous with error in the minds of ancient writers.[23] Plato, for instance, invoked the term when speaking about ignorance, delusion, and misperception.[24] The bare and dim line contrasted with the fullness and accuracy that color confers on any image. This negative connotation carried over in Christian anti-Jewish rhetoric, most typically in describing the Mosaic Law or the Old Testament as a "shadow of the good things to come, not the very image of the things."[25] As Chrysostom says elsewhere, one knows little with certainty from a sketch "until the truth of the color comes."[26] He illustrates his point by invoking how an imperial image unfolds. "Come, let us consider the images that painters delineate. You have often seen an imperial image covered with blue color [a reference to a primer that formed the background]. Then the painter traces white lines and makes an emperor." Still, the shadow is far from the truth:

> As you see things being sketched (*skiagraphoumena*), you do not know the whole [composition] . . .Who the emperor is, and who the enemy, you do not know exactly until the true colors have been applied, making the image clear and distinct. . . . In the same way you should consider the Old and New Testaments.[27]

More than embellishment, color renders truth, while the uncolored image remained incomplete and temporary.[28] Clearly, Christian discourse was not immune to those negative connotations. Nor, however, was it confined by them. For Christian preachers also appealed to the positive dimensions of picture-making. To illustrate the wider connotations of *skiagraphia* and painting, I turn to their use in sermons intended mainly for lay Christians.

## Preachers and the Painterly Self

One preacher who made ample use of painterly metaphors was John Chrysostom (ca. 347–407), deacon then presbyter in Antioch until he was appointed bishop of Constantinople in 398. The process of sketching, draw-

23 *PGL* s.v. "*skiagraphia*,"1238b.

24 Plato, *Laws* 663B; *Phaedo* 69B; *Rep.* 365C, 583B, 586B; in Pollitt, *Ancient View,* 247–49, 253–54.

25 John Chrysostom, *Hom. on Hebrews 17* (PG 63:130; ET: NPNF 1.14.448).

26 Chrysostom, *Hom. on 1 Corinthians 10:1 4* (PG 51.247), discussed in Mitchell, *Heavenly Trumpet*, 54 n.94.; cf. *PGL* s.v. "*skia*" 1238a-b.

27 Chrysostom, *In dictum Pauli, Nolo vos ignorare* (PG 51.247 ; ET: Mango, *The Art of the Byzantine Empire,* 47).

28 James, "Color and Meaning," 225–26.

ing, and coloring shaped John Chrysostom's presentation of the Christian life to his congregations.[29] His sermons, he claimed, were composite portraits, the fruits of a collaborative enterprise between his tongue as stylus and the Holy Spirit as real painter.[30] Moreover, church attendance was likened to a "dyer's vat" (*bapheion*). For some, the colors set beautifully. For others, they did not take.[31] Beyond painting and dying, he also likened his sermons to a stamped image, likening the soul to a "sort of wax. For if you apply cold discourses, you harden and make it callous; but if fiery ones, you melt it [ . . . ] form it to what you will, and engrave the royal image on it."[32]

The process of picture-making also appeared in a child-rearing manual he composed, in which he advised parents to regard their offspring as art in the making. For, "just as we see the artists adorn the images and statues with great precision, so we must care for these wondrous statues of ours. Painters when they have set the canvas on the easel paint on it day by day to accomplish their purpose."[33] By this steady application of color parents shared in the painter's and sculptor's vigilant gaze. Not content with the fleeting glimpse of a casual beholder, Chrysostom called on parents to bring eye and hand together to correct and perfect a malleable and incomplete wonder.

Even babes in the faith might benefit from this metaphor. Like Diadochus, who likened baptism to sketching and painting, Chrysostom invoked *skiagraphia* as a fitting metaphor for conversion.[34] During Lent, a time when candidates enrolled and prepared for baptism, he advised his charge with this appeal to portrait painting:

> Let the same thing happen now which occurs in the case of painters. They set forth their wooden tablets, draw white lines around them, and trace in outline the royal images before they daub on the true colors. They are perfectly free to erase and to substitute another instead,

[29] Much of what follows is indebted to Margaret Mitchell's thorough and insightful analysis of Chrysostom's pictorial language in the context of ancient philosophical and epistolary conventions. Mitchell, *Heavenly Trumpet*, 34–68.

[30] *Hom. on Acts 30.4*, quoted in Mitchell, *Heavenly Trumpet*, 40 n. 30.

[31] *Hom. on Acts 29* (PG 60.218; NPNF 1.11.186); on dipping in dye (*baphê*) as a metaphor for baptism, see *PGL* s.v. "*baphê*" 294b.

[32] *Hom. on 2 Thessalonians 2* (PG 62.478; ET: NPNF 1.13.383b).

[33] *On Vainglory and the Right Way for Parents to Bring up Their Children* (Anne-Marie Malingrey, ed. SC 188 (1972) 106–8; ET: M.L.W. Laistner, *Christianity and Pagan Culture in the Late Roman Empire* [Ithaca: Cornell University Press, 1951) 96. Cf. *Hom on Ephesians 21* (PG 62.154; NPNF 1.13.156–7): parents deserve the same honor as royal sculptors and portraitists. Whereas the latter depict kings, the former strive to depict the "king of kings" in their offspring.

[34] Montfaucon 2 (PG 49.235); ET: Paul Harkin, *St. John Chrysostom: Baptismal Instructions*, ACW 31 (New York: Paulist, 1963) 179–80; Hom. 12.23-24.

> correcting mistakes and changing what turned out badly. But after they go ahead and daub on the pigments, they can no longer erase again and substitute, since they injure the beauty of the image by doing so, and it becomes a matter for reproach. You do the same thing. Consider that your soul is an image. Before daubing on the true color of the Spirit, erase the bad habits. . . . The bath takes away the sins, but you must correct the habit, so that after the pigments have been daubed on and the royal image shines forth, you may never thereafter blot it out or cause wounds or scars on the beauty which God has given you.[35]

No step of the process has been omitted in his description, so much so that the initiand is held responsible for the creation as well the conservation of one's own image. Already in these brief examples Chrysostom extended the notion of sketching and coloring to consider how a violation of the process damaged the image.

More than art critic, however, Chrysostom is probably better remembered as a verbal portraitist. In a recent study, Margaret Mitchell offers a rich study of his portraits of the apostle Paul. His most intriguing use of the metaphor appears in his thirteenth *Homily on 1 Corinthians*, in which he invites the audience into the painter's workshop: "Now let's assume our tablet is Paul's soul." The tablet was dirty and its bare lines lacked color, "it wasn't through carelessness and laziness that Paul was drawn this way, . . . for he had zeal, but the colors were not there." Grace, however, conferred "the bright tincture of truth" on that image "and all at once he exhibited the imperial portrait."[36] As John continues, "For after receiving the colors and learning the things of which [Paul] was ignorant, he . . . immediately appeared as an excellent artist." Invoking the contrast between shadow and image we encountered in his contrast of Old and New Testament, Chrysostom used the trope to show the continuity and discontinuity between Paul's former self and new life in Christ. For color not only enhances the sketch, but animates it. Beyond this familiar supersessionist trope, however, there is a subtler shift. Noteworthy here is that what began as the image has become its own artist, an elision that, in Mitchell's words, marks the "tension between a frozen, fixed icon and a living, growing, changing presence."[37]

The remainder of the praise offers a serial description of body parts taken from Paul's letters. He begins with the head in this panel portrait, then plunges to the missionary's feet, the belly, the hands, and finally the back, before proceeding to describe the apostle's garments and ornaments. As Mitchell

35 Ibid.

36 ET and commentary from Mitchell, *Heavenly Trumpet*, 53–55, 104–21, esp. 54–55.

37 Ibid., 55.

rightly observes, Chrysostom shifts pictorial metaphors, from two-dimensional panel portrait to three-dimensional full-body statue.[38] In addition to the two images, there are also two bodies invoked here, as Paul's body and the body of Paul's letters become intertwined in this passage. With this rhetorical body, Chrysostom constructs a meditative map for Christian devotion to the apostle.[39] He cues scriptural memory to each body part, constituting the apostle's body from the corpus of letters. Like *spolia,* the fragments of older statues and monuments incorporated into new ones, Chrysostom has constructed a Pauline edifice from fragments of letters.

One might expect this mixing of bodies and image types to occlude the painterly process involved. Oddly, it does not. In this extended portrait, Chrysostom never let the audience forget that image-making is a slow and collaborative process. By fixing attention to the process, Chrysostom not only praised the apostle, who like John, addressed a congregation buckling under the call to perfection. The pictorial metaphor served Chrysostom's efforts to forge a domestic(ated) asceticism designed to suit the realities of urban and family life.[40] Whereas the apostle appealed to the body as a metaphor for the interdependence of the community's members (1 Cor 12:12-27), Chrysostom appealed to the components of an image to show how some draw, others paint, some clean, while others protect. In both cases, the roles are many, the body/image, one. Nor is any task the exclusive right of God, priest, or Christian. For some, God makes the preliminary sketch, for others, grace adds the colors. What remained constant, however, was John's resistance to the idea of a solitary artist or an image bearing no traces of its manufacture.

Chrysostom's stress on the collaborative effort is not unique to his Pauline interpretations. It also appears in other sermons, as in his opening to a sermon delivered after an extended absence:

> Just as artists (*zôgraphoi*) mix together a variety of colors (*chrômata*) and create the images (*eikonas*) of bodies, I too blended your enthusiasm for our assemblies, your willingness to listen, your love for the speaker, and all your other achievements like different colors (*chrômata*) of virtue, and I sketched (*hupograpsantes*) the character of your soul; and putting this image before the eyes of my thoughts, I received through this mental image enough consolation during this time of separation.[41]

[38] Ibid., 111.

[39] On such meditative maps to control the wandering mind in ancient and medieval memory, see Mary Carruthers, *The Craft of Thought: Meditation, Rhetoric, and the Making of Images, 400–1200* (Cambridge: Cambridge University Press, 1998) 82–84.

[40] Mitchell, *Heavenly Trumpet,* 59.

[41] Chrysostom, *On repentance,* 1 (PG 49:277); ET: Gus George Christo, *St. John Chrysostom:*

Here, he enlists his audience in the process of his mental image-making. He claims responsibility for sketching the image and mixing the colors. Yet, the congregation supplied the color. More precisely, their exemplary behavior in church were those colors that rendered the image sufficiently vivid to overcome the distances separating preacher from audience.

This limited sampling of Chrysostom's painterly metaphors reveals the multiple steps involved in making images: drawing, tinting, mixing, painting, and repainting. Moreover, the metaphor also implied the display and scrutiny and copying of images. It is puzzling, then, that such a fertile metaphor should have fallen out of use in later Christian discourse. For, as we shall see, the painterly metaphors are displaced in sixth-century sermons such as those composed by Romanos the Melodist.

## From Image to Text: Romanos the Melodist

Romanos lived in Constantinople during the first half of the sixth century, where he composed versified homilies, typically dialogue poems, performed by one singer who sang the voices of multiple characters. The liturgical setting for these sermons was somewhat different from Chrysostom's homilies. Whereas most of Chrysostom's sermons were delivered in some connection with the eucharistic liturgy, Romanos's *kontakia*, as these sung sermons are now known, were reserved for church vigils connected to specific feast days.[42]

References to image-making are rare his hymns. For instance, Romanos remarks that "God paints (*zôgraphei*) the virtues just as he traces (*stêlographei*) your vices while showing in your sleep images (*eikonas*) of temptations."[43] Here we find the many steps invoked, but only one hand, as God wields both stylus and paintbrush. The fleeting reference renders the audience into passive viewers of images set before them. For Romanos, biblical characters, like the Samaritan woman at the well, render images. "For me," the melodist says,

> the woman of Samaria . . . appears like the painter of two images (*duo eikonôn zôgraphos*) of the Church and of Mary. Therefore let us not hurry past her, for she has great attraction . . . How fair are the words

*On Repentance and Almsgiving,* FC 96 (Washington, D.C.: Catholic University of America Press, 1998) 1.

42 José Grosdidier de Matons, "Liturgie et Hymnographie: Kontakion et Canon," *Dumbarton Oaks Papers* 34/35 (1980–81) 31–44, esp. 37–39.

43 Romanos 43.2; Paul Maas and C. A. Trypanis, editors, *Sancti Romani Melodi Cantica: Cantica Genuina* (Oxford: Clarendon, 1963) 340.

> of my woman of Samaria as they sketch out (*huposkiagraphousin*), upon the well, the font from which he receives his maidservant.[44]

Here, Romanos credits one painter with two images, supplanting Chrysostom's collaborative trope, in which (at least) two artists prepare one image. The departure from Chrysostom is even more striking when one recalls the timing of this hymn in the liturgical calendar. Sung during the Easter season, Romanos calls attention to baptism as a painterly moment. Yet, for Romanos, the font, rather than the initiand, now bears the picture. Choosing the fixture over the faithful, Romanos interprets sketching for its proleptic quality. As he proclaims in the *Samaritan woman*, "O wise riddles, O wise images (*charaktêrôn*). By the faith of the holy woman all those of the Church are depicted in true colors (*zôgrapheitai ek chrômatôn*) that do not age."[45] The truth of an image is in its prefiguration rather than its preparation. Thus, Romanos has no use for the slow and deliberate process of making images or the notion of an incomplete image.

That is not to say that Romanos has no concern for depiction. In a recent article, Derek Krueger notes the role of hands in Romanos's hymns. The finger of Doubting Thomas, as it penetrated Christ's wound, was likened to a reed dipped in an inkwell. His hand "became like a pen of a swiftly writing scribe,"[46] a signature authenticating the resurrection body. When John hesitates to baptize Jesus in the Jordan, Jesus explains, "I am painting (*zôgraphô*) for you the fair and radiant form of my Church, granting to your right hand the power that after this I shall give to the palms of my friends and the priests."[47] As Krueger comments, "The disciples, and after them the priests, have this power to paint the Church through the act of baptizing, marking the identity of the Church upon the faithful."[48] Yet, the mark lacks the lines and colors so vividly detailed in baptismal descriptions from the fourth century. Romanos's stress on illumination has washed out the hues by which the faithful once participated in the production of images.

In opting for a mark that bears no trace of its manufacture, Romanos points to a larger shift in Christian rhetoric of images. Whereas the impe-

44 Romanos 9.7.1, 8–9; Maas-Trypanis, *Sancti Romanos*, 66; ET: Ephrem Lash, *St. Romanos the Melodist, Kontakia: On the Life of Christ* (San Francisco: HarperSanFrancisco, 1995) 66; cf. John 4:7-42.

45 Romanos 9.12.1-3; Maas-Trypanis, *Sancti Romanos*, 68; Lash, *St. Romanos*, 68 (modified).

46 Romanos, 30.3.1-3; Maas-Trypanis, *Sancti Romanos*, 235; Lash, *St. Romanos*, 184; discussed in Derek Krueger, "Writing and Redemption in the Hymns of Romanos the Melodist," *BMGS* 27 (2003) 2–44, esp. 32–38.

47 Romanos 5.13 (Maas-Trypanis, *Sancti Romanos*, 39).

48 Krueger, "Writing and Redemption," 37–38.

rial portrait, a prominent metaphor in John Chrysostom's preaching,[49] invited allusions to image-making, Romanos preferred a different type of image: that transferred by "palms," but not necessarily created by artists' hands. His hymns reflect a mounting interest in his own day with a class of images called *acheiropoiêta,* "not made by human hands." One such image was the Camouliana image, named after a town in Caesarea, where a woman found an image of Christ on a cloth in her garden. A copy, also regarded as *acheiropoiêtos,* was eventually transferred to Constantinople in 574, where the image gained renown as the cause of subsequent military victories.

More apt is the evolution of legends surrounding the Holy Face of Edessa.[50] Already in the fourth century, Christians were familiar with the legend of how Abgar, king of Edessa, converted to Christianity. Both the church historian Eusebius and later the pilgrim Egeria reported knowledge of a letter thought to have been written by Jesus to King Abgar of Edessa.[51] In the letter, Jesus declined the king's invitation to come to Edessa and cure him, but promised to send a disciple. That envoy, Thaddeus, also called Addai, healed the king and thereby converted all the Edessenes. By the fifth century, however, the *Doctrina Addai* offered a similar version of the story, but with two innovations: a messenger and a portrait. The king's envoy, called Hanan, not only delivered the letter also "took and painted the portrait of Jesus with choice pigments, since he was the king's artist and brought it with him to his lord King Abgar."[52] By the sixth or seventh century, the making of the portrait changed. In the *Acts of Addai*, Hanan was unable to paint the image, so Christ asked for water to wash his own face. As he dried his face, the moisture left an impression of his face on the towel. That cloth is famously known as an image "not made by human hands" (*acheiropoiêton*).[53] By the end of the

49 Mitchell, *Heavenly Trumpet*, 55–64.

50 What follows is based on Averil Cameron's reconstruction in "The History of the Image of Edessa: The Telling of a Story," in *OKEANOS: Essays Presented to Ihor Sevcenko on his Sixtieth Birthday by his Colleagues and Students*, edited by Cyril Mango and Omeljan Pritsak, Harvard Ukrainian Studies 7 (Cambridge, Mass.: Ukrainian Research Institute, 1981) 80–94, esp. 81–86. See also, Kessler, "Configuring the Invisible," 70–71. The idea was not limited to impressions of Christ. A mid-sixth century description of the Cathedral of Edessa likened the smooth and shining marble covering the walls to "the image not made by human hand"; see "The Cathedral of Edessa," 9. Syr. text ed. H. Goussen, *Le Muséon* 38 (1925) 117–36, trans. in Mango, OKEANOS, 57–58, esp. 58.

51 Eusebius, *Ecclesiastical History* 1.13; Egeria, *Travels,* 19; cited in Cameron, "History of the Image," 81–82.

52 *The Teaching of Addai*, trans. George Howard, TT 16 (Chico, Calif.: Scholars, 1981) 8–11.

53 See Hans Belting, *Likeness and Presence: A History of the Image before the Era of Art*, trans. Edmund Jephcott (Chicago: University of Chicago Press, 1994) 49–57.

sixth century, Christian writers credited the miraculous image with saving Edessa from Persian attack. The story of the Holy Face of Edessa goes well beyond the two-hundred-and-fifty-year trajectory I have recounted here. Its evolution is noteworthy: from the tale of a famous letter into the legend of a painted portrait, and finally a miraculous image produced by contact with the portrayed. Or, as Averil Cameron summarizes the transformation, "Paint was not enough."[54]

For Romanos, too, "paint was not enough." Romanos's depictions are no longer made by human hands. Instead, the hands have become scribal. Romanos's hymn on the leper illustrates this shift toward the scribal. As Derek Krueger points out, Romanos transforms a gospel account about an oral petition into the presentation of a written petition (*deêsis*), prepared by a professional scribe. The hand here is no longer that of the painter, but instead the hand of a professional scribe "extremely skilled and trained in using words."[55] It is no longer a matter of selecting and preparing paints, but of carefully choosing words.

The decline of painterly metaphors points to a connection with the rise of the non-manufactured image. Chrysostom's detailed descriptions of the slow and painstaking process of image-making gave way to a moral discourse drawn to a form of representation that stressed "contact between the portrait and the portrayed."[56] That the process of human image-making should fall out of use among preachers close to the time when *acheiropoiêta* images gained celebrity is a connection I can only raise but not fully investigate here. Even so, the turn away from image-making toward image-taking in Christian preaching reminds us of the importance of tending to the fate of interior images as well as exterior ones in the history of Christian spirituality.

The story I have been telling here begins with Chrysostom's painter and concludes with Romanos's scribe. This shift from the paintbrush to the pen calls to mind modern fiction writer Italo Calvino's remarks on the evolution of his stories:

> The first thing that comes to my mind is an image that for some reason strikes me as charged with meaning . . . the written word little by little comes to dominate the field. From now on it will be the writing that guides the story toward the most felicitous expression, and the visual imagination has no choice but to tag along.[57]

[54] Cameron, "History of the Image," 86.

[55] Romanos 8.10; Maas-Trypanis, *Sancti Romanos*, 61; Lash, *St. Romanos*, 55.

[56] Charles Barber, *Figure and Likeness: On the Limits of Representation in Byzantine Iconoclasm* (Princeton: Princeton University Press, 2002) 24.

[57] Italo Calvino, *Six Memos for the Next Millennium* (Cambridge: Harvard University Press,

Following Calvino's modus operandi, it may appear that Chrysostom's image had "no choice but to tag along." Yet, thanks to the work of Margaret Miles, we know that the visual imagination does far more than birth our stories and then trail them. Her scholarship inspires us to rethink what paths mental images introduced for historical Christians. It is in gratitude for this rich journey that I dedicate this essay to this cherished teacher and scholar.

1988) 88–89. On the Roman satirist Lucian of Samosata's use of artistic metaphors for defining his own compositional technique, see James Romm, "Wax, Stone, and Promethean Clay: Lucian as Plastic Artist," *ClAnt* 9 (1990) 74–98.

# Using Philosophers to Think With

## *The Venerable Bede on Christian Life and Practice*

Arthur G. Holder

"THE overriding concern of most historical Christians was primarily a practical concern: how to live a Christian life in the face of the expectation of an inevitable judgment in which their destiny of everlasting reward or punishment would be decided by an omniscient and unbiased judge."[1] For Margaret Miles, historic Christianity's intrinsically practical character invites the historian to consider manuals of popular (and especially lay) devotion along with theological treatises. But as she rightly points out, theological texts are likewise concerned with the interrelationship of doctrinal concepts and religious practice—though often only implicitly[2]. My intention here is to apply her insight to the learned biblical commentaries of the eighth-century Anglo-Saxon author known as the Venerable Bede and to suggest that even his treatment of classical philosophy and philosophers evidences a very practical concern with issues of devotion and virtuous behavior in the Christian life.

Scholarly assessments of Bede's attitude toward classical philosophy have varied considerably over the years, with differences of opinion and emphasis often turning on the interpretation of some key passages in his biblical commentaries. More than forty years ago, Pierre Riché declared in his magisterial Education and Culture in the Barbarian West that "Bede placed himself outside the tradition of the Fathers, who had hoped that the liberal arts would be used in the service of Christian thought."[3] Riché based much of his argument

1 Margaret R. Miles, *Practicing Christianity: Critical Perspectives for an Embodied Spirituality* (New York: Crossroad, 1990) 5–6.

2 Ibid., 6.

3 Pierre Riché, *Education and Culture in the Barbarian West: From the Sixth through the Eighth*

on Bede's commentary on 1 Samuel, where the eighth-century Anglo-Saxon monk castigated Christians who descended from the heights of Scripture to the plains of secular learning; compared classical literature to thorns on a rose or a stinger on a bee; recalled the dream in which Jerome was accused of being more Ciceronian than Christian; and warned his readers against following the example of Jonathan, who disobeyed his father King Saul by tasting the sweet honeycomb that is a figure of pagan eloquence.[4]

More recent scholars have read these and other exegetical passages in a markedly different way. Noting that Bede criticizes Saul for ordering a complete fast before battle in a pagan land, Roger Ray sees him as an advocate for moderation in the use of secular wisdom—even going so far as to take Bede's reference to the beneficial effects of having tasted the flower of a Tullian text as an indication that Bede was himself an avid practitioner of Ciceronian rhetoric.[5] George Brown doubts Ray's claim that Bede knew Cicero's *De inventione,* but he agrees that Riché was too quick to conclude that Bede saw no positive value at all in philosophy, dialectic, or rhetoric. For Brown, Bede's attitude toward secular learning may best be described in terms such as "ambivalent," "complex," and "depending on the context, relative."[6] This stress on a contextual reading of Bede's exegesis has been further developed by William McCready, who concludes judiciously:

> If Bede speaks contemptuously of worldly philosophy, what is at issue is philosophy that would offer itself as a substitute for faith, the kind of enquiry undertaken by those who, without committing themselves to the Christian life, would presume to pronounce on the meaning of human existence or the source of ultimate blessedness.[7]

The current consensus, then, is that Riché was wrong to see Bede as a rigorist ascetic who condemned all liberal arts other than grammar; McCready, Brown, and Ray all note that Bede's commentary on 1 Samuel refers approvingly to the examples of Moses and Daniel studying with the Egyptians and

*Centuries,* trans. John J. Contreni (Columbia, S.C.: University of South Carolina Press, 1976) 388. (The original French edition was published in 1962.)

4 Bede, *In Samuhelem* 2,8,20 (CCSL 119: 112, lines 1853-57); 2,14,24 (CCSL 119: 119, line 2147); 2,14,27 (CCSL 119: 120, lines 2176-79); 2,14,28-29 (CCSL 119: 120–21, lines 2200-21).

5 Roger Ray, "Bede and Cicero," *Anglo-Saxon England* 16 (1986) 1–16; *Bede, Rhetoric, and the Creation of Christian Latin Culture,* Jarrow Lecture, 1997; the Ciceronian reference appears in Bede, *In Samuhelem* 2,14,29-30 (CCSL 119: 121, lines 2227-30).

6 George Hardin Brown, *Bede the Venerable* (Boston: Twayne, 1987), 30-31; *Bede the Educator,* Jarrow Lecture 1996, 10–13.

7 William D. McCready, *Miracles and the Venerable Bede* (Toronto: Pontifical Institute of Medieval Studies, 1994) 7–19; the quotation appears on pages 15–16.

Chaldaeans, and of Paul quoting Greek poetry.[8] But these scholars agree that Bede was no strong advocate for philosophical speculation.

This is hardly surprising, since he had been exposed to virtually none of it in his own monastic education. He was able to identify a few individual philosophers who were named in his patristic sources, including Pythagoras, Plato, Aristotle, Diogenes the Cynic, Epicurus, Cicero, Celsus, and Panthenus the Stoic, who was said to have debated with Clement of Alexandria.[9] But he had read none of their writings (unless Roger Ray be right about Bede's knowledge of Cicero's *De inventione*) and his knowledge of their distinctive teachings was sketchy at best. Commenting on the Epicureans and Stoics who debate with Paul in the Book of Acts, Bede echoed Augustine's note that Epicureans put human happiness in the pleasure of the body, while Stoics found happiness in the virtue of the mind.[10] In his commentary on the Catholic Epistles, Bede quoted Epicurus as saying, "After death there is nothing, and death itself is nothing."[11] The commentary on Mark contains an extended quotation from Jerome that notes in passing that Plato located the principal part of the soul in the head, whereas Christ put it in the heart.[12] Beyond tidbits such as these, Bede's writings show no substantive engagement with ancient philosophical thought. As Gerald Bonner has observed, the most important difference between Bede and the earlier Latin Fathers was that Ambrose, Augustine, Jerome, and Gregory the Great were Roman citizens and native speakers of Latin, all of them well educated in the classical tradition. Bede was none of those things; as Bonner puts it, "In describing the dangers of the classics he was denouncing a peril to which he had never been exposed."[13]

8 Bede, *In Samuhelem* 2,14,28-29 (CCSL 119: 121, lines 2212-16).

9 The references are given by Charles Plummer, editor, *Venerabilis Baedae opera historica* (Oxford: Clarendon, 1896) 1:50–52.

10 Bede, *Expositio Actum Apostolorum* 17,18 (CCSL 121: 71, lines 19-21), trans. Lawrence T. Martin in *The Venerable Bede: Commentary on the Acts of the Apostles* (Kalamazoo, Mich.: Cistercian, 1989) 141–42.

11 Bede, *In Epistolas VII Catholicas,* on James 4, 16 (CCSL 121: 216, lines 170-71), trans. by David Hurst in *Bede the Venerable: Commentary on the Seven Catholic Epistles* (Kalamazoo, Mich.: Cistercian, 1985) 54.

12 Bede, *In Marcum* 2, 7, 20-21 (CCSL 120: 522, lines 1329-31).

13 Gerald Bonner, "Bede and Medieval Civilization," *Anglo-Saxon England* 2 (1973) 83. (The same point is made by Riché in *Education and Culture,* 393.) A few pages later (p. 89), Bonner notes that Bede did not even have access to Christian philosophical theology such as Augustine's *De trinitate*, the works of Marius Victorinus, or anything by Boethius. But both Victorinus and Boethius, along with Aristotle and Cicero, appear among the authors whose works were in the library at York later in the eighth century, according to Alcuin's *Versus de patribus, regibus, et sanctis Euboricensis ecclesiae,* ed. and trans. by Peter Godman (Oxford:

Why, then, did Bede refer to philosophy or philosophers some forty times in his biblical commentaries–usually, but not always, with critical intent? Not, I would argue, because he was worried that his monastic readers were going to read Aristotle instead of Augustine, or Plato instead of Prudentius. Bede wrote about the philosophers because he found them (as Levi-Strauss said of animals used as totems) "good to think with."[14] Here I want to focus attention not on what Bede says about philosophers but rather on what he is trying to say *with* them—that is, *by means of* his references to them. Modern scholars have tended to begin with abstract questions such as "What was Bede's attitude toward classical philosophy?" or "How did he feel about Christians making use of pagan learning?" But that was not the way the issue appeared to him, nor was it how he dealt with philosophers in his writings. For Bede, the questions were more often of a practical nature, such as, "What role did the ancient philosophers play in God's plan for the salvation of humankind?" and "What can Christians today learn—both positively and negatively—from observing the examples of philosophers in history?"

The first thing we should note is that Bede did not reserve the word *philosophia* for speculative thought derived from classical antiquity, and when he did use the word in this sense he frequently used a qualifying adjective such as "pagan" or "secular" before "philosophy." On at least four occasions, he used either *philosophia* or *philosophus* in a wholly positive sense, within a strictly biblical or Christian context:

1) When Solomon in the Book of Proverbs admonished his sons to listen to the discipline of the father, he was exhorting them "to philosophy."[15]
2) When Mary the sister of Martha and Lazarus humbly sat at Jesus' feet, the "better part" she was choosing was that of "heavenly philosophy."[16]
3) At Caesarea in Palestine, Origen initiated two young bishops-to-be into "divine philosophy."[17]
4) In Bede's History of the Abbots, the Greek Theodore of Tarsus, who becomes archbishop of Canterbury, is praised as being a man learned in "both secular and ecclesiastical philosophy."[18]

Clarendon, 1982) 124, lines 1548-50.

14 Claude Levi-Strauss, *Totemism,* trans. Rodney Needham (Boston: Beacon, 1963) 89.

15 Bede, *In Proverbia Salomonis* 1, 4, 1 (CCSL 119B: 45, lines 1-3).

16 Bede, *In Lucam* 4, prol. (CCSL 120: 231, lines 10-11).

17 Bede, *De temporum ratione* 66 (CCSL 123B: 504, lines 1250-52).

18 Bede, *Historia abbatum,* Plummer, *Venerabilis Baedae,* 1:366. This interesting point is lost in D. H. Farmer's translation of the text in *The Age of Bede* (Harmondsworth: Penguin, 1983),

Thus we must suppose that Bede was fully aware of the positive connotations of the Greek word meaning "love of wisdom" and that he heartily approved of philosophy in that sense. But which philosophy is the true and efficacious love of wisdom and to which lovers of wisdom will God grant their heart's desire? These are the "philosophical" questions that preoccupied Bede, and they appear again and again in his commentaries in relation to a cluster of favorite themes: the relationship between Jews and Gentiles in salvation history, the threat of heresy, the need to pursue right behavior for the sake of the proper heavenly reward, and the place of humility in the Christian life. Let us briefly consider how Bede uses philosophers to "think with" as he engages these four themes.

## Jews and Gentiles

A prominent feature of Bede's account of salvation history is the complementarity of roles afforded to Jews and Gentiles as the "two peoples" from whom the Christian church was derived.[19] As a group, philosophers figure in this scheme because they represent the highest and best that the Gentile world had to offer, comparable to the doctors of the law among the Jews. Thus when Bede came to the verse in 1 Samuel that reads "And behold there came Saul, following oxen out of the field," he explained as follows:

> And behold there came the Lord, the helper in due time in tribulation (Ps. 9:10, Vulg.), who was born into the world after the experts in the law and the doctors of philosophy, yet by his teaching of things heavenly he drove quite a few of them from the field of outdoor liberty to be brought within the walls of the church.[20]

Similarly, John the Baptist eating locusts and wild honey can be understood as a figure of Christ, who chose both Jews who wavered in pursuit of heavenly things like locusts that fly but short distances and Gentiles "who knew only the taste of earthly philosophy."[21]

187, where *philosophia* is rendered as "learning." There is apparently no instance in Bede's writings of *philosophia* used as a simple equivalent of "the monastic life," although that usage was very common in the Early Middle Ages in the Latin West, as shown in Jean Leclerq, "Pour l'histoire de l'expression 'philosophe chrétienne'," *Mélanges de Science Religieuse* 9 (1952): 221-26.

[19] Diarmuid Scully, "Introduction," in *Bede: On 'Tobit' and on the 'Canticle of Habakkuk,'* Seán Connolly, trans. (Dublin: Four Courts, 1997) 17–37.

[20] Bede, *In Samuhelem* 2, 11, 5 (CCSL 119: 95, lines 1140-44). Cf. 1, 2, 4 (CCSL 119: 23, lines 488-91), where the "bow of the mighty" is identified as both the prideful intention of the Jews and the loquaciousness of secular philosophy.

[21] Bede, *Homelia* 1,1 (CCSL 122: 4, lines 108-17), trans. by Lawrence T. Martin and David Hurst in *Bede the Venerable: Homilies on the Gospels,* 1:5.

The parallelism in these passages implies an evenhanded criticism of Jew and Gentile before their conversion, but in other places Bede stressed the distinctive positive attributes of Christian leaders drawn from the two peoples. When Solomon built the temple, he chose some workers from Israel and borrowed some from Hiram, king of Tyre, just as Christ took ministers of the word from among Gentiles as well as Jews. The craftsmen sent by Hiram remind Bede of Gentiles like Dionysius the Areopagite and Cyprian, "philosophers converted to true wisdom, people who because of their learning might deservedly be put in charge of people to govern them."[22] Solomon set Hiram's craftsmen to hewing timber, but only in the company of his own Hebrew servants, symbolizing that a converted philosopher like Dionysius "was better able to refute the false teachings of Athens whose syllogisms . . . he knew since a boy," but still needed to be guided by a Jewish apostle like Paul, who "had a better knowledge of the mystery of the Gospel."[23]

The priority of the biblical revelation given to the Jews is maintained also in Bede's commentary on the Song of Songs, where he says that although the church of the Gentiles has individual members who are skilled in speaking, either from natural talent or from philosophic training, nevertheless the ministry of preaching must be founded upon the silver bulwarks of Holy Scripture.[24] The same commentary contains an extended passage in which the bride seeking "him whom my soul loved" (Song 3:1) is interpreted as the Gentile church before her conversion, searching for truth in the schools of the philosophers but finding the beloved (who is Christ) only with the aid of the Jewish Christian apostles who are represented by the "sentinels who guard the city" in Song 3:3.[25] Passages such as these confirm what various scholars have written about the limited, but real, value of philosophy for Bede. Nevertheless, philosophers are not themselves the focus of his attention, but rather one set of players among many, each with its appointed role in the history of salvation. What Bede is doing here is to use the category of "philosopher" to represent the flower of the Gentiles in the ancient world, with some particular messages for missionary preachers from among his own Gentile

22 Bede, *De templo* 1 (CCSL 119A: 149, lines 91-96) trans. by Seán Connolly in *Bede: On the Temple* (Liverpool: Liverpool University Press, 1995) 8.

23 Bede, *De templo* 1 (CCSL 119A: 149-50, lines 104-27), trans. by Connolly, 8-9. Cf. Bede, *Expositio in actuum apostolorum* 17,34 (CCSL 121: 73-74, lines 93-97): "This is the Dionysius who was afterwards ordained bishop and gloriously governed the church of the Corinthians. Also he left many volumes containing his insights and they remain even now apposite to the church's benefit." Bede does not appear to have had access to the pseudo-Dionysian corpus, though he would have found references to it in the writings of Gregory the Great.

24 Bede, *In Cantica Canticorum* 5, 8, 9 (CCSL 119B: 351, lines 514-22).

25 Bede, *In Cantica Canticorum* 2, 3, 1-3 (CCSL 119B: 230-32, lines 1-64).

nation, who like Dionysius and Cyprian need to depend upon the gospel message rather than trusting in their own eloquence and oratorical skill.

## Philosophers and Heretics

Another topic that Bede often connects with philosophy is that of heresy. In the commentary on 1 Samuel he put it succinctly, quoting a famous line from Tertullian: "A certain one of ours nicely remarked that philosophers are the patriarchs of heretics, polluting the purity of the church with their perverse doctrine."[26] Twice in his commentary on Ezra and Nehemiah, Bede refers to heretics devoting themselves to the study of philosophy, rhetoric, and dialectic.[27] In his mind, then, heretics and philosophers are linked in their fondness for sophistry and argumentation. The devil's haughty city is built upon the foundation of secular eloquence, whether in the form of deceitful philosophy or heretical craftiness; the practitioners of such falsehood can be identified as the angels of Satan, who are messengers of death, or the foreign wives that corrupted the children of Israel.[28]

Both philosophers and heretics are always fighting among themselves; like the divided nations at Babel they speak in a confusion of various tongues, as contrasted with the simplicity and unity of the gospel.[29] But most importantly, they are constantly contending against the authoritative doctrine of the church. When Bede writes of the Council of Nicaea in his commentary on 1 Samuel, he recalls two debates: one between Athanasius and the heretic Arius and another between some Christian teachers and a certain Gentile philosopher armed with Aristotelian arguments.[30] This is but one concrete example of an unholy alliance that Bede considers an endemic threat to the orthodox Christian faith, as philosophy and heresy make common cause against the truth. He seldom deals with specific philosophical arguments; indeed, as we have seen, his knowledge of such argument was extremely limited. It was the contentious and arrogant spirit animating both philosophy and heresy that

26 Bede, *In Samuhelem* 4,31,1 (CCSL 119: 267, lines 2346-47).

27 Bede, *In Ezram et Neemiam* 1 (CCSL 119A: 286, lines 1784-85); 3 (CCSL 119A: 391, lines 283-84).

28 Bede, *In Genesim* 3,11,8-9 (CCSL 118A: 159, lines 607-10)*; In proverbia Salomonis* 2, 6,14 (CCSL 119B: 92, lines 89-90); *In Ezram et Neemian* 2 (CCSL 119B: 327, lines 1589-91). See also *In Proverbia Salomonis* 2,21,22 (CCSL119B: 110, lines 93-99), where "the arguments of philosophers and heretics" are overthrown by wise and faithful teachers in the church.

29 Bede, *In Genesim* 3,11,8-9 (CCSL 118A: 162-62, lines 699-706). Cf. *In Samuhelem* 2, 11, 7 (CCSL 119: 95, lines 1149-52), where the "simplicity, truth, and humility of the gospel" destroys the wisdom of secular philosophy as well as the Jews' observance of the carnal law.

30 Bede, *In Samuhelem* 4,30,9-10 (CCSL 119: 262-63, lines 2155-67); Riché, *Education and Culture,* 389, n. 186, identifies the source as Socrates, *Historia ecclesiastica* 1, 8.

aroused Bede's concern, for he knew that such a spirit could wreak havoc on the peace and unity of the church.

## Right Behavior and Heavenly Reward

As Pierre Hadot has reminded us, ancient philosophy was not a merely speculative science, but a way of life incorporating a set of rigorous spiritual exercises designed to effect the transformation of the individual in pursuit of the ultimate goal of wisdom.[31] Was Bede aware of this practical dimension of philosophy? It would seem that he recognized that philosophy claimed to be a transformative way of life, but he denied its efficacy. In a homily for the feast of Benedict Biscop, Bede commented on St. Peter's declaration to Jesus in Matthew 19: "Behold we have left all things and followed you." It is not enough, Bede notes, simply to leave all things; in order to be a true disciple, one must also follow after the Lord. He continues:

> For it is unquestionably foolish to follow Plato, Diogenes and other philosophers in trampling underfoot the riches of this life, and not to do this in order to secure eternal life, but [merely] to grasp after the empty praise of mortal men; it is foolish to take on additional hardships in the present without hope of future rest and peace.[32]

The key point here is that the philosophers, in Bede's estimation, limited their sights to the things of this world. Even when they renounced possessions, they were seeking to exchange them for an earthly reward. In his exegesis of Proverbs 19:4, Bede asserted that the riches of the heavenly kingdom are denied to the philosophers and the other teachers of the Gentiles, since they are ignorant of that certain blessedness promised in the world to come.[33] Commenting on the "pods that the swine ate" in the story of the Prodigal Son, he strikes the same note:

---

[31] Pierre Hadot, *Philosophy as a Way of Life: Spiritual Exercises from Socrates to Foucault*, ed. with an introduction by Arnold I. Davidson, Michael Chase, trans. (Malden, Mass.: Blackwell, 1995). For the case of a Neoplatonist philosopher with great influence on Christianity, see Margaret R. Miles, *Plotinus on Body and Beauty: Society, Philosophy, and Religion in Third-century Rome* (Oxford: Blackwell, 1999).

[32] Bede, *Homelia* 1,13 (CCSL 122: 88, line 8-13), Martin and Hurst, trans., *Bede the Venerable,* 125. A similar criticism of Diogenes and his followers appears in the commentary *In Ezra et Neemian* 1 (CCSL 119A: 265, lines 969-75).

[33] Bede, *In Proverbia Salomonis* 2,19,4 (CCSL 119B: 100, lines 36-38). Cf. *In Genesim* 2, 7, 20 (CCSL 18A: 119, lines 1661-64), where carnal philosophy is castigated because it knows how to dispute with subtlety about the word's creatures, but has nothing to say about the Creator and the things above the world in which the life of the saints consists.

> The servants of the father have bread in abundance, because those who strive to perform good works with a view to future reward are refreshed by the daily sustenance of heavenly grace. But those who, excluded from the father's dwelling, eagerly fill their bellies with pods, perish from hunger, for living without faith they seek after the blessed life by the vain study of philosophy. . . . [The pod,] which does not nourish the body but fills it . . . is not inappropriately compared to secular wisdom, whose discourse resounds to the applause of eloquence, but is void of the virtue of utility.[34]

Philosophy may claim to be a way of life leading to wisdom and bliss, but if it does not acknowledge the fundamental reality of a heavenly reward, it is not truly wise and can never make its practitioners truly happy. For Bede's hearers and readers, the message is clear: keep your eyes on the prize and let your ascetic discipline be motivated by a fervent desire for eternal life.[35]

## Humility in the Christian Life

A final criticism that Bede levied against the philosophers was that they were arrogant and prideful. No wonder that the Philistine giant Goliath was said to have a height of six cubits and a palm, because the devil boasts of his great height and proclaims through his philosophers that he is able to provide both the perfection of works (as in the six days of creation) and a happy end.[36] Ignorant of the divine law, those who instruct in secular philosophy fancy themselves to be their own masters in what they teach.[37] Such arrogance needed to be taught a lesson, as Augustine explained in two homiletic passages that Bede chose to include in his excerpts on the Pauline epistles. Christ chose his first disciples from among the "weak, poor and unlearned" precisely in order to keep the "strong, wealthy, wise and noble" from supposing that they had been chosen on account of their assets instead of on account of God's grace.[38]

---

34 Bede, *In Lucam* 4,15,16-17 (CCSL 120: 289, lines 2348-58), McCready, trans., *Miracles and the Venerable Bede*, 15.

35 As Margaret Miles observed in *Fullness of Life: Historical Foundations for a New Asceticism* (Philadelphia: Westminster, 1981) 91–95, Bede's focus on the rewards of heavenly life did not lead him to deny the importance of life in the body in this material world. On the contrary, as Miles says on p. 92: "Not only is the natural world in general the medium and evidence of the operation of God's power in the sensible world, but the human body itself, when the utterly incredible gift of continence has been matched by spiritual acumen, become the place of immediate sensible evidence of the already transformed body of the resurrection."

36 Bede, *In Samuhelem* 3,17,4 (CCSL 119: 147, lines 440-43).

37 Bede, *In Samuhelem* 4,15,2 (CCSL 119: 232, lines 855-56).

38 Bede, *Excerpts from the Works of Saint Augustine on the Letters of the Blessed Apostle Paul,*

> He did not choose kings or senators or philosophers or orators; instead he chose persons from the lower class, people poor and unlettered, fishermen. Peter was a fisherman, Cyprian an orator—if the fisherman had not gone first in faith, the orator would not have followed in humility.[39]

Thus far, we have been considering how Bede used philosophers to "think with"—how he was using the mental construct "philosopher" to address what he saw as the pressing needs of the church in his own day. Is there some particular point to his criticism of philosophical arrogance, other than a general call to Christian humility? I believe there is, and that the clue can be found in the preface to Bede's commentary on the Song of Songs. This preface is a sustained theological polemic (quite rare in Bede's corpus) directed against the fifth-century Pelagian bishop Julian of Eclanum. Since Bede thought that Julian was the author of the Epistle to Demetrias, which we now know to be the work of Pelagius himself, the preface includes a refutation of key points in that treatise, including the argument that the virtues evident in the lives of pagan philosophers prove that humankind after the fall has retained some form of natural good. To this Pelagian argument, Bede replies:

> Although he says that many of the philosophers have patience, chastity, modesty and other virtues from the good of nature, it is evident that none of the philosophers who are ignorant of "Christ the power of God and the wisdom of God" (1 Cor. 1:24) can have any true virtue or any true wisdom.[40]

As we have seen, Bede was willing to acknowledge that the philosophers represented the best that the pre-Christian Gentile world had to offer. But apart from Christ, that best was far from good enough. Paradoxically, by giving the outward appearance of virtue, the philosophers were of all people the most at risk of vice, since they would be tempted to boast of their own goodness apart from God's grace. It seems quite possible, then, that at least some of Bede's animus toward philosophers in his biblical commentaries was motivated by his anti-Pelagian zeal. This was in fact suggested many years ago by Pierre Riché,[41] but he did not go on to explain that for Bede and his Anglo-Saxon contemporaries the theological debate over Pelagianism was intimately bound up with the controversy over the dating of Easter, since

132. David Hurst, trans. (Kalamazoo, Mich.: Cistercian, 1999) 112. This translation is based on a preliminary critical text prepared by the translator; there is no critical edition available in print.

[39] Bede, *Excerpts from Augustine on Paul* 133, Hurst, trans., 112.

[40] Bede, *In Cantica Canticorum,* perf. (CCSL 119B: 177, lines 406–10).

[41] Riché, *Education and Culture*, 390.

the Irish were accused (wrongly, as it happens) of observing the paschal feast during the Jewish Passover, thus symbolically denying their need for the grace of Christ's resurrection.[42] So what appears to us as Bede's quarrel with the pagan philosophers may well have been a transposition of his debate with the Pelagians, which was in turn a transposition of his passionate advocacy of the Roman method for finding the date of Easter.

At first blush, it may seem that our examination of Bede's references to philosophy and philosophers has ended in a decidedly "impractical" conclusion. If a good deal of his criticism of philosophers turns out to be part of an argument about the proper date of Easter, is this not simply another instance of a theologian obsessed with matters of abstraction and theory, far removed from the practice of Christian living? Not at all! For Bede and his eighth-century Northumbrian church, there were few matters as utterly practical as the date of the Paschal observance with its associated regulations for bodies in community. In the Lenten season before Easter there was fasting, abstinence from sex, extended night vigils, and the rigorous scrutiny of candidates for baptism. After Easter there was feasting, relaxation of disciplines regarding sex and sleep, and the welcoming of the newly baptized into communion with the faithful. A disagreement about the timing of the Easter celebration had quite recently caused serious division in Bede's local church, with political overtones that lingered to his own day.[43] If denouncing the pridefulness of philosophers was an indirect way of criticizing the alleged Pelagianism of those who celebrated the Irish Easter, this was for Bede an urgently topical issue with practical implications for the Christian life.

[42] Dáibhí O'Cróinín, "'New Heresy for Old': Pelagianism in Ireland and the Papal Letter of 640," *Speculum* 60 (1985) 505–16.

[43] Henry Mayr-Harting, *The Coming of Christianity to Anglo-Saxon England,* 3d ed. (University Park: Pennsylvania State University Press, 1991) 103–13; Walter Goffart, "Bede and the Ghost of Bishop Wilfrid," chap. 4 in *The Narrators of Barbarian History (A.D. 550–800): Jordanes, Gregory of Tours, Bede, and Paul the Deacon* (Princeton: Princeton University Press, 1988) 235–328.

# "As long as that song could be heard"

## *Eternal Time in the* Trinity *of Augustine*

Peter Manchester

PLATO'S *Timaeus* famously tells us that when the father and maker wanted the already-moving and fully ensouled All to be a still more perfect image of its paradigm, he made time "an image of eternity moving according to number" (37D). The later Plotinian exposition of this doctrine that time is a 'moving image' of eternity is summed up brilliantly in the remark of Iamblichus, a generation afterward, that the moving of time is not a motion among the motions, a sensible motion, nor, as Plotinus had shown at length in his critique of Aristotle, is it something 'running alongside' sensible motions and measuring them, but it is motion "with respect to eternity alone."[1]

Iamblichus lived into the fourth century; Augustine was born some twenty years after his death. In their treatments of time both of them brought especially the problem of number into question, specifically time-number, in a way that went beyond Plotinus. Augustine in particular made original contributions to the topic, of far-reaching consequence.

I like to call our topic "numbersomeness." The whole ancient Greek tradition—Old Pythagoreans like Archytas, Plato in *Timaeus*, Aristotle in *Physics*—agreed that time is a certain numbersomeness about motion. Augustine himself calls it "numerosity" (*numerositas*).

Augustine's application of musical number to time begins in the early dialogue *On Music*, extends the concerns of its Book VI into *Confessions* X and XI, where *Music*'s featured example *deus creator omnium* returns, and culminates in *On Trinity*. There, Augustine writes a sentence using *numerositas* that I find surprisingly rich. It is one of those sentences in Augustine

[1] Commentary on *Timaeus*, Fragment 64 (Dillon). *Iamblichi Chalcidensis in Platonis Dialogos Commentariorum Fragmenta*, ed. John M. Dillon (Leiden: Brill, 1973).

that stops you dead, a remark that pulls away all to itself, like a sentence by Heraclitus that moves when you hear it so that you hear it then again, in ever-widening registers of meaning. In the treatise *On Trinity*, Augustine writes in Book XII:

> Or if one were to apprehend the rhythm of any artificial or musical sound, passing through certain intervals of time, as it rested without time in some secret and deep silence, it could at least be thought as long as that song could be heard (XII, 14, 23, trans. Arthur West Haddan).
>
> *Aut si alicuius artificiosi et musici soni per moras temporis transeuntis numerositas comprehendatur sine tempore stans in quodam secreto altoque silentio, tamdiu saltem cogitari potest quamdiu potest ille cantus audiri* (CCSL 50:377).

I have long thought it could be an adventure to trace out the background and implications of this remark, and for this occasion I want to give it a try.[2]

This is a difficult text and we need first to take a moment adjusting the translation. Arthur West Haddan's ear makes his my preferred translation, but he buries Augustine's key word *numerositas,* the subject of the sentence, with the otherwise nicely chosen "rhythm." Edmund Hill, O.P., notices the importance of the reference to number in "numerosity," but basically just puts it back into Greek: "Or if the sheer *arithmetic* of a beautiful piece of music that passes through a temporal rhythm . . . ." Since "arithmetic" no longer has any musical associations, he forces moras (intervals) to mean rhythm, though the term belongs not to what Augustine calls rhythm, but meter. For our purposes I translate as literally as I can:

> Or if the numbersomeness of some artful and musical sound passing through intervals of time were to be comprehended standing without time in some high and secluded silence, it could at least be thought as long as that song could be heard.

Turn now to the difficulty of the thought. With regard to its passing through "intervals of time," music features a numbersomeness of some sort. Whatever this is, it is apprehended or thought first and last in the hearing of the song, the actual hearing of the performance. But it can also, and appar-

[2] This paper revisits the comparison of Augustine's trinitarian image *memoria, intelligentia, voluntas* in *On Trinity* with the ecstatic-horizonal temporality of Heidegger's *Being and Time* in the author's dissertation, "The Doctrine of the Trinity in Temporal Interpretation" (Ph. D. diss., The Graduate Theological Union, 1972), from the standpoint gained in the project begun in 1975 called *The Syntax of Time: the Phenomenology of Time in Greek Physics and Speculative Logic*, completed 2003 and in final preparation for publication.

ently simultaneously, be "comprehended," which suggests some higher act of attention, and indeed comprehended "standing without time," which is familiar shorthand for "in eternity" or "in its eternal aspect." And what would be the timeless character, the eternal aspect of the numbersomeness of time? Silence. A silence thought in the hearing of music.

To unfold this thought we need two steps. First, we need to sketch the position on eternity and time of Plotinus, who deeply affects Augustine from *Confessions* on, but who all but suppresses the dimension of number in his discussion lest he seem to support Aristotle. Second, we need to show how Augustine brings number into the picture from his own experience of music, leading to a reversal of the Plotinian perspective that I call ecstatic. I close with a brief third section sketching what would become the future of that experience.

## Plotinus in Augustine

Plotinus begins his treatise *On Eternity and Time* with the prototype of Augustine's famous gambit in *Confessions,* "don't ask me, I know; ask me, I don't know," observing that we talk familiarly enough about eternity and time,

> . . .and at once and as if by a fairly continuous application of our concept of them, we think we have a clear and distinct experience of them in our own souls, as we are always speaking of them and using their names on every occasion. Of course, when we try to concentrate on them and, so to speak, to get close to them, we find again that our thought runs into difficulties (III, 7, 1: 4-9, trans. Armstrong).

How this anticipates *Confessions* XI, 14 needs no rehearsal.[3] Less often noticed is that Plotinus himself is reprising the beginning of Aristotle's treatise on time in *Physics*. Aristotle begins (IV, 10) with a rehearsal of "common assumptions" (*exôterikôn logôn*) about time, and the various conundra that befall them. He then moves to the survey of predecessor opinions that is so regular a part of an Aristotelian syllabus. And that is just what Plotinus says we do next:

> we consider the statements of the ancient philosophers about them, who differ one from the other, and perhaps also different interpretations of the same statements; and we set our minds at rest about them

[3] We know that Augustine had studied *Ennead* III, 7 *On Eternity and Time* before *Confessions,* because he uses Plotinus's concept *distentio (diastasis)* when he identifies time as a "distention of the soul" (XI, 26). But the engagement with Plotinus is even more far-reaching in *Trinity,* where, for example, X, 5, 7 expands upon but follows chapter 11's derivation of time from eternity word for word.

> and think it is sufficient if we are able, when we are asked, to state the opinions of the ancients; and so we are satisfied to be freed from the need of further research about them. Now we must consider that some of the blessed philosophers of ancient times have found out the truth. But it is proper to investigate which of them have attained it most completely, and how we too could reach an understanding about these things (*sunêsis*, literally a 'coming together' with them) (*loc. cit.*: 9-16).

In this case, the "blessed philosopher of ancient times" who has found out the truth is Plato at *Timaeus* 37D, time: the moving image of eternity. Plotinus accepts this text as guidance, but goes on to seek direct comprehension of our own, *synêsis* or union with the things themselves.

As he sets out to seek eternity and time themselves, Plotinus observes that because they have the relationship of paradigm and image, one could expound in either direction: from eternity to time, or from time to eternity. One might suppose that time, being more familiar, and ostensibly "where we are," would make the more natural beginning, but Plotinus decisively starts with eternity instead, continuing for five chapters (*Enneads* 2–6). Only in chapter 7, where he finally turns to time, do we learn why.

> But what it means to be in time and what it means to be in eternity may become known to us when we have discovered time. So, then, we must go down from eternity to the enquiry into time, and to time, for there our way led us upwards, but now we must come down in our discourse, not altogether, but in the way in which time came down. (7: 6-11)

The order of exposition is suited to the nature of time, which is itself a "coming down" from eternity, one that does not come down "altogether" (*pantê*) but holds eternity in reach, so to speak. Moreover, not just "what it means to be in time" but also "what it means to be in eternity" require us to have discovered time. Time is an eternal movement from eternity into time, a perpetual "vertical" arrival into its own "horizontal" spread or *diastasis.* This is the sense of Plotinus's formulation that time is the "life of soul" (*zôê psychês*) in a "motion of transition (*kinêsis metabatikê*) from one way-of-life (*bios*) to another" (*Enneads* 11: 43). One way-of-life is that of *Nous*, eternity, the other is that of sensible motion. Time for Plotinus is not sensible motion nor "along" sensible motion, but is its "medium" (*to en hô*), the enveloping power of Soul, reaching from eternity into its own stretching-out (*diastasis*), expressing intelligible being (the *logoi*) in the unfoldings of sensible life. The descent of the soul is nothing like downfall; it is the creative outreach of life itself, and time is the very engine of Platonic participation, so to speak, mediating intelligible into sensible being.

Despite the distracting fact that Soul is heard from throughout the pivotal chapter 11 in the first person plural, it is not individual souls, not even that especially noble individual soul She-of-the-All (*hê tou pantos psychê*), whose life (*zôê*) is time, but the sheer condition-of-existence of Soul in general (*pasa psychê*). It is sometimes agreed that Augustine accepts the Plotinian identification of time with the life of the soul, with the difference that, for Plotinus, it is the world-soul; for Augustine, his own individual soul. Something like this may be correct (though if one wishes to stress the role of individual souls in Plotinus, there is as much reason to look to "we ourselves" as to the soul-of-the-all), but the true sense of the shift in Augustine is phenomenological, not ontological. In *On Trinity*, Augustine completes a movement that was latent in *Music* and incipient in *Confessions*, more as practice than as theoretical reflection: he explores the relationship between eternity and time from within the horizons of ecstatic temporality.

## Number and the Ecstatic in Augustine

In broadest outline, Augustine shares what Plotinus finds already in *Timaeus*, the conviction that eternity and time are one topic, not two. They are extremes of something like a space, a range, a hierarchical series that maps the inner life of the soul. At one extreme, the highest or most inward, is pure contemplative mind (*nous* or *mens animi*); at the other, lowest or most outward, are embodied action, perception, and imagination. Eternity is not timeless in the sense of being a logical contrary to time. As the paradigm of which time is the image, it is paradigmatically timelike, and present in and for time in that relationship.

In *Timaeus* this is expressed in the relationship between unity and number: more specifically, in the configuration of Soul as a number series incorporating arithmetic and harmonic means that corresponds to a Pythagorean musical scale extending over four octaves and a major sixth (35B–36B). This range or dimension provides the number-space for the motions of the heavens, the simple unitary motion of the heaven of the stars that is the icon of eternity, and the sevenfold motion of the planets, the "music of the spheres," which mediates intelligible motion into the sub-lunar dimension of coming-to-be and perishing. The inner life of Soul is number, Pythagorean number, number as music and power. If time then is music, the "abiding in unity" (*menontos en heni*) (37D) of eternity is silence—a silence that is not the opposite of sound, but its source and plenitude.

Plotinus has very little to say about number in *On Eternity and Time*, despite the centrality of its role in *Timaeus*, perhaps because of his extended critique of the Aristotelian application of the "number of motion" definition to the measurement of motion, which makes time into a kind of magnitude (*Enneads*, chapters 8–10). Augustine's reflections on time, on the other hand, grew from the beginning out of his experience of music and reflection on the power of number expressed in it.

In *On Music*, the discussion of time-number was not at all shaped by the problem of scale construction, but rather by the pattern of intervals or "times" in the quantitative metric of Latin poetry. Using his favorite example, and underscoring to mark the long syllables, consider *deus creator omnium*. If the long syllables are given intervals twice the shorter, then the line has twelve times comprising four iambic feet of three times each, in the pattern one time, two times. These are its "numbers," and Augustine associates them with structure and meaning more than measurement per se, about which he is very little concerned. In Book VI of *Music*, he expands the discussion of numbers and numerosity into a hierarchical series of kinds of numbers that are all simultaneously alive in the soul in the hearing and understanding of sound as meaningful and beautiful. To give them in the order of his summary: judicial numbers, advancing numbers (*progressores*), reacting numbers (*occursores*), memorial numbers, sounding numbers (VI, 6, 16). These are kinds of numbers in the sense of kinds of time, or better dimensions within lived time, the highest or most interior being the judicial numbers, sounding numbers the most outward. Above the judicial numbers are the numbers in eternity, where they are from God as "author of all fittingness and agreement" (VI, 8, 20).

If this is to order them by rank, Augustine's own order of exposition is decidedly the reverse, in many ways anticipating the direction of the series of "turns within" that mark the ascending course from outer to inner man, and indeed from more outward to more inward aspects of each, that takes place in Books XI through XIV of *On Trinity*. This in itself expresses what I am calling the ecstatic standpoint, its rootedness in embodiment—"as long as that song could be heard."

More telling is that higher numbers are a kind of "silence" relative to the numbers below them, in the sense that they are an active latency or power that can enact at its own level all possible numbers presented "from below." What makes this silence ecstatic is that it is *heard in* the sounding numbers, or along with them, so to speak. Because of number, hearing is carried upward, inward through more inward silence, but only from an embodied beginning. The numbersomeness of a pleasing musical sound, for example, doesn't enter the soul from outside, but is enacted within the enlivened body, enjoyed, and finally judged lovely in that same numbersomeness, at the level above which the only silence remaining is eternity.

The sentence from *On Trinity* about "comprehending the numbersomeness" of some artistically accomplished musical performance as though "standing without time in some high and secluded silence" therefore means apprehending it, in its beauty, under its eternal aspect, grasped ecstatically from within time itself: "as long as that song could be heard." Indeed, I would add that from *Music* onward, it is essentially the performing of music, not its passive appreciation, in which Augustine experiences the creativity of the soul in agency, hence in embodiment, hence as mortal beauty.

It is Augustine's ecstatic experience of eternity that shapes his reversal of Plotinus's systematic strategy, which begins with eternity and "comes down" with time as it opens itself out, and then descends into that openness. Augustine begins within the openness itself, grasping the ecstatic character of its second dimension and finding in that his own eternal aspect.

The ground of Augustine's ecstatic experience of eternity is his powerful and original encounter with memory. Already in his discussion of the layers of time-numbers in *Music*, where memorial numbers are second lowest in the list, they are not left behind as he continues past them. They keep floating upward, so to speak, and it is their precedence in the series against which each of the higher and higher numbers gets tested, reaching finally the level where the question becomes memory of eternity—where Plato in *Meno* embraces the Orphic myth of preexistence of the soul. Augustine's breakthrough, which allowed him finally in the *Trinity* to let go of preexistence altogether (XII, 15, 24), was an ecstatic experience of the priority of memory, not as dealing with the past, but as an horizon of present experience itself. Radically, in the *Trinity* memory becomes the "first hypostasis" of the mind, a retention or "holding" from which all attention, whether sensory or intellectual, derives. But something of that ecstatic projection of consciousness itself as something founded is already discernible in *Music*.

In a context reminiscent of *Meno*, where the dialogue between master and disciple concerns how one cannot be reminded by questioning unless somehow the content is already present in memory, the master sums up by asking,

> Is it not evident that he, who under another's questioning moves himself within to God to know the unchangeable truth, cannot be reminded by any outside warning to see that truth, unless his memory hold fast his own same movement? (VI, 12, 36)
>
> *eum qui alio interrogante sese intus ad deum movet, ut verum incommutabile intelligat; nisi eumdem motum suum memoria teneat, non posse*

> *ad intuendum illud verum, nullo extrinsecus admonente revocari?* (PL 32:1183)

The thought is difficult because of the phrase "his own same movement," whose antecedent is more evident in the Latin than in Taliaferro's translation. The movement in question is the "movement within to God" and unchangeable truth, and it is that movement that is "held in memory"—not as recollected past experience, but as a condition of present possibility. This anticipates the position of Book XIV *On Trinity* that memory is the founding moment of self-sameness itself and therefore the dimension in which we approach or turn from God. In between lies *Confessions*, where Augustine gives himself over to an extended encounter with memory as ecstatically bringing the mind "before itself" (*ante se*), in the double sense of a constitutive priority and of being brought to appear. And insofar as the soul is brought to appear for itself in ecstatic memory, it is brought to appear before God, which is to say, in its eternal aspect.

## Ecstatic Temporality and the Future

Eternity is not something "extensive" about time, the ultimate container of all its various lengths, say, in which case it is the everlasting, for which there is a separate concept: in Greek, *aïdios*, in Latin, *sempiternus*. Eternity is something "intensive about" time. To approach it, one has to know how to go inside time.

In *On Trinity*, Augustine goes inside all the way to the pure disclosure space of ecstatic temporality itself, the image of divine trinity. This has the schema that the present is taken to be "begotten" from having been, in the overarching unity of an eschatological future. In the way he finds it psychologically, in the search for God in time and memory he began in *Confessions*,[4] the inside of time has the following structure: we only know as we remember, but we only remember as we love.

This development of trinity as a *perichôrêsis* among past, present, and future horizons of ecstatic temporality, in the image of the divine life, surfaces again centuries later in chapter 3 of Kierkegaard's *Begrebet Angest* (1844) (in English *The Concept of Dread* or *The Concept of Anxiety*). Kierkegaard argues that past, present, and future cannot be found within time itself, but only in time "synthesized" with eternity, which can happen in three ways: an eternity of the past, corresponding to the aesthetic moment; an eternal present at the root of the ethical moment; and a culminating and transforming futural

[4] John S. Dunne, *A Search for God in Time and Memory* (Notre Dame: University of Notre Dame Press, 1967), especially the section "Augustine and the Story of Experience," 45–57.

eternal, impending as the apocalyptic *Ojebliket / Augenblick* / "twinkling of an eye" of the religious moment.

As adapted by Kierkegaard, Augustine's ascription of priority to the future, specifically to the future of love as "gift of God" (subjective genitive), the "relation" that defines the Holy Spirit, becomes "existentialism," notably the interpretation by Rudolf Bultmann of the Jesus of the Gospels as the paradigm for existence in faith. The core theme of authenticity in the face of death became the crux of Martin Heidegger's temporal interpretation of finite human historical existence. In short, Augustine's precocity and originality in regard to the problem of temporality—the problem of the ecstatic unity of past, present, and future—are fruit of his tenacious and finally ecstatic meditation on the numbers of time, the music he heard them in, and the music he made of his own.

# Interlude

# Toward a Pedagogy for Comparative Visual Studies

Deborah J. Haynes

## Introduction

This essay concerns what Ernest Boyer called "the scholarship of teaching."[1] The issues I address have broad roots in discussions about pedagogy in arts education, particularly as it relates to the study of religion. Consideration of the nature of education in the visual arts is ongoing, but I see now a reemphasis on the question of what a dynamic and holistic arts education should be. For many years, my scholarly work has focused on the interrelationships of art and religion: first, making art that grew out of a broadly religious impulse; then studying world religions, theology, and art history; and now teaching what I call "comparative visual studies" to art history and studio art students. I believe that responsible pedagogy in the arts includes a global and comparative approach to visual studies and that the integration of art history and the study of religion with the practice of art is crucial to this approach.

The purpose of the essay is to articulate, first, what comparative visual studies means; second, to describe its methodology; and third, to describe briefly two new course initiatives that seek to embody these methods. The essay thus moves from the general and theoretical toward the specific. Before getting into these discussions, however, it will be useful to consider a fundamental question.

[1] Ernest Boyer, *Scholarship Reconsidered* (Princeton: Princeton University Press, 1990) 23–25.

What do students most need to learn right now, at the outset of the twenty-first century? I am convinced that aspiring artists must learn to deal with moral, religious, and metaphysical ideas. This conviction was born of my own artistic work, nearly thirty years of contemplative practice, and sustained study of the world's religious and cultural traditions. I believe that, in addition to rigorous technical training, young artists need to develop a relationship to tradition. Many people, including artists, express deeply felt cynicism and nihilism about the world in which we live. Such attitudes can only be challenged by developing a more comprehensive perspective on the present and by developing alternative visions of the future. Training for aspiring artists in observation, contemplation, and visualization can have a profound affect on their intellectual and spiritual development. An important foundation for artistic creativity involves the cultivation of such skills.

In addition, students need thorough training in visual literacy, which will prepare them for analyzing contemporary culture. Much has been written about the rapidly changing media culture that dominates our lives today, but education in the arts and technology is just beginning to address this issue. Comparative visual studies offers one avenue for helping students understand, analyze, and criticize the impact of our consumer-based media culture.

## What is Comparative Visual Studies?

Recently an analysis of what is being taught in art schools appeared in the journal *Art News*.[2] This magazine is addressed to a wide public audience that is interested in the visual arts. There are many challenges to education in the arts today, including the impact of new technologies and the emergence of quite diverse art forms that did not exist fifty years ago. Today's students and artists must therefore be trained to communicate clearly about their work and to relate that creative work to both the contemporary world and historical traditions. As Tony Jones, Dean of the School of the Art Institute of Chicago has said, "Artists today require so much more world knowledge, cultural knowledge than we've ever seen before."[3]

I share with Dutch art historian Kitty Zijlmans a sense of the importance of introducing art history in a global perspective, rather than in a narrow national European or American context. There are at least three reasons for such study.[4] First, within contemporary art, we see an increasingly global

[2] Gail Gregg, "What Are They Teaching Art Students These Days?," *Art News* (April 2003) 106–9.

[3] Gregg, "What Are They Teaching," 107.

[4] Kitty Zijlmans, "The 'Art History' of non-Western Cultures," lecture given at Edinburgh

orientation. The various large international exhibitions from *Documenta* to the *Venice Biennale* have provided important contexts for looking at the art of diverse peoples. But what about the art that is produced locally, in regions from central Australia to the Middle East, from the Southwest to the Pacific Northwest coast? Our curiosity can be the guide in exploring and finding out about this art. Second, many people already have easy access to the entire world, if not through travel, then through the technologies of mass communication from television to the Internet. If we have the resources, we can travel, learn others' languages, and see their art. Yet, I realize that this "if" is huge, for the privileges of race, ethnicity, and class often define the ability to travel. Third, the populations of many countries, including the United States, are increasingly multicultural, and this is reflected in the art that is exhibited in galleries. In June 2003, for instance, the Museum of Contemporary Art in Denver, Colorado, hosted its biennial exhibition. The show featured twenty artists from diverse cultural backgrounds—including Hispanic, African American, and Asian American artists—all of whom are, first of all, Americans living in Colorado.

Comparative visual studies builds on this rationale for a global art history. But just what do each of the terms in this title mean?

There are certainly many reasons for using a *comparative* methodology. Jonathan Z. Smith, an historian of religions, has written vividly about the cognitive importance of comparison: "The process of comparison is a fundamental characteristic of human intelligence. Whether revealed in the logical grouping of classes, in poetic similes, in mimesis, or other like activities—comparison, the bringing together of two or more objects for the purpose of either similarity or dissimilarity, is the omnipresent substructure of human thought. Without it, we could not speak, perceive, learn, or reason."[5] In short, comparison allows us to speak about and ultimately to understand what we see.

Yet comparing examples of art from different visual traditions is also problematic, for too often scholars settle for emphasizing similarities and not acknowledging differences. I have come to understand this through my own experience of focusing more on similarities between Russian Orthodox icons and Himalayan Buddhist *thangkas* during my initial years of studying them, and less on important cultural differences.

Analyzing the similarity, unity, and universality of images across cultures has provided powerful insight for generations of students, but learning

College of Art, conference titled "Framing Art History: Reflections on the Discipline," March 13–15, 2003.

5 Jonathan Z. Smith, *Map Is Not Territory: Studies in the History of Religions,* SJLA 23 (Leiden: Brill, 1976) 240.

to respect and understand difference has become even more important in contemporary society under the impact of globalization. More than anything else, offering students the opportunity to compare the art of unique cultural traditions helps them to develop both perceptual and analytical skills.

Comparative *visual* studies considers how we see the world and how we see images and representations of the world. It focuses on the interpretation of what we see, looking beyond the confines of traditional Eurocentric art history and beyond traditional approaches to studying world art.

It may be distinguished from *visual culture* studies, which also is comparative and often cross-cultural. Visual culture studies is a hybrid and complex inter-disciplinary enterprise that formed at the convergence of a variety of disciplines and methodologies.[6] Visual culture itself is an ever-moving and constantly changing entity and process, especially as artists and non-artists alike grapple with the evolution of new technologies. As Nicholas Mirzoeff put it, "Visual culture is the study of the hypervisuality of contemporary everyday life and its genealogies."[7] The term does not usually imply either a particular national culture, or distinctions between high and low, elite and popular, historical and contemporary cultures.

By contrast, visual studies seeks neither to define "culture," which is one of the most complex words in the English language,[8] nor does it focus so explicitly on contemporary life. Visual studies examines the interrelationships of artist-creator, object, and viewer within specific contexts. To paraphrase Gayatri Spivak, the questions we ask produce the field of inquiry, not some *a priori* body of materials that determine what questions can be asked.[9] Comparative visual studies examines visual phenomena, as well as the way particular art forms address the body, mind, and spirit of the viewer within particular cultural contexts, but "culture" in all of its intricacies is not the primary focus.

Nevertheless it is important to remember that, as Karel van Kooij notes, "waves of culture" may be a more appropriate phrase to use than "areas of

6 See, for instance, discussions in John A. Walker and Sarah Chaplin, *Visual Culture: An Introduction* (New York: Manchester University Press, 1997) 1–4; and Nicholas Mirzoeff, *An Introduction to Visual Culture* (New York: Routledge, 1999). Both books contain extensive bibliographies. An excellent resource on the arena of visual studies is James Elkins, *Visual Studies: A Skeptical Introduction* (New York: Routledge, 2003). His discussions of visual studies and visual literacy are superb, and we share many fundamental values about how visual studies might be developed in art programs and art schools.

7 *College Art Association News* 28 (July 2003) 7.

8 Raymond Williams, *Keywords: A Vocabulary of Culture and Society* (New York: Oxford University Press, 1983) 87–93.

9 Gayatri Spivak, quoted by Irit Rogoff, "Studying Visual Culture," in *The Visual Culture Reader*, ed. Nicholas Mirzoeff (New York: Routledge, 1998) 16.

culture."[10] For instance, we could discuss the influence of Islam across the European continent, as well as in Africa and Asia. This term, "wave of culture" acknowledges that there are no fixed artistic definitions, and that links are forged and broken between constantly changing areas and cultures. I have wondered, for example, if there was early contact among Buddhists from the Himalayas, traveling the Silk Road on horseback with *thangkas* strapped to their saddles, and Russian priests, iconographers, and holy people who might have traveled that same route, carrying their icons. The fact that the traditional training of both icon writers and *thangka* painters has so much in common has led me to ponder these possibilities.

In the wider scheme, cultures are not autonomous, but instead are mutually connected and at certain points can be compared with each other.[11] We must therefore reexamine traditional art historical assumptions that there is a fixed hierarchy within the arts, a model where most of the world is seen as subordinate to the European West, and where certain art forms such as painting have priority. Such an approach provides fruitful opportunities for students to think about the interrelationships of geography and history, religion and art.

Comparative visual *studies* can be based on a number of methodologies and disciplinary perspectives, including those derived from art history, art theory, the study of religion, and anthropology of art, as well as studio practice. It can be based on particular themes such as color, cultural myths, or symbolic systems or on careful study of the affinities and differences between the arts of diverse cultures. My comparisons are explicitly based upon the affinities, analogies, and differences between the artistic practices of quite disparate traditions. From this point of view, individual disciplines and their analytical methods become tools to be used, with care and conscious understanding.

Another aspect of comparative visual studies is the reintegration of studio practice and the study of art history. We need to ask what kind of knowledge comes from looking and what comes from making. Can visual literacy be authentic if the body and mind, eye and hand, are not connected? Motor and sensory-based training developed through drawing, for instance, can greatly help a student to see. Understanding the cultural significance of color is greatly aided by studying not only the European color theories of Goethe, Johannes Itten, and others, but also by experience and experimentation with Tibetan color theories such as that of the fifteenth-century scholar Bo-dong

10 Noted in Zijlmans "Art History." Van Kooij is an art historian at Leiden University.

11 Zijlmans, "Art History."

Pan-chen. Such knowledge is best developed pragmatically, through studio exercises.

My point here is to try to reveal the starting point and assumptions that may guide work in comparative visual studies. Hopefully, this will help to create space for a dialogue about other possible approaches and concepts of art, art's histories, and practices.

## Methodology

It is probably easier to describe what comparative visual studies is and could be than to define a specific methodology for teachers and students to use in their study. I am reminded of Mary Daly's cautions against what she calls "methodolatry," an idolatry of method that can cripple creativity and seem to offer easy answers about how to approach challenging material.[12] I have learned much from the work and writing of Margaret R. Miles in this arena, especially about how to understand images and their power to create and inform the self and how images teach and inculcate culturally specific values. Much of what follows is modeled on her published work.

I would identify five key factors in a methodology for comparative visual studies:

1) developing a "hermeneutics of generosity" combined with a "hermeneutics of suspicion"
2) cultivating a practice that Miles calls "reading for life"
3) consistently linking texts and images to their social and historical context
4) selecting and developing a personal repertoire of images
5) incorporating contemplative practice as a key pedagogical element.

### *Developing a Complex Hermeneutics*

Usually, hermeneutics is based on the assumption that interpretation and understanding develop through a circular process. The nature of this hermeneutical circle has been variously described by Friedrich Schleiermacher, Martin Heidegger, Rudolf Bultmann, Hans Georg Gadamer, Paul Ricoeur, and others. Understanding evolves through a back-and-forth movement between reader and text, between parts of a text and the whole text, between viewer and image, between the past and present. It involves awareness of both the presuppositions of the text or image and its author or creator, as well as the

12 See Mary Daly's definition of methodolatry in *Websters' First New Intergalactic Wickedary of the English Language* (Boston: Beacon, 1987) 82.

presuppositions of the reader, viewer, and critic. Interpretation should also take account of the historicity of both text and reader, image and viewer.

But a more complex hermeneutics would combine both generous and critical or suspicious interpretations. In traditional textual interpretation, as Miles has pointed out, a hermeneutics of generosity would lead to trying to understand critically the meaning of ideas presented in a text, but without particular attention to the author's political commitments, institutional loyalties, or assumptions about gender and other markers of difference.[13] Such a hermeneutics of generosity would not attempt to articulate either the complex relationship of language use to implicit and explicit power structures or issues of racism, sexism, or gender asymmetry in a text. By contrast, a hermeneutics of suspicion would address these issues directly. Keeping in mind how a hermeneutics of suspicion may be tempered by a hermeneutics of generosity leads to more nuanced interpretation and understanding.

## *Reading for Life*

Clearly, reading refers to textual practices and to literature, but we might well talk about images as texts to be read or about their intertextual qualities. Traditionally, reading and viewing or watching are considered to be passive activities, while writing and speaking are more active and effective ways to learn. However, in her 1997 book, *Reading for Life*, Miles used the metaphor of reading to offer a comprehensive methodology for approaching texts of all kinds, including visual images and works of art. To read "for life" is to train the habit of attentive listening and critical evaluation that we need in all dimensions of life.[14]

There are a number of characteristics of or ingredients in reading for life. We learn to identify the serious, gathering pictures of the world, including warnings, detailed information, and instruction about how to proceed in our daily lives. We practice (re)imagining the self, learning that each of us has a responsibility in relation to the crises and critical issues of our time. We learn to read and to view generously, trying to hear what the author or artist is trying to communicate. We acknowledge that being interconnected with all of life requires active moral responsibility, and we begin to understand that reading is practice for living responsibly. We encounter and perceive great beauty, which is connected to generosity of spirit and responsibility. As Miles wrote so eloquently in her 1996 DuBose lectures, "If perceptions

13 Margaret R. Miles, "Theological Education in a Religious Diverse World," *ThEd* 23 (1987).

14 Miles, *Reading for Life: Beauty, Pluralism, and Responsibility* (New York: Continuum, 1997).

of beauty really do produce spontaneous generosity which, in turn, augment responsibility, it is crucial to know how these effects might be generated and stimulated."[15] *How* we read and *how* we look affect *how* we live.

## *Linking Texts and Images to Their Context*

Many forms of analysis and criticism now take for granted that civil, economic, and social life, history, geography, and a variety of other factors form a matrix that must be taken into account when studying cultural artifacts. This is essential in comparative visual studies if students are to have more than a rudimentary ability to identify works of art from diverse cultural contexts.

Images always convey particular meanings to particular viewers and are as significant as verbal language in conveying senses of self, relationship, and community. We must understand, however, that the visual experience of historical viewers differed from that of people today in several ways. The understanding of and theories about vision were different. In the past, images were often experienced in the context of worship and piety. There has also been a tremendous increase in the quantity and impact of visual images. In interpreting images, whether historical or contemporary, we need to look at their reception and not only at the intentions of patrons, commissioners, or artists.

A key element in understanding particular cultural contexts is religious and cultural pluralism. Whether dealing with individual and cultural differences, differences among religious traditions, differences between historical and contemporary arts, or differences among artistic practices, we should oscillate between acknowledgment of particularity and unity, between differentiation from and identity with "the other," in whatever guise we encounter otherness. Such ideas have profound implications for both our public and private lives.

In addition, some images are used in devotional practice, while others are more aptly described as promoting contemporary media spectatorship. In both studying about and creating artworks, students learn that all images can be manipulated. Images inform, socialize, and attract or repel us. Although the meanings of images change dramatically over time, their power over us does not. It therefore behooves us to help students develop sophisticated methods for interpreting images that take into account when, where, and why they were made.

[15] Miles, "Reading for Life: Hermeneutics of Generosity and Suspicion," (The William Porcher DuBose Lectures) *STR* 41 (1997) 51.

## *Developing a Repertoire of Images*

Elsewhere I have written about a formative experience in a graduate art history seminar at Harvard University.[16] Professor Oleg Grabar urged us to learn about monuments of world art. It did not matter what our particular cultural or historical interests were. To paraphrase his exhortation: "Choose ten monuments from around the world . . . and learn everything there is to know about them." Over the subsequent years, I have developed a repertoire of images from various times and cultures that I use in my teaching and creative work. These monuments serve as points of reference, touchstones for interpreting the present and for thinking about the power of art in the future.

But it is not enough simply to urge students to learn in depth about individual works of art. How does one train oneself and one's students to choose and use images? We must become aware of the messages we receive from images, question images presented in the media, and develop an understanding of how representation functions.

Images have the power to provoke repression, but as Miles has shown, there is also the productive role of feeling, emotion, and the body in our responses to works of art. In *Carnal Knowing*, she most vividly articulated her view that an accurate understanding of the power of representation must include a social theory of the subject; that is, a theory of how socialization, subjectification, and sexualization are developed using both verbal and visual languages.[17] Building on the work of Michel Foucault, Miles argued that a repression hypothesis is inadequate for understanding either the power of images or the construction of women's subjectivity. Productive forces of attraction and regulated desire also help individuals to create a self. As Miles put it, "Formation by attraction, or the creation and direction of an individual's desire, is effective, economical, and problematic because particular forms of socialization appear to be chosen and pursued rather than imposed as external requirements."[18] Using Foucault's categories of weak and strong power, she emphasized that whereas weak power uses threats and physical force, strong power stimulates and attracts the individual. Images function most effectively to attract and thereby regulate our desire, and scholars must be attentive to this process. This is one of the major reasons for helping students select and develop a repertoire of images to aid in visualizing personal and social transformation.

[16] Deborah J. Haynes, *Art Lessons: Meditations on the Creative Life* (Boulder, Col.: Westview, 2003) 11–12.

[17] Miles, *Carnal Knowing: Female Nakedness and Religious Meaning in the Christian West* (Boston: Beacon, 1989).

[18] Ibid., 188.

## *Incorporating Contemplative Practice*

Up to this point I have been describing, albeit briefly, a methodology that scholars and teachers in many disciplines would find congenial. In turning to contemplative practice as a pedagogical method, I move into less familiar territory; therefore, the following discussion is more thorough. Contemplative skills include:

1) *mindfulness*: bringing a careful ongoing awareness to the present moment
2) *the ability to detach from normal modes of cognition and perception*: to suspend ordinary trains of thought, and to sustain mindful attention
3) *concentration*: being able to let go of distracting thought and to become absorbed
4) *equanimity*: mental and emotional evenness in place of normal reactivity; and
5) *energy and zest*: in this and all endeavors.[19]

In general, we can cultivate such capacities through silence, prayer, meditation, and a variety of spiritual practices. In my teaching, I explore how to integrate such practices into the classroom.

Before turning to more concrete discussion of how particular course initiatives have evolved, however, I want to describe two ways of understanding contemplative practice as a pedagogical method. The first concerns how we educate the person—body, mind, and spirit. The second concerns our epistemology.

At the beginning of our new century and new millennium, and at this time of global crises and war, I am inclined to ask big questions. To paraphrase colleague Peter London, who teaches at the Massachusetts College of Art in Boston, Massachusetts: What would a human being be like, if deep mindfulness were cultivated? What would an education in and through art look like, if it were concerned with the whole human being?[20]

The body is a highly intelligent system. "Its pattern recognition is uncanny," as London has written, "its awareness is constant, its manufacturing agility without peer, its ability to surmise from the scantiest of evidence

[19] This description comes from Daniel Goleman, "The Contemplative Mind: Reinventing the News," available at www.contemplativemind.org/goleman.html.

[20] Peter London, "Towards a Holistic Paradigm of Art Education," lecture given at School of the Visual Arts, New York City, October 2001.

unrivaled. It can improvise, heal itself . . . and so on."[21] The body constantly monitors itself, interprets critical information, and acts autonomously on its own behalf. If we are sensitive, we observe these processes. But mostly they are opaque to us. A holistic education will attend to, and cultivate, the body's multiple intelligences. There are many sophisticated systems—from yoga and *tai-chi* to *qigong*, dance, and mindfulness-based stress reduction in American medicine—that seek to educate us about the body. All of these traditions begin by quieting the noisy mind and twitching body so that more subtle energies can be experienced.

The artful mind is a holistic mind, as London has observed. A sense of wonder and awe, a rich intuition and imagination, access to dreams, fantasies, and the unconscious: all of these are states of mind familiar to and cultivated by artists and creative people in general. But our formal educational systems have largely expunged them from the curricula. Certainly in the United States, with recent emphasis on teaching to standardized tests, the importance of teaching the whole person is not recognized.

In our fast media-saturated culture, we need to encourage students to feel wonder and awe and to fantasize and dream. We need to call upon these innate capacities within each person, to acknowledge their importance, alongside instrumental reason and cognition, and alongside the tendency to watch television passively and manipulate digital media. If we do not teach a student how to access and discipline the creative imagination, then it will languish, subject to the seductions and ever-increasing speed of ubiquitous media images.

So, how do we nurture mindfulness, in both daily life and education? Especially, how can we evoke and nurture matters of the spirit in art education?[22] We must raise the perennial questions, as Paul Gauguin did in his famous 1897 painting, *Where Do We Come From? What Are We? Where Are We Going?* In contemporary vernacular language, we might ask, what is of ultimate value? How shall we get where we want to go, as individuals and as a people? How will we know when we have arrived? Are we nearing the end of life as we know it on the earth? To engage students with such questions is to engage in the deepest kind of educational mission. The visual arts can provide a powerful means for exploring these questions.

When all aspects of the human being are in concert, natural human behavior *is* artistic behavior. This seemingly radical proposition can be evidenced in many different forms of creativity, from cultures of all times and around the globe. The integration of body, mind, and spirit is implicit in the

[21] London, "Towards a Holistic Paradigm."

[22] This is a paraphrase of Peter London's questions, which are also my own.

training of artisans, artists, and architects and in the art produced in many cultures—in Russian Orthodox icons and Himalayan Buddhist *thangkas*; in aboriginal Australian rock carving and painting; in Haida and Tlinglit totem poles of the Pacific Northwest; in the sandpaintings and rituals of Navaho healers and shamans; in traditional Shaker architecture and artifacts; in Zen gardens such as Ryoanji in Kyoto; and in Celtic and Islamic manuscript traditions. Thus, I teach students about these arts.

Because of the strong church-state separation in public education in the U.S., it is difficult to bring religion into one's pedagogy. Obviously, this differs from the situation in many other countries and in seminaries and other educational institutions with a religious foundation. But in a secular context, two approaches have been effective. One is called "mindfulness-based stress reduction training," which is mainly offered in medical schools and has been widely publicized by Jon Kabat-Zinn; the other is called "contemplative practice as a pedagogical method," which is pertinent to my own disciplines and location in a public secular university.

Let me approach this question of contemplation as a pedagogical method from another angle, with the help of Arthur Zajonc, professor of physics at Amherst College in Massachusetts. Zajonc's radical agenda includes reframing our methods of inquiry to include the insights of contemplative practice.[23] Certainly, there is an important place for discussing religious pluralism outside of the classroom, but it is rare to speak about bringing the contemplative and spiritual back into the classroom. How this is done is obviously very important, and Zajonc suggests that we begin by considering our models of knowledge and cognition.

For instance, the modern conception of cognition is based on analytical and critical reasoning. Most of our knowledge is based on this conception of analytic, critical and rational thought, or valid inference. But there is another dimension of cognition, based on what he calls "the synthetic capacity for perceptive judgment."[24] We need to put more emphasis on direct perception and perceptive judgment, so that there is a balance among ways of knowing. Feminist philosophers and psychologists have written extensively and with great nuance about epistemologies and theories of knowledge. For instance, received knowledge, subjective knowledge, procedural knowledge, and constructed knowledge differ from one another; and each constitutes a particular mode of knowing.[25]

23 Arthur Zajonc, "Spirituality in Higher Education, Overcoming the Divide," *Liberal Education* (Winter 2002) 50–58.

24 Zajonc, "Spirituality in Higher Education," 55.

25 See Mary Field Belenky et al., *Women's Ways of Knowing* (New York: Basic Books, 1986) for one important articulation of these categories.

Contemplation can also be a way of knowing. A contemplative methodology has several features. First, experience should be granted central significance, and should not be explained away in terms of other so-called primary qualities. Second, we must recognize that cognition is always participatory and that we cannot eliminate the subject who knows. Third, direct perception should be considered an ultimate goal of cognition. This requires that we cultivate faculties that make us capable of genuine seeing. These first three points apply both to sense-based experience and to spiritual experience and insight. Developing insight is a valid goal for the art student who practices contemplative seeing, or what some art historians have begun to call "beholding." True education should be less about teaching information or data, and more about shaping and extending the faculties of knowing.[26] The artist Paul Cezanne knew this and insisted that nature is the true teacher: "Literature expresses itself by abstractions, whereas painting by means of drawing and color gives concrete shape to sensations and perceptions. . . . Get to the heart of what is before you and continue to express yourself as logically as possible."[27] We are, in most of our lives, disconnected from nature. Through cultivating our perception and attending to the natural world, we can align ourselves with the world. This will have an enormous impact on our imagination and creativity. Finally, action can then be based on moral judgments that are grounded in an empathetic connection to the world in which we live. This basis for action is very different from a cost-benefit analysis or calculating the utility of someone or something.[28]

Where are the contemplative role models in our culture? In the arts traditions that students may study. The courses I have developed have little to do with preaching particular religious dogmas or faith traditions. Rather, to paraphrase Zajonc, I seek to help students extend their powers of attention, compassion, and skillful action. In our media- and image-saturated culture, there are only a few places for developing contemplative qualities, all of which need silence and quiet time and space. The religious sanctuary, artist's studio, and scholar's study are three such locations. I believe that it is necessary to restore a balance between manipulating data and information and fostering creative action in the world. My teaching focuses on how contemplative practice is central to the cultivation of aesthetic and moral imagination.

---

[26] Zajonc, "Spirituality in Higher Education," 57.

[27] Paul Cezanne, in a letter to Emile Bernard, May 1904, in *Theories of Modern Art: A Source Book by Artists and Critics,* ed. Herschel Chipp (Berkeley: University of California Press, 1971) 20.

[28] Zajonc, "Spirituality in Higher Education," 56.

## New Course Initiatives in Comparative Visual Studies

Over the past few years, I have developed two new courses that take seriously the methodology I have been discussing and that further define a pedagogy for comparative visual studies. Comparative study demands both a complex hermeneutics, including analysis, criticism, and even a healthy suspicion, as well as a generous point of view that is open to the cultures of others. My courses emphasize how the traditions we study are applicable to students' own creativity and creative work. I encourage students to develop a repertoire of images that can become points of reference for understanding not only the history and culture of the past, but also their own lives.

The first course, "The Art of Contemplation," is primarily focused on two historical traditions, Russian Orthodox icons and Himalayan Buddhist *thangkas*. The second course, "The Contemplative Artist," is more oriented to studio practice, and involves study of a broader range of cultural traditions. In all cases, the art to be studied is created in a contemplative and ritual mode and/or for a contemplative audience.

In general, both courses focus on four major dimensions of the art that is studied. First, the role of and training of the artist. For example, examination of the roles and practices of *thangka* painters and icon writers emphasizes four aspects: anonymity of the artist, long training, a sense of spiritual mission and calling that informs the work, and contemplative practices such as prayer and meditation. We study the relevance of such models of the artist and ask if and how they may be reappropriated in our time. Second, aesthetic issues related to the object, such as iconography, use of color, and materials. Both icons and *thangkas* use complex iconography; and I work with students to begin to understand their visual languages and representational strategies in these traditions. Third, the audience or viewer for which the work was intended. How do ritual practices in Russian Orthodox churches differ from rituals in Tibetan temples? How are contemporary practices in both contexts changing under the pressures of commercialization? Fourth, the context of the work, including art history, religion, and social history. For example, what do we know about when and how icons and *thangkas* were first made? As they explore these questions and ideas, students work in small groups over the course of the semester to share resources, conduct research, and develop oral presentations.

Each course has a number of objectives: to introduce students to specific examples of contemplative art in their cultural and historical settings; to help them develop a vocabulary for visual analysis that is applicable to cross-cultural study; to help them learn to express themselves more fluently and powerfully in writing and in oral presentation; to offer opportunities to conduct research, using personal observation and experience, library resources, and the Web; and to encourage students to integrate and express their understanding in studio art projects. Each of these objectives would be considered fairly standard in many art history and visual culture studies courses.

A sixth objective—to introduce students to contemplative practice—is probably less familiar to most teachers. My courses offer students the opportunity to be part of an innovative national movement to integrate contemplative practices such as mindfulness meditation and yoga into academic study, an initiative that has been sponsored by a number of foundations and organizations.[29] During most class meetings during a semester, some time is devoted to contemplative practice and tools of internal exploration and mindfulness.

From Hindu and Buddhist forms of yoga we learn that the difference between outer sight and inner vision depends upon sustained development of the powers of imagination and visualization. In these yogic traditions, imagination (*kalpana*) is generally understood as one of the perceptual and mental processes that must be overcome in traversing the stages of practice. Like sense perception and memory, the spontaneous drifting of imagination must be stilled before other visualization techniques can be learned. In short, imagination, as it is often understood within the European and American contexts, is a deterrent to deeper awareness. By contrast, yogic inner vision is a highly trained ability to call forth visual images in the imagination. The goal of teaching art students yoga and meditation techniques, especially breath awareness, is to cultivate such powers of visualization and creativity. The actual practices vary, from sitting on a chair and following the breath, to the body scan exercise developed by Jon Kabat-Zinn and his medical collaborators, to standing, walking, and various eye exercises.

As noted above, "The Art of Contemplation" focuses on interdisciplinary and cross-cultural study of visual art from two traditions: Russian Orthodoxy and Himalayan Buddhism. In considering the models of the Orthodox icon writer and the Buddhist *thangka* painter, my goal is neither to compare nor to extol them uncritically. These traditions provide inspiration and insight for artists who are seeking an alternative to the materialist and commercial values that drive the contemporary art world. After reading about and discussing the historical contexts for these traditions, we examine how they are relevant to our broadly pluralistic context.

The second course, "The Contemplative Artist," uses similar questions and issues, but focuses on a broader range of cultural traditions, as I mentioned earlier. In addition to *thangkas* and icons, we study Celtic and Islamic manu-

29 More information on this program, which was developed by the Center for Contemplative Mind in Society, The Fetzer Institute, the Nathan Cummings Foundation, and the American Council of Learned Societies, is available at www.contemplativemind.org.

scripts, Hindu *darshan* (specifically *Devi puja*), and Navaho sandpaintings. I specifically select artistic practices from several religious traditions—Hindu, Buddhist, Christian, Muslim, and Native American. During the course we use a case-study approach in examining specific examples of these artistic traditions. The course is organized around three themes: Contemplating the word: writing and the book; Contemplating the symbolic image: sacred painting; and Contemplating ritual: performance and place. Unlike the more historical focus of "The Art of Contemplation," this course encourages students to explore what they are learning in their own studio practice and artwork, with exercises such as artist books, drawing and painting, and installation and performance.

Feedback on the courses thus far has been extremely positive. Students have written to me that the incorporation of contemplative practice in the courses has changed their approach to their school work and their lives more generally, as these three brief comments demonstrate.

> *The contemplative practice portion of this class is extremely helpful. The extra dynamic it adds keeps me attentive and eager to learn more.*

> *I think the practice is useful and relevant. It gives me a chance to slow down and take in what I am doing in a setting that is usually chaotic.*

> *I believe strongly that it [contemplative practice] is an important thing for young people to learn and an important foundation for artists.*

## Concluding Comment

This essay describes my vantage point as a professor who is concerned about what students are learning and what they most need to learn. Alongside traditional discipline-based scholarship and creative work, attention to the scholarship of teaching is crucial. In our contemporary media culture—a culture that transcends national and international boundaries—I think that little is as important as cultivating skills of perception, visualization, and interpretation. And no discipline trains us better in this arena than comparative visual studies when it is informed by a deep contemplative sensibility.

## Calypso, Revisited

Here, the weaving was not unraveled
night after night. What did he expect?
Time fell in reams. I cut it from the loom,
restrung a new fabric, until the magic
of my own youth bored me,
my tired music soured on the wind.
So I grew older, came to be less taken with a man
dogged for his dream, licking the sores
of his old loyalties, the loves he tore
into wounds, the cold shoulder he was always
looking over, the letters he would not write.
At last, in some Spring's rains,
the old thatch fell from the beach hut
where we used to idle,
Snakes nest under the floor. He came back there to find me,
after Penelope died, sailing from home, milky eyes
shocked by ruin, expecting to be remembered
in tended mementos of wood and skin, to remember
himself in my remedying flesh, finding only
the smell of amnesia, damp, the litter of mice.

I hadn't been back in an aeon.
I keep a small hostel now, up north. Some traders arrive
in favorable weather for a little mother-comfort.
I cook and do their small linen,
holiday in the South Aegean when winds are mild.

Go back
to Ithaca old man of twists and turns,
back over your singing dark blue wave,
go home and make your peace
with slaughtered suitors on the earthy bed
of the wife who did not quite turn them away.
I never held you here by force.
It was your own longing for more than one
life at a time. Dawn's fingers blanche
with gripping on the night, and Father Atlas
long ago laid down his pillars, loped off
to the west. The sky did not slump down
over the earth to crush us, only,
my dreams changed while yours
remained the same.

—Jennifer M. Phillips

# Religion and Culture

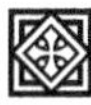

# Lay Asceticism as Social Critique

## *The Sixteenth-Century Anabaptists and Twenty-First-Century Dissent*[1]

Paula M. Cooey

MARGARET Miles had just finished her doctoral work at Berkeley and taken a job at Harvard Divinity School when we first got to know each other; I was a doctoral student in the Graduate School of Arts and Sciences at the time. It was the late seventies and feminism generated enormous intellectual excitement throughout Boston. It was a heady time, full of hope for how women, granted equity with men, could transform the world for the betterment of all, across racial, class, and sexual differences. Feminist scholars and scholars of gender analysis were exploding philosophical and theological assumptions about gendered polarities of masculine and feminine as identified respectively with spirit and nature, mind and body, intellect and feeling, aggression and passivity. A revolution that was both intellectual and practical was taking place.

Margaret Miles had written her dissertation on Augustine's view of the body right at the front-end of a total cultural re-evaluation of matter, physicality, and sentience. In her dissertation, Miles had argued that, while ambivalent, Augustine nevertheless viewed the body positively, particularly given his own historical context.[2] Miles, herself in the process of becoming a feminist, was challenging a then-held cherished feminist assumption that Augustine's view was strictly negative, a view that essentially reduced all of his thought to misogyny. This would not be the first time Miles challenged the

1 This essay represents a highly abridged and revised excerpt from Paula M. Cooey, *Jesus, Desire, and Dissent* (Minneapolis: Fortress, forthcoming).

2 Margaret Miles, *Desire and Delight: A New Reading of Augustine's Confessions* (New York: Crossroad, 1992).

reigning view of things, whether feminist or mainstream. For example, when most of us as feminists focused on the centrality of relationships, she wrote on the courage to be alone.[3] I remember one conversation in which she, much to my surprise, defended monastic asceticism. We argued over the significance of such practices as fasting, flagellation, and other mutilations of the body. I held the popular view that asceticism, particularly in its monastic forms, was at its heart a matter-hating, sexuality-fearing, woman-despising retreat from the world. She responded that, while indeed such elements might characterize some forms of asceticism, there were other features as well, chief among them a critique of a corrupt culture, characterized by violence, excessive consumption among the elite, and massive social upheaval.[4] I didn't buy it at the time. Now, however, given the continued corruption, violence, consumerism, and social upheaval that mark our own times, I see things differently. As usual, Margaret Miles was ahead of the curve. This piece is my response, now that I have begun to catch up a little. In a sense, it picks up where we left off over twenty years ago, though I shift the subject matter from monastic asceticism in the early Christian churches to lay asceticism in the sixteenth century.

The Anabaptist movement of the sixteenth century serves as a case study for a type of lay asceticism, one of the fruits of which was to contribute to what we now recognize as the secular right to dissent. In other words, what looks like (and indeed was) a separatist movement that grew out of a critique of a corrupt culture, redounds back on the dominant culture, helping to transform it, albeit slowly, over time. In this respect, an intentional communal act of separation from the dominant culture helps to create the space for dissent from within the culture. My point is not to argue historical influences. Others have already done so. Rather, I will develop the case for the further purpose of theological reflection on its significance for dissent today. While U.S. culture of the early twenty-first century obviously differs greatly from European culture in the sixteenth century, reflection on the Anabaptist response to European culture—a response that forms part of the legacy of our own contemporary dissident movements—provides an excellent occasion for interrogating how dissent now takes place. This reflection permits us the op-

3 Margaret Miles, "The Courage to be Alone—In and Out of Marriage," in *The Feminist Mystic, and Other Essays on Women and Spirituality*, ed. Mary E. Giles (New York: Crossroad, 1982) 5–17.

4 Miles was not alone in arguing that practices of self-denial surrounding food and the treatment of the body registered dissent against the dominant culture. See relevant work of Caroline Bynum, *Holy Feast and Holy Fast: The Religious Significance of Food to Medieval Women* (Berkeley: University of California Press, 1987) as example from the time and more recently Michelle Lelwica, *Starving for Salvation: The Spiritual Dimensions of Eating Problems among American Girls and Women* (New York: Oxford University Press, 1999).

portunity to be self-critical about our own assumptions and motivations that drive us to dissent or prevent us from doing so.

## Sixteenth-Century Europe

The sixteenth century saw tumultuous change in Europe. With the Christian defeat of the Muslims in Spain and the ascension of Ferdinand and Isabella to the Spanish throne at the end of the fifteenth century came widespread colonial expansion by virtually all western European countries into Africa, Asia, and what are now known as the Americas. With colonialism came Christian evangelism. Meanwhile the corruption of Christian institutions accelerated. Exposure to non-Christian and pre-Christian cultures, along with the invention of the printing press, the use of vernacular tongues as written language, particularly the translation of the Bible into the vernacular, and the extension of literacy produced an explosion in knowledge and its transmission. Scholars of the time began to employ philological methods to approach antiquity, both Greco-Roman and Hebrew, an approach to the past that was to begin the intellectual journey that ultimately produced what we now call historicized consciousness. This explosion, of course, had its roots in earlier shifts in thought and activist movements. The philosophical theologies of William of Occam and Duns Scotus, along with earlier movements protesting Roman Catholic hegemony initiated by the Cathars, the Waldensians, and the followers of John Wycliff and Jan Huss, had previously set the scene for generating what was to become successful, widespread protest. Dissident movements further resulted in religious schism and ultimately in internal reform within the Roman Church. Colonialism, technology, corruption, and its critique conspired to produce a time both filled with promise and fraught with terror.[5]

To be more precise, the sixteenth century in Europe, commonly known as the Protestant Reformation, was an age of several religious reformations within Christian traditions. In addition to the Protestant Reformation, these included the radical reformation movements of Anabaptists and Unitarians, among others, and the reform efforts within the Roman Catholic Church, marked especially by the Council of Trent and the founding of the Jesuit Order. Without question the upheaval of the times resulted from a variety of material conditions including new technologies, colonial expansion, and disrupted patterns of labor due to rising capitalism. At the same time, this period also saw great, public theological debates over human salvation in relation to human freedom. These debates ultimately shifted how ordinary peo-

5 The next four paragraphs appeared in slightly modified version in Cooey, "Immigration, Exodus, and Exile: Academic Theology and Higher Education," *JTTRS* 3.3 (2000) 125–32.

ple came to understand their ethical, political, and spiritual agency. This shift redefined their relations to their immediate communities, to religious and political authority, to the cosmos, and to God. We live today with the legacy of this redefinition. Furthermore, the process of redefinition continues.

Studying such a time, then, provides a laboratory for witnessing how theological ideas and religious institutions, practices, and identities are both the product and co-producer of human culture and society. Studying the primary texts, in their historical context, allows a glimpse of the growth, if not the birth, of modernity. We catch in process the development of both capitalism and socialism, of democracy, of individualism, and of literacy among laity, all in the midst of colonial expansion, institutional deterioration and corruption, fanatical apocalypticism, and religious and political torture and massacre.

In retrospect, the tumult of the sixteenth century and its legacy for the twenty-first century serve especially well as a laboratory for studying dissent in a variety of manifestations. I have chosen to focus here on the Anabaptists in particular because they represent ordinary lay people driven by extraordinary vision and commitment. They sought to live out nothing less than the values of the Kingdom of God on Earth as they interpreted it through scripture. Their vision of the kingdom permitted internal differences within certain limits. Within this realm, when internal differences transgressed those limits, they addressed them nonviolently. It was a counterculture they were willing to die for.

## Anabaptists

The Anabaptist movement represents dissent in the form of intentional separatism from the dominant culture.[6] This sixteenth-century dissident movement was founded on the premises of adult baptism (the believers' church) and the separation of religion and state. The Anabaptists emerged in protest against the Protestant movement, specifically the Reformed Church in Switzerland. When the Reformed Church resisted the efforts of the Anabaptists to purify its practices and executed, persecuted, or exiled them, the survivors sought, largely through separation from the surrounding culture, to form new, voluntary religious communities based solely on biblical principles, as they understood them. Although the term *Anabaptist* means "rebaptizer," it would be more accurate to call the members of this initially heterogeneous movement "Baptists," for they rejected the efficacy of infant baptism altogether.

[6] See G. H. Williams, *The Radical Reformation* (Philadelphia: Westminster, 1962); and Hans J. Hillerbrand, editor, *The Protestant Reformation* (New York: Harper & Row, 1968) 122–52.

The movement began in opposition to the Swiss Protestant Huldrych Zwingli in 1525. Frustrated by the slowness with which Zwingli executed change within the Reformed Church in Zurich, a group of his one-time followers, led by Conrad Grebel and Felix Manz, among others, began baptizing one another, initially by sprinkling, later by immersion. Meeting for prayer in private homes, the group sought a revival or spiritual awakening among those in attendance. In addition, they regularly celebrated the Lord's Supper, stripped almost entirely of all formality. Thus, these house fellowships established separate communions outside the governance of both the Reformed Church and the Zurich magistracy. In 1526 the government responded with a macabre sense of symbolic action by ordering all of the participants drowned. The movement nevertheless spread throughout Switzerland, Germany, the Netherlands, and Moravia. Because of Anabaptist commitment to separation of religion and state, Catholic and Protestant religious and political leaders alike considered them, along with spiritualists and anti-Trinitarians, to be radicals—potentially if not actually seditious and heretical. The radicals as a whole covered a range of often conflicting beliefs, practices, and lifestyles. Within this range, the Anabaptists themselves were diverse. By the mid-sixteenth century, unable to sustain heterogeneity, the Anabaptists soon split into three distinct communities—the Swiss and South German Anabaptists, the Mennonites of Holland and North Germany, and the Hutterites in Moravia.

Though Anabaptist attempts to sustain heterogeneity ultimately failed, the movement sought at one point to clarify the range of its theological diversity through a document known as *The Schleitheim Confession of Faith*, which grew out of a meeting held in 1527 at Schleitheim, located on the Swiss-German border. This confession, along with other assorted documents including a letter from a Dutch Anabaptist martyr, allow us insight into the rationale for separatism as a type of dissent.[7]

The *Schleitheim Confession* set out the norms of most, if not all, Anabaptist communities at the time.[8] The document begins with words of consolation and assurance to all those across the Anabaptist communities. The point is to clarify the limits of what is acceptable practice and belief. The focus is on communal and personal life as it should be lived in relation to God through Christ. First and foremost the writers dissociate themselves and their movement from the libertine practices of some of its members. The libertines included persons or communities who "have turned aside from the

7 See Hillerbrand, *Protestant Reformation*, 129–52.

8 Hillerbrand, *Protestant Reformation*, 129–36. See also John C. Wenger, "The Schleitheim Confession of Faith," *Mennonite Quarterly Review* 19 (1945) 243ff.

faith in the way they intend to practice and observe the freedom of the Spirit and of Christ . . . [who] think faith and love may do and permit everything."[9] The writers admonish their members to separate themselves from the "perverted."[10]

The document then proceeds to expound, among other things, seven articles on which the writers, representing their communities, agree. These include: adult baptism; the exercise of the ban or excommunication; the restriction of communion to the legitimately baptized; separation of the believers from all who are not members of the community, particularly with respect to religious differences; the proper calling of pastors; rejection of political involvement with the state and with it any use of violence; and the prohibition against swearing oaths. The practice of baptizing or rebaptizing adults, the prohibition against taking oaths, the exercise of the ban, and the injunctions on religious and political separation are of particular relevance to a discussion of dissent.

The restriction of baptism to consenting adults and, therefore, the rebaptism of those so persuaded constituted acts that directly challenged religious authority, Catholic and Protestant alike. From the perspective of theological orthodoxy, the restriction to consenting adults put infants and older children at risk of eternal damnation, should they die before reaching adulthood. That believers within the movement rejected the efficacy of their own infant baptisms and confirmations and instead baptized one another, by constructing new communities out of such activity, directly challenged the institutional structures and authority of Catholicism and Protestantism as holders of the keys to salvation. Thus the practice stood in open defiance of both doctrine and polity. Similarly defiant, but in a different arena, refusal to swear oaths challenged among other things, the legal system and the authority of the state. This refusal further constituted a rejection of loyalty to the state.

The articles addressing the separatism of the communities flow logically from the rejection of normative religious and civil authority and deserve extended attention. The injunction to withdraw from interaction with the dominant culture assumes a dualism of good and evil in which the wider culture, respecting both its religion and its politics, is evil, under the rule of the

[9] While there were groups that indulged in libertine practices, they were by far a minority. It was typical of both Catholic and Protestant polemic to tar all the radicals with the same brush by accusing them of excess. Protestants in particular sought to distinguish themselves from the radical sects as paragons of order for the purpose of legitimating their cause. See for example, John Calvin's letter to Francis I at the beginning of the *Institutes of the Christian Religion,* 2 vols., ed. John T. McNeill, Library of Christian Classics 20 (Philadelphia: Westminster, 1960) 1:9–31.

[10] Hillerbrand, *Protestant Reformation*, 130–31.

devil. To the authors, ". . . truly all creatures are in but two classes, good and bad, believing and unbelieving, darkness and light, the world and those who have come out of the world, God's temple and the idols, Christ and Belial; and none can have part with the other."[11] From the believer's perspective the issue is to avoid the contamination of a holy people by a corrupt and sinful world. God has called such a community into existence to live in Christ according to God's rule as revealed in scripture. Whatever is not addressed explicitly in scripture, rather than being a matter of indifference as the Protestants would have it, is in fact expressly forbidden.[12] Thus there should be no compromise; neither should there be contact with those who believe otherwise.

Violence is of central concern in the rejection of the wider culture associated with nonbelievers. In respect to rejecting Catholic and Protestant religious authority, the writers acknowledge that they are, by virtue of their separation, inviting violence, but they instruct their fellow believers not to respond in kind.[13] The discussion of the rejection of state authority, referred to metaphorically as the sword, includes a more extensive articulation of why the Anabaptists reject violence as a viable response to oppression, one that is grounded christologically.[14] The communities are to remain nonviolent because Christ teaches nonviolence both by example and by explicit statement. Jesus' interaction with the adulterous woman from John 8:2-11 serves as the authority for nonviolence in the face of state persecution. They are to cultivate an attitude of mercy and forgiveness, one that counsels against sin but is otherwise nonjudgmental.

This attitude should carry over into ordinary disputes, both external and internal. Resort to civil authority to settle such disputes is eschewed. Indeed, members are instructed to reject official political involvement of any kind. The writers appeal to Christ's rejection of kingship (Matt. 4:1-11; Luke 4:1-13) and to his injunction to the disciples to take up his cross and follow him (Matt. 8:24-26; Luke 9:23-27) as authoritative support against assuming political office.

The cultivation of an attitude of mercy, forgiveness, and warning extends further to self-governance as well. The lapsed or heretical members will receive first private, then public admonishment to repentance and renewal

[11] Ibid., 132.

[12] Infant baptism was a particular sticking point here. From an Anabaptist perspective, there is no scriptural example or support for the practice. For further elaboration on the Anabaptist position see the letter to Thomas Muntzer from the Zurich Anabaptists in Hillerband, *Protestant Reformation*, 124. See also George H. Williams, editor, *Spiritual and Anabaptist Writers* (Philadelphia: Westminster, 1957) 73–85.

[13] Hillerbrand, *Protestant Reformation*, 133.

[14] Ibid., 134–35.

of their faith (Matt. 18). Should the admonished prove incorrigible, they will be banned, but they may not be treated with violence for their recalcitrance. Ecclesiastical and political authorities viewed Anabaptist practices of adult baptism and the rejection of oath taking, as well as the separatism of Anabaptist communities, as acts of heresy or alternatively as an acts of sedition. In Germany, by 1530, Catholic and Protestant princes alike agreed to invoke an ancient Roman law against heresy. Membership in an Anabaptist community was subject to punishment by death, though the evangelical provinces tended to regard membership as seditious and to seek first the deportation of the dissenters before executing them.[15]

Persecution and martyrdom without respect to age, gender, or status subsequently followed Anabaptists wherever they went in Europe. The *Schleitheim Confession* makes clear that the authors knew well what would befall them at the hands of the world. The rationally expounded rejection of materialism, earthly power, and violence as associated with Catholicism and Protestantism alike, as well as with civil government in any form, reflect highly intentional dissent. The affirmation of the cross, along with the suffering and sacrifice it entailed, justified and authorized this dissent, while providing solace in the face of present persecution and encouraging a focus on the heavenly kingdom to come. A letter by a Dutch woman named Elizabeth Munstdorp, written as a last will and testament to her newly born daughter Janneken, further confirms both the deliberation of Anabaptist commitments and the christology that authorized it.[16]

Facing imminent death, Elizabeth begins the letter with the words "written to Janneken my own dearest daughter, while I was (unworthily) confined for the Lord's sake, in prison, at Antwerp, A. D. 1573." The events leading up to the letter include Elizabeth's marriage to Janneken's father, their life together for six months, his seizure and execution, her imprisonment while pregnant, the removal of the child, now a month old, and her placement with other relatives. Elizabeth interprets all these events as the will of God and to be expected in light of Jesus' death on the cross. She writes:

> . . . my dear child, if we would with Christ seek and inherit salvation, we must also bear His cross; and this is the cross He would have us bear: to follow His footsteps, and to help bear His reproach; for Christ Himself says: "Ye shall be persecuted, killed, and dispersed for my name's sake." Yea, He Himself went before us in this way of reproach,

[15] For a classic overview of these events, see Williston Walker, *A History of the Christian Church*, 3d ed. (New York: Scribner, 1970) 326–32.

[16] Hillerbrand includes this letter in abridged form in *The Protestant Reformation, op. cit.* For the full text see Thieleman van Braght, *The Bloody Theater or the Martyr's Mirror* (Scottdale, Pa.: Herald, 1951) 984–87.

> and left us an example, that we should follow His steps; for, for His sake, all must be forsaken, father, mother, sister, brother, husband, child, yea, one's own life.[17]

Of herself, Elizabeth goes on to explain, "So I must now pass through this narrow way which the prophets and martyrs of Christ passed through, and many thousands who put off mortal clothing, who died for Christ."[18] She holds out hope, though very little, for deliverance from death, if it be God's will.

One of her major concerns is to leave her daughter a remembrance of her mother, so that Janneken might grow up to fear the Lord and choose the same path. Elizabeth instructs her child in regard to the virtues Janneken should practice, among them, to avoid the ways of the world and "look at the little flock of Israelites, who have no freedom anywhere, and must always flee from one land to another, as Abraham did."[19] She counsels her to honesty, chaste speech, humility, resistance to violence in the face of inevitable persecution, obedience to her caretakers, and frugality. Elizabeth's primary concern, however, is with the significance of persecution itself. The text reveals a christology of Christ as exemplary suffering servant and martyr who demands nothing less of his followers. Such demands necessitate that the followers will be few in number, a chosen few identified with the Israelites particularly in terms of their suffering as wanderers, enslaved, and in exile. Nevertheless, these are the very people of God, whose holiness will ultimately bring them eternal life with God.

The "remembrance" Elizabeth left her daughter ("This do in remembrance of me!") was the legacy of her own dissent, an example for Janneken to follow. Generations of Anabaptists, quite ordinary people by most standards, inherited this legacy and passed it along to those who followed. Thus, a christology of the cross, combined with a concern for communal holiness or purity, produced dissent as nonviolent but adamant refusal to conform to worldly authority of any kind, even at pain of death.

## Anabaptists and Dissent in the Twenty-First Century

Dissent as we know it today in the United States, that is, as an individual right guaranteed by the First Amendment of the U.S. Constitution, assumes a religiously plural, secular state, one prohibited from requiring, establishing, or inhibiting (within certain limits) religious expression. Dissent fur-

17 Hillerbrand, *Protestant Reformation*, 148.

18 Ibid., 150.

19 Ibid., 149.

ther assumes free speech, free assembly, and a free press, likewise guaranteed. Its exercise constitutes one form of political resistance among many, just as dissent manifests itself in a variety of ways. Dissent may be intentional or inadvertent, communal or individual, conventional as in "public" or non-conventional, as in "private." Dissent can take both legal and illegal forms. It can be violent or nonviolent. Indeed it can begin nonviolently and erupt into unintended violence. Thus dissent in practice crosses and blurs the lines that distinguish reform, rebellion, and revolution from one another. That dissent is legally protected (up to a point) implies that its exercise is not only a legal right, but, under some circumstances, a moral obligation. The Anabaptists as lay ascetics understood this essential element of moral obligation in ways from which we have much to learn today.

Though Anabaptists chose to separate themselves from the dominant culture, they did so under duress, at least early on. Their dissent was intentional, their separatism initially a last recourse in the face of a violent response. They had initially sought reform from within with no success. In choosing to separate, they knew they were inviting violence, a violence that they refused to return in kind. To live in accordance with their values accorded them no other choice.

In the long run, their separatism provided a space to preserve and live out those values, some of which were in turn eventually co-opted back into the dominant culture, among them religious tolerance and the right to dissent. Speaking more generally, separatism functioned to redefine boundaries by transgressing culturally established limits. Though separatist movements never entirely escape the culture they challenge by virtue of sharing its language, they do stretch it in new directions. To deny one's community or oneself participation in what are viewed as the corruption and excesses of a dominant culture may ultimately transform the dominant culture, even as the dominant culture co-opts the counterculture that seeks to escape it.

This interaction proves ambiguous, however, in a contemporary capitalist society. Co-option means that what can be turned into a commodity will be, to be marketed and sold, thus undermining the initial intent of the values co-opted.[20] The marketing and selling of religious tolerance as New Age spirituality quickly comes to mind as a more recent example. The status of the value and practice of dissent, nevertheless, remains much more contested than religious tolerance.

Dissent as practiced today, though legal within certain limits, remains at the very least unpopular, particularly dissent against government policy.

[20] R. Laurence Moore, *Selling God: American Religion in the Marketplace of Culture* (New York: Oxford University Press, 1994).

Regarded by many citizens as unpatriotic, even treasonous, collective political dissent still reflects one or more residual countercultures, even though they are not necessarily separatist.[21] To sustain such movements requires a relative, disciplined self-denial, albeit often secular in form. The lifestyle and the practices associated with sustained dissent continue to invite violence ranging from ridicule and economic sanctions (for example, loss of work) to police action and possible brutality (for example, the violation of due process now justified since 9/11 by the Patriot Act). Many of these dissident movements are voluntary, critical of the dominant culture, persistently nonviolent, democratically structured collectives that reject the accumulation of wealth, consumerism, and waste. To the extent that the participants are willing to take the social and legal consequences of their rejection of the dominant culture, these movements share distinctive features of lay asceticism characteristic of the Anabaptists, even if they do not necessarily express them in theological discourse.

The self-denial necessary to sustain dissent and the sense of group identity required by participation in a movement furthermore stands directly in tension with some of the goals of the movements themselves. Sustained dissent may well require a willingness to put one's own self-fulfillment on the back burner. Seeking to extend self-empowerment beyond boundaries defined by nationality, race, ethnicity, socioeconomic status, gender, and sexual orientation may require that the dissident modify, if not give up, some of her own individual aspirations.

At the same time, to recognize one's own community as a besieged minority, a remnant set aside as a people to exemplify and to carry on a holy cause, however just, carries certain inherent totalitarian tendencies, if not countered by other qualities. Such self-identification may degenerate quickly into tyrannical self-regulation, as well as sanctimony toward nonparticipants, if not held in tension with the Anabaptist more universalistic trajectory of extending toward all mercy, forgiveness, and a refusal to judge others moralistically.

Most importantly, self-denial in combination with group identity centered by its status as a besieged minority—said another way, by its own martyrdom—may degenerate quickly into pretense, self-satisfaction, lack of creative self-critique, rigidity, and morbidity. Although taking up Jesus' cross lay at the heart of Elizabeth Muntsdorp's legacy to her daughter Janneken, Muntsdorp understood this as a way of life as well as a way of death. What she left her daughter was a legacy in which the way of the cross was driven

[21] Ann Coulter, *Treason: Liberal Treachery from the Cold War to the War on Terrorism* (New York: Crown Forum, 2003).

by a ministry to others that connected directly to a vision of God's rule on earth.[22] That she might move on to a second, happier life in a realm beyond death did not militate against her focus on this one, though it clearly emboldened her to carry on. That this living might place one at risk of dying for one's practices and beliefs required a focus on the significance of death in ways that likely seem alien to more secularized dissenting movements of the twenty-first century. For one thing, constitutional guarantees have lulled us into the self-deception that one is no longer vulnerable to such deaths, though depending on class, race, and gender, some of us are clearly more vulnerable than others are. We may not share the Anabaptists's view of the cross or of the resurrection. All the more important then, we would do well to consider what does indeed drive us to dissent or keep us from it in terms of the interrelation of life, death, and the future we will not live to see.

22 Womanist theologians have rightly pointed out the dangers, particularly with regard to African-American women, in disconnecting the crucifixion from Jesus' ministry. See Delores S. Williams, "Black Women's Surrogacy Experience and the Christian Notion of Redemption," in *After Patriarchy: Feminist Transformations of the World Religions*, ed. Paula M. Cooey et al. (Maryknoll, N.Y.: Orbis, 1997) 1–14; and Kelly Brown Douglas, *The Black Christ* (Maryknoll, N.Y.: Orbis, 1994).

# Expressing Life

## *Dancing Toward the Feminist Philosophy of Religion*

Kimerer L. LaMothe

*Authorship is moral responsibility.*[1]
—Margaret R. Miles

A moral fiber weaves through every page of Margaret Miles's texts, connecting scholar, argument, and context. This thread is provocative and unsettling, for Miles never lets us forget our responsibility as readers and writers—never allows us the luxury of imagining that we think and write in a vacuum. This commitment is evident in her choice of issues to study, as well as in the questions she asks, the strategies of interpretation she adopts or invents, and the conclusions she draws for our understanding of Christian history, our contemporary lives, and our ongoing education as scholars and theologians. Miles's persistent attention to the responsibility embedded in our selection of topics and methods has inspired and encouraged me in turning to the early American modern dancers and in developing the theoretical tools needed to discern the significance of their work for the feminist philosophy of religion.

## Following Miles

More precisely, in her choice of topics, Miles trains her eye to moments in Christian history that crystallize a troubling contradiction she perceives between the doctrine of "incarnation" with its appeal to "embodied self-un-

1 Margaret R. Miles, *Image as Insight: Visual Understanding in Western Christianity and Secular Culture* (Boston: Beacon, 1985) xi.

derstanding" or "carnal knowledge,"[2] on the one hand, and on the other, an evident hostility towards human bodies, especially female bodies, manifest not only in the theologies, liturgical practices, and religious imagery of the western Christian world, but also in the strategies of scholars in religious studies who privilege the religious experiences and expressions of those she calls "language users."[3] In response Miles works the problem from both ends. From one end, Miles seeks to loosen the clutch of dualistic thinking evident in both scholarly and theological interpretations of Christian religion. For example, in early Christian asceticism she finds an affirmation of human bodies as integral to the pursuit of Christian goals;[4] in Augustine's embrace of continence she finds patterns of male desire and delight.[5] Yet far from excusing Christianity, Miles works the other end of the problem as well. She interrogates representatives of Christianity who have identified female with body and male with mind and demonstrates how individuals and communities have reinforced this identification by denying women access to the tools and realms of language production. By seeking to unravel "the still-puzzling nexus of women's simultaneous empowerment and subordination" within Christian communities,[6] Miles thus points her readers forward, towards more just societies, by providing them with a critical appreciation of their Christian history, its resources, and its limitations.

Moreover, in seeking to unravel the paradoxes surrounding Christian attitudes towards (female) embodiment, Miles calls for new methods of scholarship–methods that imply nothing less than a thoroughgoing revaluation of how we theorize religion and educate future scholars. She calls for scholars not only to attend to materials other than texts, but also to learn how to approach them through the perspective of those who use or used them. Miles herself attends to visual images in art and cinema, seeking to discern how the messages they communicate qualify or contradict theological teachings and societal norms. Scholars have a moral responsibility, she avers, to become critical image-users.[7]

In short Miles reclaims as vital for our understanding of religion what Foucault calls "subjugated knowledges," knowledge "disqualified as inade-

[2] Miles, *Carnal Knowing: Female Nakedness and Religious Meaning in the Christian West* (New York: Vintage, 1991) 8.

[3] Miles, *Image as Insight*, 9.

[4] Miles, *Fullness of Life: Historical Foundations for a New Asceticism* (Philadelphia: Westminster, 1981).

[5] Miles, *Desire and Delight: A New Reading of Augustine's* Confessions (New York: Crossroad, 1991).

[6] Miles, *Carnal Knowing*, 23.

[7] Miles, *Image as Insight*, 146, 154.

quate . . . or insufficiently elaborated" as a "naive knowledge . . . located low down on the hierarchy, beneath the required level of cognition or scientificity;"[8] and she calls scholars to task for employing theories and methods that reproduce these hierarchies. Guiding the moral fiber through her work is what she perceives at the heart of the Christian message: "We, in our fascination with intellectual insight, often forget that to be a Christian is to affirm an incarnational orientation to life whereby what we *do* is as important as what we *think*."[9]

I follow Miles's lead in my work in the feminist philosophy of religion. Here, scholars are challenging topics, methods, and educational practices that have functioned to deny women access to the religious beliefs and scholarly authority available to men.[10] Impelling this project is a commitment Miles describes: to enable women to claim a "rich subjectivity," by representing the "female body, not as erotic—as 'erotic' has been culturally constructed—not as the object of fascination and scorn, but as revelation and subjectivity. It is to present the flesh, not made word, but given voice to sing its own song."[11] As Grace Jantzen elaborates, a feminist philosophy of religion must not only critique "the bias and sterility of masculinist (supposedly neutral) pursuits" but also engage in "the creative effort of developing a feminist imaginary which will enable the divine becoming of women." Drawing on Luce Irigaray, Jantzen explains that "becoming divine" does not involve recuperating masculinist religion nor "playing God" but rather projecting ideals as horizons for bodily subjectivity "according to our gender"; it is a critical, creative, open-ended task of "realizing divinity in our individual and collective lives."[12]

A question Jantzen and Miles raise is this: what kind of representational practices are capable of delivering such critical, creative imaging of female

8 Michael Foucault, *Power/Knowledge: Selected Interviews and Other Writings 1972–1977*, edited and translated by Colin Gordon (New York: Pantheon) 80–81.

9 Miles, *Fullness of Life*, 163.

10 For an introduction to the feminist philosophy of religion, its concerns and representatives, see *Hypatia: Special Issue: The Feminist Philosophy of Religion* 9 (4), a special issue devoted to the feminist philosophy of religion. In the Introduction, Nancy Frankenberry explains the rather late development of feminist work in the philosophy of religion, and sets an agenda for future work (1994). See also Grace Jantzen, *Becoming Divine: Toward a Feminist Philosophy of Religion* (Bloomington: Indiana University Press, 1999); Luce Irigaray, *Sexes and Genealogies*, trans. Carolyn Burke and Gillian C. Gill (New York: Columbia University Press, 1993); Luce Irigaray: *An Ethics of Sexual Difference*, trans. Carolyn Burke and Gillian C. Gill (Ithaca: Cornell University Press, 1993); Amy Hollywood, *Sensible Ecstasy: Mysticism, Sexual Difference, and the Demands of History* (Chicago: University of Chicago Press, 2002).

11 Miles, *Carnal Knowing*, 185.

12 Jantzen, *Becoming Divine*, 17, 27.

embodiment? Under what conditions can "the flesh" "sing its own song"?[13] What forms could such imagining assume?

The early American modern dancers—Isadora Duncan, Ruth St. Denis, and Martha Graham among others—found in *dance* a medium of experience and expression capable of catalyzing, in those who practice or observe, a knowledge of bodily movement as "revelation and subjectivity," as the locus for human encounter with the infinite or divine. As such, their dancing and writing about dance offer cases of women who wrestled in, with, and against the Christianity they knew to generate images of (their female) bodily selves as divine; their work also offers scholars in religious studies guidance in how to acknowledge the role that aesthetic and bodily dimensions of religious life play in the formation of fe/male subjects.

In what follows I focus on one of these dancers, Isadora Duncan, to argue a thesis my reading of Miles predicts: the project of revaluing (female) bodily being as a site and symbol of revelation and subjectivity must proceed hand in hand with a critique of *writing* as a privileged model of and for religious expression.

## Introducing Isadora

Isadora Duncan (1877–1927), born and raised in California, achieved fame as a dancer in Europe during the first decade of the twentieth century.[14] Despite—or perhaps because of—an eclectic education in both religion and dance, Duncan arrived at the unprecedented prediction that her dance creations would catalyze a renewal of religion in the West. Hers was a double vision. She rejected extant forms of both dance and religion as inadequate, largely because the forms of each were deformed by their forced separation from those of the other.[15] She did not argue that her dance belonged to any

13 Miles identifies two necessary conditions: access to the means of public self-representation and a collective voice containing the "resources and support necessary for self-criticism and self-correction." Miles, *Carnal Knowing,* 170–71.

14 For two noted biographies on Duncan's life, see Ann Daly, *Done Into Dance* (Bloomington: Indiana University Press, 1995); and Frederika Blair, *Isadora: Portrait of the Artist as a Woman.* (New York: McGraw-Hill, 1986). Unless noted, biographical details are drawn from these works.

15 For discussions of relevant contexts within which Duncan moved, see Elizabeth Kendall, *Where She Danced: The Birth of American Art-Dance* (Berkeley: University of California Press, 1979) for an account of American dance, theater, and social practices; see Ramsey Burt, *Alien Bodies* (London: Routledge, 1998) for a discussion of European modernism and nationalism; see Ann Wagner, *Adversaries of Dance: From the Puritans to the Present* (Urbana: University of Illinois Press, 1997) for a discussion of U.S. Christian attitudes toward social dancing as publicized by clergy.

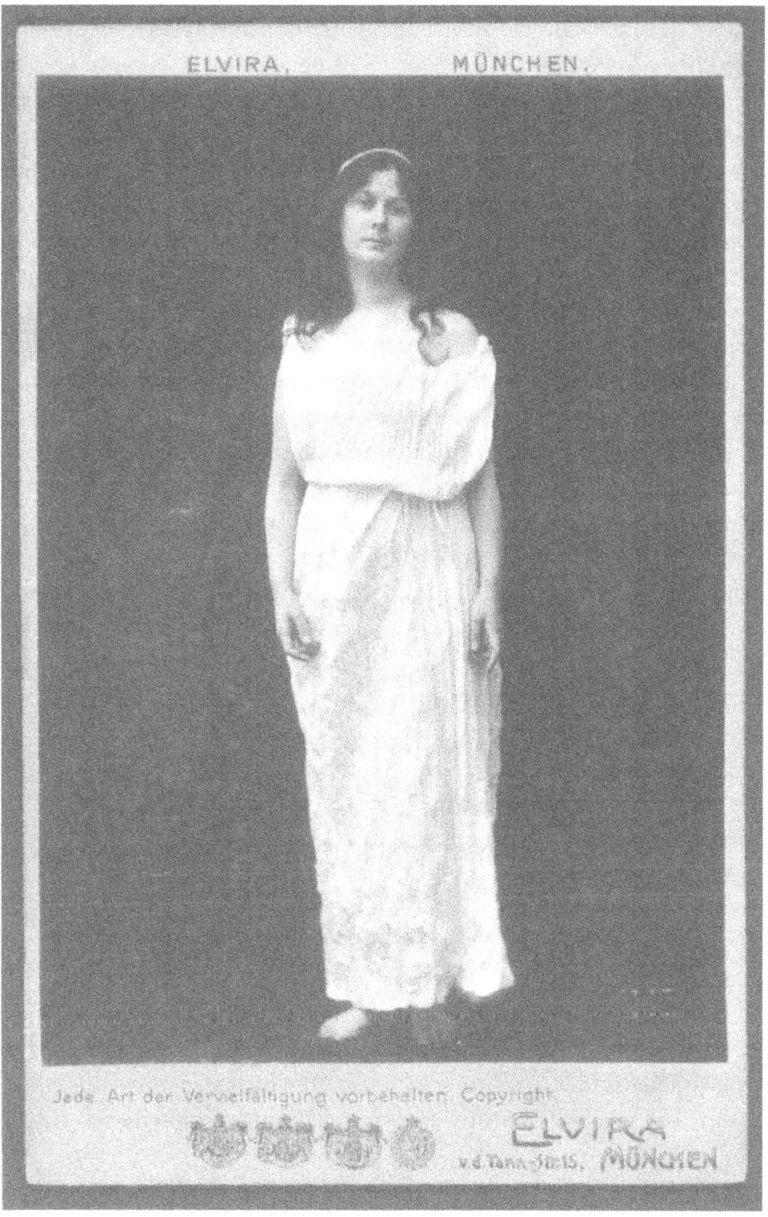


Isadora Duncan. Publicity Postcard for European Performances, ca. 1903. Courtesy of the Harvard Theatre Collection, Houghton Library, Harvard College Library. Used with permission.

one religious tradition and she denied allegiance to any established dance tradition. She rather urged the mutually interdependent regeneration of what she and her contemporaries recognized as dance and as religion. Dance, she avers, will initiate the change: a dance like hers that expresses "the highest and most beautiful ideals of man"[16] will give rise to beliefs and rituals of religion that affirm the beauty and holiness of the female body. Duncan's mission was to find the seed movements capable of generating such dance forms and to educate the children capable of cultivating them.[17] As she affirms in her published manifesto, "The Dance of the Future" (1903), "The dance is not a diversion but a religion, an expression of life."[18]

Hints of what Duncan means by religion and expression of life may be gathered from what we know of her eclectic religious education and dance training. Born as the fourth child to an Irish Catholic mother and her Episcopalian husband, Duncan's first Christian sacrament was her last: she was baptized at five months old. Around that time, the bank her father had founded failed; he fled the law—and his family. Her mother, Dora Gray Duncan, soon renounced her Catholic upbringing, divorced her husband, and turned instead to the lectures of the atheist Robert Ingersoll and her beloved arts. To support the family, Dora taught piano lessons. In the evenings she would play classical music for her children (Beethoven, Schumann, Schubert, Mozart, Chopin), read literature and poetry aloud (Shakespeare, Goethe, Shelley, Keats, Burns, Whitman), and teach about the visual arts. Duncan describes her mother's instruction as "my real education . . . These hours were to us enchanted." Moreover, the family did not simply absorb this education intellectually, they enacted it, learning to play and sing and act. Forming a family theater troupe by the time Isadora was sixteen, Elizabeth, Augustin, Raymond, and Isadora, with mother on piano, traveled the coast of California, performing dramatic scenes and what Isadora remembers as "my religious dances."[19]

The young Duncan's immersion in the arts and letters of the romantic enlightenment undoubtedly exposed her to "religion" as a word used in the generic to refer to that essence or criterion to which all expressions (theological, liturgical, symbolic) of any tradition claiming to be religious (including

16 Isadora Duncan, *Art of the Dance* (New York: Theatre Art Books, 1928) 56.

17 Duncan corrects those commentators who perceive her as an ambitious solo artist, eager to found a performing troupe. Her primary mission, she insisted, was to educate children into her vision for dance (as religion). Performing was a means to raise the funding for this end by demonstrating and sharing the fruits of such education.

18 Duncan, *Art of the Dance*, 142.

19 Isadora Duncan, *My Life* (New York: Liveright, 1928) 10.

and especially Christianity) must be held accountable.[20] Further, many of the artists she embraced identified the artist, the poet in particular, as the person most capable of revealing this defining core. The artist was a mediator, a modern prophet, expressing not herself per se, but new and vital images of (her) relationship with the divine—of religion. Yet Duncan was also aware that this desire for pure living religion, while critical of Christianity, itself had a long Christian history, even in the United States. While railing upon the "Puritan Spirit of America" for the "disastrous" effects of its taming impulse on American artists, she acknowledges her own puritan impulses, admitting "my gods are Beauty and Love."[21] Imbibing this array of ideas, fully supported by her loving family, Duncan nourished a sense of her self as an artist whose moral responsibility was to strip away the encrusted beliefs and stale formulas of modern western Christianity and generate new religious ideals and practices.

Why Duncan picked dance as the art form through which to realize her moral responsibility cannot be fully explained by her religious education or haphazard dance training. While audiences at the time were accustomed to women acting, singing, and dancing on public stage (as in classical ballet), and even to women performing solo dances of their own creation (such as Maude Allen and Loie Fuller), no other stage performer at the end of the nineteenth century framed her solo, publicly performed dance creations as fulfilling the promises of revelation and religious renewal limned by poets and philosophers of the romantic enlightenment.[22] At the end of the nineteenth

20 To artists, theologians, and philosophers in the early nineteenth century, in Germany, France, and England in particular, religion represented the relationship of an individual human to the divine. For example, while Kant identified religion with "rational belief"; Schleieremacher associated religion with a "sensation and intuition of the universe." In these and other cases, philosopher and theologians used the term "religion" both to affirm and defend a core Christianity capable of withstanding the rising tide of scientific inquiry, and at the same time, critique those aspects of Christianity which did not appear as rationally defensible. Duncan repeats a similar logic in her use of the term–wielding it to identify and defend a "good" (Christian) religion over and against those aspects that sustain antipathy towards dance as a medium of religious expression and experience.

21 Duncan, *My Life*, 78; Walter Terry, *Isadora Duncan: Her Life, Her Art, Her Legacy* (New York: Dodd, Mead and Co., 1963) 91. Although historians debate whether there actually was such a creature as "Puritanism," the term was one that had meaning for people at the turn of the century as a way to name an image of a repressive, punitive Christianity they were eager to move beyond. One might say that Duncan, as an Irish American, embodied a lingering tension within Christianity between its Catholic and Protestant expressions, rejecting both the elaborate ritualizing of one and the over-intellectualizing of the other.

22 Ruth St. Denis developed a similar defense of dance as art and religion several years after Duncan, based on her research into South Asian religions and their dance traditions. After 1910 their paths unfolded in different directions, with St. Denis touring the United States in

century, as during the romantic enlightenment, few considered dancing a fine art, not to mention a religion. Dancing, most often, meant social dancing, and counted, at least for the elite, as an essential ingredient in a child's etiquette education. Duncan herself learned social dances from her older sister Elizabeth and Irish jigs and reels from her mother's parents. She may have taken some lessons in ballet, and dabbled in the exercises of the Delsarte craze sweeping the United States. When asked, Duncan insisted that she learned to dance by visiting her beloved California beaches, where she moved with the rhythms of wind, water, and trees.[23]

One answer is that Duncan perceived dance as the art most capable of catalyzing a renewal of Christian religion along the trajectory opened by her critical engagement with its beliefs and practices. Duncan sought to reform the ideas and practices that identified women's bodies with a sinful sexuality and thus justified the social control of women.[24] Deeply influenced by her

---

the interest of developing an American dance audience, and Duncan traveling across Europe in search of a permanent home for her "School of Life." See Suzanne Shelton, *Divine Dancer: A Biography of Ruth St. Denis* (Garden City, N.Y.: Doubleday, 1981); and Ruth St. Denis, *Ruth St. Denis, An Unfinished Life* (New York: Harper, 1939). While Mallarme celebrated the dancer as the ultimate artistic and religious symbol, her ability to serve this purpose depended upon her lack of consciousness. While very few ministers supported the use of dance in religion, they did so within the setting of the church (Wagner, *Adversaries of Dance*).

[23] Of course, this motif of learning from nature is itself characteristic of the romantic enlightenment. Daly emphasizes how Duncan wanted to project an image of her dancing as natural. However, I take Duncan seriously in this sense—her descriptions of dancing in nature witness to the sheer joy of moving, which most dancers will explain as the reason for pursuing the art. In representing her training as "of nature," Duncan is identifying what she hopes her dances, as cultural creations, to recreate and communicate: an experience of our capacity to realize a relationship to the natural world characterized by a sense of continuity. For Duncan such an experience is Dionysian in a Nietzschean sense–as devastating and tragic as it is empowering. Nature is indifferent to the individual. See Friedrich Nietzsche, *The Birth of Tragedy and The Case of Wagner*, trans. Walter Kaufmann. (New York: Vintage, 1967), a book Duncan called "my bible."

[24] Debates concerning the nature of women were frequently raised in the enlightenment and post-enlightenment debates over artistic and religious education. Rousseau more than anyone, perhaps, framed the "Frauenfragen" to which Mary Wollstencraft in England and the romantic circles in Germany responded. While authors differed widely on whether women could or should receive education, rights, and freedoms equal to men, the arguments always rested on a conception of how women are different from men. Reformers demanded access to education and freedom on the grounds that it would make women better wives and mothers. See Mary Wollstonecraft, *A Vindication of the Rights of Woman* (New York: Everyman's Library, 1992 [1792]) for a defense of women's rights in response to Rousseau. See Ruth D. Richardson, *The Role of Women in the Life and Thoughts of Early Schleiermacher (1768–1806)* (Lewiston, N.Y.: Mellen, 1991) for a discussion of women in the life and thought of Schleiermacher. For parallel debates in American culture, see Nancy Cott, *The Bonds of Womanhood: 'Women's Sphere' in New England, 1780–1835* (New Haven: Yale University Press, 1977). For Duncan's claims about dance, religion, and the emancipation of women see Isadora Duncan: *Isadora Speaks*, ed.

mother's disappointment in marriage, and by the social reprobation met by an aunt who wanted to be an actor, Duncan decried marriage as a practice that robbed women of religious, legal, economic, and artistic autonomy. She railed against religious teachings that linked holiness with thinness and educational systems that denied women equal access to the production of ideas. She rejected fashions and exercise regimes that bound women's bodies into artificial shapes and sizes. In short, Duncan vehemently criticized social and religious conventions that led women to believe that their roles and responsibilities were dictated by their sex.[25]

In response, not only did Duncan endorse the right of women to have sex with whomever they chose and to bear children out of wedlock (she did both), she encouraged women to dance. By learning to dance, as Duncan wrote and taught and lectured, a woman could acquire knowledge of her difference from both men and the distorting images of woman as determined by (her) sex. A dancer could project an image of a female form—of herself—as perfect and beautiful and holy. Dancing could thus provide a woman with a practice for resignifying her own embodiment as site and symbol for divine encounter. As Duncan avers: "If my art is symbolic of any one thing, it is symbolic of the freedom of woman and her emancipation from the hide-bound conventions that are the warp and woof of New England Puritanism."[26]

---

Franklin Rosemont (San Francisco: City Lights,1981), *My Life*, and *Art of the Dance*.

25 At the same time Duncan rejected the image of the "New Woman"—a professional and public individual—and refused to support the movement for women's suffrage. She was in good company. Many women and men were rejecting the image of the professional, political, socially active "New Woman" as a "mannish lesbian" (Carroll Smith-Rosenberg: *Disorderly Conduct: Visions of Gender in Victorian America* [New York: Knopf, 1985] 272) as someone who not only rejected motherhood, but rejected men and heterosexual sex. As Smith-Rosenberg suggests, this critique proved effective. While feminist modernists sought to embrace the image, they did so in ways that alienated the previous generation of women reformers. While Duncan endorsed women's difference and their unique roles as lovers and mothers, she remained a fierce advocate for the professional visibility and freedom the "New Woman" represented. Moreover, in her appeal to female bodies, she was not an essentialist. Seen in the context of her dancing, her claims offer resources beyond the constuctionist/essentialist debate current in feminist philosophy (see section "Dancing Religion" in this essay). See Smith-Rosenberg, "The New Woman as Androgyne: Social Disorder and Gender Crisis 1870–1936," in *Disorderly Conduct*. For further reflections on whether Duncan's feminism was "recuperative" or "revolutionary," see Sally Banes, *Dancing Women: Female Bodies on Stage* (London: Routledge, 1998) 92; and Susan Manning, "The Female Dancer and the Male Gaze," in *Meaning and Motion*, ed. Jane Desmond (Durham, N.C.: Duke University Press, 1997) 164. For a helpful summary of the constructionist/feminist debate see Linda Alcoff, "Cultural Feminism versus Post-Structuralism: The Identity Crisis in Feminist Theory," in *The Second Wave*, ed. Linda Nicholson (London: Routledge,1997) 330–55.

26 Duncan, *Isadora Speaks*, 48.

As Miles's work with visual images suggests, understanding the meaning of Duncan's call for dance to renew religion requires inventing a methodological approach that accounts for the role played in determining that meaning by Duncan's experience of dancing.[27] Duncan was a dancer. While she read avidly it was work in the studio that provided her with the test of whether any idea about religion or dance had merit. Her double vision and her techniques of dance training and performance developed in tandem, reflecting and reinforcing one another. Focusing on the first decade of her solo career (1900–1910), I demonstrate how attention to this interdependent development illuminates what she calls the first principle of her art: dance is religion when it flows from an awakened soul.[28]

## Dancing Soul

Duncan claims to have discovered her sense of soul in the studio, in the course of her first trip to Europe (1901–2). In search of audiences and inspiration, with family in tow, Duncan traveled to London and then Paris, visiting museums and libraries, immersing herself in all of the images of dance she could find and performing wherever possible. She spent hours in the British Museum imitating figures she observed in the Elgin Marbles from the Parthenon and days at the Louvre studying the figures on Greek vases. She read works of philosophy and evolutionary theory and debated her emerging theories with a wide array of intellectuals and artists.

Amidst this flurry of activity, Duncan also waited. She explains: "I spent long days and nights in the studio seeking that dance which might be the divine expression of the human spirit through the medium of the body's movement. For hours I would stand quite still, my two hands folded between my breasts, covering the solar plexus."[29] What finally appeared to her was an impulse to move, arising in her solar plexus. She interpreted this experience as an awakening of her soul and as the key to what makes dance religious.

[27] While there are a number of excellent theoretical works offering conceptual tools for both acknowledging and interpreting dance, most of these theories conceive dance as a form of language, or "bodily writing," whose codes, grammar, syntax and signs can be read even if not completely translated. See for example, Susan Foster's edited volume *Choreographing History* (Bloomington: Indiana University Press, 1997) and her essay in particular. My sense is that the model and metaphor of writing does not go far enough in helping scholars appreciate the transformation of bodily experience that dance involves and its implications for our sense of self.

[28] Most scholars explain away Duncan's soul language as a savvy "rhetorical strategy" aimed at securing credibility for dance; as a "cultural habit" for naming certain kinds of deep emotional experiences (Daly, *Done Into Dance*, 31–32); or as poetic "flowering" (Terry, *Isadora Duncan*, 95).

[29] Duncan, *My Life*, 75.

Soul, she insists, has its "temporal home" in the solar plexus.[30] Why this interpretation?[31] By closely attending to the cluster of verbal images Duncan uses to elucidate this experience, as well as to exercises and dance creations she derives from it, I develop the concepts of physical consciousness and kinetic image to argue that soul, for Duncan, refers to an awareness of one's bodily movement as revelation and subjectivity.

Most often Duncan describes how, as soul awakens, a dancer's "body becomes transparent."[32] As the impulse to move wells in her solar plexus and flows through her body, she experiences her flesh as "light and transparent,"[33] no longer seeming dense, opaque, and material. In fact, her moving body enables sight: a dancer sees *with* her body; she sees *through* her body. And what she sees, as Duncan asserts, *is* her body: she sees the meaning of her solar plexus as "the central spring of all movement, the crater of motor power, the unity from which all diversions of movements are born, the mirror of vision for the creation of the dance."[34] By implication she experiences (the rest of) her body as rays streaming out from this central spring.[35] In other words, this experience of transparency is one in which Duncan discovers her body as double—as both a material substance moving and as the image of herself as transparent, which the movement makes possible. At the same time both dimensions of her bodily being are, in that moment, one. Further, the effort

30 Ibid., 341.

31 Scholars have debated which external influences governed Duncan's choice of the solar plexus as the source of dance movement. Duncan may have been primed for her discovery by exposure to the Delsarte system of exercise (for example, Terry, *Isadora Duncan*, Part I). In Delsarte's program, the body is composed of three zones: head, torso, and limbs, each of which in turn is composed of three zones. In the case of the torso, the three are the upper chest or heart, the solar plexus, and the lower abdominal region. Movements that begin in the torso carry emotional and moral significance; those beginning in the solar plexus do so exclusively. Thus Duncan may have learned from Delsarte both to appreciate the spiritual significance of any movement in relation to its physiological source, and second, to appreciate the solar plexus in particular as the seat of emotion. As Delsarte taught: "Nothing is more deplorable than a gesture without a motive, without meaning." See Ted Shawn, *Every Little Movement: A Book About Francois Delsarte* (Pittsfield, Mass.: Eagle, 1954; reprinted 1976) 24; also Genevieve Stebbins, *Delsarte System of Expression* (New York: Werner, 1902 [1885]). However, as my analysis suggests, for Duncan, movement sourced in the solar plexus did more than express emotion.

32 Duncan, *My Life*, 165.

33 Duncan, *Isadora Speaks*, 51.

34 Duncan, *My Life*, 75.

35 Note as well that the solar plexus itself is movement–the site of a flexing and release that accompanies each act of exhalation and inhalation; that is involuntary yet subject to conscious control; and that enables and mirrors every moment of an individual's life through alterations in its pace, pattern, and quality.

of following the movement impulse changes her body, opening capacities for future movements. Thus, in this moment of soul awakening, Duncan experiences her body as a rhythm of continual becoming, fueled by its own (receptivity to) movement. A body is what it does and whatever it does is always changing it into what it will be—and will be able to do.

When perceived in the context of her dance experience, Duncan's soul language appears as an argument as common as it is contested in religious studies: the act of dancing (or religion) enables a kind of knowledge that cannot be conveyed through other—especially verbal—means. Yet, that knowledge is neither of an "inner" nor "wholly Other" reality. It represents what I call physical consciousness: a bodily sense of one's bodily being as itself consciousness, that is, as a movement of self-reflection, a medium of experience and expression. It represents an increased vulnerability and responsiveness to movement impulses arising (in this case but not necessarily always) in the solar plexus. Physical consciousness is thus not an awareness of one's body as an object (whether as body image, reflection in the mirror, site of social inscription, a cauldron of unconscious desires, etc.); it rather represents a way of being (in one's) body. For Duncan, a person whose soul is awake moves differently; what she knows and can communicate intellectually is that she can move differently, and that the difference is significant to her for what she learns about her self.

Duncan's exercises for educating dancers support this interpretation of soul as physical consciousness. Duncan intended her classes to guide students in awakening a bodily sense of how to receive and respond to movement impulses arising in the solar plexus.[36] In a basic exercise, students draw their hands together and up through the center of the body. As a dancer's hands move across the solar plexus, open towards the sky, and circle around again, his movements map patterns of energy flowing from and returning to the solar plexus. The mental and physical effort required to make these movements focuses the dancer's attention such that he not only begins to notice movement impulses arising in the solar plexus, but more importantly, learns how to respond to them, move with them, and allow the impulses to radiate through each limb and beyond. Each movement he feels in his body and follows with his gaze reveals something new to him about his bodily being, opens up a possibility for further movement, and thus expresses his ongoing life, his evolving strength, and his freedom.[37]

36 Duncan, *My Life*, 75.

37 Sondra Horton Fraleigh develops an aesthetics of dance in which she argues that dance enacts human freedom–the capacity to choose to act. See Sondra Horton Fraleigh, *Dance and the Lived Body: A Descriptive Aesthetics* (Pittsburgh: University of Pittsburgh Press, 1987).

A dancer trained in this manner, Duncan suggests, will make movements that harmonize with his or her particular body. The image she uses to describe this form that soul takes is a wave.[38] A dancer who practices sensing movement impulses arising in the solar plexus experiences her bodily movement responses as amplifying and transmitting these impulses—as making them visible in her flesh. She experiences these impulses as currents of infinite energy originating beyond her and continuing through her. Movements that arise from (and give rise to) this physical consciousness may look natural, not because they represent what any untrained body does, but because they abide by the limits of the dancer's body. In so doing, the movements project an image of bodily being as wave, that is, as actively participating in a greater rhythmic continuity. Thus, a dancer trained in this technique does not learn steps; she learns how to enter into any movement she does with the expectation of learning from that movement who she is (becoming). In Duncan's words, a dancer who moves with an awakened soul knows a "power within," where that power consists in the ability to enact—to both represent and realize—one's bodily "relationship to the universal rhythm."[39] Insofar as her movements realize these impulses, then, they project an image of her bodily self as "one with the great movement that runs through the universe."[40]

In choreographing dances Duncan sought to recreate and communicate her experience of wave forms so as to make visible and visceral for herself and others the sense of being the movement through which (her relation to) divine continuity of the universe comes into view. From her early crowd-pleaser, *Blue Danube* (1902), to the later solos *Mother* (1924) and *Revolutionary* (1924), Duncan's dances feature movements that pulse and flow continuously from one shape to the next, from one part of the body into and through the next, even in moments of punctuated stillness. Insofar as a dancer cultivates her ability to make wave movements, she demonstrates that a rhythmic continuity exists, that it courses through her, that she can recognize and

[38] Duncan, *Art of the Dance*, 51. This image of body as wave reflected Duncan's fascination with the idea that all dimensions of the universe—whether light, electricity, sound, matter, human desire, emotion or will—appear in the form of waves, as their "ground-plan" (Duncan, *Art of the Dance*, 68). This commonality she explains as a function of participation in a shared force field: "the attraction and resistance of the law of gravity" (Duncan, *Art of the Dance*, 69).

[39] Duncan, *Art of the Dance*, 52.

[40] Ibid., 52, 68.

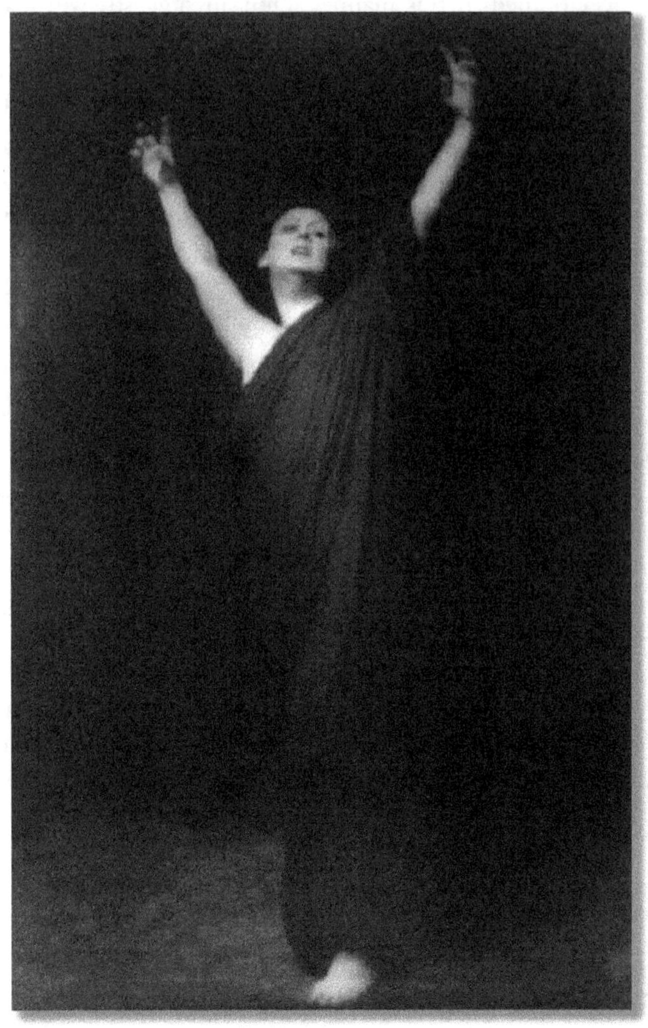

Isadora Duncan. Photography by Arnold Genthe, 1915–18. Courtesy of the Harvard Theatre Collection, Houghton Library, Harvard College Library. Used with permission.

recreate its forms wherever they occur, and that her doing so is what makes that continuity real—in the very least as the condition for her dancing. *Her dancing enhances consciousness of the conceptual and experiential webs that make it possible.*[41]

[41] John Blacking, in *How Musical Is Man?* (Seattle: University of Washington Press, 1973), develops this argument in relation to music.

Duncan's wave-form-movements represent what I call kinetic images. A kinetic image is a pattern of physical consciousness; it is what a person with an awakened physical consciousness uses that consciousness to create. As "kinetic" the image can never be fully present in a figurative or conceptual form; it appears as an "image" only across time, in the fleeting moment of its execution. A kinetic image represents a potential for moving. However, it does not just represent the potential for making a specific movement shape (as in body memory), but rather the potential for making a movement in a way that expresses physical consciousness. By repeating movements that begin in the solar plexus and pass through the body, Duncan developed an ability to mobilize these wave patterns—and all they meant to her in her experience of physical consciousness—as the impetus for any movement or choreographic challenge she faced. Regardless of theme, music, character, or mood, a dance composed of wave-form kinetic images will, according to Duncan, "express life" and reveal the value of whatever is being represented for the project of "becoming divine." In her words, a dancer whose movement flows in waves speaks out of her self and out of something greater. Her dance is in this sense a prayer, seeking to bring into being the sense of divine continuity it represents: "Each movement reaches in long undulations to the heavens and becomes a part of the eternal rhythm of the spheres."[42]

In sum, Duncan's genius was to recognize that the capacity for kinetic image-making is a medium in and through which a person can become her "self," a more "perfect" and "beautiful" body, by enacting her bodily participation in the process of sensing and realizing (kinetic images of) inclusive, open-ended ultimacy.[43] Moreover, by interpreting Duncan's appeal to soul in terms of physical consciousness and kinetic image, it is possible to resist interpretations of her as perpetuating racial and religious elitism.[44] If Duncan had elevated dance as an activity for celebrating embodiment alone, she would

42 Duncan, *Art of the Dance*, 52, 56–57.

43 In some respect the repetition of any dance technique, religious practice, or daily task may serve to develop a physical consciousness and the kinetic images that enable that activity. Duncan strove to become conscious, in this sense, of what every human is always already doing in order to live.

44 Commentators often read Duncan's disparaging remarks about the Black Bottom, Foxtrot, Charleston, and other "modern dances" as evidence of an elitist effort to reproduce bodies and social divisions "along the lines of class and race" in order to ensure that "dance" be preserved as a force of moral purity and social order (Daly, *Done Into Dance*, 113–34, 217–19). My reading of Duncan's religion language suggests that Duncan's concern was less with racial order and purity per se than with forcing the redefinition of these ideals. She criticized forms of "modern dance," which she perceived as preserving social divisions and conceptions of moral order inimical to dance by reinforcing a perception of dancing bodies as occupying a different realm than that of religious souls.

have reinscribed the conceptual matrix that privileges religion (and soul) over and against dance (and bodies) and sustains oppression against women and others. Duncan rather calls upon dance to serve as a practice within which women (and others) can redefine the meaning that soul (as the symbol of a highest self) has for them and to redefine that meaning as a function of physical consciousness—that is, of the transformed sense of their own bodily movement as vital source, receptor, and creator, which Duncan intended her dance to enable.

## Dancing Religion

Duncan's double vision for religion and dance sheds light on an issue debated by feminist philosophers of religion: how to conceive of transcendence. The debates are often framed as a discussion of whether Irigaray's call for a "sensible transcendent" succeeds in retaining the critical perspective on systems of oppression offered by concepts of transcendence, without reinscribing the dichotomy between transcendence and immanence that grounds female bodies.[45] The question persists, nonetheless, of how "sensible" and "transcendent" can or should be related.

Reading Duncan's vision of soul as a physical consciousness awakened to the power of its kinetic imagination suggests a logic for thinking this relationship. Duncan uses soul language to point to a paradox she intends her dancing to animate: dancing affirms individual human bodies as self-reflexive wave movements capable of bringing into being the divine continuity of a meaningful, harmonious world.[46] In a moment of dancing a person both affirms his individuality (as he executes movements with grace and strength) and stages the dissolution of that individuality in the greater rhythms he makes visible. In this sense a dancer enacts a continuous self-transcendence. Yet this transcendence does not represent a departure from the body but rather a deepening and refining of his sense of bodily being as the movement through which he constantly refigures and realizes his connection to the constitutive energies of the universe. When Duncan envisions a dance that will

[45] Irigaray develops this term in *An Ethics of Sexual Difference*. For commentary, see Margaret Whitford, *Luce Irigaray: Philosophy in the Feminine* (London: Routledge, 1991) 154ff. and Elizabeth Grosz, "Irigaray and the Divine," in *Transfigurations: Theology and The French Feminists*, ed. C. W. Maggie Kim et al. (Minneapolis: Fortress, 1993).

[46] This analysis leaves open the question of whether Duncan adequately dissolves the hierarchical dimension of the relationship between body and soul even as she redefines soul as a transformed sense of embodiment. She does not. Yet, insofar as the soul she envisions represents an overcoming of body/soul opposition and an increased attention to bodily movement as a locus of revelation, then the moments of the hierarchy appear to represent stages on a trajectory towards developing physical consciousness.

"develop and show the ideal form of woman," that will celebrate "new nakedness, no longer at war with spirituality and intelligence, but joining with them in a glorious harmony,"[47] she is not making claims about the essential nature of the body, nor ensconcing any one idea of transcendence. Rather, she is affirming the power of dance flowing from an awakened soul—of a trained physical consciousness—to be the medium through which women and men enact kinetic images of (their own) transcendence. Morever, as a kinetic image, any ideal projected by her dancing is inherently dynamic. Not only does the ideal of divine continuity, for example, appear as real only in the moment of bodily performance, but the performance of that ideal alters what it includes —namely, the dancing body. While any ideal represents the abilities and limits of the dancer dancing as the condition for its possible articulation as ideal, every performance of a movement changes those limits and abilities, opening new spaces of sensation and new possibilities of expression.

In short, Duncan frames dancing as the art form capable of realizing a religion that affirms female embodiment as revelation and subjectivity. For Duncan, dancing is and models the process by which our sense of divinity—whatever it is—emerges in relation to us as real for us. Further, dancing enables us to know something about this "other" and about our relation to it that cannot be known any other way. That knowledge appears in the form of physical consciousness and the kinetic images that allow us to sense, express, and thus know our bodily participation in the ongoing realization of (our own) divinity. Dance in Duncan's world is incarnating activity–a practice in which a self becomes sensible by transcending her sense of opposition to her own embodiment.

This description of dancing, if honored, offers a response to a question posed to Irigaray by Hollywood and others: if we know that we are projecting images of divinity or sensible transcendence, how can they function for us as divine?[48]

Attention to Duncan's dancing suggests that feminist philosophers of religion need to resist thinking about projection as an intellectual act. Such models reproduce the sense of the body generated by the practice of writing. Writing is an embodied activity whose success depends upon forgetting that fact. Writing requires a careful choreography of bodily posture and forward gaze, a bodily stillness allowing for maximum mobility of front limbs and frontal lobes. Writers cultivate a sense of being a *mind* in a *body*—a physical

47 Duncan, *Art of the Dance*, 61, 63.

48 See Hollywood and Serene Jones, "This God Which is Not One: Irigaray and Barth on the Divine" in *Transfigurations*, for versions of this critique. Both suggest that Irigiray, in endorsing Feuerbach's notion of projection as the source of a new religious imaginary, fails to address Feuerbach's claim that projection works only when the mechanism is hidden.

(un)consciousness. Correlatively, where scholars conceive the projection of a feminist religious imaginary as a mental act that operates at a distance from its life-world by identifying and representing desirable traits, their theories continue to represent and thus reproduce the sense of self as mind over body honed, however unwittingly, by persons educated as readers and writers.

The projection involved in Duncan's dancing works through the medium of bodily movement. Here it is the bodily action through which a symbol is generated—and which the symbol thus re-presents—that gives that symbol its meaning. From the point of view of Duncan's dance, intellectual assent to a symbol's meaning is one moment in a rhythm, representing a thought that becomes possible due to what a dancer knows in physical consciousness as true. Describing the dancer she envisions, Duncan writes: "her movements will become godlike, mirroring in themselves the waves, the winds, the movements of growing things, the flight of birds, the passing of clouds, and finally the thought of man in his relation to the universe."[49] Her movements will become a mirror for the thoughts they enable. For Duncan, such thoughts, in turn, will stand or fall based on their ability to honor and encourage dancing as necessary to the production, projection, realization, and constant evolution of such thoughts. The implication is not that feminist philosophers of religion should not write, but rather that they must conceive the process of generating a new religious imaginary as an embodied project. As such, writers may need to engage in some activity that encourages them to awaken a physical consciousness of their own bodily being as integral to the process of inventing new images of female and human flourishing. Some of these images will need to be kinetic.

This analysis carries implications for scholars in religious studies as well. At least some scholars have a moral responsibility to become critical kinetic image-users. Too often the task of understanding religion is perceived solely as an intellectual one. A scholar can easily lose sight of how his choices of topics and methods re-present the physical (un)consciousness that the practice of writing requires and sustains. As Miles is well aware, it is conceivable that in different times and cultures the bodily activity in relation to which verbal expressions themselves had meaning was not writing. As such the patterns of physical (un)consciousness opened through writing, while possible and valuable, may not afford a thinking person sufficient resources for understanding the bodily dimensions of human life that enable any text to have the meaning it does. If not, the success of a scholar in understanding religious phenomena may depend upon cultivating kinds of bodily awareness that writing does not. Otherwise, our disciplines will continue to reinforce the dualistic mod-

[49] Duncan, *Art of the Dance*, 63.

els generated unconsciously by those disciplined by the task of writing. Here the phenomenologist of religion Gerardus van der Leeuw would agree with Duncan. We should learn to appreciate dance, he writes: "It is high time; it is a theological and ethical necessity."[50]

50 Gerardus van der Leeuw, *Sacred and Profane Beauty: The Holy in Art,* trans. David Green (New York: Holt, 1963) 74.

# A Samaritan, a Mother-in-law, and an Addict

## *Insights on Vision and Attention*

Martha Ellen Stortz

## Introduction

If my own story is any indication, Margaret Miles has mentored more people than she knows. Before I had ever met her, I came to rely on her intellectual compass. When I turned to the topics that have irresistibly attracted my scholarly attention, I was relieved to find that Miles had been there already. She had sifted the secondary literature, probed the primary texts, and rendered a judgment that was modest, fair, and above all charitable. I felt better when I located the Miles article on the topic I happened to be researching. It meant I was on the right track.

Studying Miles's *Practicing Christianity* deepened my own thinking on Christian practices. I re-read Augustine's *Confessions* through the eyes of *Desire and Delight* and *Augustine on the Body. Image as Insight* refocused my ideas on vision and imagination. A passing article on infancy, parenting, and nurturing in the *Confessions* opened a new perspective on Augustine's understanding of childhood.[1] Miles brings the historian's craft to bear on a matter theologians ignore to their peril: the concrete experience of human bodies. She invites her reader into a world steeped in both strangeness and familiar-

[1] Margaret R. Miles, *Practicing Christianity: Critical Perspectives for an Embodied Spirituality* (New York: Crossroad, 1988); *Desire and Delight: A New Reading of Augustine's "Confessions"* (New York: Crossroad, 1992); *Augustine on the Body* (Missoula, Mont.: Scholars, 1979); *Image as Insight: Visual Understanding in Western Christianity and Secular Culture* (Boston: Beacon, 1985); "Infancy, Parenting, and Nourishment in Augustine's Confessions," *JAAR* 50 (1983) 349–64.

ity. As the plates between past and present thrust sideways, the reader experiences two sharp jolts. One is a shock of recognition, when the reader recovers a shard of her own soul in texts and images from centuries long gone; the other, a shock of alienation as the strangeness of a lost world reorients her own settled presumptions. I always emerged from a Miles article or book with a different angle of vision. A once-familiar view altered irrevocably.

In this essay I draw on Miles's investigation into Augustine's optics to illumine the work of two philosophers for whom vision was pre-eminent, Simone Weil and Iris Murdoch. In Miles's hands, Augustine finds common cause across centuries with these two twentieth-century philosophers. Though operating out of very different understandings of the physics of seeing, the three find consensus on the essential attribute of attention. Moreover, all three focus on the eye exercises necessary to develop a habit essential to the good life.

Miles elaborates Augustine's optics in a compelling article, "Vision: The Eye of the Body and the Eye of the Mind in Saint Augustine's *De Trinitate* and *Confessions*."[2] Drawing on a Platonic optics, Augustine understands vision as volitional act initiated by the spectator. A particular object attracts the eye, and the spectator chooses to focus on it. The eye then sends out a ray of light to embrace the object and then return, bearing the impression of the object into the soul of the spectator. Vision is selective, unitive, even erotic. We attend to what attracts us, and it becomes a part of us.

In his *Confessions*, Augustine relates the story of his good friend Alypius, who was addicted to the violence of the coliseum. Although Alypius had sworn off such spectacles, his friends dragged him to a contest in order to test his resolve. He found it impossible to avert his gaze, and Augustine evaluates the consequences: "he opened his eyes, and his soul was stabbed with a wound more deadly than any which the gladiator, whom he was so anxious to see, had received in his body."[3] Alypius falls off the wagon as he drinks in the bloodfest in the arena below. Only through a combination of grace and sheer grit is he able to shake his habit. Miles emphasizes that, in readying the soul to glimpse the *visio dei*, a vision of God, Augustine relies on a combination of divine illumination and human discipline. She focuses on the latter, and here her careful reading has direct bearing on contemporary discussions of vision and attention.

Miles trains her analysis on the dimension of human responsibility. For Augustine had not read the corpus of Martin Luther, nor did he share

[2] Miles, "Vision: The Eye of the Body and the Eye of the Mind in Saint Augustine's *De trinitate* and *Confessions*," *JR* 63 (1983) 125–42.

[3] Saint Augustine, *Confessions* 6.8, trans. R. S. Pine-Coffin (New York: Penguin, 1961) 122.

Luther's intense aversion to "works righteousness," though this is a point many Protestant interpreters of Augustine tend to overlook. Miles carefully elaborates the eye exercises that Augustine demands of the good Christian who would gain practice in the exercise of attention. First, relying on faith, the Christian trusts that there is something to be seen. Second, from the riot of visual impressions, she selects and brings into focus images that will structure the soul. Finally, she orients her life around a "holy longing," whereby she searches with the eye of the soul for a glimpse of the divine. We are what we attend to—and we have some choice in the matter.

Miles positions Augustine for conversation with two twentieth-century philosophers for whom vision was paramount: Simone Weil and Iris Murdoch. Both would have felt at home in Augustine's neo-Platonic cosmos and both explore the discipline that attention demands. Yet each feels compelled to juxtapose vision and choice, a false dichotomy for their fourth-century conversation partner. For Augustine, vision *is* a kind of choosing, while for these two latter-day philosophers, vision offers an alternative to choice. I propose a three-way conversation among these thinkers in an effort to probe the whole notion of attention and to contribute to a developing discourse among moral philosophers on the question of vision.

## The Significance of Vision for the Moral Life

Questions of vision appear at the intersection of several current discussions in contemporary moral philosophy. Neo-Aristotelians like Martha Nussbaum argue the importance of discernment and perception in the moral life.[4] Critics of impartiality insist that there are only partial perspectives; they train the moralist's gaze on the particulars of a situation.[5] Proponents of "responsibility ethics" situate moral claims in relational contexts that depend on rightly "seeing" the other.[6] Feminist ethicists present "attention," described as a "just and

4 Martha Nussbaum, *Love's Knowledge: Essays on Philosophy and Literature* (New York: Oxford University Press, 1990), especially the essays, "The Discernment of Perception," 54–105 and "Perception and Revolution: The Princess Casamassima and the Moral Imagination," 195–219.

5 Donna Haraway, *Simians, Cyborgs, and Women* (New York: Routledge, 1991), especially the essay "Situated Knowledges," 183–202; Seyla Benhabib, "The Generalized and the Concrete Other," in *Feminism as Critique,* ed. Seyla Benhabib and Drucilla Cornell (Cambridge: Polity, 1986); Bernard Williams, *Moral Luck* (Cambridge: Cambridge University Press, 1981); Lawrence Blum, *Moral Perception and Particularity* (Cambridge: Cambridge University Press, 1994); Margaret Urban Walker, "Moral Understandings: Alternative 'Epistemology' for a Feminist Ethics," in *Explorations in Feminist Ethics: Theory and Practice,* ed. Eve Browning Cole and Susan Coultrap-McQuin (Bloomington: Indiana University Press, 1992).

6 H. Richard Niebuhr, *The Responsible Self* (New York: Harper and Row, 1963); William Schweiker, *Responsibility and Christian Ethics* (Cambridge: Cambridge University Press, 1995);

loving gaze" fixed upon another, as central to the moral task.[7] Throughout these diverse writings references to Simone Weil and Iris Murdoch surface both as sources of inspiration and as sounding boards for further constructive positions.

Yet while these projects adopt Weil's and Murdoch's emphasis on vision, they fail to notice a coordinate emphasis in both Weil and Murdoch on how vision is formed and how attention is developed. Without this emphasis, an ability to distinguish moral from immoral vision and to discriminate eyes that behold from eyes that devour vanishes. We have difficulty discerning what to look at and, more importantly, what to look for. Vision, it seems, must be tutored, and both Murdoch and her mentor in moral optics, Simone Weil, prescribe precise practices for sharpening moral vision.

Clear lines of influence link the two philosophers. Murdoch read Weil in the 1950s, and one might track the influence through her mention of the visual metaphor of "attention." Attention surfaces in an early paper, entitled "Vision and Choice in Morality,"[8] but almost as an afterthought, "attention to detail," and without reference to Weil. Attention commands more copy and express acknowledgment to Weil in *The Sovereignty of Good;*[9] it dominates *Metaphysics as a Guide to Morals* in the form of the "concentrated attention" toward which all religious practices should point.[10] In her two major philosophical works, Murdoch adapts Weil's language and softens Weil's angularity to elaborate her convictions. Both philosophers, however, juxtapose seeing and choosing, a dichotomy that Augustine presents as false.

But it is odd to talk about vision without something to see. In elaborating Weil and Murdoch on the subject of vision and attention, I present two stories as verbal visual aids. Weil's paradigmatic story is a scene of suffering: the arresting parable of the Good Samaritan. Murdoch's paradigmatic story

---

Robert Goodin, *Protecting the Vulnerable* (Chicago: University of Chicago Press, 1985); Hans Jonas, *The Imperative of Responsibility* (Chicago: University of Chicago Press, 1984).

7 Sara Ruddick, *Maternal Thinking* (New York: Ballantine, 1989); Margaret Urban Walker, "Moral Understandings," 165–75.

8 Iris Murdoch, "Vision and Choice in Morality," *Proceedings of the Aristotelian Society* 30 (1956) 32–58. The article responds to one of the same name and published in the same volume by R. W. Hepburn, 14–31. Both are reproduced in *Christian Ethics and Contemporary Philosophy,* ed. Ian T. Ramsey (London: SCM, 1966).

9 "I have used the word 'attention,' which I borrow from Simone Weil, to express the idea of a just and loving gaze directed upon an individual reality," Murdoch, *Sovereignty of Good*, 34.

10 E.g., "Emphasis is laid by Zen, partly in its instruction through art, upon the small contingent details or ordinary life and the natural world. Buddhism teaches respect and love for *all things*. This concentrated attention implies or effects a removal from the usual egoistic fuzz of self-protective anxiety," Iris Murdoch, *Metaphysics as a Guide to Morals* (New York: Penguin, 1992) 244.

captures the bustle of English village life, as she examines the less dramatic and more ordinary, complex, and messy trajectory of a relationship between a mother and her daughter-in-law. The narrative gap between these two stories itself speaks volumes about the differences between two philosophers who nonetheless share common commitments to the importance of vision in the moral life.

## Weil on Vision and Attention

Gerard Manley Hopkins revels in a world "charged with the grandeur of God."[11] Weil presents a world charged with the absence of God. For her the defining mark of the Divine is kenosis: the divine ability to pour itself out in creation, incarnation, crucifixion, and love. She regards creation as an act of renunciation and restraint. The Creator could have retained control over the creation, but instead withdrew, leaving necessity and free will to govern in the breach. Incarnation is but another kenotic act: the Divine renouncing its divinity, taking human form, and residing in the world. The crucifixion shows an omnipotent God refusing to control and a compassionate God suffering. Every human act of love that exercises similar renunciation replicates this divine kenosis.

While her template for tracking God seems thoroughly Christian, Weil wrestled with the Roman Catholic Church and finally identified herself as one whose loyalty would best be shown by remaining on the outside. She mined other religious traditions for their practices of attention and singled out four practices or "forms of the implicit love of God": love of neighbor, beauty, love of religious ceremonies, and friendship. Of these practices Weil observes: "Even the most narrow-minded of Catholics would not dare to affirm that [these loves]. . . . belonged exclusively to those centuries and countries that recognized the Church."[12] These four practices count as eye exercises for developing the habit of attention.

In describing the first of these practices, love of neighbor, Weil turns to the parable of the Good Samaritan. She exegetes the story as a parable of attention. The visual dynamics, not the ensuing actions, capture her attention. Weil provides clues for understanding what each character in the story sees and how their various views are shaped.

What do the priest and the Levite see? They see enough to cross to the other side of the road; they see enough to avert their gaze. They cannot at-

11 Gerard Manley Hopkins, "God's Grandeur," in *Poetry and Prose* (London: Everyman, 1998) 44.

12 Simone Weil, "Reflections on the Right Use of School Studies with a View to the Love of God," in *Waiting for God*, trans. Emma Craufurd (New York: Harper & Row, 1951) 113.

tend to the suffering man and they move away from him.[13] For Weil, seeing or not seeing the suffering man amounts to seeing or not seeing God. The grandeur of the self eclipses everything these two men might glimpse, including a vision of the God they purport to worship. The *visio dei* demands a kind of "unselfing," which Weil calls "decreation." Decreation enacts the divine kenosis on a human scale. It moves the self from center stage, where it blocks the view of anything else. Attending to the suffering man entails getting one's self out of the line of sight, and the priest and Levite simply cannot do this. Preoccupied by duties, they move away from what is in front of them; they avert their eyes.

Weil examines the kind of tutelage these men would need if they were to see what lies in front of them. They would have to divest themselves of attachments, illusions, and something that for Weil almost never has positive significance: imagination. While Murdoch will distinguish between true and false imagination and regard the former as an essential element of attention,[14] Weil links imagination with the delusion of someone who places herself at the center of the moral universe. She calibrates the value of everything else in terms of proximity to that central point. To see God and to see the suffering man would mean dethroning the self. The priest and the Levite cannot afford that; they choose not to see.

What does the Samaritan see? He sees the suffering man and does not avert his eyes. This kind of seeing demands attention, which issues from looking—a quiet, receptive vision of what is in front of one. The Samaritan attends to what is before him and that vision alone compels him. The actions that follow—the bandaging, the transport, the paid convalescence—follow from his attentive gaze.

But what does the suffering man see? Weil attends to the most invisible figure in this knotty tale. The man suffers from affliction, which Weil describes as having three components: physical pain, social degradation, and spiritual alienation.[15] Physically, his body implodes in pain, collapsing in upon the soul. Socially, he watches his own invisibility, as priests, Levites,

13 With this, we cross into perhaps the only space Weil allows for will and choice in her moral philosophy. She likens this range of choice to a plant, stuck somewhere in the ground: "The plant does not have any control or choice in the matter of its own growth. We, however, are like plants which have the one choice of being in or out of the light" (*Waiting for God*, 130). While her schoolmate Jean Paul Sartre proclaimed the power of the solitary will, Weil could only claim its immobility, constricting decisively its range. She calculates the range of choice visually and weights it spiritually.

14 She does so brilliantly in "The Darkness of Practical Reason," 49–50, and *Metaphysics as a Guide to Morals*, 315. See also her plea for political imagination, 321ff.

15 Weil presents a phenomenology of suffering and graphically describes its three components in a powerful essay, "The Love of God and Affliction," in *Waiting for God*, 117–20.

and commentators across centuries all avert their eyes. But spiritually, the suffering man searches for God from the place of abandonment that compelled the dying Christ to cry, "My God, my God, why have you forsaken me?"(Matthew 27:46; Mark 15:34) Suffering requires attention from the one suffering. If the suffering man continues to wait upon God, "loving in the emptiness," he will see God.[16]

The one who waits on God may not gaze upon the Divine face-to-face; the *visio dei* will be mediated. Weil turns to the final point of view, the mysterious presence of God who watches at infinite remove. Rerouting his path, rearranging his plans, ultimately displacing his self, the Samaritan creates a space into which God descends to regard the man lying beaten and bloodied by the side of the road. The Samaritan bears the face of the Divine and mediates God's gaze. As he looks into the face of the Samaritan, the suffering man sees God. Simultaneously, he discovers himself to be the object of divine attention.

How is such attention tutored? One gains practice in the exercise of attention early on and in a familiar arena: school studies and homework. Weil distinguishes sharply between vision and choice in the simple exercise of doing homework. Handmaiden of choice, the will labors in vain over geometry problems and Latin translations, its muscular efforts stymied. These tasks, however, submit to vision, particularly the receptive waiting that Weil calls attention. Weil's formula for finishing homework borders on the mystical:

> In every school exercise there is a special way of waiting upon truth, setting our hearts upon it, yet not allowing ourselves to go out in search of it. There is a way of giving our attention to the data of a problem in geometry without trying to find the solution or to the words of a Latin or Greek text without trying to arrive at the meaning, a way of waiting, when we are writing, for the right word to come of itself at the end of our pen, while we merely reject all inadequate words.[17]

Weil turns homework into a kind of ascetic discipline, a yearning for the right answer, rather than a dogged and willful pursuit for easy solutions.

The prescription for school studies and the spiritual life are the same. Attention culminates in prayer, which is waiting for God. Weil elaborates in lapidary fashion:

> Not to try to interpret [the problems], but to look at them till the light suddenly dawns. . . . In our sense perceptions, if we are not sure of what we see we change our position while looking, and what is real

[16] Weil, "The Love of God and Affliction," 121.

[17] Weil, "Right Use of School Studies," 113.

> becomes evident. In the inner life, time takes the place of space. With time we are altered, and, if as we change we keep our gaze directed towards the same thing, in the end illusions are scattered and the real becomes visible.[18]

Waiting for God requires unselfing; unselfing calls for practice. While the priest and the Levite moved themselves out of the way of the suffering man, so that they would not have to see him, the Samaritan literally moved his *self* out of the way of the suffering man, precisely so that *he could see him better.* This unselfing was for him such a habit that it became a certain sort of obedience, something he was "unable not to do."[19]

In her exegesis of the parable of the Good Samaritan, Weil educates the reader in a kenotic way of seeing, which empties the self in order to better observe the other and to mediate the gaze of God. She trains the moral agent to see suffering, to notice the outcast, to look to the periphery. It is rigorous training, but one learns discrimination, discernment, and focus.

## Murdoch on Vision and Attention

Weil's world is intense, compressed, almost claustrophobic; her writing, like a Buddhist koan, is loaded with paradox. With Iris Murdoch, one walks into the bustle of village life, no less complex, though decidedly less dramatic. Everyday life and ordinary people crowd her novels and inform her philosophy. For Murdoch, what doesn't ring true in the everyday, probably isn't. Throughout her work she argues the importance of vision rather than choice in effecting that moral change that makes us, if not great moral philosophers, then at least, better people. An ordinary story from *The Sovereignty of Good* sums up her approach:

> A mother, whom I shall call M, feels hostility to her daughter-in-law, whom I shall call D. M finds D quite a good-hearted girl, but while not exactly common yet certainly unpolished and lacking in dignity and refinement. D is inclined to be pert and familiar, insufficiently ceremonious, brusque, sometimes positively rude, always tiresomely juvenile. M does not like D's accent or the way D dresses. M feels that her son has married beneath him. Let us assume for purposes of the example that the mother, who is a very 'correct' person, behaves beau-

18 Simone Weil, *Gravity and Grace*, trans. Emma Craufurd (New York: Routledge, 1998) 109.

19 Writing on obedience, Weil describes obliquely the situation of the Samaritan: "We should do only those righteous actions which we cannot stop ourselves from doing, which we are unable not to do, but, through well directed attention, we should always keep on increasing the number of those which we are unable not to do." Weil, *Gravity and Grace*, 39.

> tifully to the girl throughout, not allowing her real opinion to appear in any way. We might underline this aspect of the example by supposing that the young couple have emigrated or that D is now dead: the point being to ensure that whatever is in question as happening happens entirely in M's mind.
>
> . . .
>
> Thus much for M's first thoughts about D. Time passes, and it could be that M settles down with a hardened sense of grievance and a fixed picture of D, imprisoned (If I may use a question-begging word) by the cliche: my poor son has married a silly vulgar girl. However, the M of the example is an intelligent and well-intentioned person, capable of self-criticism, capable of giving careful and just attention to an object which confronts her. M tells herself: 'I am old-fashioned and conventional. I may be prejudiced and narrow-minded. I may be snobbish. I am certainly jealous. Let me look again.' Here I assume that M observes D or at least reflects deliberately about D, until, gradually her vision of D alters. If we take D to be now absent or dead this can make it clear that the change is not in D's behaviour but in M's mind. D is discovered to be not vulgar but refreshingly simple, not undignified but spontaneous, not noisy but gay, not tiresomely juvenile but delightfully youthful and so on. And as I say, ex hypothesi, M's outward behaviour, beautiful from the start in no way alters.[20]

In unpacking her parable of the Good Samaritan, Weil probes each character's perspective to display multiple points of view. In Murdoch's story, there are multiple points of view, but they coinhere in M's mind. Is D to be seen as a "silly, vulgar girl"? Or as "refreshingly simple, spontaneous and gay, delightfully youthful"? M's view of D alters, as she struggles to see truthfully. Sadly, M does not make an appearance in Murdoch's later philosophical work, *Metaphysics as a Guide to Morals,*[21] where Murdoch deals explicitly with moral change. But if M had, one might pose two questions related to her change in point-of-view. Why did M's vision of D alter? More importantly, how?

Following Weil, Murdoch credits attention rather than will for M's change in perspective. As for Weil, vision and not choice leads to moral change. M does not will herself to behave differently toward her daughter-in-law. Rather, her view alters. Murdoch discusses the practices of attention that

[20] Iris Murdoch, *The Sovereignty of Good* (New York: Schocken, 1970) 17–18.

[21] "Moral change comes from an *attention* to the world whose natural result is a decrease in egoism through an increased sense of the reality of, primarily of course other people, but also other things." Iris Murdoch, *Metaphysics as a Guide to Morals* (New York: Viking Penguin, 1992) 52.

moral change demands. Unselfing alters M's perspective. Like the Samaritan, she disposes of shards of self-interest that block her view of D: "I am old-fashioned and conventional. I may be prejudiced and narrow-minded. I may be snobbish. I am certainly jealous." M suspects that her view of D is tainted by "the fat relentless ego"; she resolves to look again and attend to D.[22]

Such attention requires practice. Though Murdoch remarks upon the humbling and unselfing potential of learning a language like Russian in middle age, she does not turn school studies into a prelude to prayer. She proposes art and meditation as tutors in moral vision.

Good art instructs us in how to perceive truthfully. Taking art as a clue to morals,[23] Murdoch draws Rilke into the discussion, as a lyrical illustration of vision unclouded by the self. Rilke describes a portrait of Cezanne: "[H]e made a replica of himself with so much humble objectiveness, with the credulity and extrinsic interest and attention of a dog which sees itself in a mirror and thinks: there is another dog."[24] Above all, Rilke appreciated Cezanne's ability always to paint, not the willful "I like this," but as a statement of simple truth: "Here it is." The distinction confirms the disjunction Murdoch sees between vision and choice. M may or may not know Rilke or Cezanne, but she does firmly suspect that her view of D is colored by selfish sentiment, as in "I *don't* like this." She is practiced in identifying and discarding self-interest. She resolves to look again.

But art is not the only practice Murdoch prescribes for instruction in moral vision. In both *The Sovereignty of Good* and *Metaphysics as a Guide to Morals*, the apostle Paul enters as a tutor in identifying appropriate objects of attention: "Whatsoever things are true, whatsoever things are honest, whatsoever things are just, whatsoever things are lovely, whatsoever things are of good report, if there be any virtue, if there be any praise, think on these things." (Philippians 4:8 KJV).[25]

Where Paul would probably locate all things in terms of proximity to the cross of Christ, Murdoch counsels attention to the everyday and prescribes certain practices for its exercise. She calls for Zen Buddhist meditation, which teaches one to perceive purely, transcend the self, and see one's surroundings. Writing toward a "religion without God," she proposes "a 'natural way of mysticism,'. . .[which] involves a deepened and purified apprehension of our surroundings. . . . I really see the face of my friend, the playing dog,

22 Murdoch, *The Sovereignty of Good*, 52.

23 Murdoch concludes a review of Stuart Hampshire's *Freedom of the Individual* with this comment. See her article, "The Darkness of Practical Reason," *Encounter* 27 (1966) 50.

24 Murdoch, *Metaphysics as a Guide to Morals*, 246.

25 Ibid., 301.

Piero's picture."[26] While M is probably not practiced in the skills of Buddhist meditation, she is probably someone who has spent time "thinking on these things" to which the apostle Paul pointed. She is someone who can see herself, see through her pettiness and jealousies, see someone else without her own "fat relentless ego" standing in the way.[27] Murdoch insists on the "endless task" of "good vision: unsentimental, detached, unselfish, objective attention," which she calls love.[28]

With Weil, Murdoch regards delusion as stemming from self-absorption. With Weil, she wages war against a habit of mind that calibrates everything in terms of proximity to the self. Both philosophers worry about placing the self at the center of the universe; both would rally behind Weil's challenge to regard all other selves as centers equal in value. The two philosophers part company over the whole notion of God. Weil's kenotic God has withdrawn from the universe in order to let free will and necessity reign. God is present precisely as an absence. Murdoch empties God from her philosophy entirely, proposing a "religion without God"—at least without the "old God" of Christian theism.

Meditation offers an alternative religious view. Murdoch's world is truly "charged with grandeur." Although hers is not the "grandeur of God" that Hopkins clearly imagined, one finds in Murdoch a solid delight in the created world. The practice of meditation offers exercise in attending to things purely and without delusion. Beauty unselfs us, and Murdoch chooses an example that refuses to compete with Weil's dramatic flair, but persuades the reader with its sheer ordinariness:

> I am looking out of my window in an anxious and resentful state of mind, oblivious of my surroundings, brooding perhaps on some damage done to my prestige. Then suddenly I observe a hovering kestrel. In a moment everything is altered. The brooding self with its hurt vanity has disappeared. There is nothing now but the kestrel. And when I return to thinking of the other matter it seems less important. And of course this is something which we may also do deliberately: give attention to nature in order to clear our minds of selfish care.[29]

Attending to beauty emerges as an important exercise in developing attention.

For Murdoch, truthful vision draws on imagination and Murdoch's positive valuation of imagination marks another place where she both softens

[26] Ibid.

[27] Murdoch, *The Sovereignty of Good*, 52.

[28] Ibid., 28, 65–66.

[29] Ibid., 84.

and departs from Weil. Weil regards imagination as only another insidious form of self-absorption, feeding delusion and fantasy. Murdoch distinguishes between true and false imagination.[30] True imagination she defines as the "effortful ability to see what lies before one more clearly, more justly. . .and to respond."[31] This is not only the issue of contemplative practices Murdoch recommends, but has immediate implications for the political realm. Political imagination is two-fold. We not only see the other, but we are encouraged to see as the other sees, i.e., see what the other sees from her point-of-view. Regard overrides M's suspicion as she learns not only to see D as she really is, but to imagine the world the way D does, and by imagining, to see the world D sees. When one extends the horizon beyond village life, into the nursing home, the streets of the Bowery, the sweat shops in Malaysia, imagination becomes an important part of political life, and we begin to see the world from multiple points of view.

## Conclusion

The work of Weil and Murdoch continues to shape contemporary moral philosophy, as scholars of various stripes and diverse agendas explore the significance of vision for the moral life. As they continue the conversation, I would hope they take two points into consideration.

First, I hope these same scholars attend as carefully as did Murdoch and Weil to the ways in which vision must be tutored. The two thinkers passionately attend to that instruction, because vision shapes the moral life.

1) Both discriminate between a vision foreshortened by self-absorption and a vision freed to see another person or thing. Weil sees the other person or thing as a mask of God; Murdoch focuses on the ability to "really see" the other person or thing in their unique particularity.

2) Both describe practices that constitute eye exercises for remedying moral myopia. For Weil, those practices are inculcated in school exercises and culminate in prayer. Waiting for the appropriate solution to a geometry problem habituates one to wait for God. For Murdoch, good art, art that presents things as they are, guides one's gaze away from "the dazzling object" that is the self toward one's

30 Murdoch, "The Darkness of Practical Reason," 46–50; *Metaphysics as a Guide to Morals*, 308ff. Martin Andic argues that Weil's use of imagination is elusive enough to admit some positive place for it in the moral life. See his essay, "Discernment and Imagination" in *Simone Weil's Philosophy of Culture: Readings Toward a Divine Humanity*, ed. Richard H. Bell (Cambridge: Cambridge University Press, 1993) 116–49.

31 Murdoch, *Metaphysics as a Guide to Morals*, 322.

surroundings.[32] Meditation compliments art in directing the gaze away from the self and toward the other. Finally, for both philosophers, beauty serves as a handmaid for unselfing.

3) Both tell us what to look at and what to look for. Murdoch counsels a "just and loving gaze" on what crosses our field of vision, though she has been charged with a form of "social conservatism" on precisely this point.[33] Weil urges a gaze that sweeps toward the periphery, recognizing that we might need to "change our position" to gain this vantage point. From Weil, one learns to see the afflicted, the marginalized, and the poor, and her view corrects Murdoch's near-sightedness. Weil would ask—and Murdoch—not only how each regards her daughter-in-law, but the man who picks up her trash, the gypsy-woman begging in the Metro station, or the starving child in Somalia.

Second, I hope that moral philosophers revisit the sharp dichotomy Weil and Murdoch draw between vision and choice. Though both dismiss choice and the will as servants of "the fat, relentless ego," is it really so simple as all that? Their own arguments for the sovereignty reveal elements of choosing.

Choices move vision from merely looking to the settled disposition of attention. The agent of vision is choice, and here choice is not a wild moment of choosing, but a habit that is etched into the soul over time. Augustine's addicted friend Alypius merely looks at the suffering he sees in the arena. He sees it—and is not moved to do anything. The Samaritan, by contrast, acts on what he sees and what moves him to action is choice. For all her brilliant visual exegesis of the parable, Weil fails to see the Samaritan's compassion. He sees—and he is moved by what he sees "in his guts," as the Greek puts it. His care for the dying man is not simply the product of vision, but the product of a vision tutored by a lifetime of choosing to be compassionate. After all, Alypius has looked on far more suffering, but failed to act. The Samaritan acts because he chooses to attend. He attends because he has been so disposed by compassion.

By the same token, M's behavior is elegant—but inexplicable. Murdoch fails to address why M decides to look again. Surely, this is not simply a gambit to regain her son's good graces, but rather a tendency to review first impressions that may be tainted by self-interest. M did not stumble upon that tendency; she acquired it over a lifetime.

[32] Murdoch, *The Sovereignty of Good*, 31.

[33] Cf. Sabina Lovibond, *Realism and Imagination in Ethics* (Minneapolis: University of Minnesota Press, 1983).

The dichotomy between vision and choice cannot be as sharply drawn as Murdoch and Weil make it. Here they need counsel from Augustine, particularly the Augustine that emerges in Margaret Miles's reading of him. For Augustine, vision is a kind of choosing, not an alternative to choice. Moral agents choose to believe what they see is true; they select what they look at; they long for the broadest horizon of vision possible. For Weil this would be the *visio dei*; for Murdoch, a gaze at things "as they really are."

At some point, Alypius tired of his bloodlust or exhausted his pocketbook. He chose to turn away. Grace staged his recovery, but he also acknowledged the intervention and assented to it. The working of divine illumination and human responsibility coalesce in a rich, thick description of moral vision.

Murdoch, Weil, and the philosophers under their influence may need to review their posited dichotomy between vision and choice, lest they present vision as magical and moral agents as captive to what they see. Choice is what distinguishes moral vision from merely looking and that choice is a habit of seeing things that one develops over a lifetime. We are what we attend to—and we have some choice in the matter.

# On Doing Theology during a Romantic Movement[1]

Owen C. Thomas

I believe that we, in the United States and England at least, have been in a Romantic movement since the 1960s, similar to the first one in the late eighteenth and early nineteenth centuries. This movement influences in varying degrees all aspects of our lives and our culture. Since this is not widely recognized, this influence is all the more effective. Romantic movements are ambiguous, having both beneficial and destructive effects in society and culture. They have been usually correct in their criticism of the cultural situation and dubious in their extremes and some of their assumptions. Many of the negative effects result from the fact that Romantic movements are based in part on what has been called the perennial philosophy, the traditional esoteric metaphysics that has been at the foundation of Gnosticism, later Neoplatonism, theosophy, and related movements. The current Romantic movement has influenced Christian theology of both scholars and others reflecting on their faith. This has tipped the table of argument in a particular direction, making it easier to argue in one direction and more difficult in another, or making some theological proposals seem more plausible and others less so. We need to become more aware of the current Romantic movement and its influence on us so that we can affirm its positive side and avoid its negative results.

This is clearly a tall order for a short essay, especially since Romantic movements are highly amorphous and debatable in their definition, themes,

[1] For almost thirty years, Margaret Miles has been my gentle and persistent teacher in the history of Christian thought and related studies and also a beautiful example for me of the Christian academic life in her honesty, openness, generosity, conscientiousness, seriousness, and dedication, all order by her principle. "Delight orders the soul" (Augustine, *De musica,*VI. II.29).

and extent. Arthur Lovejoy has complained about the sloppy use of the term and warned against its careless application.[2] Nevertheless I will hazard some generally accepted descriptions of Romanticism. W. T. Jones has described Romanticism as a complex syndrome of "biases" in the direction of what he calls the dynamic, the disordered, the continuous, the soft-focused, the inner, and the other-worldly. He exemplifies this through an analysis of the poetry of Coleridge, Goethe, Keats, Wordsworth, Shelley, and Byron; the metaphysics of Schopenhauer; and the political theory of Edmund Burke.[3] Crane Brinton portrays the Romantic temperament as "sensitive, emotional, preferring color to form, the exotic to the familiar, eager for novelty, for adventure, above all for the vicarious adventure of fantasy, reveling in disorder and uncertainty, insistent on the uniqueness of the individual to the point of making a virtue of eccentricity." The phases of Romantic thought include "exaltation of intuition, spirit, sensibility, imagination, faith, the immeasurable, the infinite, the wordless."[4]

A number of cultural analysts have argued that we are involved in a new Romantic movement. The main one is the historian Theodore Roszak in his books *The Making of a Counter Culture* (1969) and *Where the Wasteland Ends* (1972). In the first book Roszak explores the youth movement of the 1960s, but the interpretation of it as a new Romantic movement is only a sub-theme. In the second volume, however, this interpretation of the youth movement is the major thesis. To support his thesis Roszak offers an analysis of the themes of the first Romantic movement in the work of Blake, Wordsworth, and Goethe. Then he shows how these themes have been adopted by the youth movement, seen especially in its critique of the dominance of science and technology in industrial society and the resulting rationalization, secularization, bureaucratization, and dehumanization of life. Furthermore, Roszak finds the basis of both the old and new Romantic movements in what he calls the "Old Gnosis." This includes the hermetic tradition, Islamic and Hindu mysticism, Kabbalah, Zen, I Ching, Tarot, Taoism, magical, alchemical and occult traditions, astrology, shakra yoga, Buddhist Tantra, as well as ancient Gnosticism.[5] Rozak often appeals to Jung, especially in his studies of hermeticism and alchemy. Philip Rieff offers an interpretation of the Romantic

[2] Arthur O. Lovejoy, "On the Discrimination of Romanticisms," in *Essays in the History of Ideas* (Baltimore: Johns Hopkins Press, 1948) chap. 12.

[3] W. T. Jones, *The Romantic Syndrome: Toward a New Method in Cultural Anthropology and History of Ideas* (The Hague: Nijoff, 1961) chaps. 5–7.

[4] Crane Brinton, "Romanticism," in *The Encyclopedia of Philosophy*, 8 vols., ed. Paul Edwards (New York: Macmillan, 1967) 7:206b, 209b.

[5] Theodore Roszak, *Where the Wasteland Ends: Politics and Transcendence in Postindustrial Society* (Garden City, N.Y.: Doubleday, 1972).

themes in Jung's writings; namely, feeling versus intellect, spontaneity versus restriction, the unconscious as savior, introversion, the creative disorder of the interior life, and especially fantasy, which Rieff describes as "the Jungian successor to Christian faith."[6]

In a 1977 volume on the holocaust, in a section entitled "The New Romanticism and Biblical Faith," Michael D. Ryan finds evidence for the new Romanticism in Robert Jay Lifton's concept of "protean man," who embraces many loyalties and commitments in a single life.[7] He also finds it in Charles Reich's book *The Greening of America* in which Consciousness I represents the old Romanticism, Consciousness II the technocratic managerial revolution, and the emerging Consciousness III, which rejects Consciousness II and reaffirms Consciousness I.[8] Ryan finds further evidence of the new Romanticism in William Irwin Thompson's book *At the Edge of History*.[9] Thompson's book is a wide-ranging critique of the scientific, technological, industrial society, which he believes has blinded itself to the possibilities of a deeper understanding of human life and history available in the myths of Atlantis and native Americans; in the prophecies of Edgar Cayce; the poetry of William Blake; and the science fiction of J. R. R. Tolkien, C. S. Lewis, and Arthur Clarke, author of "2001: A Space Odyssey."

In the same section of this volume, in an essay entitled "Romantic Consciousness and Biblical Faith," Edith Wyschogrod describes Romanticism as a metaphysics of consciousness and biblical faith as a metaphysics of event. She argues that the metaphysics of consciousness expands the role given to individual consciousness with the goal of unlimited freedom and the tendency to identify the self with God, as in Hegel. This leads Romanticism to an apotheosis of the undetermined, of chaos, and finally to a valorization of death, which, she argues, was the contribution of Romanticism to Nazism. Wyschogrod states, "In the cult literature of the New Romanticism Hitler's orgies of destruction are interpreted as a regrettable but necessary antidote to Western rationalism, as demonic possession [is] the price man must pay to inaugurate the new age of giants." She continues: "Another strategy [of the New Romanticism] is to return to a Neoplatonic or Vedantic devaluation of the body by acquiring spiritual powers which bypass the body and depend upon transcendent principles. . . . The true self and the body are radically

6 Philip Rieff, *The Triumph of the Therapeutic: The Uses of Faith After Freud* (New York: Harper & Row, 1966) 118.

7 Eva Fleischner, editor, *Auschwitz: Beginning of a New Era?: Reflections on the Holocaust* (New York: Ktav, 1977), part 7.

8 Charles A. Reich, *The Greening of America* (New York: Random, 1995).

9 William Irwin Thompson, *At the Edge of History* (New York: HarperCollins, 1971).

dichotomized, the demise of the body is no way experienced as jeopardizing the life of the spirit."[10]

It is interesting to note that in his first book Roszak also worries about this darker side of the new Romanticism. He is concerned that "liberating the non-intellectual powers of the personality," which he favors, may lead to a "rampant, antinomian mania, which in the name of permissiveness threatens to plunge us into a dark and savage age." Here he refers to Peter Viereck's book *Metapolitics: The Roots of the Nazi Mind,* which he describes as a "thorough attempt to spell out the connections between Nazism and Romanticism."[11] Roszak's worries, however, disappear in *Where the Wasteland Ends.*

Also, in an unpublished essay written in 1971 and entitled "Romanticism as a Religious Movement" the historian Sydney Ahlstrom states,

> Many observers have pointed to a pronounced romantic element in the new interests that mark the 1960s. A short unelaborated enumeration will suffice as a reminder: 1) the revival of Novalis' plea that youth must bring in the new day; 2) the surge of interest in Far Eastern religion that Herder and Friedrich Schlegel pioneered; 3) the commitment to history that Hegel personified and which Herbert Marcuse and the Marxist revival betoken; 4) the renewed interest in astrology, hermetic philosophy and the occult which Saint-Martin and Oettinger championed; 5) the interest in subjectivity, the subconscious, and openness to others associated with Rousseau's *Confessions* and dozens of romantic autobiographical expositions; 6) the search for the meaning and realization of an organic sense of community and a general enlivening of organic metaphors as an antidote to materialism, individualism, and mechanism; 7) a widespread attack on conventional morality which also reverberated in [Rousseau's] *La Nouvelle Héloise* and [Schlegel's] *Lucinde*; 8) a return of interest in Hermann Hesse who himself recapitulated many of these themes–not least a deep regard for Hölderlin–in his poetry and fiction; and 9) a new reverence for Nature.

Although these two historians refer solely to the German and English versions of the first Romantic movement, a similar case can be made from the American version exemplified in Ralph Waldo Emerson and the transcendentalists. They were influenced by the European versions as well as by the perennial philosophy tradition and they combined them in novel ways.

Finally, three British sociologists confirm the judgment of these historians. Bernice Martin states "At the heart of the radical movement which

10 Fleischner, editor, 335. (Here she cites the influence of the work of Sri Aurobindo.)

11 Roszak, *The Making of a Counter Culture: Reflections on the Technocratic Society and Its Youthful Opposition* (Garden City, N.Y.: Doubleday, 1969) 73.

will be the focus of my attention is the so-called 'counter-culture' of the late 1960's. My argument is that it served as a dramatic embodiment of certain crucial Romantic values which in the subsequent decade became intimately woven into the fabric of our culture."[12]

It should be noted that postmodernism in literary and cultural critical theory, which emerged in the 1960s, can be considered to be an aspect of the current Romantic movement. Postmodern authors often refer to figures in the first Romantic movement, such as Goethe, Blake, and Burke, as forerunners of postmodernism. This is not surprising, as both movements involve a strong critique of the Enlightenment tradition.

I turn now to more specific evidence of the current Romantic movement in American culture. Over the past two years I have collected many examples of this from the media, but I will mention only a few of them.[13] A reviewer of "The Lord of the Rings" in the *New York Times* attributes its success to the fact that "fantasy has become the order of the day in contemporary popular culture." Picking up on a phrase of Crane Brinton's mentioned previously, namely the Romantic preference "above all for the vicarious adventure of fantasy," I refer to the vast popularity of novels, movies, and television shows since the 1960s that focused on fantasy; these popular entertainments involve mythic places, plots, young characters with magical powers in epic struggles with evil powers, the supernatural and paranormal, aliens, ghosts, angels, etc. In an article entitled "A Hunger for Fantasy, an Empire to Feed It," A. O. Scott notes that four recent movies, "Spider-Man," "Star Wars: Episode II - Attack of the Clones," "Harry Potter and the Sorcerer's Stone," and "Lord of the Rings: The Fellowship of the Ring," have already grossed more than one billion dollars in domestic sales alone, not counting overseas box office, DVD and video sales, and the vast merchandising of all the accompanying paraphernalia. Moreover, these box office hits are parts of series, extending their scope and influence. Scott concludes, "Perhaps more than ever before, Hollywood is an empire of fantasy."[14] A reviewer in *The New Yorker* describes the devotees of Harry Potter as "obsessed, incurable die-hard romantics."[15] Another

[12] Bernice Martin, *A Sociology of Contemporary Culture Change* (New York: St. Martin's, 1981) 2. See also Frank Musgrove, *Ecstasy and Holiness: Counter Culture and the Open Society* (Bloomington: Indiana University Press, 1974) 65; and Colin Campbell, *The Romantic Ethic and the Spirit of Modern Consumerism* (Oxford: Blackwell, 1987) 3. I will return later to Campbell's thesis about the relation of the new Romanticism and consumerism.

[13] When I searched "new Romantic movement" on the Web, I received 217,000 items in .07 seconds on the new Romanticism in art, music, literature, literary criticism, etc.

[14] A. O. Scott, "A Hunger for Fantasy, an Empire to Feed It," *New York Times:* Arts and Leisure (June 16, 2002) 1.

[15] Bruce McCall, "Not Scared of Harry Potter," *The New Yorker* (December 10, 2001) 54.

reviewer summarizes the significance of the "Lord of the Rings" trilogy in this way: "They revive the art of Romantic wonder."[16] Furthermore, sales of video games based on these movies and similar science fiction fantasies approached thirty-five billion dollars in 2002. Although these examples of a current Romanticism in popular culture are rather sketchy, I will leave it to the reader to assess whether or not they tend to confirm my thesis.

Closely associated with these manifestations of the new Romantic movement is a new intensity of consumerism. In 1970 Erich Fromm stated, "Man is in the process of becoming a *homo consumens,* a total consumer. . . . This vision of the total consumer is indeed a new image of man that is conquering the world."[17] Noting that American consumer debt now exceeds $2 trillion, one commentator puts it this way: "U.S. shopping centers now outnumber high schools and the attract 20 million shoppers a month. In as many as a dozen states, the biggest tourist draw is not a historical, cultural or natural attraction: It's a mall. . . . The nation's largest temple to malldom [is] the 4.2 million-square-foot Mall of American in Minnesota."[18]

British sociologist Colin Campbell sees this consumerism as a manifestation of the current Romantic movement, even as the first Romantic movement facilitated the emergence of the consumerism that fueled the Industrial Revolution in the late-eighteenth and early-nineteenth centuries. He states that although consumption would seem to be at the opposite pole of life from Romanticism, "There is one significant modern phenomenon which does indeed directly connect the two. This, of course, is advertising, for even the most cursory examination of the pages of glossy magazines and the contents of television commercials will serve to reveal how many advertisements are concerned with the topic of 'romance', or with images of copy which deal with scenes which are 'remote from everyday experience', 'imaginative' or suggestive of 'grandeur' or 'passion'."[19] [These quotations are taken from the OED definition of the word "romantic."]

I believe that the influence of the current Romantic movement can also be seen in the contemporary neoconservative movement that informs the administration of George W. Bush. The mentor of the neoconservative theorists

[16] Alex Ross, "The Ring and the Rings," *The New Yorker* (December 22, 2003) 162b.

[17] Erich Fromm, Problems of Surplus," *The Essential Fromm,* ed. Rainer Fund (New York: Continuum, 1995).

[18] Vicki Haddock, "Lessons in Human Buy-ology," *San Francisco Chronicle* (December 19, 2004) D1. See also these important studies of the new consumerism: Juliet Schor, *Do Americans Shop Too Much?* (Boston: Beacon, 2000), and *Born to Buy: The Commercialized Child and the New Consumer Culture* (New York: Scribner, 2004); Juliet B. Schor and Douglas B. Holt, *The Consumer Society Reader* (New York: The New Press, 2000).

[19] Campbell, 1.

and their disciples in the Bush administration is the political philosopher Leo Strauss (1899–1973). Strauss's impact has been described as the largest academic movement in the twentieth century, and he has been called the godfather of the Republican Party's 1994 "Contract with America." Strauss's political thought shows the influence of the Romantic political philosophers Edmund Burke and Jean Jacques Rousseau and he praised Romanticism as the strongest German protest against liberal modernity. He was also influenced by the Romantic reactionaries, such as Oswald Spengler, Carl Schmitt, Ernst Jünger, and Martin Heidegger. His thought was marked by certain Romantic themes and tendencies: the esoteric character of his teaching (which has been described as having a profound similarity to that of the Kabbalists—see below for a discussion of the current fascination with Kabbalah); antimodernity; rule by an elite who are considered godlike; the state as sacred; an hierarchical ordering of society; antipathy to liberal democracy; abhorrence of egalitarianism; the importance of religion as the basis of a society; and an emphasis on rootedness in the soil and on militarism and war.[20] I am suggesting that Strauss's political thought was influenced by the first Romantic movement and that its widespread influence today is strengthened by the current Romantic movement. It represents the darker side of Romanticism mentioned previously.

How has the current Romantic movement influenced Christian theology? I believe that the emphases of Romanticism mentioned by Jones and Brinton are apparent in contemporary theology. I have observed a suspicion of clarity, precision, analysis, and rationality, and a favoring of vagueness, complexity, the irrational, the anarchic, the chaotic, the wild, the Dionysian, the exotic, the esoteric, the heretical, the ancient, the primitive, the apophatic, the holistic, the mystical, and the divine darkness. Some years ago a graduate student in theology told me she did not like distinctions. When I tried to explain that the making of distinctions was an essential of rational thought, she responded that rational thought always dichotomizes and creates separations and alienations, whereas she preferred holism. I have encountered several examples of these Romantic attitudes among younger theologians.

In 1980 the Dean of a seminary published an essay on theology and religious renewal that exemplifies the current Romantic movement. He stated that renewal requires us "to move, at times, to the edge of chaos," to have "a confrontation with the abyss. . . . felt and intuitive meaning borders on chaos, whereas thinking is several steps removed from chaos." Theology and religion

[20] See Shadia Drury, *Leo Strauss and the American Right* (New York: St. Martin's, 1997) 2, 3, 41; idem, *Alexandre Kojève: The Roots of Postmodern Politics* (New York: St. Martin's, 1994) 155; and idem, *The Political Ideas of Leo Strauss* (London: Macmillan, 1988). Professor Drury has stated that she agrees with my interpretation of Strauss.

need "the willingness to get dirty together." Also he calls us to embrace "the threat" and "the antistructural." "We must intentionally move into the darkness, the surd, the unknown behind our systems." He offers three illustrations that identify the darkness into which we must intentionally move: "our grim fear of our own sexuality," the need for the archaic, the bizarre, and the vulgar in the liturgy, and "formation in the wilderness." He says that academic theologians will accuse him of "Romanticism, Transcendentalism, alchemy, the neo-Gothic revival," etc.[21] He was correct in this prediction since his essay illustrates many Romantic themes.

More recently a professor of spirituality and editor of a major journal of spirituality has published an article exploring "what it means to see the wild and the sacred as part of a single, indissoluble mystery," and "learning again to see and imagine the wild world as alive and sacred and whole." There are many positive references to mystery, immersion in the larger whole, sacred yearning, ground of being, and negative references to the arrogance of knowledge and objectifying perception. He focuses on the environmental movement and especially on trees "those wild, ancient luminous beings which are for me the most necessary traces of the sacred in the world." He continues, "The *trees* hold me. And I hold them. . . . I find myself increasingly asking myself this: what does it mean to hold and be held by a tree? . . . To ask this question is really to ask: what is a tree? . . . Perhaps it is time to begin thinking of and responding to trees, as, well, trees."[22]

Both Jones and Brinton mention a bias toward the disordered or reveling in disorder as an aspect of Romanticism. One example of this theme appears in contemporary theology in the current interest in creation out of chaos and criticism of the traditional view of creation out of nothing. This is based on an interpretation of Genesis 1:2: "The Earth was formless and void (*tohu wabohu*) and darkness covered the face of the deep (*tehom*)." Historians generally see this passage as a reflection of the Babylonian creation myth, the *Enuma elish*, in which the young male god Marduk defeats the primeval mother goddess Tiamat (= *tehom*) in a story of rape, murder, and dismemberment, and out of this primeval chaos he creates the world order. Paul Ricoeur interprets this myth as one of the four great myths of evil, in which evil is identified with the chaos out of which the world is made. Thus evil is built into the order of things, is not a matter of human responsibility, and is irredeemable.[23]

21 Urban T. Holmes, "Theology and Religious Renewal," *ATR* 62 (1980) 3–19, see esp. 16–19.

22 Douglas Burton-Christie, "The Wild and the Sacred," *ATR* 85 (2003) 494, 501, 506–7, 509.

23 Paul Ricoeur, *The Symbolism of Evil* (Boston: Beacon, 1967), part 2, chap. 1.

Sjoerd Bonting criticizes the doctrine of creation out of nothing and affirms creation out of chaos on the basis of the Genesis texts, Justin Martyr, Clement of Alexandria, and modern chaos theory in physics. He applies this to all the main topics in theology and concludes that, although chaos itself is morally neutral, it is also the cause of moral and physical evil.[24]

A more fully developed theology based on a theory of chaos is presented in James Huchingson's book *Pandemonium Tremendum: Chaos and Mystery in the Life of God*, which was discussed by a panel at the 2002 Annual Meeting of the American Academy of Religion.[25] In it the Romantic themes of imagination, disorder, anarchy, complexity, mystery, and critique of the Enlightenment receive special emphasis. He makes creative use of information, communication, and systems theory to offer a perspective and vocabulary for the development of a novel theology of chaos as the basis of God and creation. Like Bonting, Huchingson begins with an interpretation of Genesis 1:2 that speaks of the formless, the void, and the deep.

Huchingson's main thesis is that chaos or the *Pandemonium Tremendum* is the foundation of both God and the creation. He states that chaos is "an infinite field of variety, of complete indeterminateness filled with potency, the source of all created things and one aspect of divine abundance." Furthermore, "The *Pandemonium Tremendum* is the state antecedent to the creation, the comprehensive, unconditioned, and indeterminate source or ground of diversity among determinate things. It is the formless and the void of the *tohuwabohu* and the agitated deep of the *tehom*." What then is the relation of the chaos or *Pandemonium Tremendum* to God? It is the source of "grounding" for the "chaos-God-creation system. . . . The chaos is the *Ungrund* [Boehme], the fundament and basin [basis?] of the divine life, the ground and groundlessness of God, eternal and uncaused, at once the answer to the cosmological question and the most profound mystery." God must, however, shield the creation from chaos. For the *Pandemonium Tremendum* is "nothing but trouble. . . . It cannot behave itself." God therefore must "contain the chaos. . . . The order of the cosmos is divinely protected from being swept away" by the chaos. Furthermore, God can release the chaos or the *Pandemonium Tremendum* as the instrument of divine judgment, wrath, and retribution. Huchingson is aware that "chaos is traditionally identified as evil." But he argues that "the primordial chaos, the *Pandemonium Tremendum*, suffers the

24 Sjoerd L. Bonting, *Chaos Theology: A Revised Creation Theology* (Ottawa: Novalis, 2002). For a similar view from the perspective of process philosophy, see David A. Griffin, "Out of Chaos and the Problem of Evil," *Encountering Evil: Live Options in Theodicy*, new ed., ed. Stephen T. Davis (Louisville: Westminster John Knox, 2001) 108–44.

25 James Huchingson, *Pandemonium Tremendum: Chaos and Mystery in the Life of God* (Cleveland: Pilgrim, 2001).

undeserved reputation of being evil. Evil is to be located in the character of systems that generate destructive chaos, the chaos that does not liberate but obliterates." It is not clear how this is different from the *Pandemonium Tremendum.*[26]

Catherine Keller follows a similar line but with quite different sources and style in her book *Face of the Deep: A Theology of Becoming.*[27] She offers a different argument against creation out of nothing and for creation out of chaos that is more clearly an expression of contemporary Romanticism than either Bonting or Huchingson. Many Romantic themes receive constant reiteration: depth, darkness, chaos, disorder, fluidity, multiplicity, mystery, mysticism, gnosticism, apophasis, and silence. Also various Romantic heroes are regularly cited: Dionysius, Eckhart, Nicholas of Cusa, the unknown author of *The Cloud of Unknowing*, Blake, and Schelling.

Keller's goal is to develop what she calls a tehomic (deep) theology that constitutes a fundamental critique of the tradition of creation out of nothing that has promoted the "dominology" of the transcendent male person structure of Christian orthodoxy and its destructive effects on all of creation. Although her style is meditative, allusive, poetical, vague, and often elusive, her central theological proposal, which she calls "apophatic panentheism," is fairly clear. She affirms Whitehead's concept of "creativity from which both creator and creature emerge as mutual differentiations. . . .Creator and creature create, effect *each other*. . . .This radical interdependence would take place within the 'infinite creativity'. . . .The tehomic deity remains enmeshed in the vulnerabilities and potentialities of an indeterminate creativity. As Tehom it *is* that process; as deity it is *born from and suckles* that process."[28]

Finally, Philip Hefner, drawing on Plato, the *Enuma Elish*, Boehme, Berdyaev, and Tillich, analyzes the types of experience that are associated with the second law of thermodynamics on entropy. These are the experiences of running down, degeneracy, chaos, the irreversibility of time, and the emergence of new possibilities. In the tradition of Plato they have usually been interpreted negatively and dualistically. Hefner, however, sides with the tradition of Boehme, Berdyaev, and Tillich, which interprets them positively. Hefner concludes that our experience of the basic polarity of being and non-being, order and chaos, good and evil, possibility and actuality, point to the very foundation of reality in God.[29]

26 Ibid., 105, 109, 131, 132, 127, 128, 127–28, 210.

27 Catherine Keller, *Face of the Deep: A Theology of Becoming* (London: Routledge, 2003).

28 Ibid., 218, 226.

29 Philip Hefner, "God and Chaos: The Demiurge Versus the *Ungrund*," *Zygon* 19 (1984) 469–85; see also Stuart Chandler, "When the World Falls Apart: Methodology for Employing Chaos and Emptiness as Theological Constructs," *HTR* 85 (1992) 467–91; and James I.

The main problem in these four interpretations of chaos, besides their lack of clarity, is whether or not they can overcome the dualistic implications of creation out of chaos, which have been analyzed in detail by Paul Ricoeur. In any case, however, they illustrate the fascination with chaos that is characteristic of the current Romantic movement.

Another bias of Romanticism has been in favor of complexity, richness, and mystery as against rational simplicity and unity. I believe that this bias can be seen in the revival in contemporary theology of the ancient Eastern doctrine of the Trinity that now seems to have become the majority view. This is the social analogy of the Trinity emphasizing the distinctions of the persons in the Godhead as contrasted with the Western psychological analogy emphasizing the unity of the Godhead. This can be seen especially in the work of Jürgen Moltmann, Catherine La Cugna, and Elizabeth Johnson. Here the ancient concepts of *perichoresis* and *circumincessio* are sometimes interpreted as the dance of the divine persons in the eternal Godhead that constitutes the mystery of the Trinity. Moltmann, for example, sees monotheistic Christianity as heretical, as in the cases of Arius and Sabellius. He describes the inner life of the Trinity in the following way: "John Damascene's doctrine of the eternal *perichoresis* or *circumincessio* of the trinitarian persons . . . grasps the circulatory character of the eternal divine life. An eternal life process takes place in the triune God through the exchange of energies. . . .It is a process of the most perfect and intense empathy."[30] This kind of fascination with the mystery of the divine complexity is redolent of Romanticism. (See O'Regan on Moltmann in the next paragraph.)

I expect indirect confirmation of the influence of Romanticism in contemporary theology in the work of Cyril O'Regan. He has begun a vast seven-volume project described by the title of the first volume, *Gnostic Return in Modernity*.[31] His thesis is that the Valentinian Gnosticism of the second and third centuries has returned in the philosophy of the seventeenth-century German mystic Jacob Boehme, in the philosophy of Hegel and Schelling, in German and English Romanticism, and in the twentieth-century theology of Berdyaev, Tillich, Altizer, and Moltmann. (O'Regan states that "the essentially Valentinian [Gnostic] narrative is trinitarianly framed and landscaped" in Moltmann.[32]) I say indirect confirmation, because, if as O'Regan argues,

McCord, "Editorial: The Blurred Vision," *ThTo* 28 (1971) 271–77, in which he refers to our "moving out of one age into another," and to one reaction to this as the "romantic left," which in its fears of the "promised land of technology" represents a "flourishing romanticism."

30 Jürgen Moltmann, *The Trinity and the Kingdom,* trans. Margaret Kohl (San Francisco: Harper & Row, 1981) 174–75.

31 Cyril O'Regan, *Gnostic Return in Modernity* (Albany: SUNY Press, 2001).

32 Ibid., 233.

Romanticism is a manifestation of Gnosticism and Gnosticism is present in contemporary theology, then the latter will constitute prima facie evidence of the influence of Romanticism in contemporary theology.

I believe, however, that the clearest and most massive evidence of the current Romantic movement in contemporary theology is the current spirituality movement. It emerged about three decades ago, and it has grown very rapidly into a vast multimillion- dollar industry involving thousands of full-time professional specialists, many new retreat and conference centers, a large number of new professorial chairs of spirituality in seminaries and other graduate schools, and a vast new publishing enterprise producing hundreds of new books on spirituality every year, which has resulted in the creation of new sections on spirituality in almost all bookstores. There is, of course, some overlap between the new spirituality movement and the continuing tradition of the churches' practice of teaching and formation in the Christian life. They shade into each other. This is a result of the fact that Christianity has almost always been an unstable synthesis of what can be called the biblical-religion tradition and the perennial-philosophy tradition, on which one side of Romanticism has been based.[33]

The marks of the current spirituality movement include many of those of the first Romantic movement mentioned by Jones and Brinton. I will focus on a few of them: an emphasis on the interior life as distinct from the outer life of the body, the community, and history; a focus on the individual and private life rather than public life; a sharp distinction between religion, which is disparaged, and spirituality, which is honored; and an emphasis on feeling rather than rationality. Along with these more fundamental marks go more tangential elements: the fascination with the ancient, the primitive, the exotic, the esoteric, the mystical, the apophatic, and the heretical. All of these characterize both the current spirituality movement and the new Romantic movement of which it is in large part a product.

First, both the current spirituality and Romantic movements strongly emphasize the importance and centrality of interiority or the interior life.[34] Jones has noted its centrality in the first Romantic movement.[35] One of the most important publications of the spirituality movement is the twenty-five volume series entitled *World Spirituality*. In the "Preface to the Series" in each of the volumes, the general editor, Ewert Cousins, states, "This series focuses on that inner dimension of the person called by certain traditions 'the spirit.'

[33] See Owen C. Thomas, "Christianity and the Perennial Philosophy," *ThTo* 43 (1986) 259–66.

[34] See Owen C. Thomas, "Interiority and Christian Spirituality," *JR* 80 (2000) 41–60.

[35] See Jones, *The Romantic Syndrome,* 125–26.

This spiritual core is the deepest center of the person."[36] In a recent study Michael Downey comments on contemporary currents in Christian spirituality as follows: "The common perception is still that spirituality is primarily concerned with the life of the soul, the inner life, one's prayer life, one's spiritual life, as a separate compartment of the Christian life. The tendency to equate the spiritual life with the interior life is particularly prevalent in our own day."[37]

Brinton has noted the emphasis in Romanticism on the individual and the fundamental importance of individuality. Jack Forstman states that the early German Romantics were "overwhelmed and exhilarated by the awareness of individuality."[38] This appears in the current spirituality movement in its similar emphasis on the individual spiritual life as distinct from communal and historical life, an emphasis on private life rather than public life. Any consideration of the implications of spirituality for politics, for example, is extremely rare.[39]

One of the key affirmations of the current spirituality movement is the sharp distinction it makes between spirituality and religion, a distinction in which religion is disparaged and spirituality honored. While spirituality is understood to deal with the inner life, religion is seen to treat the outer life of institutions, creeds, traditions, and moral codes. Recent surveys of religious attitudes have often come across statements such as the following: "I'm probably not very religious, but I consider myself a deeply spiritual person."[40] Roszak is quite clear that the Christian religion is one of the main problems rather than the solution, which he finds in the "old Gnosis."[41] This is taken to an extreme in the thought of Diarmuid Ó Murchú, a Roman Catholic monk, who is a leader of the spirituality movement. (He was the keynote speaker at the annual conference in 2002 of Spiritual Directors International, the largest professional group at the heart of the spirituality movement, with over four thousand members.) According to Ó Murchú, spirituality emerged

36 Ewert Cousins, editor, *World Spirituality: An Encyclopedic History of the Religious Quest* (New York: Crossroad, 1985–).

37 Michael Downey, *Understanding Christian Spirituality* (New York: Paulist, 1992) 105.

38 Jack Forstman, *A Romantic Triangle: Schleiermacher and Early German Romanticism* (Missoula, Mont: Scholars, 1970) xii.

39 Owen C. Thomas, "Political Spirituality : Oxymoron or Redundancy?," *Journal of Religion and Society* 3 (2001) (an electronic journal).

40 See Meredith B. McGuire, "Mapping Contemporary American Spirituality: A Sociological Perspective," *Christian Spirituality Bulletin* 5: 1 (1997) 1c. See also Wade Clark Roof, *The Spiritual Marketplace: Baby Boomers and the Remaking of American Religion* (Princeton: Princeton University Press, 1999) 81, 173–79.

41 See Roszak, *Where the Wasteland Ends,* xxxi, 391, 405.

forty thousand years ago in the paleolithic period as "a cosmological synthesis imbued with a highly developed holistic, intuitive and spiritual consciousness" devoted to the worship of the Great Mother Goddess.[42] Religion, however, appeared only five thousand years ago and has been the source of all our alienation and inhumanity. "Religion in its essential essence is about alienation from the Earth and the cosmos. . . Religion thrives on perpetuating that state of exile and alienation." The end of religion is "a likely possibility and a highly desirable one." Ó'Murchú hails "the probable decline of formal religion and the revival of spirituality."[43]

Generally speaking, in the current Romantic movement, traditional Christianity is often seen as a massive conspiracy against anything new, fascinating, liberating, and heterodox. This is exemplified in the wide popularity of Elaine Pagels' books *The Gnostic Gospels* (1979) and *Beyond Belief: The Secret Gospel of Thomas* (2003) and the 2003 fiction best seller *The Da Vinci Code* by Dan Brown, whose theme is the marriage of Jesus to Mary Magdalen, the birth of their child, and the desperate suppression of all this by the Church. This is a repetition of the attitude toward religion that often appeared in the first Romantic movement. For example, the intended audience of Schleiermacher's *Speeches on Religion* appears in the subtitle of his work, *To the Cultured Among its Despisers*, referring especially to his friends, Schlegel and Novalis, the founders of the German Romantic movement, who had turned away from organized religion toward Gnosticism and theosophy.[44]

A new study brings together three themes of the current Romantic movement that have been mentioned before, namely, spirituality, consumerism, and neoconservatism. The authors argue that the spirituality movement has been taken over and further individualized, privatized, and commodified by neoliberal, multinational, corporate capitalism in order to sell its worldview and its products. This has removed any concern in spirituality for community, social justice, or politics. This privatization and commodification has been accomplished through contemporary humanistic psychology and the colonization of Asian religious traditions in New Age forms. In order to further the goals of neoliberal corporate capitalism, this individualized and privatized spirituality is now widely used in educational and professional institutions, including health care, counseling, business training, management theory, and marketing.[45]

42 Diarmuid Ó'Murchú, *Religion in Exile: A Spiritual Vision for the Homeward Bound* (Dublin: Gateway, 2000) 29.

43 Ibid., vii, 14, 65, 66.

44 See Forstman, *A Romantic Triangle*, chaps. 2 and 3.

45 See Jeremy Carrette and Richard King, *Selling Spirituality: The Silent Takeover of Religion* (London: Routledge, 2005).

Another theme of the first Romantic movement was the emphasis on feeling, passion, and sentiment. The hero of Goethe's *Faust*, the "Bible of the [first] Romantic movement," (Barzun) cries, "Feeling is all." Sentiment, emotion, and the heart are constantly praised over against reason and the mind in Rousseau's Romantic novel *La Nouvelle Héloise*. This theme has been strongly echoed in the current spirituality movement and the Romantic movement of which it is a product. This is also exemplified in the human potential movement of the 1960s and '70s and its focus on feeling, emotion, and sensitivity training pioneered by the National Training Laboratories and the Esalen Institute.

The spirituality movement has a fascination with the ancient, the exotic, the mystical, and the esoteric. This reflects a similar attitude in the first Romantic movement, exemplified in Novalis's idealization of the Medieval; Schopenhauer's devotion to Hinduism; and the interest of Saint-Martin and Oettinger in astrology, hermetic philosophy, and the occult, as mentioned by Ahlstrom. In the spirituality movement this fascination can be seen in the newfound interest of Protestants in such figures and movements as the Desert Fathers, Celtic spirituality, the Kabbalah, Eckhart, and the medieval mystics. It is also exemplified in the great popularity of the new multivolume series *Classics of Western Spirituality*, which includes volumes on *The Cloud of Unknowing*, Pseudo-Dionysius, and Boehme and Swedenborg, who were deeply influenced by the perennial-philosophy tradition. This can also be seen in the program of the 2001 Annual Meeting of Spiritual Directors International, which featured institutes and workshops on such topics as the Kabbalah, the sacred labyrinth, and two on the Enneagram, as well as "Praying through the great elements of Earth/Air/Fire/Water."

Especially typical of the new Romantic movement is the recent surge of interest in Kabbalah, the collection of texts of medieval Jewish mysticism with alleged sources in the second century. It arose in Provence in the thirteenth century and was influenced by the Neoplatonist and Gnostic traditions. A recent newspaper article described Kabbalah as "arcane, obscure, and inaccessible. . . . Its inaccessibility is what makes it attractive."[46] Kabbalah has been taken up by various celebrities, such as Madonna, Barbra Streisand, Courtney Love, Roseanne Barr, and Britney Spears. It is promoted by the Kabbalah Centre International, which has twenty-three offices worldwide and claims 18,000 students in its classes; 90,000 active members in the United States; and 90,000 visits to its website every month.[47] Kabbalah as ancient, esoteric,

[46] Patrician Yolllin, "New Interest in Jewish Mysticism," *San Francisco Chronicle* (December 26, 2003) A21, 25.

[47] Debra Nussbaum Cohen, "A Surge in Popularity in Jewish Mysticism," *New York Times* (December 13, 2003) A15.

mystical, heretical, and exotic is a perfect example of and vehicle for the current Romantic and spirituality movements.

Although perhaps not central to the spirituality movement but constituting its left wing and clearly a manifestation of the current Romantic movement are phenomena such as the Fourth International Conference on Science and Consciousness held in 2002 and sponsored by thirty-five organizations including the Parapsychology Foundation, The Anthroposophic Press, The Mind Science Foundation, the Holographic Repatterning Association, the American Society for Psychical Research, the Academy of Intuitive Studies and Intuition Medicine, and the International Society for the Study of Subtle Energies and Energy Medicine. The conference featured workshops on many aspects of the relation of spirituality and science including "Electromagnetism and Sacred Indwelling," "The Science of Alchemy and the Art of Tantra," "The Genome Approach to Spiritual Transformation," "Trance Surgery," "The Chakras of Telecommunication," "The Frequencies of Higher Consciousness," and "Accessing Noumenal Consciousness." This conference and many similar ones are examples of the spirituality movement, its basis in the current Romantic movement, its foundation in the perennial philosophy, and the fascination of all of these with the exotic and the paranormal.

This conference and other points mentioned here indicate an important difference between the two Romantic movements in their diverse attitudes toward science. The first Romantic movement in its emphasis on disorder, uncertainty, the soft-focused, the exotic, fantasy, the inner, and the otherworldly, attacked the Newtonian science celebrated by the Enlightenment. This was more evident in England than in Germany, where Goethe and Schopenhauer had some interest in and knowledge of science. In England, however, Blake and Wordsworth in particular were unremitting in their attack on Newtonian empirical science.

In the current Romantic movement, however, the attitude toward science has occasionally been more affirmative. The main reason for this has been the emergence early in the last century of what has been called postmodern science, in particular relativity and quantum theory and later chaos theory. Relativity theory holds that there is no absolute and fixed space-time system as in Newtonian physics. Quantum mechanics is usually interpreted to mean that our knowledge of the most fundamental level of matter is strictly limited by the uncertainty principle; that events with no physical cause are pervasive in matter; and that non-locality or unmediated action at a distance is also pervasive.

These developments in modern physics were quickly adopted by the current Romantic movement, since they seemed to support the main emphases of this movement. One of the first books was Fritjof Capra's *The Tao of*

*Physics* (1976), which argued that modern physics demonstrated the truth of Eastern mystical religious thought. This was followed shortly by Gary Zukav's book *The Dancing Wu Li Masters* (1979) with a similar argument. More recently we have Danah Zohar's books *The Quantum Self: Human Nature and Consciousness Defined by the New Physics* (1990) and (with Ian Merchall) *The Quantum Society: Mind, Physics, and a New Social Vision* (1994). Most recently we have Diarmuid Ó'Murchú's book *Quantum Theology: The Spiritual Implications of the New Physics* (1997), which explores these ideas further. All these works are examples of the current Romantic movement and its spin-off in the spirituality movement. The appendix in Ó'Murchú's book on "Principles of a Quantum Theology" is a fine summary of both. I have suggested that Romantic movements have tended to be correct in their criticisms of the contemporary culture and dubious in their extremities and some of their assumptions. The first Romantic movement was valid in its criticism of the one-sidedness of the Enlightenment and neo-classical traditions. W. T. Jones describes the Enlightenment as a syndrome of biases toward the static, order, discreteness, a sharp focus, the outer, and the this-worldly. According to Jones, the biases of the first Romantic movement were the exact opposite of these and constituted a critique of their exaggerations.[48] Friedrich Schlegel, the leader of the German version of the first Romantic movement, was "convinced that the day of enlightened rationality and detachment, of neo-classical ideals and decorum was over." He and his colleagues "challenged the cool rationality and spectator attitude of the Enlightenment."[49]

The English Romantics were appalled at the scientific-technological attitude toward the natural world. Blake chastised the "single vision" of Bacon, Newton, and the new natural science. Worsdworth cried that natural scientists "murder to dissect" nature. All of this was a valid criticism of the ideals of the Enlightenment and of the worldview of modern science and technology. The Romantics attempted at least to restore a measure of balance by emphasizing the place of feeling, emotion, intuition, fantasy, and imagination in human life and culture. But of course, they went to extremes, since extremity was their middle name.

The same can be said of the current Romantic movement. It is a valid critique of the dominance of scientism, technology, and industrialization and the resulting over-rationalization, bureaucratization, and dehumanization of human society and culture. As to the dubiousness of their extremities and their assumptions, we have noted Wyschogrod's and Roszak's warnings about the dark side of Romanticism, its tendency toward a valorization of chaos

48 Jones, *The Romantic Syndrome*, 117, chaps. 6–7.

49 Forstman, *A Romantic Triangle*, x.

and death, and its antinomian mania, which tends toward savagery. To this we should add its tendency to melancholy, disenchantment, and to political messianism, extreme nationalism, militarism, imperialism, and racism, which became evident in the Fascism and hate groups of the past century.

I believe, however, that the most significant problem in Romanticism and the main source of its negative implications is its grounding in the perennial philosophy, in what Roszak calls "the old Gnosis." By the perennial philosophy I refer to a Weberian ideal type, a heuristic construct that serves to organize certain historical data. This particular ideal type was described by Weber as the exemplary type found mainly in Eastern religion in distinction from the emissary type found in biblical religion in the West.[50] Peter Berger refers to these as the interiority and confrontation types.[51] The perennial philosophy is the religio-philosophical worldview exemplified by later Neoplatonism and Vedanta and by the philosophical foundations of Gnosticism, Rosicrucianism, Theosophy, and similar movements, and propounded in the modern period by such philosophers as René Guénon, Frithjof Schuon, S. H. Nasr, Huston Smith, and many others. The implications of the perennial philosophy are that individuality or personhood tends to be understood as ambiguous, evil, or unreal; that bodily life and the natural world are viewed with suspicion; that human communal life and history lack any meaning; and that human fulfillment is found only in escape from the body and the world and in reunion of the human spirit (which is divine) with the divine.[52] I will first give some examples of the grounding of the first Romantic movement in the perennial philosophy.

Goethe, the father of the German Romantic movement, states in his autobiography that he was influenced by Arnold's *History of the Church and of Heretics*. And that "what particularly delighted me in his work was, that I received a more favourable notion of many heretics." He states that every man has his own religion and that he was moved to form his also. He describes it as follows: "The Neo-Platonism lay at the foundation; the hermetical, the mystical, the cabalistic, also contributed their share." He goes on to describe "a Godhead which has gone on producing itself from all eternity." First is produced a Second, which is the Son; then a Third, which completes the circle of the Godhead. But the work of divine production continues with the

50 See Max Weber, *The Sociology of Religion*, trans. E. Fischoff (Boston: Beacon, 1963) 456–50.

51 Peter Berger, ed. *The Other Side of God: A Polarity in World Religions* (Garden City, N.Y.: Anchor, 1981), vii-viii, 3–6.

52 For fuller elaboration of these points, see Owen C. Thomas, "Christianity and the Perennial Philosophy," *ThTo* 43 (1986) 259–66; and idem, "Tillich and the Perennial Philosophy," *HTR* 89 (1996) 85–98.

appearance of a Fourth, which is Lucifer, who embodies a contradiction as unlimited but contained in the Godhead, and who creates the angels who are contained in him. Then Lucifer forgets his higher origin and attempts to find himself in himself, and this causes the Fall of the Angels and the production of matter, which is heavy, solid, and dark. But since matter is descended by filiation from the Divine Being, it is unlimited and eternal. Next the Elohim give to the Eternal Being the power of expansion to produce the creation and also man, who acts the part of Lucifer and produces the second fall. Finally, in order to restore the creation, the Divinity takes the form of man. Thus "the whole creation was nothing but a falling from and returning to the original."[53] This seems to be a version of the Valentinian Gnosticism analyzed by O'Regan.[54]

Novalis (Friedrich von Hardenburg), the leader of the first German Romantic movement, was a follower of Jacob Boehme, Plotinus, and what he called "the mysteries of the East." As a follower of later Neoplatonism he envisioned all of reality as a process of separation from the primordial unity and an ultimate return to a higher and richer unity. He saw this world as a prison, a realm of polarity, opposition, separation, and boundedness, from which we are released only by death. It is only the poet, who through the power of imagination, can lift the veil that the world casts over the true reality of the spiritual world. This, however, requires deification, since "God is known only by a god." According to the mystery tradition, this is accomplished by an initiation that involves the recognition and enhancement of the part of man that is divine. Then the poet, the divinized high priest of this cosmic religion, lifts the veil of illusion by means of dream, fantasy, imagination, and magic and leads us back to our eternal home. Novalis is a perfect example of the perennial philosophy.[55]

Arthur Schopenhauer, the "arch Romantic" (Brinton), was attracted by Buddhism and mystical elitist esotericism, but he was primarily a Vedantist. He referred to the Vedas as "the most profitable and sublime reading that is possible in the world." The Upanishads were his main devotional literature. He held a dualistic view of the body and the world, which he said was created by a devil. He held that the world is a hell surpassing that of Dante. He said "No" to the Romantics who delighted in nature. The eternal soul had been banished into the body, but the better and eternal self could be saved by

[53] See *Autobiography of Johann Wolfgang von Goethe,* trans. John Oxenford (New York: Horizon, 1969) 379–82.

[54] For O'Regan's summary, see "Valentinian Narrative Grammar," in *Gnostic Return in Modernity,* 137.

[55] See Forstman, *A Romantic Triangle,* chaps. 3, 4; and Jones, *The Romantic Syndrome*, chap. 6.

turning away from life in the body and the world through renunciation and resignation, aided by art, especially music.[56]

The thesis of Denis de Rougemont about romantic love suggests a continuity between the first and second Romantic movements. He argues that such a continuity is based on Catharism, a dualistic heresy in the tradition of Gnosticism and perennial philosophy, which flourished in Provence in the twelfth century. Catharism was persecuted by the Inquisition, went underground, and appeared again in the guise of courtly love expounded by the poems and songs of the troubadours. This embodies what de Rougemont calls the myth of romantic love, which affirms that passionate romantic love is the true human fulfillment that exalts and transforms the lovers through death. He traces the myth through French literature to German Romanticism and Wagner's *Tristan and Isolde* with many references to Neoplatonism, Goethe, Novalis, and Schopenhauer, among others. His point is that the romantic myth with its hidden Catharist basis has continued to dominate all areas of Western culture down into the twentieth century.[57]

Roszak also argues that the current Romantic movement is founded on "the old Gnosis" or the perennial philosophy, more specifically on the hermetic tradition, Islamic and Hindu mysticism (Sufism and Vedanta), and ancient Gnosticism. Ahlstrom sees hermetic philosophy and Eastern religion at the basis of the current Romantic movement. Wyschogrod finds one foundation of the new Romanticism in Neoplatonism and Vedanta. Finally, since O'Regan argues that the first Romantic movement was at least in part a manifestation of Gnostic return, then he would presumably agree that a current Romantic movement would be subject to the same interpretation.[58]

It should be stated, however, that there is a side of both the old and perhaps the new Romanticism that is not based on the perennial philosophy in any of its versions. It is quite clear, for example, that Schleiermacher, although clearly a Romantic and the first Romantic theologian, opposed and distanced himself from the views of Novalis.[59] And O'Regan considers Coleridge, the most philosophical of the English Romantics, among the anti-Gnostic authors. Finally, some of the themes of the perennial philosophy seem to be less evident in at least one side of the current Romantic movement; note, for ex-

[56] Rudiger Safranski, *Schopenhauer and the Wild Years of Philosophy*, trans. Edward Osers (Cambridge: Harvard University Press, 1960) 58–59, 63, 93, 201–2, 228, 321.

[57] See Denis de Rougemont, *Love in the Western World*, trans. Montgomery Belgion (New York: Harper & Row, 1956). See also Owen C. Thomas, "Beatrice or Iseult? The Debate about Romantic Love," *ATR* 79 (1997) 571–80.

[58] Cyril O'Regan, *Deranging Narrative: Romanticism and its Gnostic Limit* (Albany: State University of New York Press, forthcoming).

[59] Forstman, *A Romantic Triangle*, chap. 6.

ample, a dualistic attitude toward human nature and the natural world, and human fulfillment as escape from the body, the community, and the world.

If the above argument has any validity, what are the implications for Christian theology, both lay and professional? In sum, we need to become aware of the current Romantic movement in its various aspects and influences, to assess how much we have been influenced by it, to affirm the positive aspects without their extremities, and to avoid the negative aspects. Among the positive aspects I find: first, the critique of the dominance of scientism, technology, and industrialization and the resulting over-rationalization, bureaucratization, and dehumanization of life and culture; second, the affirmation of the centrality in human life and culture of feeling, emotion, sentiment, intuition, and imagination; third, the affirmation of the fundamental importance of individuality and subjectivity; and fourth, the affirmation, on one side of Romanticism, of the goodness and beauty of the natural world and the human body. However, the extremes of these aspects must be avoided: a Romantic retreat from modern life and responsibility; an overemphasis on feeling to the exclusion of a proper rationality; the extreme individualism of contemporary life noted by many commentators; and the Romantic divinization of nature often found in Neo-pagan movements.

The negative aspects of the current Romantic movement are: first, the darker side mentioned by Roszak and Wyschogrod exemplified in the prevalence of many hate groups based on racism, nationalism, and militarism and, second, the negative influences of the foundation of one side of the current Romantic movement in the perennial philosophy mentioned here. It is clear, however, that one side of the current Romantic movement has avoided some of these results.

Finally, if we have in fact been in a Romantic movement since the 1960s that has influenced the character of our reflection on Christian faith, what is our responsibility as lay and professional theologians? Obviously, we need to be aware of this influence, affirm the positive aspects, and be on our guard against the negative. This means that we are called to interpret new theological proposals with generosity, that is, in the best possible light, and then subject them to critical analysis in the light of our norms. This may be difficult, since the influence of the current Romantic movement on theology has been to tend to disparage clarity, precision, analysis, and coherence, and to tend to commend vagueness, the irrational, the chaotic, the apophatic, the heretical, and mystery. The task of theology, however, has always been difficult, and in fact recent Romantically influenced theology has sometimes given us examples of important critical and constructive theological work.

# Asceticism or Formation

## *Theorizing Asceticism after Nietzsche*

Richard Valantasis

I owe my academic interest in asceticism to Margaret Miles. Her lectures on the history of Christian thought at Harvard always attended to asceticism and the body, and as a clergyperson just taking courses, I was hooked. Margaret Miles opened to me a world of study—gender, critical theory, historical theology, the arts—that transformed for me the study of asceticism from the arid religious practices of the past into living traditions that challenged and enhanced living. The publication of her book on asceticism, *Fullness of Life: Historical Foundations for a New Asceticism,*[1] not only put asceticism on the academic agenda, it launched me into ascetical studies for my entire academic career. Margaret Miles has moved on to other studies and issues, but I have stayed the ascetical course. It is an honor to dedicate this latest incursion into historical and cultural perspectives on asceticism to the woman whose presence and writing inspired it.

The word "asceticism" is not a common part of popular or scholarly discourse. It conjures for many ancient and medieval practices intended to mortify the body. Mortification, or the punishment of the body, might require lice-infested hair shirts worn in secret next to the body, or intense fasting and the rejection of the pleasures of food and drink, or abstinence from sexual pleasure and the rejection of marriage with its attendant sexual engagement, or the rejection of society and the pleasures of normal social relations in favor of dark caves and isolated monasteries in some remote site in Egypt or Syria. These practices are indeed ascetical, but when viewed as isolated practices they tell only part of the story.

[1] Margaret R. Miles, *Fullness of Life: Historical Foundations for a New Asceticism* (Philadelphia: Westminster, 1981).

In order to get to the heart of an ascetical discipline, one must ask questions about the intent or the purpose or the goal of a practice. To what end does an ascetic wear a hair shirt? What kind of body does fasting fashion? What kind of intimacy does chastity construct? What kind of society is created by withdrawal from normal social relationships? The ascetic practices always connect to some larger purpose, to a wider conception of human existence or human potential, to a different understanding of society and world. The goal of the practice relates to creating this different person, whose life (at least in the common understanding of asceticism) depends on discomfort, renunciation, and withdrawal to create a more holy or more perfect person. This essay explores the wider context for ascetical theorizing by distinguishing formation from asceticism as a basis for developing an alternative genealogy for the study of asceticism in the postmodern world. The distinction between formation and asceticism, as well as the new genealogy for the current interest in ascetical studies, both depend upon the development of a subjectivity in a specific context.

Both formation and asceticism posit the construction and reconstruction of the subject: formation constructs a subject for the dominant society or culture, while asceticism constructs one for an alternative and subversive society or culture. Let me begin with the ascetic. The ascetic performs the emerging subversive subjectivity in specific practices. When a person decides to wear a lice-infested hair shirt next to the body, that person chooses to redefine the self. There is some intimation that the person not wearing the hair shirt is less desirable, or less acceptable, or (in more theological language) less holy than the person who chooses to wear the hair shirt. The decision to engage in the ascetical activity immediately posits two identities, two different ways of articulating a subjectivity: the first identity, the received subjectivity that does not require a hair shirt, is a given in the society in which the person lives; the second person, an emergent subjectivity, imagines that through the wearing of a hair shirt a different person will emerge, a person significantly more improved than the received identity of the majority of people among whom the ascetic lives. Ascetical practice relates to the process of defining a new person in opposition to a received and normative subjectivity promulgated in any social and cultural context. Formation relates to the process of developing a subjectivity capable of functioning within the dominant society. The presence of two subjectivities, one given in a society and one contrary to the given, points to two different systems toward which a subjectivity orients itself. The practices constitutive of the dominant subjectivity I term formation, those of the subversive or alternative society, I term asceticism.[2]

[2] For a more complete explanation of my theory of asceticism, see Richard Valantasis,

The early part of the twenty-first century eagerly engaged the important question of alternative subjectivities. The creation of an alternative identity in a wider culture perceived as being at odds with the dominant society became a hallmark of the times. The evidence for the pervasiveness of the ascetical context of the twentieth century may be amassed simply by listing some of the important movements whose aims were to construct alternative identities within the dominant culture: Black power, the feminist movement, gay activism, libertarian communities, right-wing Christian separatists, religious and political communes, the ecology movement, and the many ethnic movements that promulgate the development of a counter-cultural Chicano/a, Asian, Pacific Rim, or Native American identity in the United States. And there are many others. Each of these groups or movements find themselves caught between the two subjectivities—one received from the wider cultural context and one developed in opposition to that dominant subjectivity in order to articulate or define an alternative way of living.

The twenty-first century, bathed as it is in the blood of the clashing of various subjectivities, must address the questions of the relationship of conflicting conceptualizations and enactments of the self. Pluralism, which is the ability of many diverse people to live together harmoniously, depends upon the capacity for diverse people to create and sustain identities at variance with each other, but also identities who can live together. Religious pluralism demands that various religious identities cohere in a social and political environment without either losing the distinctiveness of their own identity or creating some identity that belongs to no one person in particular. Asceticism, which I present here as the practices that create these alternative identities, stands at the heart of pluralist religious, social, and political life.

The postmodern context, however, needs to recognize the difference between training for the dominant society and training in subversive identities. Asceticism, the creation of an alternative identity, must be distinguished from formation, the creation of an identity equipped to function in the dominant society. That is the first step. Then, based on the distinction I propose a new genealogy for the postmodern attention to asceticism that picks up other strands of the twentieth- and twenty-first-century phenomena based upon the construction of alternative subjectivities. That genealogy begins with two literary figures (Kazantzakis and Genet) and ends with two religious movements (the Branch Davidians and the human bombs of September 11).

"Constructions of Power in Asceticism," *JAAR* 63 (1995) 775–821.

## Formation or Asceticism

The following incident describes a formative process. On the eve of July 1 in Greece, the beginning of the feast of the dual saints of healing, Cosmas and Damian, who are called the "Holy No-Silver Ones" (οι άγιοι ανάργυροι)—because, according to the popular legend, they never asked for payment as did the secular healers of their day—the Greek Orthodox community on the island of Paros in the Kyklades gathers for a festival evening, at a remote and no-longer inhabited monastery perched high above the village on a mountain top. The festival begins with vespers followed by a community supper and concludes the next morning at sunrise with the celebration of the Eucharist. The little chapel, normally dark and deserted (although always well-kept and clean) is decorated for the occasion: the icons on the walls are garlanded as they were in pre-Christian antiquity with red and white carnations; embroidered and crocheted white cloths are hung below each large icon to cover the old wood of the icon screen; the brass hanging lamps are cleaned of their year's accumulation of olive oil; the candlestands are cleaned and prepared to receive the beeswax candles of the hundreds of pilgrims who will come for the celebration. At vespers, the tiny chapel is packed with worshippers. Hundreds of candles illumine the space and make seeing in the otherwise dark chapel possible. On a small table in the middle of the cramped space stand five enormous loaves of bread (at least two feet in diameter) that will be blessed during vespers and distributed to the assembly after the service. The vesper service itself begins about 9:30 p.m. (although it is announced for about 8:00 p.m.) and it continues until just about midnight.

Unless one has some understanding of Orthodox religious ethos, this event would remain troublesome, boring, long, and without any apparent logic. However, once the participant learns some of the traditions associated with the festival, the celebration becomes clearer. Those traditions include the inauguration of a two-day festival with vespers on the eve of the saints' day, the blessing of loaves at the vespers as part of the commemoration of the biblical feeding (of the Israelites in the desert and of the five thousand by Jesus) and as an act of communal thanksgiving to God for sustenance and blessing, and the commonly known fact that Greeks normally do not even think about eating their dinner until about midnight. Supplied with this information, the outsider then begins to understand the festival: it coheres and displays the community's corporate sense of religious identity. Festivals are carefully planned and orchestrated events celebrating the spirituality of the community.

Various systems of formation exist for a group to communicate the systems necessary to understand and participate in its corporate life. The Parian islanders, reared in an environment of festival celebrations, learn these systems from their earliest youth through their lifelong participation. Knowing something of the religious environment from Greek Orthodox practice in the United States where I was born, I could quickly pick up the particularities and nuances peculiar to the customs practiced in Greece more generally, to Paros more specifically, and to this specific festival on the feast of the dual saints Cosmas and Damian more concretely. A tourist unfamiliar with Greek culture would probably neither know about the festival (the tourist would need to be familiar not only with the Greek Orthodox kalendar of saints, but also with the names of local shrines and monasteries on the island), nor would the tourist understand the various elements of the customary festival of a feast day (the festival would look like a late-night picnic delayed by a church service).

To those who have knowledge either as an insider or even as an outsider, the practices and traditions of the community bear witness that various systems of formation do indeed exist. A person must undergo a process of formation in order to understand and to participate in a cultural event. Those processes of formation are not always self-evident. Michel Foucault (1926–84), more than any other theorist of the postmodern era, has explored and documented the formational systems, both visible and submerged, that enable members of a society to be constituted as a subject of that society. But what Foucault describes as "asceticism" is perhaps best called "formation." Foucault's study of the "care of the self" in the Greco-Roman period explored the means by which predominantly entitled male members of a society cultivated themselves in order to develop for themselves a mode of being consistent with the societal norms in which they lived. Foucault's concept of the care of the self "is what one might call an ascetical practice, giving the word "ascetical" a very general meaning, that is to say, not in the sense of abnegation but that of an exercise of self upon self by which one tries to work out, to transform one's self and to attain a certain mode of being."[3] What Foucault here calls asceticism ought more properly to be called cultural or social formation. The systems engaged in the care for the self are systems that enabled the entitled males of the Greek and Roman period to form themselves as significant parts of the dominant society by acquiring "the knowledge of a certain number of rules of conduct or of principles which are at the same time truths and regulations. To care for self is to fit one's self out with these truths."[4] The social

[3] Michel Foucault, "The Ethic of Care for the Self as a Practice of Freedom: An Interview with Michel Foucault on January 20, 1984." Interview by Raúl Fornet-Betancourt, Helmut Becker, and Alfredo Gomez-Müller, trans. by J. D. Gauthier, S.J. in *The Final Foucault*, ed. James Bernauer and David Rassmussen (Cambridge: MIT Press, 1994) 2.

[4] Ibid., 5.

formation that motivated these Romans revolved about the development of a socially acceptable *ethos*. Foucault defines that *ethos* as "the deportment and the way to behave. It was the subject's mode of being and a certain manner of acting visible to others." This ethos, Foucault argued, is directly related to the dominant social world in that "*Ethos* implies also a relation with others to the extent that care for self renders one competent to occupy a place in the city, in the community or in inter-individual relationships which are proper—whether it be to exercise a magistracy or to have friendly relationships."[5] In Foucault's thought, the care of the self aligns the person with a role and function in the dominant society. The wider context for the construction of an identity holds great importance: it is one thing to be trained to become part of the dominant culture and entirely a different thing to construct an identity to subvert that culture. Since some practices orient the person toward the society and other practices orient a person against that dominant society, the distinction between formation and asceticism becomes essential. The distinction here is between exercises and practices intended to integrate a person into the dominant society (formation) and exercises and practices intended to create a subjectivity alternative and subversive to the dominant structure (asceticism). Foucault develops a theory of formation. This essay explores the basis for a theory of asceticism.

The distinction between formation and asceticism is one that, curiously enough, an important and influential source for Foucault articulated. Friedrich Nietzsche (1844–1900), beginning his third "Untimely Meditation"[6] entitled *Schopenhauer as Educator* with a similar excursion into a tourist's visit to a different land, articulates a distinction between the lazy person who accepts his socialization into the common mass-culture and the liberated person who strikes out free from the constraints of custom to construct his own identity. Nietzsche characterizes the lazy person as one who acts "(f)rom fear of his neighbor, who demands conventionality and cloaks himself with it" and who is constrained "to think and to act like a member of a herd" with "indolence, inertia, in short that tendency to laziness." This lazy person remains "fettered by the chains of fear and convention." In contrast to this person is the "youthful soul" who understands the conventionality as far distant from its true self because "its liberation gives it a presentiment of the measure of happiness allotted it from all eternity." This liberated person "knows quite well that, being unique, he will be in the world only once and that no imaginable chance will for a second time gather together into a unity so strangely variegated an

5 Ibid., 6.

6 Friedrich Nietzsche, "Untimely Meditations," in *Schopenhaurer as Educator,* ed. Daniel Breazeale, trans. R. J. Hollingdale, Cambridge Texts in the History of Philosophy (Cambridge: Cambridge University Press, 1997) 125–94.

assortment as he is."[7] This youthful person constructs the way proper only to the individual—singular, unique, unfettered, and far distant from the person society constructs for itself; Nietzsche instructs this youthful soul:

> Let the youthful soul look back on the life with the question: what have you truly loved up to now, what has drawn your soul aloft, what has mastered it and at the same time blessed it? Set up these revered objects before you and perhaps their nature and their sequence will give you a law, the fundamental law of your own true self. Compare these objects one with another, see how one completes, expands, surpasses, transfigures another, how they constitute a stepladder upon which you have clambered up to yourself as you are now; for your true nature lies, not concealed deep within you, but immeasurably high above you, or at least above that which you usually take yourself to be.[8]

Nietzsche draws a stark contrast between the person formed by the dominant social paradigm for the mass-culture, the person whose primary identity is provided by the social convention of the day, and the other person who actively subverts that conventional formation to develop a self that actualizes the unique qualities and interests and gifts of an identity no longer constrained by convention or society. Nietzsche has framed an issue central to twentieth- and twenty-first-century people: the differentiation between formation and asceticism. Nietzsche's lazy person's training properly should be termed formation and his "youthful soul's" alternative, asceticism.

The differentiation of formation and asceticism is crucial for understanding the construction of both ancient and postmodern identities. Formation orients itself toward dominance; asceticism orients itself to alterity and subversion. Formation, the primary means whereby a person becomes a functioning member of a dominant group or society includes such systems as etiquette, social propriety, participation in ceremonial events and activities, as well as other customary practices. Members of a group are socialized, integrated, taught various appropriate behaviors and modes of thinking, and molded into a person capable of seamlessly participating in the life of the group. These groups may be of a wide variety including, political, recreational, religious, educational, and civic, among many others.

## A Genealogy of Ascetical Studies

If one does not include Foucault among the ascetical theorists of the twentieth century, then how did asceticism come to the fore of academic and public

[7] Ibid., 127.

[8] Ibid., 129.

life? Four particular phenomena in the twentieth century, two literary and two political, seems to have thrust asceticism into modern and postmodern life. The first phenomenon is the ascetical exercises of Nikos Kazantzakis (1883–1957) who in 1922–23 created the first post-Eastern-Christian, secular ascetical theology. Kazantzakis, writing during a period of clashing cultures, political structures, and intellectual foment, promulgated an ascetical discipline intended to create a new and different understanding of modern identity precisely to address the problems of modern existence. The second phenomenon of my genealogy revolves about the novels and plays of Jean Genet (1910–86), who translated Western ascetical practice into gay life, and from gay life, it found its way into French critical theory, including the work of Roland Barthes (1915–80) and Foucault. Genet connected his efforts at defining a new identity to the Black Power movement in the United States, the gay activist movements in Europe, and the Palestinian effort to maintain a subversive identity in the context of the creation of the State of Israel. Genet's literary identities provided the context for the exploration of ascetical identity in the midst of seriously conflicted modern identities. The third event of my genealogy is more recent: the Branch Davidians in Waco, Texas. The Branch Davidians brought alternative religious identity to the fore of American attention. Their religious alterity, linked with their libertarian political views and their apocalyptic religious beliefs and practices, at once condemned normative American values and practices and showed that some Americans were willing to risk everything to live by a different set of rules. Their alternative subjectivity ultimately resulted in their willingness to train themselves to become "all fire," a tradition, as we will see, with ancient roots among the Egyptian desert monks. The fourth event in my genealogy is even more recent, the Muslim "martyr heros" who were trained to turn themselves and their fellow passengers into human bombs in the terrorist attack on the United States on September 11, 2001. These human bombs, when they practiced the identity for which they had so carefully been trained, became an effective display of the extent to which alternative religious and political practices contend with dominant subjectivities in order to assert their differences. Kazantzakis and Genet, though literary leaders of their generation, have been intellectually marginalized, especially as regards their ascetic teaching, but the Branch Davidians and the September 11 terrorists have captivated global attention in an unprecedented way. I contend that just as these four events forced me to think carefully about asceticism, so also these four elements conspire to force Western people to understand asceticism.

## *Nikos Kazantzakis*

In the latter part of the twentieth century the Western world came to know Nikos Kazantzakis primarily through the cinematic renditions of two of his most influential novels, *The Last Temptation of Christ*, which presented a view of Christ's own emergence as a Savior often against his own will, and *Zorba the Greek*, which dramatized the character that became quintessentially "the Greek man" struggling against an interior and exterior Fate. The dramatic characterizations of Jesus, Paul, Mary Magdalene, Zorba, and the many other characters, both major and minor, in these novels and films attracted the attention of artistic leaders and the imagination of the general public.

Kazantzakis based his characterization on a specific theory of asceticism that he had developed early in his career. In 1922–23 Kazantzakis produced the first post-Christian ascetical theology in his book entitled *ΑΣΚΗΤΙΚΗ: Salvatores Dei*, which has been translated into English as *The Saviors of God: Spiritual Exercises.*[9] His ascetical work became a centerpiece, perhaps more appropriately a manifesto, for his philosophical, theological, political, and literary productions because each of his subsequent works presents various aspects of the theories and practices advocated in his ascetical theology. Kazantzakis considered his ascetical theology central to his intellectual, political, literary, and spiritual projects, but it has remained largely unknown.

Significantly, Kazantzakis wrote a post-Christian ascetical theology. Being nurtured in a highly ascetical religious environment of the Greek Orthodox Church in Crete, and having spent formative time living among the ascetics of Mount Athos, Kazantzakis nonetheless rejected Christianity as the primary conduit of ascetical behavior. For Kazantzakis asceticism provided the means to transubstantiate the flesh, to transform materiality into spirit.[10] His post-Christian ascetical theology moved toward the founding of

[9] The Greek edition is *ΑΣΚΗΤΙΚΗ: Salvatores Dei* (Athens: Eleni Kazantzakis, 1985); the English translation is Nikos Kazantzakis, *The Saviors of God: Spiritual Exercises*, trans. Kimon Friar (New York: Simon and Schuster, 1960). When he wrote the book in 1922–23, Kazantzakis originally entitled the work with the Latin "Salvatores Dei" followed by the Greek feminine adjective form of the adjective "ascetical." When he revised the book, however, he inverted the Latin and Greek titles. The use of the adjectival form implies that it is intended to be either "the ascetical theology" or "the ascetical book," as both "theology" and "book" are feminine in Greek.

[10] Peter Bien, *Kazantzakis: Politics of the Spirit* (Princeton: Princeton University Press, 1989) 34–38. Bien argues that this concept was one taken from the work of Henri Bergson with whom Kazantzakis studied in Paris. The very mystical concept, according to Bien, resonated with Kazantzakis's own intellectual formulations. To my mind, the concept agrees to a great extent with the long tradition of transformation of self evident in the Greek ascetical tradition. Bergson provided the Western conceptual frame, but Orthodoxy provided the substance for the concept. The word "transubstantiation," however, is the Western Christian term for the

a new religious perspective resonant with all the currents of the period between the World Wars by combining in various ways Marxism, Communist theory and practice, radical Greek identity, the philosophy of Nietzsche, the teaching of Bergson, and readings in Buddhism. It was written as a post-Christian response to the rise of nationalism, the fall of the Ottoman Empire (and the consequent creation of modern Turkey), the spread of Communism in Eastern Europe, and the modern critical intellectual climate of Germany and France. Kazantzakis understood that the new world order, and the new ways of thinking about personality, society, and politics, required a different understanding of subjectivity. According to Kazantzakis, the world could not survive without a drastic reordering of the role and significance of individual effort in order to advance the human state to the next level of its evolution. His ascetical theology provided a scheme for this reordering of self, society, and the symbolic universe. His vision was prophetic for the beginning of the twenty-first century.

The center of Kazantzakis's ascetical agenda revolves about the "super-human struggle" (ο υπερανθρωπινός άγωνα).[11] Based on an understanding of the evolution of material culture toward some spiritual end, Kazantzakis understood human endeavor as the propelling agent that could force evolution to its next logical step. His ascetical program included five states: preparation (η προετοιμασία); the walk along the road, or the march (η πορέια); the vision (το όραμα); practice (η πράζη); and silence (η σιγή). Further elaboration of his ascetical system need not detain us here.[12] What is important is that Kazantzakis developed and articulated a full ascetical system as a response to the significant changes in the society around him. That ascetical system recognized the important role of the transformation of an individual subjectivity as the means whereby further social and political development could occur.

Kazantzakis lived at the perimeter, on the boundary (this is an important image for him taken from the Byzantine figure Digenes Akritis) of many worlds: Eastern and Western philosophy, Ottoman and modern political structures, Eastern Christianity and Western, agricultural life and industrial society, among many others. It is precisely this sense of being neither one nor the other that led him to articulate an ascetical theology. His goal was to

---

transformation of the elements of the Eucharist (bread and wine) into the Body of Christ (body and blood) through the prayers of the priest at the Eucharist. Eastern Christian eucharistic theology places more stress on the invocation of the Holy Spirit over the gifts, which is commonly called "consubstantiation." Kazantzakis blends Eastern and Western traditions in his emphasis on the transubstantiation of flesh into spirit.

[11] Kazantzakis, *Saviors of God*, 55; Greek text, 19.

[12] For a full description and analysis of Kazantzakis's system, see Bien, *Kazantzakis*, 67–78.

provide a conceptual frame for people, including himself, to move forward amidst remarkably divergent systems of power and in the midst of dramatic social and political changes. The old structures that nurtured him and the West, in its youth, no longer could sustain themselves. Some new way of living, of being an agent in the world, of forming social alliances and families, and of conceptualizing the meaning and significance of the cosmos was necessary. For Kazantzakis, these new things begin and end in human transformation, in the creation of a subjectivity capable of carrying self, society, and world to a new level of spiritual and political awareness. Kazantzakis's instinct toward asceticism, probably arising in his border experience as an Eastern Orthodox-trained intellect engaged in Western philosophy, put the question of formation on the modern agenda. Although we know his asceticism primarily through the characters he developed to dramatize his ascetical theory, we have nonetheless been invited into an ascetical world that has held our fascination.

## *Jean Genet*

In contrast to Kazantzakis's move toward a post-Christian ascetical theological system, Jean Genet took up the question of the construction of a new subjectivity in literature that invoked Catholic Christianity. Genet opened new possibilities for experiencing new subjectivities by taking the reader into the minds and experiences of characters (often with autobiographical referents) who display their ability to create new identities out of the often harmful elements of their true lives.

Genet's own ascetical formation has two formative loci.[13] First, he was raised as a foundling placed into a foster family in the rural village of Alligny-en-Morvan. Rural life for the Regnier family revolved about the local Roman Catholic parish where Genet was a chorister and acolyte and where Genet was baptized, received a Catholic religious education, and received his first communion. This youthful formation in the rituals, practices, festivals, and music of the church resonates throughout Genet's novels. His characters take on religious significance (one queen in *Our Lady of the Flowers*[14] is called "First Communion," while another, "Divine," "rises at cock's crow to go to communion, the Quite-Repentant"); characters even observe traditional ascetical disciplines in a completely gay context (the narrator relates: "Now, the fact is that Divine wore next to her skin a clinging hair shirt, unsuspected

[13] I base this section on the superb biography by Edmund White, *Genet* (London: Chatto & Windus, 1993).

[14] Jean Genet, *Our Lady of the Flowers*, trans. Bernard Frechtman (New York: Grove, 1976).

by Darling and the clients").[15] Genet applies his religious experience and his formative ascetical practices to the life of his gay characters.

The second locus of Genet's own ascetical formation took place at Mettray, an agricultural reformatory for young offenders of the law. Mettray's program of reformation revolved about the rigorous monastic style regimen of hard work, enforced religious training, and harsh discipline for those breaking the rules, in an all-male environment. This ascetical and severely disciplined life fused with the Roman Catholic religious asceticism of his youth to produce a uniquely gay asceticism modeled on ecclesiastical practices but applied in an entirely different context of male homosexuality.

Genet's asceticism revolved about a program to enact a gay identity, or more properly gay identities, in the context of a gay community. His characters act out their gay life, referring to each other in the feminine (a process that is enhanced by the narrator at various points by providing the masculine birth names of his characters when they are brought into court), revealing their inner thoughts and especially their sexual desires, and living out their lives in the context of male homosexual love, prostitution, transvestitism, and society. In the process, Genet creates a gay culture, parallel to the heterosexual dominant society in France, but entirely subversive of it. This gay world that he creates resonates with the vibrancy of a subversive (and often dangerous) counterculture in which male homosexuals dominate and in which the male-female roles of the dominant French culture have been translated into the pimp-queen and into the active and passive members of gay coupling. The world in which these gay characters live does not correlate with the one into which they were born, but one into which they must be initiated by living in the subversive gay community and modeling themselves on the elder queens of the community. They follow a sort of monastic novitiate training to learn the precise practices—how to live as a queen, how to cross-dress, how to create the gestures that at once invoke feminine but bespeak gay signification and context, how to greet one another, how to relate to one's pimp; in short, a complete novitiate training in gay culture and life.

Genet accomplishes his ascetical agenda in his novels and plays by piecing together what Richard Schechner, the performance theorist, calls "malleable bits of experience."[16] In writing Genet's biography, Edmund White repeatedly shows how Genet refracts events or elements of his life in the life, character, gestures, and events of his characters. Genet does not produce simple and plain autobiography because each of the elements seems to be

15 Ibid.

16 Richard Schechner, "Magnitudes of Performance," in *The Anthropology of Experience*, ed. Victor W. Turner and Edward M. Bruner (Urbana: University of Illinois Press, 1986) 363.

changed, adjusted, refracted and in that process breaks away from the real events of his life into the fictive elements in the construction of a character. Genet creates identity out of malleable bits of experience refracted through past, present, and imaginary time. In so constructing his characters, Genet employs an ascetical modality in a literary endeavor intended to create a gay identity quite distinct from the dominant heterosexual identity assumed in French society. Genet's queens function in the context of a totalizing gay community with its own gay worldview. By employing this ascetical modality, Genet transforms the traditional religious ascetical practices of his youth into the exercises, experiences, and metaphors of a completely secularized and subversive gay identity, society, and culture.

It can easily and generally be concluded that the middle of the twentieth century witnessed the emergence of a wide assortment of subversive and alternative identities, social configurations, and conflicting worldviews. I need only point to the sexual revolution of the sixties, the emergence of the feminist movement in the seventies and eighties, and the radicalized (especially in response to the AIDS pandemic) gay activist movement of the nineties. All of these movements tended toward the construction of alternative subjectivities within a dominant society against which they defined themselves, building alternative societies and cultures that would sustain their new identity, and developing divergent understandings of the symbolic universe to support their new identities. They were all in one form or another, ascetical movements. Jean Genet provided a significant starting point in the literary scene for the construction of such alternative subjectivities.

## *The Branch Davidians*

Alternative subjectivities in the twentieth century did not remain the province of philosophical, literary, or sexual radicals. Conservative religious groups also began to form intentionally ascetic communities. The Branch Davidians of Waco, Texas provide an exemplar of such communities. The Branch Davidians move our genealogy out of the intellectual and literary world into the arena of religious politics.

On February 28, 1993, when the agents of the Alcohol, Tobacco, and Firearms division of the Federal Bureau of Investigation began their standoff with the Branch Davidians at their community center at Waco, the United States awakened to the existence of radically conservative Christian ascetical communities within its own borders. The standoff ended on April 19, 1993, when the confrontation erupted into violence and the community buildings of the Branch Davidians burst into flames killing eighty-six people, among whom were seventeen children. The Branch Davidians went nobly and fearlessly to their deaths, with only nine surviving members of the Waco community (excepting those who had been released during the standoff).

In every way, the Branch Davidians were an ascetic community. Their community was formed in opposition to the dominant religious and political culture around them in the United States and throughout the world. They held apocalyptic views of the end-times, metaphorized as a fiery ordeal in the tradition of the biblical book of the Revelation of John, views affirmed by their biblical interpretation and that led them to withdrawal from society to a sacred place apart. Their status as the elect who could rightly perceive and understand God (in contradistinction to all others) supported their living a common life of intense biblical study, common belongings, corporate meals, and mutual support and love. Their community was organized around the messianic self-understanding of their leader, who had adopted the religious name David Koresh. Their common life, focused as it was on David Koresh, organized itself as a religious militia prepared to join God in the destruction of the evil forces of the universe, an army prepared to join in the fiery ordeal that would end the beastly power of the United States and the evil governmental forces of the world. They were prepared to jump into the fiery ordeal in order to assist God in the establishment of a theocratic world government, the reign of God on earth under God's own messiah, David Koresh.

Little is known of the interior workings of this community. There is no evidence of a written rule of life nor a description of their daily life. Most of the surviving evidence revolves about biblical interpretation, the teaching of which became the central corporate act of their communal living as evidenced in the large number of transcribed tapes available from their regular bible study classes. Livingstone Fagan, one of those released from the community during the standoff, has provided a precious insight into the theory of formation operative among the Branch Davidians in an appendix to a larger biblical-interpretative piece entitled, "Intuition—The Emerging Soul."[17] Fagan describes the goal of the process as the ability "to think God's thoughts after Him, the Source of true Judgment." This ability to assimilate and to appropriate God's thinking is tied to the developing of the person, here called the "fledgling soul," that emerges from "intuition—the combined effect of the senses and seed of judgment of the fledgling soul." Intuition, together with the development of "conscience" enables and empowers one to think God's thoughts. Fagan's argument follows in this way:

[17] Livingstone Fagan, "Mount Carmel: The Unseen Reality," Appendix B, "Intuition—the Emerging Soul" at http://www.parascope.com/articles/1296/faganful.htm (accessed August 7, 2004).

> By themselves our thoughts are really ethereal labels attached to the feelings (processes and objects) of our senses. True thoughts begin with intuition and, with the aid of conscience, mature into judgments. Such judgments form the basis for true (correct) thinking, producing its corresponding thoughts. At each level—feelings, intuition, judgments, thinking—a new phase of consciousness emerges. In the light of each development, the understanding of the preceding level is completed. Becoming situated in true thinking, the soul is ready for birth.[18]

What Fagan describes here is the development of a totally new person whose soul is birthed through a process of formation. That formation consists of the reformation of thinking or thought according to a system that has been deemed "true," presumably in opposition to the false thoughts completely oriented to the senses or the physical world. The oppositions here are telling: fledgling soul versus mature, sensual versus divine thinking, lower levels of judgment versus higher levels. Intuition guides the person toward the mature, divine, and higher life that produces a new birth, a new person, a new subjectivity capable of thinking God's thoughts. In the process of being guided toward that new birth, the conscience of the person develops more fully, creating a new consciousness. This is a process gradually intended completely to reform the subjectivity of the believer.

Fagan emphasizes that the process is a complete program. It cannot be stopped before the complete transformation of the person:

> The importance of conscience in this process cannot be underestimated. It is like the umbilical cord of the developing child in the womb. The fledgling's link [*sic*] to the soul of the universe from which it is nourished and takes its form. Cut prior to maturity, and the soul fails of coming to birth. It dies and ultimately returns to nothing. As with a soul, so with a nation.[19]

Two issues emerge as central here. The first is that without the formation found in the community of believers, a person cannot thrive. Without the formation available in the community, the fledgling is doomed to death. Wisdom, salvation, health, vitality flow only from the ascetical formation and practices within the community. The second issue, more striking, is the linking of the microcosmic soul's fate with the macrocosmic fate of the nation. This innocuous-seeming comment, almost a simple addendum, indicates that there is a larger and more social component to this formative process. This is not a process intended simply to create spiritually reborn people, it

18 Ibid.

19 Ibid.

is also a process intended to create a spiritually renewed nation. The ascetical disciplines at the microcosmic level create simultaneously a nation and a culture (they would probably call it a "world") at the macrocosmic level. The individual identity connects directly to a specific social environment and to a specific understanding of the goal and purpose of human existence articulated in the community's theology.

Finally, Fagan connects this understanding of human spiritual identity and the construction of a new world order to the biblical interpretation so familiar as a practice in the community:

> The matured soul combines thinking and its corresponding thoughts, the one male and the other female. The perfect image of god. At the birthing they are placed in separate forms, and are one, completely in touch with every aspect of each other. Perfectly mated. This is God's ideal of marriage, of which Adam and Eve in their innocence were an example. His being formed first was an object less[on] in order. Her being the more beautiful, it was necessary for her to be formed from living substance, rather than raw dust. The majesty of femininity. This ideal has been blighted by sin and has degenerated to what we have today. The plan of salvation incorporates its restoration. Of a truth, the soul is created from nothing, coming via dust. In the Kingdom of God we are born perfectly mated.[20]

Here Fagan provides us with the theological rationale for the whole system emergent from an interpretation of the purpose of human existence in the first two chapters of Genesis. The system of formation, so non-biblical in its language and metaphor, becomes biblical because it is identified with the proper understanding of Adam and Eve's creation in Genesis. Chillingly, the metaphor of marriage opens the possibility of sexual abuse of women and children by the messianic figure, but the metaphor becomes naturalized in the interpretative process so that the concepts of restoration, of perfect mating, of a divided whole (presumably brought together in coitus), of the image of God all flow logically and properly from their biblical interpretation. Fagan claims that he merely explains the deeper meaning of scripture. This deeper level of understanding, however, provides the glue to all the other elements of the formative process. It is the creation of a symbolic universe that sustains the alternative subjectivity and gives depth and meaning to the construction of an alternative society or nation.

What ended in the fiery ordeal at the Branch Davidian community center in Waco was the logical conclusion to an intensive and complete ascetical formation. The members of that community were trained to become living

20 Ibid.

warriors, willing to die in the heavenly conflagration that was to befall this sinful and evil world. David Koresh trained and equipped his religious community to become living fires, living flames that were intended to birth a new nation, a new era, a new Kingdom of God.

## *The Terrorists of September 11, 2001*

It is but a short jump from becoming a living flame inaugurating the Kingdom to becoming a human bomb in honor of God. I began writing this essay in the aftermath of the September 11, 2001 bombing of the World Trade Center buildings in New York, the Pentagon in Washington, D.C., and the destruction of the airplane in Pennsylvania, and during the intense fighting between Israel and the Palestinian Authority in Spring, 2002. After the terrorist attacks on American soil, the nature of American identity, power, and self-awareness—so long lived as dominant and unquestionably supreme—shifted weight permanently in the face of what have been called "martyr heroes" of the jihad. These human bombs provide the fourth political, social, and cultural event that has put asceticism on the (post)modern agenda.

In an article, Nasra Hassan[21] reported on the training of *shaheed batal* (martyr heroes) of the Palestinian uprising against Israel. Her account, without ever mentioning the word or the concept, relates an ascetical regime for young men to train themselves not only to become human bombs, but also to become martyrs for the cause of the holy war. The training in martyrdom,[22] as Hassan reports them, revolved about a nexus of important elements: the promise of immediate entrance into Paradise upon their self-imposed death; a "constant state of worship" as one of the martyrs-in-training described it; the attractiveness of a spiritually uplifting project; the close support of a cell of people (*al khaliyya al istishhadiyya*, [martyrdom cell]), whose life acquires an intensity based on a common holy calling; the love for the holy scriptures that gives contours and depth to the actions of the martyrs; the fame and blessing bestowed upon the family and community of the martyr; the clear sense of a calling—by clerics indirectly or from Allah directly—to a holy office and offering; and finally, the joy of knowing that there will be victory over the enemies of Islam. The young men selected for this office are carefully trained. The religious guides employ videos of exemplars of martyrs that model be-

21 Nasra Hassan, "An Arsenal of Believers," *The New Yorker* (November 19, 2001); cited at http://www.newyorker.com/fact/content/?011119fa_FACT1 (accessed August 7, 2004).

22 See also Bruce Lincoln, *Holy Terrors: Thinking About Religion after September 11* (Chicago: University of Chicago Press, 2003). Lincoln includes a translation of the letter, copies of which each terrorist had in his possession, that provided the theology and instructions to the terrorists.

havior, attitudes, and postures as they prepare themselves for their sacrifice. The guides reinforce such visual imagery with recitation and memorization of the qur'anic passages that justify and glorify their mission while emphasizing the rewards of their sacrifice on behalf of Allah. Recited questions and responses that train the mind in new ways of thinking of themselves and their world reinforce the learning and help the martyrs-in-training to image themselves in their chosen vocation. Signs and posters glorifying previous martyrs and their successes provide visual and verbal support from the religious and secular community around them to encourage the martyrs in their preparation (even though members of the community do not know specifically who those being trained are). And, of course, the profound sense of oppression from the enemy both in their personal experience and in the indoctrination of the martyrs' guides grounds their determination to become martyrs. This sense of oppression of the dominant society provides the greatest impetus and drives the martyrs-in-training to overcome their fear of death—and more importantly, fear of failure—through the exercise of their religious strength and determination. It is a complete ascetical formation provided to youths willing to accept the community's call to fight the holy war.

What emerges from Hassan's description is a classic ascetical system. The new subjectivity, immersed as it is in passages from the Qur'an, emerges as a result of specific training and specific individual and corporate practices. That new identity stands in stark contrast not only to the infidel identity and society, but also to other Muslim people and groups. The new subjectivity, to become a living bomb, belongs to a select group of religiously elect who constitute an elite religious society. The process of constructing that identity resembles that of the Branch Davidians, the gay people of Genet's novels, and the ascetical theology of Kazantzakis. These are Kazantzakis's superhumans who transfigure materiality through their efforts and who transform their own bodily existence into a holy, fiery presence.

## Theorizing Asceticism after Nietzsche

By moving forward from Nietzsche's initial differentiation in *Schopenhauer as Educator* between the lazy person, blindly being constructed as a person of his age, and the youthful soul, energetically defining himself from within himself and rejecting the inherited societal norms, this essay has pursued Nietzsche's youthful soul into the ascetical construction of subjectivities opposing the dominant culture. I have argued that what characterizes validly ascetical activity is precisely this creation of an alternative identity in the face of a dominant and given social identity. The other side of the equation, Nietzsche's lazy person and Foucault's self-formed person, being oriented toward the dominant culture and their ability to function within it seamlessly, consists not of asceticism, but of formation. Formation prepares people to participate in the dominant society by equipping them with the requisite tools. Foucault's theories, exciting as they are, apply not to asceticism but to social formation, and that among primarily elite and entitled males in ancient society.

Once Foucault and his theory have been displaced from the discussion of asceticism proper, then the pursuit of a genealogy of subversive identity construction may begin anew. That genealogy, beginning with Nietzsche's youthful soul and moving through the undercurrents of the next two centuries' social and intellectual movements, emerges as an interesting combination of philosophical, literary, religious, and political movements. The genealogy develops through the expression of an undercurrent of subversive identities: Kazantzakis's superhuman, Genet's queens, David Koresh's fiery community, and the human bombs of September 11. Although these events are not necessarily directly related to one another, they form a progression from theory, to literary imagination, to community life that explains how many of the movements of the twentieth century created their alternative subjectivities. The interaction of theory and practice among the various subversive movements—feminists, people of color, ethnic groups, religious communes, ecological advocates, animal rights protagonists, to name just a few—locates them precisely in this ascetical stream, and not the formational one. These movements oppose the dominant culture and perspectives of their time in order to create something new, a new identity, different communities, and structures of meaning to support them in their new life. These movements fill in the genealogy from Nietzsche to September 11, providing ample proof that ascetic subjectivities will emerge to counter the hegemony of a dominant perspective.

The Feast of the Holy No-Silver Ones in Paros with which I began this essay takes place in a monastery. The monks of the monastery were ascetics—they withdrew from society in order to construct a new identity in God. The people attending the festival, however, received formation, cultural information and practices to enable them to enter the dominant life of the Greek society of which the Church is a part and to enjoy the riches of hegemony. These two perspectives, formation and asceticism, stand as related and yet very different processes. Each orients itself in radically different ways to the dominant culture and each forges new subjectivities in response to that dominant culture, but each constructs its identities in decidedly different ways.

# Interlude

# Insight as Image

## *My Ongoing Conversation with Margaret Miles*

Lynn Randolph

*While language necessarily begins with a universal experience that it imposes on the particular, images begin with an expression of the particular and evoke the universal, inviting the viewer to participate in a symbolic expression that gives universal significance to the particular experience of human beings.*[1]
—Margaret Miles

IN 1989–90 I spent a year as a painting fellow at the Mary Ingraham Bunting Institute (now known as the Radcliffe Institute) in Cambridge, Massachusetts along with forty-two other women from all over the world. My project was entitled "A Return to Alien Roots: Painting Outside Mainstream Western Culture." One day I was having a discussion with a young historian whose work concerned a sixteenth-century Spanish nun. My excitement for her work and my personal take on contemporary uses of religious images provoked her to suggest that I read a book called *Image as Insight* by Margaret R. Miles. I was profoundly struck by the book and the correspondence in our ways of thinking and seeing. Margaret Miles was then teaching at Harvard, so I called her and asked her to come over to the Institute and talk to a group of us about her work and to visit my studio there. Thus began a wonderful friendship and an ongoing conversation about art, religion, ideas, women—life. The following is a weaving together of some of the correspondences be-

[1] All quotes are taken from two of Margaret R. Miles's books: *Image as Insight: Visual Understanding in Western Christianity and Secular Culture* (Boston: Beacon, 1985); (and the last two are from) *Carnal Knowing Female Nakedness and Religious Meaning in the Christian West* (Boston: Beacon, 1989).

tween our work. Miles is a writer who consciously finds meaning/relevance in images; I am a painter who consciously finds meaning/relevance in language.

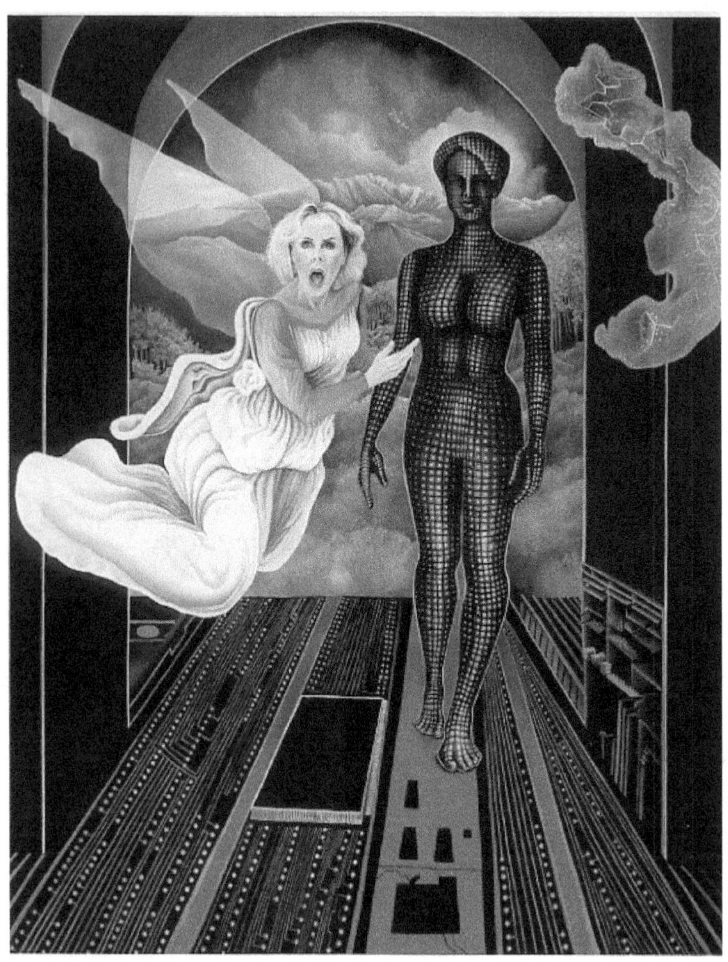

Lynn M. Randolph, *The Annunciation of the Second Coming*. 1995. (oil on canvas, 58x46 inches), in a private collection in Houston, Texas. Photo by Paul Hester. Hester + Hardaway Photographers

There are, of course, large differences between creating a work of art and writing about the history and meaning of art. Much of what goes into creating comes from understanding and appreciating the insight gained from those who think and write. Everyone's process is different. Underneath a work of art is what shaped it: the consciously consumed knowledge, life experience, attentiveness to the world, one's values and reflections, and the inspired choices that give it a life of its own.

> It is not sufficient in these days of easy availability of a variety of contemporary images—from pornography to museum art—simply to recognize that one is drawn to a particular image; rather, if the image attracts me, it speaks to me in a "significant and definite way." It has for me, "specific expressive power," that I can come to understand by being attentive to the complex of memories, associations, and longings gathered in me, over time, by the image.
>
> —Margaret Miles

This same sort of gathering and attentiveness occurs in me at the beginning of a painting.

We all have a screen in our heads; we project our dreams onto it and we repress a significant amount of the images and narratives we construct. I use the screen in my mind mostly in semiconscious states, before I go to sleep or in the early quiet hours of the morning. I run images across it; the images are paintings in process. They are of people I know, places I've been, the things that enchant me, as well as ones I imagine. There are many images or fragments of images waiting to make themselves known. It is as if they merge and inform each other as they wait at the edge of consciousness. One thing will connect to another until I can begin materially to produce them. Occasionally I am jolted by a complete vision, an impulse that I always follow and transform into a painting. There is a sense of "rightness" about such visions, as if they had their own integrity, which I can't violate. The images are attached to my values and desires as well as what I've been thinking and reading about and watching over a wide cultural plane. While I'm painting, new images often occur; it is never predetermined but rather worked through until I can record and then abandon it.

For me art and life are inseparable and art can be about more than itself; in fact, it has to be to survive in any meaningful way. By bringing into form an informed and integrated understanding of my subjects, I hope to fashion webs of connection to others; I want to create images that trouble, resist, and disturb and offer provisional visions of love, hope, and well-being. The connection between visible surface and invisible depth is crucial. The inarticulate relationships of interior to exterior, idea to form, private pathos to public patterns, from local events to global ramifications in our twenty-first-century life, make visual skills and critical thinking necessary to artists and viewers.

Figurative "seeing" is dependent on literal seeing, and the religious life must be conceived and articulated by the use of metaphors based on natural objects if its concepts are not to remain lifeless.

—Margaret Miles

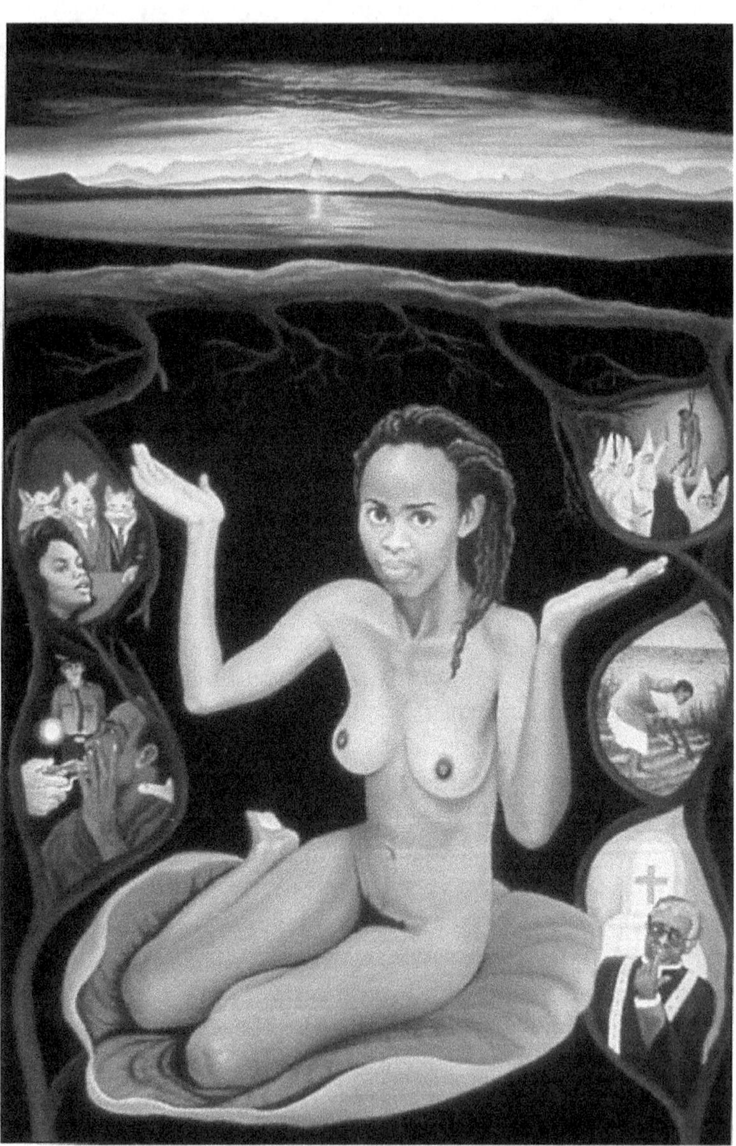

Lynn M. Randolph. *So?* 1993. (oil on canvas, 36x24 inches), collection of Arizona State University Museum, Tempe, Arizona. Photo by Paul Hester. Hester + Hardaway Photographers

I paint particular people, places and things, going from the specific subject (for instance, a figure) to the metaphysical, via the metaphoric arrangements and juxtapositions of objects in a way that binds the content or subject matter to the structures and forms in which it occurs. Every element—color, form, shape, line, texture, composition—is rendered to support, reenforce, and interpret, making the meaning visible; it actively produces consciousness of the objects it constitutes.

I call my work metaphoric realism. I'm trying to create metaphors that chart new ways of thinking and change the symbolic order. Visual metaphors call upon the beholder to combine and synthesize experience, which analysis has often fragmented or dissected. Metaphors can be a powerful means of understanding the rationally ungraspable. They offer insight into the evolution of a phenomenological sense of being in the world. They are both a mode of persuasion and a catalyst for change. Metaphors are hybrids, messy combinations that threaten a homogenous world. Metaphorology opens up a wide and truly cross-disciplinary horizon, which moves easily from the temporal zones of past and present to future and back again. Metaphors contain multiple intelligences and allow us to see how others think and feel through many lenses. In a spiritual context we are all the living manifestations of metaphors of that which is within us. Given the importance and power of metaphoric languages, we should never turn from asking, "Whose metaphors?"

> Religious "seeing" implies perceiving a quality of the sensible world, a numinosity, a "certain slant of light," in which other human beings, the natural world, and objects appear in their full beauty, transformed. The transient, intensely experienced occasions on which we experience "eyesight as insight"[2] have frequently been described as a clue to the nature and structure of reality and the first step toward realization of the ultimate fulfillment of human being as symbolized by the idea of the vision of God.
>
> The critical use of images involves understanding the particular message received from the painting; ultimately it means being able to articulate the relevance of this message to my present affective life.
>
> —Margaret Miles

2 Rudolph Arnheim. *Art and Visual Perception* (Berkeley: University of California Press, 1965), 31.

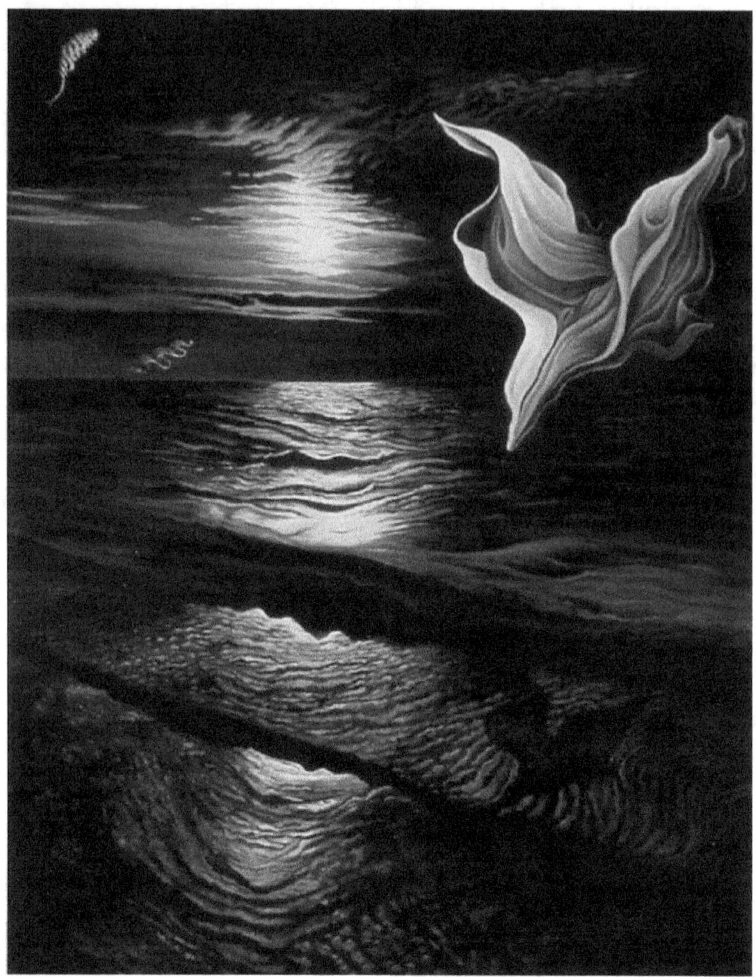

Lynn M. Randolph. *Shrouds of Light*. 2002. (oil on canvas 40x36 inches). Photo by Paul Hester. Hester + Hardaway Photographers

In one of our recent conversations, Margaret Miles and I were discussing gnosticism and she said what interested her most about the gnostics was the question of what the gnostics believed that they were willing to die for and that kept them out of the institutional church. It's often the question before the question in which she brings real value and moral challenge to a subject. Her question, of course, raises other questions about the church and where the gnostic texts differed from the orthodox texts and why. Miles is highly informed and engaged in the conversation often referred to as new critical thinking. Many of the questions she raises are ones with which I have also been concerned and they inform my paintings.

The task of representing the world becomes more complex as we come to appreciate how the social construction of reality advantages some over others and speaks to some and not to others. I want to recover much of that which has been deformed and marked by cultural institutions as unacceptable, as alien. I want to see images of value that affirm and challenge as well as confront, images that connect to the consciousness of others, images that intervene, that bring suffering to the surface, that distribute pain, that centralize the marginal, and that also resist commercialism, empower women, and magnify dreams.

> Religion, it has often been said, both articulates and responds to the life experience, the ideas, and the ultimate concerns of human beings and communities.
>
> —Margaret Miles

I think that religion can be a vital resource for making art and constructing a life. This, of course, involves an expanded sense of religion, one which "articulates and responds" to the deepest human experiences, "the ideas and ultimate concerns" of being human, a sense of religious experience that is enhanced by broadening and making relevant religious texts and images.

Much of what we are trying to overcome originated in the early discourse of religion. Ecclesiastical rule marked the beginning of the production of master narratives including the canons of art. Religious images simultaneously express some of our most noble ideals and our most debased behavior. Notions of sacrifice, transcendence, and elevation are double-edged. Many lives have been needlessly sacrificed in the name of some god and many others enslaved, tortured, and brutalized. But perhaps in attempting to deconstruct religions and religious images we have relegated to the fundamentalist-, orthodox-, and conservative-traditionalist sects some very powerful and rich ideas and images. Since we help to create each other, as we continuously produce and reproduce our common culture, I see little reason to hand over spiritual writing and seeing to those who stand for all that threatens to make religions instruments of oppression and destruction. Instead, I think that these personal expressions of the divine within is a gift of insight into the divine presence in the world.

> Although the test of a contemporary analysis is its accuracy and comprehensive treatment of the data with which it works, it must be therapeutic. The significance for us of practices and attitudes of the past is their value to corroborate and support present experience, to offer alternatives to present values and practices, or to call into question, to contradict, or to judge the present ordering—so that nothing will be lost—of the "richness of the mixture."
>
> —Margaret Miles

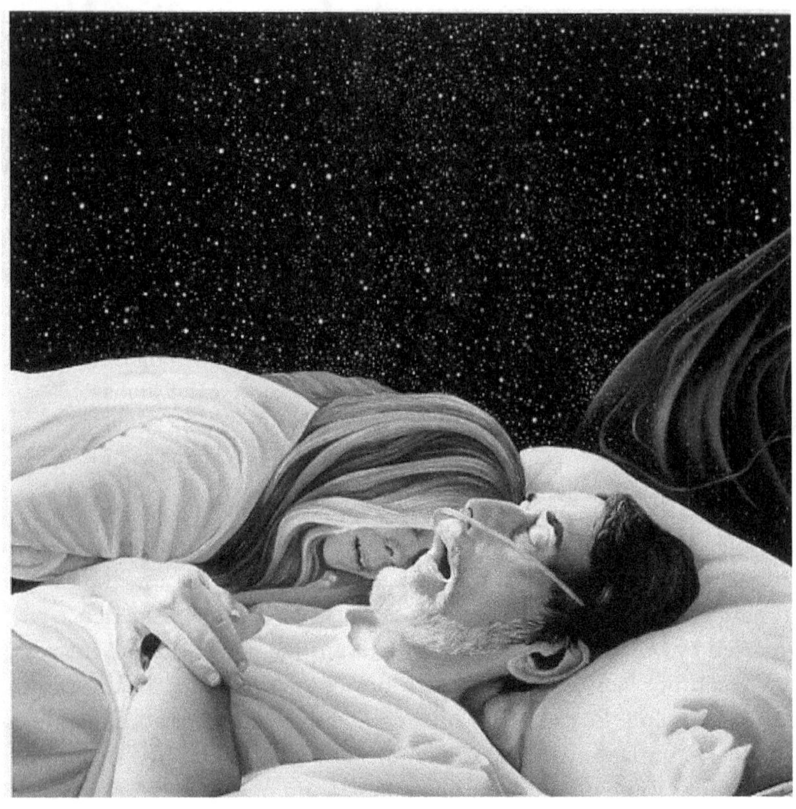

Lynn M. Randolph. *Lamentation.* 2001. (oil on canvas 29x30 inches).
Photo by Paul Hester. Hester + Hardaway Photographers

Much of the imagery that we inherited from early Christian art, to and through the Renaissance, is aesthetically beautiful, but its attachment to one story or master narrative has limited us to narrow interpretations and burdened us with images that have reduced and essentialized the total life experience to versions of the life of Christ. I suspect this could also be said of the art of all religions. There are thousands of Madonna and Child paintings; where, one might ask, are the images of a fearful, tired, playful, questing mother? Frida Kahlo's *My Nurse and Me* is a striking example of an image that challenges the stereotype. I believe confronting the stereotypes and changing them is a powerful way to engage with religion.

Three years ago, my husband died rather suddenly of cancer. I found great consolation in viewing traditional paintings of resurrections, descents from the cross, lamentations, and crucifixions. One lamentation at the Houston Museum of Fine Arts, attributed to Quentin Matssys, is special to me. I visited it regularly and felt the enormous pain it represented as my own. Viewing the passion paintings at this moment in my life was like seeing them for the first time and I found them profoundly moving. I painted my own versions and out of the experience of these paintings I began to find some peace.

Old religions need some new metaphors in order to be relevant in today's world. So I believe that turning to traditional religious images and seeing them from one's own personal state of being, as well as reinterpreting them for our time, our place, and our culture, have powerful possibilities. It is a call to not be afraid or embarrassed to spiritualize the secular or to encompass nonrational truths in our art and lives.

> By far the largest group whose history can be approached by using visual images in addition to verbal texts is women. The use of visual images as historical evidence promises to provide a range and depth of material for women's history that is simply unavailable in verbal texts, the great majority of which were neither written by nor read by historical women.
>
> When feminist artists and authors "paint the body" and "write the body" as the perfect expression of female subjectivity, this art begins to create a new kind of "spectator," a viewer whose aesthetic experience is more like making an acquaintance than like surveying an object.
>
> "Carnal knowing" refers to an activity in which the intimate interdependence and irreducible cooperation of thinking, feeling, sensing, and understanding is revealed.
>
> —Margaret Miles

There is no final portrait of any person that represents the totality of the sitter. There are only partial glimpses into the lived experience of our bodies, yet we are a society obsessed with bodily images, images and representations that are used to manipulate our bodily life. This is all too apparent in the lives of anorexic women and the commercial practices that make shopping a perpetual necessity.

If you think of the medium (paint) as costume, or script and canvas as skin, it suggests that a painting's meanings are often attached to the various levels and depths with which they reveal themselves. When I'm painting a figure—for me it is a multiple layering of thin paint, a kind of sculpting with paint, or a patient fleshing out—I can feel in my own body the body parts on which I am working. This is an important and confirming experience, which is lost when I step back to analyze what I've done. I love to be "in the paint;" I feel myself coming from behind the canvas into a new realization of the subject.

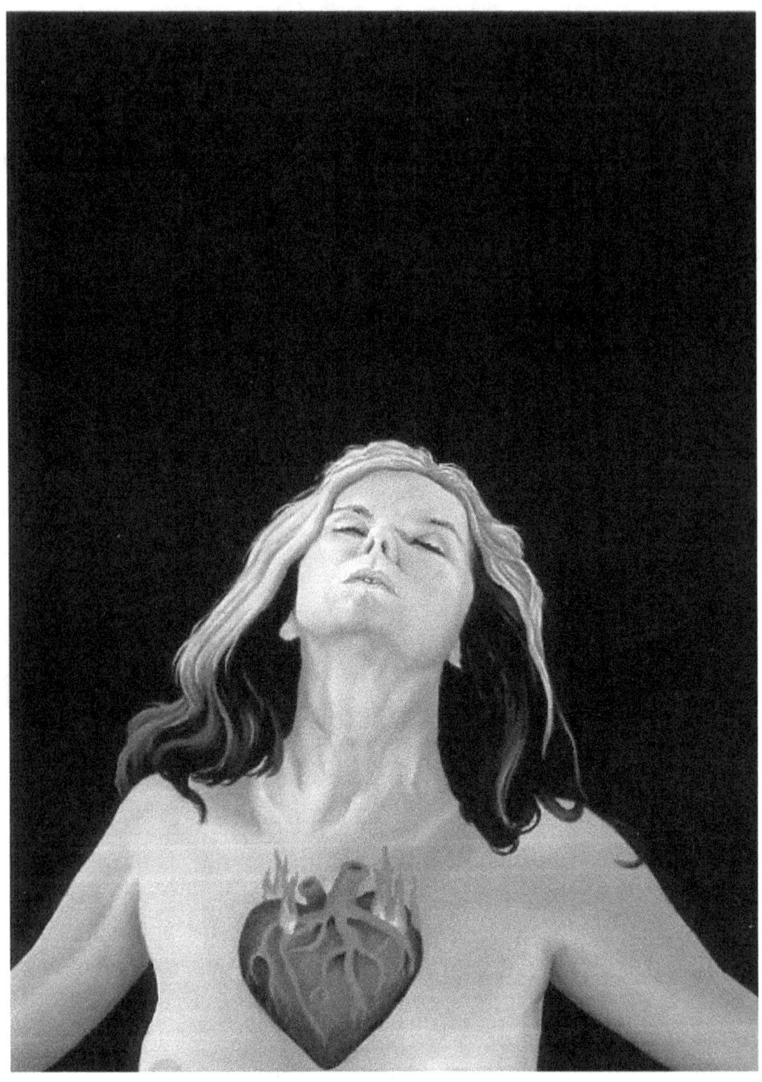

Lynn M. Randolph. *La Petite Mort.* 1992. (oil on masonite 14x10 inches). Photo by Paul Hester. Hester + Hardaway Photographers

We can't hide from or cease to exist in our bodies. In her book *Carnal Knowing,* Margaret Miles presses contemporary women artists and writers to create work that explores female subjectivity with carnal-knowing awareness that is recorded in the body—embodied self-knowing, self-loving. The mysticism represented in the texts of the mystic nuns is a distinct form of feminine culture and one of the first first-person narratives by women of historic significance. The mystic nuns unwittingly created a rich space for exploring female empowerment and carnal knowing. They claimed that they obeyed the dictates of inner voices, a claim that was hard to dispute. Their narratives represent a place to revisit as we look for possible sites and spaces to create powerful new metaphors for women's subjectivity, sexuality, and spirituality. Mystical discourse subverts the symbolic on which it rests and remains outside the logic of the linguistic system. The church felt compelled to monitor very closely the behavior and conversations of the mystic nuns. Their records, notes, and diaries contain some of the most erotic, surreal dreams and visions ever recorded by women. They lived lives of constant and heightened sensation, losing themselves and their boundaries in fantastic flights and visions. A state of being unselfconscious is a transgression. The politics and poetics of transgression are a part of the search for new ways of empowering women that do not necessarily assume unitary subjects that are essentialist nor are they traps of authoritarian attitudes. The borderlands between the sexual and the spiritual become blurred. Some nuns were excruciatingly sensitive to every body sensation. One nun could not clasp her hands for fear of the libidinal discharge this might release, another was surrounded by a horde of demons who prevented her from speech. Marie de Joseph saw her words transformed into beams of light. Saint Teresa of Avila saw a small and beautiful angel whose face was lit with a burning light. He held a long golden spear—which had a little fire on its point—that he thrust into her heart and entrails. When he drew it out, he also drew them out and left her on fire with a great love of God. This account, like many others, constitutes a space for expressing bodily pleasure that is outside the sinful. They were out of their minds.

If the self has become the sacred in a chaotic, complex post-paradigmatic world, then to create new myths and metaphors that matter we have to go to other, perhaps forbidden, places within ourselves—our wildness, our madness, our desires—to construct them. I believe it is important to reassert the presence of women's bodies; a presence that speaks to the totality of women's experience and not just as fragments, as body parts, strategically rendered grotesque in order to de-eroticize or made esoteric with theory-driven texts attached. No, I think it is important to see rich, juicy women engaged in multiple emotional, spiritual, intellectual, and physical activities. In *Carnal Knowing* Margaret Miles wrote that the first theological meaning of nakedness was innocence, frailty, and vulnerability. Representations of these have been lost in the fast-paced, smart-ass culture we live in today. When painting naked women, the intentions and distinctions—however complex—are going to be important. How a figure is contextualized and materially produced are indicators of its purpose. If one is trying to close the gap between art and life, then painting, the medium that most concretely reifies the split and the connection between flesh and image, may be singularly qualified to take on that project. I've worked to create new images of real people with undeniable presence that trump old stereotypes and static myths. The certainties with which we used to view images of the body have eroded in our recent understandings of the social construction of reality in the cultural production of gender, sexuality, and psychopathology. Past meanings, those born in the dialogue of past centuries, can never be stable or finalized. I believe there is a palpable need to rehabilitate the images of the mind and body through a process of personal interrogation that interprets the evidence of our own condition, our own time, our own metaphors for our realities, unashamedly.

## Susannah

I took my hair band and my pumice-stone
down to the garden pool sequestered by ilex,
demure twilight lowering her veil,
and it was told me after—
how the three elders closeted their gaze
among the columns, erect cypresses
and the sloven pomegranates,
knowing I would bathe.
And while I bent to pare my toenails,
lather up my grimy knees and wash the sweat
of service off me, drooling in their beards
they leered and smothered laughter,
fingering their inside jokes together,
but never gave themselves away.

Whether I let my hair down or not is hardly
the issue to me, whether the last light
glinted off me, nor how nor where the water trickled down,
while my assailants waged their quiet
combat of glances, fidgeted, broke wind.
It is, finally, to me, no matter
what they said they saw
or did not see.

—Jennifer M. Phillips

# Religion and Gender

# Religious Gender Models and Women's Human Rights[1]

Kari Elisabeth Børresen

## Human Godlikeness

THE modern concept of universal human rights derives from the European Enlightenment but builds upon the early Christian ideal of human equivalence in the order of redemption. In historical perspective, this ideal can be traced through ideas of stratified communality in the Middle Ages, religious individualism in the Age of Reform, and universal human rights for men in the Enlightenment, up to the twentieth-century shift from *droits de l'homme* to inclusive *droits humains* for both sexes.[2] In order to claim autonomous human rights, human females have to be defined as fully human beings; in Christian terms, women must be created in God's image. It is essential to observe that the recognition of this privilege to both sexes results from the Greco-Roman Church Fathers' attribution of spiritual Godlikeness also to women, using ingenious scriptural exegesis. The axiomatic incoherence between divinity and femaleness, which structures Judaism, Christianity, and Islam, is in Christian history negotiated through a gradual inclusion of female humanity in the concept of created Godlikeness.[3] This doctrinal process

[1] This essay is an enlarged version of a paper given at the Fourteenth International Conference on Patristics Studies, Oxford, August 21, 2003.

[2] See Joan Wallach Scott, *Only Paradoxes to Offer: French Feminists and the Rights of Man* (Cambridge: Harvard University Press, 1996); and Kari Elisabeth Børresen, Sara Cabibbo, and Edith Specht, editors, "Gender and Religion" ["Genre et Religion"], *European Studies/études européennes* (Rome: Carocci, 2001).

[3] See Kari Elisabeth Børresen, editor, *The Image of God: Gender Models in Judaeo-Christian Tradition* (Minneapolis: Fortress, 1995).

can be traced in three steps: androcentric monism, asexual dualism, and a holistic Godhead.

## *Androcentric Monism*

Starting with biblical texts *ad litteram* (Gen 1:26-27a; 1 Cor 11: 7), early Christian anthropology interprets the basic interaction between the man-like Godhead and Godlike man in the androcentric sense that creational Godlikeness is attributed to men only, whereas women achieve this prerogative by "becoming male" in the order of redemption, through incorporation into Christ (Col 3:10-11; Gal 3:28; Eph 4:13; cf. *Gospel of Thomas* 114). In this first doctrinal period of man-centered monism, which was normative into the fifth century and upheld by medieval Canon Law, women's sociological subordination and cultic incapability (*impedimentum sexus*) is justified by women's lack of *imago Dei* in the order of creation.

## *Asexual Dualism*

As a result, traditional Christian anthropology is based on two opposite axioms: androcentric gender hierarchy is established in this world by God's creative order and human equivalence in the sense of women's eschatological parity with men is realized through Christ in redemption.[4] This conflict between women's created inferiority and their salvational equality is confronted by "feminist" Church Fathers in order to include women in human Godlikeness even in creation, despite their God-alien femaleness. According to patristic theology, God is described as metasexual and the correlated *imago Dei* is defined as an incorporeal and consequently sexless quality, linked to the human capacity of virtue and intellect. Following this combined Platonic and Stoic God-language, Clement of Alexandria invents a feminist exegesis of Genesis 1. Here the sexual differentiation expressed in Gen 1:27b ("male and female he created them") is disconnected from the consecutive blessing of fertility in Gen 1:28 and linked to the preceding text of Gen 1:26-27a: "Let us make Adam (collective male) in our image, according to our likeness. . . . And God created Adam in his image, in the image of God he created him." Consequently, Paul's argument for men's exclusive Godlikeness in 1 Cor 11:7: "For man should not cover his head, since he is the image and glory of God, but woman is the glory of man" is disregarded. In fact, this text combines Gen 1:26-27a with God's formation of Adam from clods in the soil, blowing

[4] See Kari Elisabeth Børresen, *Subordination and Equivalence: The Nature and Role of Women in Augustine and Thomas Aquinas* (Washington, D.C.: University Press of America, 1981), updated as *Subordination and Equivalence: A Reprint of a Pioneering Classic* (Kampen: Kok Pharos, 1995).

into his nostrils the breath of life, according to Gen 2:7. Illogically, Clement invokes the negating citation of Gen 1:27b in Gal 3:28: "there is not male and female, for you are all one (collective male) in Christ," which refers to the redemptive reversal to a combined presexual and andromorphic perfection of original creation to include women instead of abolishing femaleness. In this second doctrinal period of asexual dualism, which was further elaborated by Augustine and became normative in scholastic theology, women's gender-free *imago Dei* does not affect their God-given subservience *qua* female human beings. It follows that the axiomatic incoherence between divinity and femaleness remains unchallenged by the Church Fathers' metasexual Godhead. As a result women's spiritual equivalence could only be anticipated in this world by ascetic defeminization, through virginity or widowhood.[5]

## *Holistic Godhead*

In medieval religious feminism, the ancient strategems of women becoming male in Christ or claiming asexual Godlikeness were relinquished. Perspicaciously challenging the correlated andromorphic or metasexual God-language, leading Church Mothers like Hildegard von Bingen and Julian of Norwich describe God with female metaphors in order to provide a divine model for women's *imago Dei.* This third doctrinal period of holistic Godhead was rediscovered in nineteenth-century feminist theology, first by the Norwegian Aasta Hansteen and then by the American Elizabeth Cady Stanton.[6] Taking Clement of Alexandria's strategic linkage of Gen 1:26-27a and 27b for granted, as if women were created in God's image according to the biblical text *ad litteram*, their rather vernacular exegesis argued for inclusive Godlikeness in order to obtain full civil rights for women. In fact, all established churches opposed female suffrage by invoking women's traditional subordinate status, which derived from their female lack of creational *imago Dei.* Ingeniously grasping the basic interaction between human self-

[5] See Elizabeth A. Clark, *Ascetic Piety and Women's Faith* (Lewiston, N.Y.: Mellen, 1986); Susanna Elm, *Virgins of God: The Making of Asceticism in Late Antiquity* (Oxford: Oxford University Press, 1996); and Anne Jensen, *Gottes Selbstbewusste Töchter: Frauenemanzipation im frühen Christentum?*, 2d ed. (Münster, 2003).

[6] Aasta Hansteen in *Kvinden skabt I Guds billede* [Woman Created in God's Image] (Christiania, 1878) 5–7, citation 14, affirms that man is created in the image of God the Father, woman in the image of God the Holy Spirit, and both sexes are in the image of Christ, as representing the fullness of human nature so that "human duality reflects the divine Trinity." Elizabeth Cady Stanton, in her edited volume, *The Woman's Bible* (New York: European Publishing Company, 1895) 14, argues that "The first step in the elevation of woman to her true position, as an equal factor in human progress, is the cultivation of the religious sentiment in regard to her dignity and equality, the recognition by the rising generation of an ideal Heavenly Mother, to whom their prayers should be addressed, as well as to a Father."

consciousness and God-language, Hansteen and Cady Stanton therefore described God with both female and male metaphors.

This new interpretation of holistic Godlikeness, where both women and men are created in God's image *qua* male or female human beings, was first accepted by Protestant exegesis, less from feminist motifs than by abandoning traditional dualist anthropology. Inclusive *imago Dei* was later introduced in Catholic theology after the Second Vatican Council, whereas Orthodox doctrine still upholds the patristic definition of human Godlikeness as an incorporeal and therefore asexual privilege. It is important to observe that the ensuing affirmation of women's salvational equivalence as normative for this world represents a radical innovation in the history of Christianity, where premodern bio-social gender hierarchy was constantly defined to be God's order of creation. Consequently, the theological rationale for Godlike women's human rights is now assured in the majority of Christendom.

## Patristic Innovation, Matristic Achievement

The Greco-Roman inculturation of the Church Fathers, mainly between the third and the fifth centuries, had a formative influence on traditional theology.[7] This patristic innovation was emulated by the Northern European Church Mothers' transformation of Christian God-language, mainly between the twelfth and the fifteenth centuries. I have introduced the terms "matristic/matristics" in order to designate their achievement, which was shaped by the less male-centered Germanic, Anglo-Saxon, and Scandinavian cultures.[8]

### *Augustine's Unique Creation*

It is noteworthy that Augustine is the first Church Father who explicitly confronts 1 Cor 11:7 by stating that women too are created in God's image. Since patristic exegesis understands this text as literally affirming men's exclusive Godlikeness, Augustine resolves his scriptural dilemma by an allegorical interpretation of Paul's *vir* and *mulier*. He explains that Godlike man signifies the superior element of the human soul, which is dedicated to the contemplation of eternal truth, in contradistinction to non-Godlike woman, who represents the soul's inferior element and is charged with earthly matters (*De Genesi ad litteram 111:22*). This exegetical device is inherited from Philo and Origen, who used it to explain the existence of corporality and femaleness in their theory of double creation. Although the ex-Manichean Augustine's

7 See Kari Elisabeth Børresen, *From Patristics to Matristics: Selected Articles on Christian Gender Models by Kari Elizabeth Børresen*, ed. Øyvind Norderval and Katrine Lund Ore (Rome: Herder, 2002) 15–89.

8 Ibid., 145–272.

main achievement in Western theology is the affirmation of God's unique creation, his division of women's Godlike *homo interior* and their sub-male *homo exterior* strengthens the theomorphic autonomy of the exemplary male humanity (*De Trinitate* XII: 7, 10, 12-13). Significantly, Augustine emphasizes that God's only purpose for creating the derived *femina/mulier* as man's helpmate, according to Gen 2:18, is women's subordinate and receptive role in procreation of men's offspring (*De Genesi ad litteram* IX: 5).

Nevertheless, in order to include *femina* as *homo* in God's unique creation, Augustine is the first Church Father who states that women shall not resurrect in male or sexless perfection, but will be recreated as female human beings. Describing God's final restoration of perfect humanity through a Christlike resurrection, he introduces a "feminist" exegesis of Eph 4:13. With explicit reference to creational wholeness, Augustine interprets *vir perfectus* (perfect manhood) in terms of human fulfilment according to the inclusive *homo* of Gen 1:26-27b, by combining Gen 2:7 with Gen 2:18, 21-23. Since female humanity is part of God's unique creation, women will not be restored to Christlike human nature by "becoming male," but will rise as human females, although their procreative finality will be superseded. Augustine continues his argument for female resurrection by invoking the typology of Adam–Christ and Eve–Church, with reference to Gen 2:21-22, Eph 5:32, and John 19:34 (*De civitate Dei* XXII: 17-18).

## *Augustine's Typology*

This transposition of creational gender hierarchy to the order of redemption begins with Rom 5:14: "Adam, who is a type of the coming (Christ)." The correlated nuptial symbolism of Christ–Church in Eph 5:32 (cf. 2 Cor 11:2) is amplified by Justin and Irenaeus to a salvational couple of new Adam–new Eve. Here disobedient Eve is counteracted by obedient Mary, as a complement to the Adam–Christ typology. Referring to John 19:34, Tertullian compares Eve's formation from Adam's rib during his sleep with the Church emerging from Christ's pierced side after his death on the cross. The new Eve becomes mother of the living by the sacraments of baptism and Eucharist. Since Ambrose, Mary and the Church are fused through their shared virginal motherhood in relation to Christ.

It is important to observe that this asymmetrical typology, which remains basic in traditional Christology and ecclesiology, corresponds to early Christian anthropology and is therefore elaborated before women were attributed creational Godlikeness. It is noteworthy that Augustine's application of the new Adam–new Eve typology has an aspect of androcentric feminism. Although Adam's sole responsibility for humanity's collective guilt is counteracted through Christ's redemption, according to Augustine's exegesis of Rom. 5:12, the new Eve's instrumental role in the redemptive order guarantees the salvation of both sexes. The parallel of Eve and Mary is thus invoked in order to embrace both variants of human nature, male and female (*De agone christiano* 22: 24, *De diversis quaestionibus* 83: 11). In Augustine's man-centered context, this application of redemptive typology serves to enhance creationally inferior femaleness.

Paradoxically, a so-called "iconic" argument based on the Adam–Christ parallel is now invoked against women priests and bishops in Roman and Orthodox Catholicism. In medieval Canon Law, the cultic impediment of femaleness is legitimized by women's lack of creational Godlikeness *qua* female human beings, a concept recently abandoned by Catholic theology. As a result, the current Vatican ban on women's ordination reveals an illogical disparity of updated Godlikeness and arrested typology, which is especially acute in the mariocentric feminology of John Paul II.[9]

## *Hildegard's Female Wisdom*

In this perspective of doctrinal history, the matristic achievement of metaphorical feminization of the Godhead proves to be essential for the renewal of Christian God-language. The learned abbess Hildegard's main theological work, *Scivias* (1151), describes God's revelatory *Sapientia* as a female figure.[10] The whole universe is visualized as being continuously upheld by the shaping *Creatix*, permeating *Caritas* and providing *Scientia.* When Hildegard describes God's transcendence in male imagery and God's immanence in female imagery, she builds upon a previous sapiential tradition. Connected to I Cor. 1:23-24, where God's incarnate, suffering Son and God's revealing Wisdom converge, the medieval use of female metaphors to describe Christ's human nature reformulates earlier Christology. Hildegard's vision is original in the sense that God's divine *Sapientia* provides a model of Godlike female humanity, *feminea forma.* Hildegard's mariology is consequently rather subdued, although Mary as new Eve is the prime example of female human wholeness, traditionally realized through virginity.

9 See Børresen, *From Patristics to Matristic*, 275–308; Kari Elisabeth Børresen, "Image ajustée, typologie arrêtée: analyse critique de 'Mulieris dignitatem,'" in *Women's Studies of the Christian and Islamic Tradition,* ed. Kari Elisabeth Børresen and Kari Vogt (Dordrecht: Kluwer Academic, 1993) 343–57; Kari Vogt, "Catholicisme et Islam: une rhétorique commune à propos de la femme," in *Women's Studies*, 359–65; and Kari Elisabeth Børresen, "Jean Paul II et les femmes," *Lumière et Vie* 52 (2003) 57–69.

10 Barbara Newman, *Sister of Wisdom: St. Hildegard's Theology of the Feminine* (Berkeley: University of California Press, 1987); and Elisabeth Gössmann, *Hildegard von Bingen: Versuche einer Annäherung* (Munich: Iudicium, 1995).

## *Birgitta's Co-redeeming Mary*

Like Hildegard, the successful prophetess Birgetta of Sweden (died 1373) seeks in her *Revelationes* and *Sermo Angelicus* to provide a model of female Godlikeness, but instead of metaphorically feminizing the Godhead, she attempts to divinize Mary by presenting her as christotypic.[11] Striving to rectify the gender hierarchy of traditional typology, Birgitta inserts Mary as an active partner in salvation history. This new Eve, Christ's mother, is predestined to participate in the new Adam's redemptive suffering, and the incarnate union between Christ and Mary is emphasized in terms of sharing the same heart. Unfortunately, Birgitta's original concept of salvational gender symmetry with the new Eve as co-redeemer is a christological deviation and therefore unviable. Nevertheless, her aim to validate human femaleness can inspire feminist theology.

## *Julian's God Our Mother*

In contrast, the erudite anchoress Julian of Norwich (died after 1416) is an imitable Church Mother, both in intention and doctrinal content.[12] Apparently little known in the fifteenth and sixteenth centuries, her texts have fortunately been conserved. The oldest manuscripts of Julian's *Showings*, based on a visionary experience in 1373, were identified by chance in 1909 and 1955, but even earlier a longer version from later copies was printed in 1670. Julian's theology represents an outstanding matristic achievement by healing the Judeo-Christian-Islamic rift between Godhead and femaleness. Therefore, she is increasingly valued as the most innovative theologian in Western Christianity after Augustine. Describing Christ as Mother, Julian attributes this quality not only to his incarnate human nature, but extends Christ's Motherhood to the preexistent level of the Trinity. Julian's fundamental trust in all-embracing salvation is strikingly opposed to Augustine's and later Martin Luther's anguished seeking for a merciful God. In order to verbalize her visionary experience of God's recreating love ("that all things will be well" [Short version XV]), Julian elaborates her original concept of divine Motherhood (Long version 48, 52, 54, 57-63, 83). Describing the triune Godhead at work in creation and redemption, she uses both male and female metaphors: "I saw and understood that the high might of the Trinity is our

[11] See Børresen, "Birgitta's Godlanguage: Exemplary Intention, Inapplicable Content," in *From Patristics to Matristics,* 171–230.

[12] See Joan M. Nuth, *Wisdom's Daughter: The Theology of Julian of Norwich* (New York: Crossroads, 1991); Denise Nowakowski Baker, *Julian of Norwich's* Showings*: From Vision to Book* (Princeton: Princeton University Press, 1994); and Børresen: "Julian of Norwich: A Model of Feminist Theology," in *From Patristics to Matristics,* 231–46.

Father, and the deep wisdom of the Trinity is our Mother, and the great love of the Trinity is our Lord" (Long version, 58). Julian's innovative discourse aims at correcting the androcentric duality of traditional God-language.

Julian applies her concept of divine wholeness to the human level, since original creation and redemptive incarnation unify the spiritual and bodily elements of human nature. In her *Showings*, Trinitarian interaction is verbalized by means of human wholeness, in the sense that both female and male metaphors describing God correspond to both Godlike women and men. Julian depicts Christ's maternal qualities in conformity with her cultural understanding of the female role, in which the mother is defined as protecting, nurturing, and compassionate. Nevertheless, by placing Christ's metaphorical Motherhood in his unified divine humanity, she overcomes the gender hierarchy of traditional typology, where the Church or Mary is the subordinate new Eve. Focusing on God the Mother, Julian's mariology is consequently quite discreet. As a result, the main achievement of her theology is to provide a fully Godlike, christomorphic and female role model for women.

## Religion and Gender Hierarchy

In a global perspective it is essential to observe that all main religions are structured by axiomatic gender inequality. In Hinduism and Buddhism, women are not properly human beings, but placed between men and beasts through the wheel of reincarnation or rebirth, which is determined by the ethical performance of previous existence. This ontological hierarchy is even expressed in a fundamental text of European heritage, namely Plato's creation myth in *Timaeus* (41d-42d). In contrast, the Jewish, Christian, and Islamic variants of monotheism, where each human being has only one terrestrial existence, include women in humankind, but they are defined as subordinate to serve men's procreation of offspring. Given the shared paradigm of one Creator and two sexes, the God-willed finality of female humanity is motherhood. It is important to consider that this existential gender asymmetry, with specific and separate male and female roles, is not only enforced by Islamic sexology, but is still the norm in both Roman and Orthodox Catholicism and is strongly promoted by fundamentalist Protestants.

### *Epistemological Revolution of Feminism*

It is essential to understand that women's claim to bio-socio-cultural and religious autonomy results from the epistemological revolution of feminism, where women and men are defined as human beings with equal dignity. More crucial than the previous breakdowns of geocentrism (Copernicus, Kepler) and anthropocentrism (Darwin), the actual collapse of androcentrism in

Western civilization is now spreading globally. Although less challenged than other world religions, Christianity's reaction to modern feminism ranges from ambivalent endorsement to manifest resistance, ranging from "civilized" Protestantism to Orthodox Catholicism.

It is important to note that the eighteenth-century *droits de l'homme* were not explicitly transformed into inclusive *droits humains* before the UN Conference on Human Rights (Vienna 1993) stated that women's rights are universal human rights.[13] In historical perspective, this evolution corresponds to the twentieth-century ideal of democracy, including women's political equality, which in the nineteenth century was repeatedly condemned by the established churches, with Pius IX's *Syllabus of modern errors* (1864) as a particularly retrograde example.

## *Freedom of Religion*

In contrast to universal human rights, which have roots in God-given redemptive equivalence, freedom of religion is a purely secular concept. While Jewish monotheism is ethnocentric, both Christianity and Islam are universalistic by claiming to reveal that God has supreme rights, which must be obeyed by all humankind. In this theocentric perspective, God alone ordains gender-specific rights and duties to men and women. Therefore, universal human rights cannot be based on secular international law, but must derive from *lex divina*. Nevertheless, the non-theocratic concepts of religious tolerance and freedom of religion emerged in Western civilization from the seventeenth century onwards. Codified in the Universal Declaration of Human Rights in 1948 (Article 18), religious liberty was finally endorsed by the II Vatican Council in 1965, but this novelty was primarily aimed to obtain freedom for the Catholic Church in communist states. In fact, the problem of religious liberty for individual Catholics in the Roman Church remains unsolved.

## *Religion Versus Women's Human Rights*

It follows that the persisting religious androcentrism provokes a global conflict between two incompatible human rights, where freedom of religion functions as an obstacle to gender equivalence. This basic antagonism is often strategically concealed in UN efforts to implement universal human rights through international law. The fact that Islamic *Shari'a* ordains God-given specific female rights for women as subordinate daughters, wives, and mothers, but does not grant them universal human rights, is regularly criticized

13 See Katarina Tomaševski, "Women's Rights," *Human Rights: Concept and Standards,* ed. Janusz Symonides (Burlington, Vt.: Ashgate, 2000) 231–58.

in Western debate. In contrast, the similar Roman Catholic opposition to women's human rights of reproduction autonomy and cultic capability is veiled in terms of gender complementarity.[14] Nevertheless, the combined Islamic and Vatican enforcement of divinely prescribed division in male and female functions is demonstrated by the concordant votes of the Holy See and Islamist states at the UN Conference on Population (Cairo 1994) and on Women (Beijing 1995).[15] Following this shared androcentric anthropology, the same alliance has not signed the UN *Convention on the Political Rights of Women* (1952), nor the UN *Convention on the Elimination of all Forms of Discrimination against Women* (1979), where women's voluntary fertility is explicitly defined as a human right (III, Articles 12: 1; 14: 2b; 16: 1e). In fact, the correlated sexology of traditional Christianity and Islam is currently obstructing the UN's efforts to liberate women in developing countries. Therefore, the Vatican and Islamic claims to impose man-centered theocracy by implementing Canon Law or *Shari'a* as normative in society, especially in legislation concerning the family, are main hindrances to women's fully human equivalence.

## *Christian and Islamic Sexology*

The patristic concept of human Godlikeness and christomorphic deification of humankind is alien to Islam, where God's sovereign transcendence excludes divine incarnation. According to Islamic protology, the original fall is not a catastrophe and human nature is not vitiated by the initial disobedience of Adam and his woman. God is forgiving and merciful, so there is no original sin and consequently no doctrine of redemption. God guides humanity to overcome the fault by observing his divine law, revealed through his final prophet, Muhammad. As a result the early Christian sexophobic *enkrateia* is perfectly absent, so that Augustine's transmission of hereditary guilt by orgasmic *concupiscentia* is unthinkable. His moral adage *bene uti malo,* where sinful orgasm must be neutralized by God-given fertility, is quite alien. Therefore, Islam has no doctrinal ban on contraception. Nevertheless, men's basic drive toward women must be controlled by strict separation of the sexes and female seclusion. In this man-centered context, the traditional Christian strategy of ascetic feminism is inapplicable for Muslim women, although the

14 See Børresen, "Religion Confronting Women's Human Rights: The Case of Roman Catholicism," in *From Patristics to Matristics,* 289–308.

15 See Doris E. Buss, "Robes, Relics and Rights: The Vatican and the Beijing Conference on Women," *Social and Legal Studies* 7 (1998) 339–63.

famous female mystic Rabi'a (died ca. 801) was praised as "becoming male" through her union with God.[16]

It is important to observe that Christian and Islamic eschatology converge in affirming male and female resurrection, universal judgment, and ultimate reward according to individual merit. According to the Qur'an, such gender equality before God refers to the coming world, but has been recently invoked by Islamic feminists as being valid here and now.[17] This exegetical strategy emulates Christian feminists' backdating of redemptive equivalence to the creational order.

## *Inculturated Revelation*

As a Catholic feminist theologian, I find it paradoxical that women's human rights of reproduction autonomy and cultic capability were first affirmed in a Protestant context, whereas Greek and Roman Catholicism provide the necessary doctrine of redeeming restoration of perfect humanity in Christ (*theosis*) and incarnate revelation, as historically shaped *revelatio continua*. In this perspective, I value the ancient Greco-Roman Church Fathers and the medieval Northern European Church Mothers as partners in the continuously inculturated God-language that transformed Christianity from a Jewish sect to a world religion.[18] Reconstructing theological anthropology in accordance with contemporary human rights is necessary for the Church's survival as an instrument of salvation.

In contrast to the patristic concept of God's revelatory disclosure *humano modo*, where both Scripture and tradition are conditioned by shifting human contexts of time and place, the Islamic concept of revelation is metahistorical and therefore transcultural. The God-given Arabic Qur'an is defined to be uncreated and preexistent, which was revealed to humankind through Muhammad as a passive transmitter. This immutability of divine revelation constitutes a main barrier to emerging feminism in Islam, since the sacred text persists immune from independent reasoning (*ijtihad*). Therefore,

16 See Kari Vogt, "Becoming Male: A Gnostic, Early Christian and Islamic Metaphor," in *Women's Studies*, 217–42.

17 See Shaheen Shardar Ali, *Gender and Human Rights in Islam and International Law: Equal Before Allah, Unequal Before the Law?* (The Hague: Kluwer Law International, 2000); and Jonas Svensson, *Women's Human Rights and Islam: A Study of Three Attempts at Accommodation* (Stockholm: Almqvist & Wiksell, 2000).

18 Kari Elisabeth Børresen, "Nourrir la tradition par inculturation continuée: innovation patristique et accomplissement matristique," *Bulletin ET Zeitschrift für Theologie in Europa* 9 (1998) 115–27.

historical analysis is only allowed when interpreting the prophetic tradition (*hadith*) and elaborating Islamic jurisprudence (*fiqh*).[19]

In ecumenical perspective, women's cultic *impedimentum sexus* in Roman and Orthodox Catholicism is still blocking Christian reunion. In the shared context of monotheism, it is remarkable that Reform Judaism introduced women rabbis (in 1972) with reference to the inculturated character of unfolding revelation, and that Conservative Judaism followed suit (in 1984) by stating women's Godlikeness. In global perspective, the conflict between modern human rights for women and secular religious freedom for premodern doctrinal and legal systems remains a fundamental problem.

In this emergency, I believe that the only way to counteract a current fundamentalist backlash is to emulate the patristic and matristic inculturation of Christian God-language. The doctrinal process of including women in fully human Godlikeness provides an encouraging paradigm for the indispensable feminist reformation of the Church. It is important to remember that similar examples of historical development are also available in medieval Islam, but are not invoked by Islamic reformists.[20] Quite imprecisely, they are often called modernists, although alien to the historical-critical methods of twentieth-century Catholic modernism, which managed to influence the II Vatican Council.[21]

[19] Barbara Freyer Stowasser, "Gender Issues and Contemporary Quran Interpretation," in *Islam, Gender, and Social Change,* ed. Yvonne Yasbeck Haddad and John Esposito (New York: Oxford University Press, 1998) 30–44.

[20] The historical-critical approach of Mohammed Arkoun is an exception. See Chapter IX, "The notion of Revelation" in his *Lectures du Coran* (Tunis, 1991) 257–81. See also his *Rethinking Islam: Common Questions, Uncommon Answers,* ed. and trans. Robert D. Lee (Boulder, Col., Westview, 1994). Also see Nasr Hamid Abu Zayd, *Critique du discours religieux* (Arles: Sinbad-Acts Sud, 1999).

[21] Strongly condemned by Pius X; cf. his antimodernist oath imposed in 1910, abrogated in 1967. Catholic modernism is again censured by John Paul II; cf. his *Professio fidei* in 1989 and *Ad tuendam fidem* in 1998. Also see Kari Elisabeth Børresen, "Religious Feminism and Catholic Theology," in *The Relevance of Theology: Nathan Söderblom and the Development of an Academic Discipline,* ed. Carl Reinhold Bråkenhielm and Gunhild Winqvist Hollman (Uppsala: Uppsala Universitet, 2002) 143–56.

# Gender Justice and the Transformative Power of Mutual Vulnerability

Stephen B. Boyd

*The glory of God is the human fully alive.*
—Irenaeus of Lyon[1]

## Introduction

THIS essay pursues a theme and includes methodological considerations that are central to Margaret Miles's teaching and publications—the flourishing of human beings of every gender, sexual orientation, color, ethnicity, or any other of the richly diverse conditions in which we are found. It also acknowledges the distorting character of asymmetrical power relationships between and among social groups.

I will argue that at the heart of the growing chasm within U.S. churches is a basic assumption about gender roles, or a "law of gender complementarity." I will then draw on the work of Kathy Rudy, John Dominic Crossan, and Howard Thurman to suggest a way beyond the polarization and toward gender justice and the possibility of sacramental healing and transformation.

## The Law of Gender Complementarity and the Division in the U.S. Churches

Over a decade ago, Robert Wuthnow noted that, in the last half of the twentieth century, the most significant theological differences were not between Christians belonging to different denominations, but between Christians belonging to the same denominations.[2] The conditions affecting that shift are varied. Increased migrations and intermixing of denominationally identified

1 *Adversus Haeresies* 4.20.7 (Edinburgh: T. & T. Clark, 1974).

2 Robert Wuthnow, "Old Fissures, New Fractures," in *The Struggle for America's Soul: Evangelicals, Liberals, and Secularism* (Grand Rapids: Eerdmans, 1989) 19–38.

ethnic groups, coupled with higher levels of education and intermarriage, have led to a decrease in the importance, for many, of those particular denominational identities. For example, you will find advocates and opponents of certain abortion procedures, stem-cell research, cloning, etc. within denominations and even within the same congregations and families. In other words, for most people, what denomination they belong to is less important than where they stand on these kinds of issues and who stands with them. So, the most important fault line, or lines, between and among Christians lies not between particular Protestant denominations, marked by their historically delineated doctrinal particularities, or between Protestants and Catholics, but within those communions. What Wuthnow sees is a chasm between two identifiable groups—conservatives and liberals—with fairly coherent views, contending with each other within denominations. Currently, one of the most explosive issues dividing these two groups and threatening almost every mainline denomination is the attitude toward and treatment of same-sex-oriented persons, particularly members' rights to membership, ordination, and marriage.

Underneath these questions lie, even for liberal groups, unresolved issues concerning attitudes about gender. First, let's take a quick look at some of those issues and then at how they are related to the current tensions around GLBT people.

Denominational responses to the First and Second Waves of feminism and women's demands to be treated as equals in the life of our institutions, including the church, have tended to reflect that of whichever group—conservative or liberal—predominates. Or, if there is something approaching parity between the groups, denominational adjudicatories reflect a mediating position. I would generally characterize these responses as "defensive denial" in the case of conservatives and "guilty paralysis" for liberals.

## Conservatives: *Defensive Denial*[3]

In 1984 the Southern Baptist Convention, the largest Protestant denomination in America, passed a resolution excluding "women from pastoral leadership . . . to preserve a submission God requires because the man was first in creation and the woman was first in the Edenic fall." In 1999, responding to "cultural confusion with clear teachings from the Bible," the SBC adopted, in a revision of The Baptist Faith and Message, statements on "The Family" and "The Church." Marriage is seen as a gift that provides for "one man and one woman" a "framework for intimate companionship, the channel of

[3] The following five paragraphs first appeared in slightly altered form in "On Listening and Speaking: Men, Masculinity, and Christianity," *Journal of Men's Studies* (1993) 323–45.

sexual expression according to biblical standards, and the means for procreation of the human race." Further, though the husband and wife are created in God's image, a "wife is to submit herself graciously to the servant leadership of her husband even as the church willingly submits to the headship of Christ." Consequently, "while both men and women are gifted for service in the church, the office of pastor is limited to men as qualified by Scripture."[4]

In the Roman Catholic Church, the Vatican, on the basis of the 1976 *Inter Insigniores* document, claimed that since God in Christ determined the specific nature of the sacramental sign, the Church has no right or authority to change it and admit women to the priestly order. The argument then runs: since sacramental signification requires a natural resemblance between the sign and thing signified; and since the priest, in the specific and unique act of presiding at the Eucharist is a sign; and since Christ was and remains a man; therefore, it is fitting that priestly ordination be reserved to men. The papal encyclical, *Ordinatio sacerdotalis* of 1994 reiterates that priestly ordination is restricted to men.

In both of these responses, there is a denial that the church and its authoritative structures are harmful to women, much less to men. On the contrary, the hierarchical structure must be good for all involved, including women; it is the will of God. In both, an exclusively male authority structure is speaking without listening. In fact, any listening to human voices is ruled out because that would violate the immutable voice of God, whose integrity the authority structure must defend. An implicit assumption seems to be that, though the authoritative structures are not harmful to women, women exercising leadership would be harmful to those structures.

## Liberals: *Guilty Paralysis*

On the other hand, there have been church bodies that have listened to the voices and criticisms of women, but have been slow to root out sexism or share institutional power with women. The General Board of The American Baptist Convention—the liberal Protestant counterpart to the Southern Baptists—adopted the "Resolution on the Empowerment of Women" in 1977, which called for a reversal of the declining number of positions held by professionally trained women in the city, state, regional, and national staffs.[5] However, although there was modest progress made during the decade between 1971 and 1981 on the basic professional and middle management

[4] http:/www.sbc.net/bfm, Sections VI and XVII.

[5] Elizabeth J. Miller, "Women in the American Baptist Churches: A Perspective on the Past Thirty Years," (Women in Ministry Group of the Minister and Missionaries Benefit Board of American Baptist Churches, 1986) 8–9.

levels, there was "a net decrease of one woman and a net increase of four men on the National Staff." In 1981 no women served on the National Executive Council or on the Regional Executive Ministers Councils—the most important decision-making groups in the ABC.[6] By 2003, there were 1,392 ordained women, representing 21% of clergy serving local churches. Women represented 50% of those serving on the national staff and 26% of those on regional staff. However, in thirty-seven regions, only three women served as Executive Director.[7]

The U.S. Conference of Catholic Bishops, considered by many to be more liberal than the Vatican, published the first draft of "A Pastoral Response to Women's Concerns for Church and Society" in 1988. Consequently, it declared its intention "to ensure that women are empowered to take part in positions of authority and leadership in church life in a wide range of situations and ministries." However, the bishops balked at extending the equality of women and men to priestly ordination. Responding to the negative tone of the Pope's *Ordination sacerdotalis*, the Conference issued the pastoral letter, "Strengthening the Bonds of Peace," focusing on ways women can serve the church without ordination. They see the necessary cooperation between men and women in the church as similar to the roles in marriage: ". . . equality does not imply sameness in roles or expectations, nor does it mean that two spouses will have identical gifts or character. Rather, they will respect each other's gifts and identity."[8]

In her book, *Sex and the Church*, Kathy Rudy argues that, underneath the typically polarized responses of conservative and liberal Christians to issues related to sexuality, are assumptions about gender roles common to both groups. These assumptions leave unexamined and unchallenged what might be called the law of gender complementarity, which is the root of gender injustice in our churches and in the larger culture. Conservatives are very clear that their opposition to homosexual sex is grounded in "tradition and family-centered values as the core of Christianity." For them, anything or anyone that questions, or challenges, traditional notions of differentiated and complementary gender roles is perceived to be an enemy of God and the divine order. While most conservatives believe that gay, lesbian, bi-sexual and transgendered (GLBT) people deserve compassion and often see their sexual

6 Miller, 10–12. An update in 1985 noted that the General Board, which was comprised of one-third women, voted to continue the "Resolution on the Empowerment of Women" and that two women had been appointed to significant positions on the national level since the report in 1981. See also Jackson W. Carroll, Barbara Hargrove, and Adair T. Lummis (1983) for data reflecting similar trends in other liberal Protestant churches.

7 http://www.abc-usa.org/regions/regions.html; http://www.abwin.org/statistics.htm

8 http://www.usccb.org/publishing/women.htm#bonds.

orientation as a biological given, they believe that homosexual sex is a sin and "can only support and ordain 'nonpracticing' homosexuals." Liberals, on the other hand, tend also to believe that sexual orientation is a given (i.e., biological or natural), but come to very different conclusions. Convinced that "no compassionate God would demand the impossible (i.e., celibacy)," many believe that homosexual activity can be endorsed and that gay people, sexually active or not, should be eligible for ordination. For them the core of Christianity is "inclusivity, tolerance, and social justice." However, the various documents dealing with these issues that have issued from liberal Protestant communions, while affirming the worth of gay persons and advocating more openness to them and to issues related to them, also reject the possibility of ordination for the "self-avowed practicing homosexual."[9]

Following Mary McClintock-Fulkerson, Rudy uncovers two underlying assumptions that inform a "gendered theology" common to both conservatives and liberals. First, members of both groups believe that "homosexuality is self-evident; we all know exactly what homosexuality is and can identify it both in today's milieu and throughout history." Second, there is a shared belief, as we have already seen, that "homosexuality is the result of some biological or natural phenomenon, that some people are simply born homosexual."[10] The gendered theology of which these assumptions form a part include the following, often implicit, assertions:

1) God created male and female in such a way that their complementary "parts" (both physical members and psychic aptitudes) fit;
2) what one brings to the other is needed by the other for wholeness and vice versa;
3) therefore God intended and intends for women and men to live together.

This is a gendered theology because of what is explicitly affirmed and what is implied. The notion of gender complementarity "extends far beyond the realm of sexuality into assertions about what men and women should be."

9 This particular language came from the United Methodist Church's 1993 "Report of the Committee to Study Homosexuality to the General Council on Ministries" but is characteristic of the positions of, for example, the Presbyterian Church (U.S.A.) and the Evangelical Lutheran Church in America. See Kathy Rudy, *Sex and the Church: Gender, Homosexuality, and the Transformation of Christian Ethics* (Boston: Beacon, 1997) 85–86, 88.

10 Rudy, *Sex and the Church*, 87. She cites McClintock-Fulkerson, "Gender—Being It or Doing It? The Church, Homosexuality, and the Politics of Identity," *USQR* 47 no. 102 (1993) 30.

So, the implicit notion of salvation entails fulfilling the law of gender complementarity and achieving wholeness "through reproduction of the nuclear family and the heterosexual, monogamous dyad."[11] The only acceptable lifestyle, or path to salvation, is heterosexual, monogamous marriage.

Though conservatives tend to be more explicit about the normativity of this gendered theology, it is often no less so for many liberals. By that I mean, though many liberals express toleration for same sex sexual expression, they often balk at calling a "union ceremony" a "wedding" and the result a "marriage," reserving those words for heterosexual relationships. Also, while they often express a willingness to defend the rights of gay people to have sex and even a ceremony, they don't want to hear any details, see public displays of affection, or think much about how those relationships work. My sense is that many assume that gay relationships work pretty much the way their own do—following a model of complementarity. So there may be some curiosity about who is "the man" and who is "the woman." Thus liberals share with conservatives the assumption that complementary, heterosexual sexuality is the norm; they are just more tolerant of what they, too, believe is aberrant, gay sexuality. Or they may believe that on a deeper, more significant level than that of bodies and biology, gay relationships and, therefore, gay sexuality, insofar as they mimic heterosexual ones are not really that different.[12] Consequently, the law of gender complementarity often remains unexamined among liberals, as well as conservatives.

There are a number of problems—both theological and ecclesiological—raised by this gendered theology. I'll briefly mention some of the most pressing ones.

First, the difficulties it causes for GLBT people are enormous. In this frame, homosexuality and crossing genders are symbols of "everything the Christian is not."[13] It is impossible even to outline in this brief essay the toll (including violence, discrimination, higher suicide rates, repression, concealment, and fear) this brutally (conservatives) or softened (liberals) negative message extracts from GLBT people—both internally and externally.

Second, there are a number of problems this gendered theology causes for heterosexually identified people, as well as for gay people. The results are rigidly defined gender roles that are restrictive, though with different impacts, for both women and men. Again, I cannot rehearse or even survey those ef-

[11] Rudy, *Sex and the Church*, 118. The notion of a law of gender complementarity comes from Judith Butler's work as summarized by Susan Frank Parsons, *The Ethics of Gender*, (Malden, Mass.: Blackwell, 2002) 149.

[12] This reflects the tendency of liberals to ascribe to a social constructivist approach to gender roles, while conservatives tend toward an essentialist position.

[13] Rudy, *Sex and the Church*, 119.

fects; in the last thirty years feminists have contributed much to this project, as have scholars of critical men's studies in the last fifteen.

Third, these dynamics also have tremendously debilitating effects on our relationships to our Christian brothers and sisters and to the wider communities of which we are a part. The belief that we are to find wholeness, or salvation, in one "opposite gendered other" renders Christian community essentially superfluous. The distress caused by these dynamics and the pursuit of relief in the "other" consumes a great deal of energy for many. The result is that there is often too little attention available for the work required for more just economic, political, educational, environmental, and cultural conditions in the larger community.

Fourth, the binary conceptual framework—heterosexual/homosexual—that characterizes the gendered theology of both conservatives and liberals is historically conditioned and artificial; it perpetuates, rather than redresses, gender injustice. The work of historians of sexuality such as David Halperin and Eve Sedgewick demonstrate that sexual acts between persons of the same sex or gender have not, across time and cultures, been assigned the meaning and value that is assigned today to the term "homosexuality." Consequently, queer theorists increasingly "question the categories 'gay' and 'straight' not only because they are historically inaccurate, but also because they create the possibility of oppression."[14]

Consequently, Rudy suggests a significant shift in the ethical framework Christians use to think about the morality of sexuality. Historically, there have been two central concepts in the context of which sexuality has been deemed moral or immoral—unitivity and procreativity.

## *Unitivity*

> . . . denotes intimacy, steadfastness, and one-fleshness. In the unitive nature of the sex act, two are made one; the boundaries of either individual are blurred both literally and metaphorically, such that each individual becomes, at least momentarily a part of something larger than him—or herself."[15]

The merging of body and spirit with those of another leads to transformation. This kind of transformation has traditionally been regulated by the other norm of procreation. For several reasons, procreation—understood as biological reproduction—as a central norm has become problematic and, for some,

[14] Ibid., 94. Judith Butler makes a similar argument about the gendered categories "male" and "female." See Susan F. Parson, *The Ethics of Gender* (Oxford: Blackwell, 2002) 145–50.

[15] Ibid., 111.

often conflicts with the norm of unitivity. First, in contemporary life, having a large number of children can result in a significant economic disadvantage. If contraception (considered off-limits by the procreation norm) is not an option, then "many heterosexual couples are forced to forego the goods associated with sexual relations in order to limit family size."[16] Second, there has been a growing recognition that good parenting is not simply a function of biology. The capacity to nurture new life is as critical as the capacity to produce it. Third, new technologies now make reproduction possible without physical sexual contact at all.

Rudy addresses two alternative suggestions as to a norm to pair with the transformative potential of unitivity—complementarity and mutuality. She rejects complementarity on the basis of her foregoing analysis. While affirming aspects of mutuality and its rejection of the exploitation endemic to sexual relationships between people belonging to groups with unequal power, Rudy does not believe that a notion of mutuality alone pays sufficient attention to ways of addressing those differentials in power. Given our current divorce rates, men and women seem to be having difficulty addressing the differentials in power and the alienating effects that dynamic has in heterosexual relationships.[17]

Consequently, she suggests that a notion of hospitality serve as a norm that shapes evaluations of sexual unitivity. Rudy cites canonical interpretations of the Sodom story (Ezek 16:49 and Matt 10:14-15) that make clear the behavior condemned in Sodom was a callous inhospitality. She goes on to suggest, "that what is ultimately pleasing to God about our sexuality is hospitality. If our sexual relations help us to open our hearts and our homes to lost travelers and needy strangers, they are good." For her, "the task in reconstructing a progressive sexual ethic is not to deny or sidestep power, but rather to invite others into the power of God, to welcome them into this radically transformative power which realigns the world . . . ."[18]

I think Rudy is right. To experience the transforming power of unitive relationships—genitally sexual and nonsexual—requires that we open our hearts and our homes to others that do not necessarily share our social location and the relative power and privilege attendant to it. The problem is that it is very difficult, dangerous, and potentially counterproductive for someone with relatively less power to open their hearts to those who have the power to harm or exploit that openness intentionally or unintentionally. In addition, it is difficult for someone with relatively more power to open their hearts to

16 Ibid., 115.

17 Ibid., 121.

18 Ibid., 21, 126.

those with whom a unitive relationship may well lead to a loss of power and privilege. So, we cannot deny or sidestep the differences in power between and among us. We must develop ways to create the conditions in which those with relatively more power and those with relatively less power can relate respectfully and, therefore, with an open heart.

Rudy's suggestion that we explore hospitality as a heuristic notion in this creative work is a good one. I turn now to the work of Howard Thurman and John Dominic Crossan whose reflections on the dynamics in relationships between people divided by race and class I find helpful in filling out Rudy's notion of hospitality.

## Crossan: Jesus and the Transformative Exchange between Itinerants and Householders

John Dominic Crossan, in his recent work on the sayings of Jesus, puts the sending narratives (Luke 10:1-11; 17-20; Matt. 10:5-16; Mark 6:8-13) in the social context of a growing divide between those who owned land in first-century Palestine and those who did not.[19] He focuses his discussion on the account in Luke. To remind you, Jesus sends out the seventy in pairs, preceding him to villages; tells them to carry no purse, sandals, or bag; instructs them to announce peace on whatever house they enter; and, if they are received, to stay in one house and eat whatever is served, heal the sick, and pronounce that "the kingdom of God has come near to you." If they are not received, they are to go into the streets and say, "Even the dust of your town that clings to our feet, we wipe off in protest against you. Yet, know this: the kingdom of God has come near" (Luke 10:11).

Crossan observes that this narrative should be seen in the context of some important demographic and economic shifts in Galilee precipitated by the building of Tiberius and the re-building of Sepphoris. In order to feed the large populations of these urban centers (ca. 25,000 each), wealthy landowners bought up smaller farms to facilitate mass agricultural production. The result was a growing itinerant population of the working poor and artisans, who were dependent on the landowners for their livelihoods. There was then a growing tension between what Crossan calls itinerants and householders in Jesus' home region—a class antagonism between members of two groups on opposite sides of a "dividing wall of hostility." (Eph. 2:14)

Jesus, as a carpenter, was an itinerant and was followed by other itinerants, including fishermen and tax collectors. These itinerant disciples were sent out to announce the coming of the kingdom of God and to heal the sick.

[19] John Dominic Crossan, "Jesus and the Kingdom: Itinerants and Householders in Earliest Christianity," in *Jesus at 2000*, ed. Marcus Borg (Boulder, Colo.: Westview, 1997) 21–53.

The householders were to shelter and feed the itinerants and be healed. If the householders did not receive them, the itinerants were to go into the streets, announce that the kingdom of God had come near, and then shake the dust from their sandals and move on. Crossan observes that Jesus believed that the kingdom came only when the two groups on either side of this dividing wall of hostility came together and transformed one another or were transformed by the grace of God. Neither group, on only one side of the wall, possessed the kingdom and could dispense it to the other. Persons on both sides of the wall had to participate if they were to experience it at all.

I believe that the householders were being called to extend hospitality to the itinerants. Paul refers to hospitality in Rom. 12:9, 13: "Let love be genuine, hate what is evil. . . . Contribute to the needs of the saints. Practice hospitality." The term Paul uses is *philoxenian*, which is the opposite of xenophobia: fear of the stranger; fear of the other; fear of the one who is different. Householders are to practice *philoxenian:* love of the stranger; love of the other; or love of the one who is on the other side of a dividing wall of hostility.

## Thurman: Shared Vulnerability and Transformation

One of the most compelling accounts I have read concerning an understanding of love with reference to "walls of hostility" (i.e., dynamics involving systemic discrimination, exclusion, fear, and hatred) is that of Howard Thurman. In his *Luminous Darkness,* an analysis of the Civil Rights movement and the roles both African-Americans and European-Americans played, he identifies three things he believes European-Americans (read: householders) did and should do:

1) Imagine what it like to be me. This involves a commitment to nonviolence because it "opens the heart so that what another is feeling and experiencing can find its way in."[20]
2) Report it. Report what you hear "without regard to prejudgments and private or collective fears."[21]
3) Do something about it, or, in the words of Thurman: "There must be both a spontaneous and a calculating response to such knowledge which will result in sharing of life and resources at their deepest level."[22]

20 Howard Thurman, *Disciplines of the Spirit* (Boston: Beacon, 1997) 115.

21 Thurman, *Luminous Darkness* (Richmond, Ind.: Friends United Press, 1989) 100.

22 Ibid.

With respect to the role African-Americans (read: itinerants) played in the movement, Thurman does not articulate tasks in any one passage as he does those of the members of the dominant group, but I have gleaned the following from this book and several others:[23]

1) Reject the stereotypes about you. They serve only to justify your own mistreatment by members of the householder/dominant group.
2) Announce the requirements of justice to the householders/dominant group. This is not easy, because many on the itinerant/non-dominant side of the dividing walls have given up on members in the dominant group. They do not believe householders can change, or that the system of domination can change. Why should they, then, waste their energy announcing the requirements of justice?
3) Walk away if you must. If the householders don't receive you, shake the dust and move on. Evidently, Jesus will not be stopping in that village.
4) Finally, forgive.

If itinerants announce the justice and righteousness that are the cornerstone of the kingdom and offer healing to householders who receive them, and if the householders open their hearts and homes to itinerants, then the kingdom will be imminent among them. The kingdom, then, involves reconciliation between persons separated by hostility or indifference, hatred, stereotyping, misunderstanding, and fear.

In his work, Thurman explores the possible effects of itinerant/non-dominant group members using what he calls "the tools of nonviolence" on householder/dominant.[24] He says that the courage an itinerant shows in confronting the threat of physical or psychological violence can evoke in the householder an admiration that leads to identification (cf. number one of the householder tasks). The psychological tools of nonviolence can "open the door of the heart [of an householder] so that what another [itinerant] is feeling and experiencing can find its way within."[25] This, in turn, may lead to an analysis of the causes of those experiences and feelings (i.e., the systemic, structural dynamics of a dividing wall or form of oppression). Love, or the

23 Thurman, *Disciplines*; *Jesus and the Disinherited* (Boston: Beacon, 1976); idem., *The Search for Common Ground* (Richmond, Ind.: Friends United Press, 1986).

24 We also need analyses of the effects of members of dominant groups using the tools of nonviolence on members of nondominant groups. One important part of those effects is the development of trust, necessary for working with members of dominant groups to change the institutional sources of discrimination against and disrespect for members of the nondominant groups.

25 Thurman, *Disciplines*, 115.

willingness to do what one would want another to do for oneself, leads the householder to engage in tasks two and three. It is cooperation, or co-working, that serves as a vehicle for the kinds of institutional transformations that lays the groundwork for justice and, therefore, reconciliation.

But there are also powerful effects in the lives of itinerant group members when members of householder groups renounce the institutional violence directed at the itinerant group and work with them to "share resources at the deepest level." This kind of process requires that members of both itinerant and householder groups embrace what Thurman calls "the spirit of reconciliation," at the heart of which is a willingness to be vulnerable, that is, to express one's deepest "desire and need to be cared for, to be understood." He says that doing that—exposing one's vulnerability to an "enemy"—brings a number of feelings, including fear and hatred, to the surface. However, when one embraces the spiritual tools of nonviolence, such as refusing the fight or flight instinct, one comes "face to face with his own sense of ultimate worth." When this is put "over against the implication and intent of the [any] violent act [perpetrated by members of householder groups],"[26] something miraculous happens. Thurman describes it this way:

> Then, out of some deeper region than the mind, there begins to flow up into his spirit that which gives fresh courage, new strength, and wholeness. I do not understand this. I do not know how the miracle takes place when it does—all I know is that such a triumph is possible to the spirit of man.[27]

Thurman calls it a "strange alchemy and contagion."[28] I think it can and should be called sacramentality.[29]

Thurman says that the effect of such an engagement between an itinerant and a householder is to "gentle" or "tame the wildness" out of a violent situation. The result is "to awaken conscience and an awareness of the evil of a violent system, and to make available the experience of the collective destiny in which all people in the system are participating."[30] In other words, such an engagement has an apocalyptic function. It is apocalyptic in the sense that it uncovers, or reveals, that which had been hidden to those on different sides

26 Ibid., 112.

27 Ibid., 118. I think his position makes clear that Thurman would probably, today, rethink his use of exclusively masculine language.

28 Ibid., 119.

29 See Stephen B. Boyd, "Community as Sacrament in the Thought of Hans Schlaffer," in *Anabaptism Revisited: Essays on Anabaptist/Mennonite Studies in Honor of C. J. Dyck*, ed. Walter Klaassen (1990; reprinted, Eugene, Ore.: Wipf & Stock, 2001) 50–64.

30 Thurman, *Disciplines*, 120–21.

of a dividing wall: they have one, common destiny (i.e., the kingdom of God) and that they are inextricably bound together and dependent on one another for its realization.

## Conclusion

Returning now to the growing chasm in U.S. Christianity concerning the place and role of GLBT persons, I offer the following observations and suggestions:

First, the disagreements about and the slow progress toward gender justice in congregations on both sides of the divide are rooted in a common commitment to a law of gender complementarity.

Second, the use of that law by men and heterosexually identified persons to justify violence toward and other mistreatment of women and GLBT persons creates a hostile environment that closes, rather than opens, the hearts of many heterosexually identified as well as GLBT persons.

Third, to foster the transforming opening of the hearts of people on both sides of these sexist and heterosexist barriers, there must be commitments of women and men—both GLBT persons and heterosexually identified persons—to dismantle those barriers. That dismantling calls for different tasks for women and GLBT persons than those of men and heterosexually identified persons. From women and GLBT people it calls for the courage to step out of those social, cultural, and psychic spaces prescribed by the law of gender complementarity and to speak with devastating honesty of who they are and what they need for their fullest flourishing. It calls also for them to love men and heterosexually identified people enough to expect them to work together with them "to share resources at their deepest level." This dismantling calls on men and heterosexually identified people to find the courage to drop the lenses shaped by their conditioning by this "law"; to see women and GLBT persons clearly; and to break the conspiracy of silence about their systematic mistreatment. In addition, it calls for a commitment to use their relatively greater social, cultural, and economic power to collaborate with women and GLBT people to create more just access to resources and opportunities.

Finally, it needs to be said that this kind of transgression and engagement is costly work. Men and heterosexually identified people may lose some or much of the power attendant to membership in these dominant groups. They may well have the mistreatment and violence usually directed at women and GLBT people directed at them. And they may find themselves in a position of psychic and physical homelessness between the dominant and target groups.

Women and GLBT people risk even greater exposure to sexist and heterosexist violence by their public transgression of the law of gender complementarity. In addition, by "colluding with the enemy," they may lose the confidence—and safety—of some, or many, in their own groups. Some of what needs to be changed in the world so that there is a more just access to resources can only be accomplished by the increased power achieved when GLBT and heterosexually identified people work together. Consequently, women or GLBT people may lose the compensatory sense of moral superiority when they find that other women or GLBT people are unwilling—despite their complaints about injustice—to forge the partnerships necessary to correct it. They, too, risk a kind of homelessness by their engagement with the feared or hated other.

And what about the churches? They might proclaim freedom in Christ from slavery to the law of gender complementarity and provide in their liturgies, educational programs, and other expressions of their common life sanctuaries where this sort of devastating honesty, painful recognition, and transforming mutual vulnerability might be fostered. The risk is great in the current reactionary political climate, but the risk of irrelevance is greater.

Though the personal and communal risks are great, so too are the potential rewards. Of those itinerants sent out by Jesus to engage the householders, it was reported

> The seventy returned with joy, saying, "Lord, even the demons are subject to us in your name!" And [Jesus] said to them, "I saw Satan fall like lightning from heaven. I have given you authority to tread upon serpents and scorpions, and over all the power of the enemy; and nothing shall hurt you (Luke 10:17-19).

In the engagement of itinerants and householders, of women and men, of GLBT people and heterosexually identified people, there is transformative, sacramental power to dismantle sexism and heterosexism and, I think, to create new cultural spaces that can be a more satisfying home to people on both sides of these divides.

There is also—thank God—joy.

# The Violence of "Perfection"

## *Power, Images, and the Female Body in American Popular Culture*

Michelle M. Lelwica

## Introduction

MARGARET Miles's work as a scholar of religion has made an indelible imprint on my thinking about religion, particularly as it relates to gender, embodiment, and the visual images of popular culture. A significant part of my own work has focused on the ways these images influence women's relationships to their bodies, especially when it comes to young women's pursuit of physical "perfection," as embodied in the ideal of thinness. In my research on women's food and body obsessions, I have come to see this pursuit as comprising a kind of secular religion, which I call the "Religion of Thinness."[1] In this diffuse cultural system of beliefs, rituals, and visual images, achieving the "perfect" (read: thin) female body is tantamount to salvation.

The topics of women, religion, body, and media images present a rich area for teaching undergraduate women, many of whom are themselves preoccupied with their weight and constantly wishing they were thinner. When I ask them what's so great about being thin, they typically give me the same response: "being thin means that you are in control," they explain, as if the answer were obvious. When I ask them "What's so great about being in control?" they look at me as if I were an idiot. "You can do what you want when you're in control," one young woman explains, assuredly. "You don't have to listen to what others say or worry about what they think." "If you're in con-

[1] My scholarly work on this topic appears in *Starving for Salvation: The Spiritual Dimensions of Eating Problems Among American Girls and Women* (New York: Oxford University Press, 1999). More recently, I have co-authored, with Cissy Brady-Rogers, a less academic version of this book, entitled *The Religion of Thinness* (Gurze Books, forthcoming, 2006).

trol," another student echoes, "then no one can tell you what to do. You don't have to be afraid of anything."

In this essay, I analyze the pursuit of physical perfection among American women. Using the work of Michel Foucault and feminists who have utilized his ideas, I examine the ambiguous power embedded in women's desire to be thin. And using the work of Margaret Miles, I explore the influence that media images have on this desire. The socializing power of such images has a coercive effect on some women, who engage in self-destructive practices as a result of measuring themselves against a uniform, ubiquitous visual idea. Yet such practices are not merely self-destroying; they also involve a search for freedom. Ultimately, the ambiguous power of such practices and images enables them to address the anxiety surrounding the body that has marked much of Christian history and that many women continue to experience, anxiety that stems from the body's role as both obstacle and vehicle for salvation.

## The Drive for Control and the Pursuit of Thinness

For many of my students and women like them, perfecting the body through diet, exercise, and weight loss is a way to gain more control in one's life. The allure of control is undoubtedly shaped by our culture's emphasis on this supposed virtue. We live in a culture of control, where much of daily life is oriented by a desire to get (or stay) on top of things. Many of the messages we receive from the media—from magazines, television, movies, advertisements, and newsprint—encourage us to "take control" of everything from the germs in our kitchens, to our financial investments, to the color of our hair, to the bulge in our tummies.

The association of thinness with control is vividly expressed in the discourses of women with eating disorders. One woman's statement that refusing to eat "was the only thing I felt I could control in my life"[2] echoes repeatedly in their narratives. "The thing that I liked more than anything," a former anorexic woman explains, "was the fact that I felt like I had control of what I ate and what I did, and that nobody was telling me what to do."[3] Another woman recalls: "I felt powerful as an anorexic. Controlling my body yielded an illusion of control over my life."[4] A quest for control similarly shapes the

2 Karen Twenhofel, "Do You Diet?," in *Eating Our Hearts Out: Personal Accounts of Women's Relationship to Food*, ed. Leslea Newman (Freedom, Calif.: Crossing, 1993) 202.

3 "Megan," quoted in Hilde Bruch, *Conversations with Anorexics*, ed. D. Czyzewski and M. Suhr (New York: Basic Books, 1988) 149.

4 Abra Fortune Chernik, "The Body Politic," in *Listen Up: Voices from the Next Feminist Generation*, ed. Barbara Findlen (Seattle: Seal, 1995) 78.

struggles of bulimic women, despite the loss of control surrounding their cycles of bingeing and purging: "With a feeling of relief and accomplishment, I flushed the toilet and turned to the sink to wash my hands, splash cold water on my face, and rinse the bile from my mouth. Meeting my own gaze in the mirror, I told myself: Everything is under control."[5]

The dissonance between this woman's reality and her rhetoric suggests how the drive for control that underlies the pursuit of thinness reflects more than a simple desire to be thin. It also reflects a desire for agency amid a host of unwanted and unspoken feelings: powerlessness, pain, uncertainty, fear, emptiness, and/or chaos. Women's religious and social conditioning into roles of self-sacrifice and submission makes it difficult for many of them to express and explore such feelings directly. Some of them turn to the language of food and their bodies to say what they cannot say with words: "As long as I didn't feel I could rebel in any other way," a bulimic woman explains, "the bingeing and purging was a violent release of my fears, frustrations, and anger."[6] As this woman's remarks suggest, women's pursuit of thinness embodies not just an effort to control their bodies, but also an attempt to exercise some freedom and to "rebel" against a society that limits their access to public voice and power.

Control is a form of power that seems to operate from the top down in a dominating fashion. Its structure appears to be strictly hierarchical. And yet, as the work of Michel Foucault suggests, power is never purely repressive.[7] Even the power of controlling one's appetite serves a highly *productive* function, giving a woman a sense of agency in the face of difficult feelings and a sense of accomplishment in a culture that worships thinness. Because it operates not just by saying "no," but also by inciting desires and stimulating pleasures, the violent dimension of this power is often invisible or hidden.

## The Violence of Female Socialization

The word "violence" typically conjures up scenes of guns and fists and bloodshed. Violence often refers to coercive action against another person, with or without a fight. The blatant violence that women experience at the hands of men illustrates this dynamic all too well. Every day in this country, four or five women are killed by their current or former husbands or boyfriends, and

5 Maya Brown, "Dying to Be Thin," *Essence* (June 1993) 87.

6 Caroline Adams Miller, *My Name Is Caroline* (New York: Doubleday, 1988) 96.

7 Michel Foucault, *History of Sexuality: Volume 1* (New York: Vintage, 1990 [1978]). Jana Sawicki summarizes that Foucault sees power as a force that is exercised rather than possessed, productive rather than repressive, dispersed rather than centralized. See *Disciplining Foucault: Feminism, Power and the Body* (New York: Routledge, 1991) 21–24.

at least half of all homeless women and children in the U.S. are fleeing the violence of men in their lives.[8] It's estimated that a man beats a woman every twelve seconds, and that one out of five women is the victim of some kind of sexual abuse.[9]

Such numbers point to the alarming prevalence of violence toward women in America. But they do not represent a related but different kind of violence that is at least as widespread: the kind of violence some women seem to inflict upon themselves. For these women, the pursuit of thinness involves attitudes and behaviors that are spiritually and physically debilitating, from self-starvation, to bingeing and purging, to compulsive exercise, to chronic body-hatred.

Feminists like Susan Bordo, Frigga Haug, Sandra Bartky, and Jana Sawicki have appropriated Foucault's understanding of the productive dimension of power to explain why some women seem to be drawn to the very behaviors and attitudes that hurt them. In their view, the self-scrutinizing beliefs and disciplines that women engage in their pursuit of the "perfect body" exemplify modern forms of social control wherein women are rewarded for their obedience to social norms, and where punishment for disobeying such norms is self-administered.[10]

Historically, as Foucault has shown, social control was exercised through the threat of public torture and explicit violence. Those who dared disobey the codes of acceptable social and/or religious conduct were crucified, beheaded, or burned at the stake. Such spectacles served as warnings to those who might be similarly tempted to transgress the rules of what was deemed appropriate belief and behavior within a given society.[11]

[8] Ann Jones, "Battering: Who's Going to Stop It?," *Women: Images and Realities; A Multicultural Anthology*, 3rd ed., ed. A. Kesselman et al. (New York: McGraw Hill, 2003) 449–50.

[9] Ibid., 450; and Kesselman et al., "Violence Against Women," in *Women: Images and Reality*, 445.

[10] Foucault refers to this kind of power as "disciplinary." See Michel Foucault, *Discipline and Punish: The Birth of the Prison* (New York: Vintage, 1979). For feminist applications of Foucault's notion of "disciplinary power" to illuminate women's troubled relationships with their bodies, see Susan Bordo, *Unbearable Weight: Feminism, Western Culture, and the Body* (Berkeley: University of California Press, 1993); Sandra Bartky, *Femininity and Domination: Studies in the Phenomenology of Oppression* (New York: Routledge, 1990); Frigga Haug, ed., *Female Sexualization: A Collective Work of Memory* (London: Verso, 1987); Frigga Haug, *Beyond Female Masochism: Memory-Work and Politics* (London: Verso, 1992); and Jana Sawicki, *Disciplining Foucault*. In her feminist appropriation of Foucault, Sawicki emphasizes that disciplinary power is rooted in bodily pleasures, attitudes, and practices, which are learned in relation to prevailing cultural rules and social arrangements. Sawicki, *Disciplining Foucault*, 83.

[11] See Foucault, *Discipline and Punish*.

The way social control operates today has changed. It is no longer accomplished simply through the threat of violence or coercive force.[12] It is also invisibly embedded in the process of socialization. No one is going to execute a woman for refusing to observe the dominant codes of feminine beauty. No one, for example, threatens to shoot her for failing to lose five or ten pounds.[13] And yet a woman may feel that such weight loss is imperative, given the norms for feminine behavior and appearance with which she has been socialized. And she may engage in practices that harm her in an attempt to be healthy and beautiful. Having internalized the messages our culture gives her about how her body should look and feel, she may violate—do violence to—her own well-being in an effort to "fit in."

The pressure to fit in—to be accepted in the eyes of others—can be especially heavy for minority women, who may find it easier to change the size of their bodies than the color of their skin. One black woman explains: "When I first started practicing bulimic behavior, I was very much influenced by White beauty standards . . . People treat you better when you lose weight and look beautiful."[14] The "rewards" of assimilating a dominant (white) cultural ideal such as thinness are not the only "productive" incentives for women of color who struggle with their bodies. In her multicultural study, Becky Thompson found that women of different ethnic backgrounds developed eating problems as survival strategies in the face of a variety of injustices, including racism, sexism, homophobia, poverty, and emotional, physical, and/or sexual abuse.[15] Although these women's food and body obsessions left them feeling depressed and imprisoned, such problems also enabled them to cope with the reality of violence and oppression in their lives.

In her book, *Carnal Knowing*, Margaret Miles underlines the intimate connection between the productive and repressive aspects of power, that is, between socialization and violent coercion: "socialization is anticipatory force in that it attempts, by training people to docile behavior, to forestall the necessity of coercion. Thus, no clear line can be drawn between persuasion to attitudes and behavior and the force that will be brought to bear if this

12 Foucault, *Discipine and Punish*, 216. Here Foucault describes a kind of power that is central to the maintenance of social order in modern capitalist societies like the United States, where oppression by repressive violence has been "infiltrated" by more subtle forms of domination.

13 Sandra Bartky makes a similar point in "Foucault, Femininity, and the Modernization of Patriarchal Power," in *Femininity and Domination*, 75.

14 Anonymous woman quoted by Linda Villarosa, "Dangerous Eating," *Essence* (Janurary 1994)18–21ff.

15 Becky Thompson, *A Hunger So Wide and So Deep: American Women Speak Out on Eating Problems* (Minneapolis: University of Minnesota Press, 1994) 2.

'education' is not effective."[16] In essence, Miles modifies Foucault's productivity thesis in order to highlight the close links between the creative and the destructive—the pleasurable and the violent—dimensions of power in the process of female socialization. Though losing weight may bolster a woman's self-esteem and/or give her a way to cope with difficult situations and feelings, it may also injure her health and fuel her sense of body-hatred. The danger and draw of the pursuit of perfection is that its punishments and rewards are so tightly connected. Because it seems to be self-administered, the violence embedded in this quest often goes unnoticed. Because it circulates through social norms that are internalized and taken for granted, the damage that this pursuit does to women is easily overlooked.

The connections Miles makes between the productive and repressive aspects of power point to a potential problem with understanding women's self-destructive beliefs and behaviors in terms of hidden violence. Using this term to highlight the damage women inflict on themselves in their efforts to be thin may seem to minimize the blatant violence that countless women in our society are threatened with or suffer. But this interpretation misses the point of Miles's modification of the productive thesis, namely, that these kinds of violence are related. Whether hidden or explicit, violence against women is rooted in ideologies of gender that support male dominance and in the process of female socialization through which women are rewarded for being submissive. Moreover, in a society where the threat or use of blatant violence against women is both constant and widespread, images that encourage implicit violence toward women are easily tolerated, if not emulated.

## The Power of Images

Media images of feminine perfection are some of the most notorious vehicles for female socialization today, and there is no shortage of evidence linking these images to women's well-known body discontent.[17] One survey found

[16] Margaret R. Miles, *Carnal Knowing: Female Nakedness and Religious Meaning in the Christian West* (Boston: Beacon, 1989) 190.

[17] A number of surveys document this discontent. More than three-quarters of normal-weight adult women in the United States believe they are too fat, and over half of these women report that they are currently on diets. One survey found that nearly two-thirds of high school girls were dieting, compared to sixteen percent of high school boys. Another study discovered that at least a third of twelve-to-thirteen-year-old girls are attempting to lose weight by means of dieting, vomiting, laxatives, or diet pills. These studies and statistics are cited by Jean Kilbourne in *Deadly Persuasion: Why Women and Girls Must Fight the Addictive Power of Advertising* (New York: Free Press, 1999) 125, 134. In addition, a *Psychology Today* survey found that sixty-two percent of young women between the ages of thirteen and nineteen are dissatisfied with their weight; see David Garner, "The Body Image Survey Results," *Psychology Today* 30:1 (1997) 30. Finally, a study of fourth-grade girls in the Chicago and San Francisco areas discovered that

that more than two-thirds of girls between grades five and twelve said that media images influenced their notion of the ideal body. Sixty-six percent of the 548 girls interviewed for this study said they wanted to lose weight, though only twenty-nine percent of them could be considered overweight.[18] According to studies conducted at Stanford University and the University of Massachusetts, about seventy percent of college women say they feel worse about their appearances after looking at women's magazines.[19] On a CBS news edition of *48 Hours*, Dan Rathers reported that sixty-eight percent of women surveyed said that their body image deteriorates after looking at magazine images of female models.[20] Other studies suggest that women tend to rate their own looks as less attractive after viewing media images of "model" women.[21] A meta-analytic review of twenty-five studies of the effects of exposure to media idealizations of thinness found women's body images to be significantly more negative after exposure to the glossy pictures.[22]

The high level of body dissatisfaction among consumers of popular women's magazines is further illustrated by a survey of readers of *Glamour* magazine, seventy-five percent of whom said they wanted to lose more weight, though only twenty-five percent of them weighed more than the desired weight listed on insurance tables, whose figures are already below average for women in the United States.[23] Interestingly, a survey conducted in connection with *Essence*, a magazine that targets middle-class black women, found that seventy-one-and-a-half percent of its readers were preoccupied with their bodies, and over two-thirds of them were using potentially dangerous techniques to lose weight.[24] Another study of young women with eating

---

eighty percent of them had dieted; the study is cited by Joan Jacobs Brumberg in *Fasting Girls: The History of Anorexia Nervosa* (New York: Penguin, 1988) 32.

18 Alison E. Field et al., "Exposure to the Mass Media and Weight Concerns among Girls," *Pediatrics* 103:3 e.36 (March 1999) 660.

19 These studies are cited by Kilbourne, *Deadly Persuasion*, 133.

20 This episode aired March 2, 1994.

21 See, for example, T. K. Cash et al., "Mirror, Mirror On the Wall . . . ? Contrast Effects and Self-Evaluation of Physical Attractivness," *Personality and Social Psychology Bulletin* 9 (1983) 351–58; and Nancy Wartick, "Can Media Images Trigger Eating Disorders?," *American Health* 14 (1995) 26–27.

22 L. M. Groez, M. P. Levine, and S. K. Murnen. "The Effect of Experimental Presentation of Thin Media Images on Body Image Satisfaction: A Meta-Analytic Review," *International Journal of Eating Disorders* 31 (2002) 1–16.

23 Susan Wooley and Orland Wooley, "Feeling Fat in a Thin Society," *Glamour* (February 1984) 198–201ff.

24 Villarosa, "Dangerous Eating," 19–21ff.

disorders found that nearly half of them regularly scrutinized the images of models in magazines, wanting desperately to look like them.[25]

Anecdotal comments by girls and women corroborate these surveys and studies. A fourteen-year-old reader of magazines exclaimed: "I hate how they always have pretty girls in advertisements . . . It makes you feel really ugly reading it."[26] Media images of women often provide the initial inspiration for anorexics' and bulimics' crusade for thinness. In her memoir of anorexia and bulimia, for example, Marya Hornbacher recalls imitating and comparing herself to model women: "I practiced the looks in the mirror, casting bedroom eyes at my reflection, thrusting my hips to the side and tossing my hair. My body was wrong—breasts poking through my shirt, butt jutting, all curvaceous and terribly wrong. . . . Legs too short, too round, thighs touch. *Seventeen* magazine advises that thighs should not touch. Mine touch. I suck."[27] Though the behavior of women who starve, gorge, and/or binge is extreme, this behavior typically begins in beliefs and practices that are considered normal and healthy: beliefs and practices that they learn with the help of media images.

Whether it comes in the form of negative self-talk ("I'm fat and ugly," "I suck") or in the form of physical self-destruction (starving, vomiting, compulsive exercising), the hidden violence that women inflict on themselves for failing to live up to the narrow norms of feminine perfection is inseparable from the pleasure they take in their quest to imitate the ideal. Most girls and women say that they read women's magazines for fun.[28] It is the pleasure, the attraction, the fantasy that such ideals arouse and elicit that make their influence on women so strong.

In her work with visual images, Miles found it useful to draw on Foucault's distinction between two kinds of power. "Strong power" refers to "control by stimulation," in contrast to "weak power" that works through the threat or use of physical coercion.[29] Strong power operates by attracting people to certain beliefs, ideals, and practices, while keeping the threat of punishment for disobedience hidden. Messages received through pleasurable means—for example, through visual stimulation—make a stronger, more lasting impression on the imagination than those instilled through coercive

25 This study is cited by Laura Frasure in "The Body Beautiful," *Diablo* (January 1998) 61.

26 "Rachel" qouted by Dawn Currie in *Girl Talk: Adolescent Magazines and Their Readers* (Toronto: University of Toronto, 1999) 259.

27 Marya Hornbacher, *Wasted: A Memoir of Anorexia and Bulimia* (New York: HarperFlamingo, 1998) 44.

28 Currin, *Girl Talk,* 159.

29 Miles, *Carnal Knowing*, 188.

force.[30] Images of feminine perfection have the power to grip a woman's imagination because she accepts the ideal they represent as her own, rather than something imposed by an external authority.

This acceptance is not fully conscious, which is another reason why it can be so tenacious. Although we are constantly bombarded with such images, the average person today is less aware than people in previous centuries of these images' power to influence. Miles has documented the crucial role of visual images in imaginations of medieval Christians, particularly those who could not read or write, which included virtually all women.[31] Historical Christians were highly conscious of taking and receiving lessons from the images they viewed. They *expected* to be influenced by their encounter with images. They understood the power of such visions to convey a message.[32]

By contrast, most people today imbibe thousands of images without paying much conscious attention to the messages they send or the influence they carry. Media images are more likely to be seen as sources of entertainment than as sources of power and knowledge. And yet this very lack of attention to the images' messages makes consumers highly vulnerable to the norms and values they circulate.

The power of media images is subtle. It is the repetitious, habitual, cumulative exposure to such images that allows them to get under women's skin, especially in the absence of diverse or alternative visions. When such images repeatedly enter women's minds, they eventually (pre)occupy them. How many times a day do we see them, whether or not we intentionally seek them out? A quick trip to the grocery store, a routine visit to the doctor's office, an hour at home watching TV—women need not look far to find themselves face to face with a picture of feminine perfection. Thanks to mass culture, these images are everywhere, reminding women that their bodies are their biggest asset and advising them on how best to invest in and care for this most precious (yet precarious) resource.

Perhaps the ubiquity of images of feminine perfection would not be so problematic if these images were not so homogenous. But the physical form of the "perfect" female body varies only in the slightest degree, and it has progressively gotten thinner. About thirty-five years ago, the average model in the United States weighed eight percent less than the average woman. About fifteen years ago, she weighed twenty-three percent less than the average woman, whose weight generally increased during the same period. About ten

30 See Miles's discussion of the strong power of images in both *Image as Insight: Visual Understanding in Western Christianity and Secular Culture* (Boston: Beacon, 1985) 22–24, and *Seeing and Believing: Religion and Values in the Movies* (Boston: Beacon, 1996) 26–27.

31 Miles, *Image as Insight*, 10.

32 Ibid., 7–9, 128.

years ago, most female models were about five feet ten inches and weighed one hundred and eleven pounds. The average woman in the U.S. was about five feet four inches and weighed one hundred and forty-four pounds, which means she was (on average) six inches shorter and thirty-three pounds heavier than women representing the physical "ideal."[33] Today, it is virtually shocking to see normal-sized (much less big-bodied) women featured in mainstream women's magazines. And when they appear in television or film, they are typically cast in the role of the comic or the bitch.

Because women see so few exceptions to the tall-young-thin-flawless feminine ideal, they come to believe without question that this is what the perfect body looks like. Our society's preference for thinness goes largely unchallenged because this ideal form is both uniform and ubiquitous.[34] It may vary in color, but not size. And because the thin ideal is virtually unquestioned and very widespread, this *ideal*—perfection—has become the *norm*. A norm that is anything but *normal*.

Women's habitual exposure to homogenous images of slender women sets them up to want to be thin. Through their ubiquity and uniformity, the promise of thinness persuades and pervades them. Often without knowing it, women measure themselves against the slender ideal and typically they find themselves wanting. It's not just that they want to look like the women in the pictures. They also want what these images represent. For many of their viewers, the thin female body symbolizes the happiness, success, adoration, and freedom for which they long but which they feel is lacking in their lives.

## When Salvation Hinges on Self-destruction

The power of such images of feminine perfection becomes coercive in the lives of those who engage in self-destructive beliefs and practices in their search for the happiness and freedom the images represent. One former bulimic woman recalls how the definition of happiness she learned growing up was "skinny, pretty, married, and rich." Socialized with images of the perfect female body, this woman's body-hatred grew—"the ideal of beauty represented by a fash-

33 Roberta Seid, "Too 'Close to the Bone': The Historical Context for Women's Obsession with Slenderness," in *Feminist Perspectives on Eating Disorders*, ed. Patricia Fallon et al. (New York: Guilford, 1994) 4. See also Roberta Seid, *Never Too Thin: Why Women Are at War with Their Bodies* (New York: Prentice Hall, 1989) 15. Figures comparing model women with average women are stated in the documentary film *The Famine Within*, written and directed by Katherine Gilday (1992), and in Sharlene Hess-Biber, *Am I Thin Enough Yet? The Cult of Thinness and the Commercialization of Identity* (New York: Oxford University Press, 1996) 96.

34 For an interesting discussion of the normalizing effects of the homogenization of the ideal female body, see Susan Bordo's "Introduction" to *Unbearable Weight*, 24–26.

ion model was not the figure I saw in the mirror"[35]—until she felt she had no choice but to lose weight by any means necessary.

Another bulimic woman describes how idealized images of model women shaped her understanding of success:

> Success, I firmly believed, was the key to my salvation. It would absolve me of the sins of the flesh and would lift me out of the life I hated. 'Success' meant a perfect career, perfect relationships, perfect control over my life and myself—all of which depended on a perfect me, which depended in turn on me living inside a perfect body.[36]

This woman's use of religious language (salvation, sins of the flesh) points to the quasi-religious function that images of feminine perfection serve, giving women a sense of purpose: creating the ultimate body becomes a kind of ultimate concern.[37] Although not all women who obsess about food and their bodies are directly influenced or inspired by these images, all of them have been socialized with the norms these images circulate, norms equating thinness with perfection and the salvation—the happiness and success—that accompany this state.

Despite the suffering that practices like starving or purging engenders, many women report feeling most satisfied when their stomachs are empty and growling. The connections between happiness, success, and thinness are so firmly etched in their minds and bodies that they experience each pound lost as another step toward fulfillment. Moreover, some women train themselves to experience the pain of hunger as pleasurable. Refusing to eat or digest one's food is not just a way to control one's body; it is also a means for experiencing one's body in a more concentrated way. "Appetite is more appealing than what happens after," an anorexic woman explains. Feeling hungry is full of "anticipation, fantasy and promise."[38]

The promise of hunger points to the connection between renunciation and redemption. This link is hardly new. Throughout history, Christians have practiced self-denial as a method for improving their spiritual state. In the

[35] Kim Lorton and Elena Levkin, "Re-figuring Ourselves: Two Voices on Eating Disorders," in *Eating Our Hearts Out*, 218–19.

[36] Hornbacher, *Wasted*, 231–32.

[37] This is an obvious reference to Paul Tillich's understanding of religion in terms of "Ultimate Concern." While this concept of religion enabled Tillich to see the religious dimensions of all human experiences, thus breaking down the barriers between secular and religious forms and experiences, it also led him to overlook the socially constructed character of his own concepts and claims. See Tillich, *Theology of Culture* (New York: Oxford University Press, 1959). I have found Tillich's notion of ultimate concern to be useful when understood from a *functional*, rather than *theological*, approach to religion.

[38] Sima Rabinowitz, "The Unanswered Echo," in *Eating Our Hearts Out*, 78.

third and fourth centuries, Christian ascetics were seen as "spiritual athletes," who trained and disciplined their bodies in order to achieve spiritual perfection. By giving up such pleasures as eating certain foods, drinking wine, socializing, engaging in sexual activity, and sleeping, ascetics sought to reorient their worldly desires toward an other-worldly purpose.

Many women today practice a certain kind of asceticism when it comes to food and their bodies: they find delight in self-deprivation; they feel good when their muscles ache from over-exertion; they take pleasure in the pangs of an empty stomach or a tummy that has been recently purged. And while the perfection they seek is not spiritual per se, it represents a higher state, a salvation that can only be achieved through the practice of bodily denial and self-abnegation.

Scholars of religion have noted the irony at the heart of ascetic behavior: while such self-denial seems to represent an outright war against the body, it also makes the body central to spiritual progress.[39] Fasting in particular seems to entail a denial or rejection of physical needs. And yet refusing to eat is also a way to intensify bodily experience. The method of asceticism is to conquer the body's physical cravings, and yet those who practice it depend on their bodies, cultivating a certain intimacy with their flesh, and sometimes becoming quite attached to the very thing they wish to transcend. Perhaps more than any other spiritual practice, asceticism illustrates the ambiguity of the body in Christian history: its role as both obstacle and vehicle in the quest for salvation.

The ambiguity at the heart of religious asceticism reflects the ambiguity of power: its capacity to be both productive and repressive, both punitive and rewarding, both controlling and freeing. Taken together, these ambiguities tell us something important about the religion of thinness that many contemporary women practice. Perhaps women's attempts to control their appetites reflect not just an obsequious desire to create a perfect body, but also a desire to feel empowered in the face of life's myriad challenges and changes.

[39] For scholarly works exploring the ironically central role of the body in Christian ascetic practices, see Peter Brown, *The Body and Society: Men, Women, and Sexual Renunciation in Early Christianity* (New York: Columbia University Press, 1988); Caroline Walker Bynum, *Holy Feast and Holy Fast: The Religious Significance of Food for Medieval Women* (Berkeley: University of California Press, 1987); idem, *Fragmentation and Redemption: Essays on Gender and the Human Body in Medieval Religion* (New York: Zone, 1991); Margaret R. Miles, *Practicing Christianity: Critical Perspectives for an Embodied Spirituality* (New York: Crossroad, 1988); idem, *Fullness of Life: Historical Foundations for a New Asceticism* (Philadelphia: Westminster, 1981); and Theresa Shaw, *The Burden of the Flesh: Fasting and Sexuality in Early Christianity* (Minneapolis: Fortress, 1998). In different ways, these works also highlight the ambiguity of the body in Christian thought and practice: its role as both a stumbling block and a stepping stone on the path of spiritual development.

Perhaps their efforts to lose weight represent not just a disdain for their unsightly flesh, but also an effort to retrieve and explore a part of themselves from which they feel estranged. Perhaps women's desire for thinness reflects not just a desire to diminish their bodies, but also a longing to inhabit these bodies, to live fully and deeply in the home of their own flesh. Perhaps the behaviors and beliefs surrounding the pursuit of perfection that seem so obviously self-destructive mask an even deeper yearning for salvation, a hunger for wholeness, good health, and healing.

Perhaps. Nevertheless, the irony at the heart of asceticism can turn out to be rather vicious. For some women, the attempt to deny their bodily needs keeps their bodies at the center of their attention, and their efforts to conquer their appetites tends to make them fixate on them. Many women experience the painful reversal whereby their struggle to conquer their unruly cravings makes them feel totally out of control, an experience that leads to renewed efforts to get back on top of things.

Unlike the asceticism of historical Christians, whose practices of self-denial aimed to deconstruct their social conditioning and reorient their desires toward a higher purpose, the asceticism that contemporary women practice in their efforts to be thin incorporates (rather than resists) their social training as women.[40] Although women's efforts to control their bodies give them the sense of agency and achievement, these efforts turn them into docile bodies as they imply and presume obedience to the norms and ideals of the dominant culture, particularly those that construct female salvation through implicitly violent, self-negating beliefs and behaviors.[41]

Media images of feminine perfection encourage women to seek salvation both from and with their bodies. But these images don't simply turn women into objects. They also preserve the promise of transcendence. In the mirror of such visions, female agency is narrowly oriented rather than obliterated. Ultimately, the hidden violence women inflict on themselves and their bodies as they pursue the perfect body displayed in these images is not

40 Miles writes: "For women, whose affiliation with self-sacrificial support of others has been a cultural commonplace, traditional asceticisms seem counter productive. If asceticism is for the purpose of deconstructing the socially conditioned subjectivity, it cannot serve this function if it effectively reinforces rather than dismantles cultural conditioning to femininity." See Miles's chapter "The Pleasure of No Pleasure: Asceticism," in *Practicing Christianity*, 94–104; quotation from p. 100.

41 The docile body is a concept Foucault coined to describe bodies that have been enticed and trained through a variety of disciplines and knowledges to be obedient to dominant cultural norms and thereby to support the prevailing social order. In Bordo's formulation, docile bodies are "bodies whose forces and energies are habituated to external regulation, subjection, transformation, 'improvement.'" Bordo also points out that although Foucault coined this term, feminists first articulated the ideas behind it. Bordo, *Unbearable Weight*, 166, 17–18.

purely masochistic. Such destruction conceals a tragic attempt to transform the female body from obstacle into vehicle for salvation.

# Rapt by God

## *The Rhetoric of Rape in Medieval Mystical Literature*

Julie B. Miller

In this essay I will explore how late medieval women's mystical discourse encodes rape as a spiritual act and links erotic ecstasy with the suffering of rape. In short, I will explore how it eroticizes rape and the inherent violence of this act. I propose that by eroticizing the trauma of rape in its construction of the love relationship between the soul and God, the mystical tradition has contributed to the eroticization of dominance and subordination, and hence, to the eroticization of violence against women. I will argue that by coupling together two distinct understandings of the Latin term *raptus* in its construction of the love relationship between the soul and God, the rhetoric of "rapture" in medieval women's mystical discourse contributes to the eroticization of violence, and in particular, to an eroticization of rape. Moreover, I will suggest that in this discourse we see the nascent form of a new, modern understanding of rape, understood primarily as an act of sexual violence, but, more importantly, an act in which the subordinate participant, usually a woman, is believed to find her ultimate fulfillment.

## Models of Rape and Rapture

Contemporary feminist critics of rape have determined two distinct constructions of rape operative in Western rape law throughout the last two millennia. The first is that of the theft, or property, model in which the legal victim of rape was not the woman who was violated but rather the man to whom she belonged, generally her husband or father. In this model, the woman herself is not legally considered to be a subject in her own right. Instead, she is merely the object of violence, the piece of property that was stolen from the truly offended subject, her male owner. This model of rape was operative from ancient times throughout the Middle Ages but began to shift in the twelfth century. This shift has culminated in the second construction of rape, which defines rape as the sexual violation of a person, usually a woman. In this second model, the violated woman is considered the legal victim of rape; no man to whom she may be married or otherwise connected has any legal status as a victim of a crime.

While this second model, in recognizing the subjectivity of women, certainly appears to be a great advance for women, I will argue that the parallel construction of feminine subjectivity as that which actually enjoys rape and eroticized violence found in the discourse of mystical rapture has worked to mitigate many of the advances women may have enjoyed under this new legal recognition of women's subjectivity. Further, I will argue that it is in the construction of rapture, or rape, in medieval women's mystical literature in which we see this new construction of female subjectivity fully developed. While I make no claims for any causal connection between these two developments, I do find it peculiarly interesting to note that just as women's autonomy and sexual agency were becoming increasingly recognized in the legal realm from the twelfth century onward, we find the simultaneous development of mystical discourse that eroticizes and spiritualizes the notion of rape. Previously, when rape was deemed a crime against a man, it made no ideological difference if a woman was thought to enjoy the violence of rape: the act of rape occurred even if the woman enjoyed it or consented to it, as in cases of elopement. However, as women's consent became increasingly important in determining if in fact a rape occurred or not, the parallel development of the notion of mystical rapture, in which a woman (or feminine soul) reached spiritual and erotic heights through the very act of abduction and spiritual/sexual violation serves, in my view, a significant ideological purpose. Throughout this transformation of the notion of rapture, a new ideology developed that helped to support the notion that women may actually consent to violent and brutal rape. In short, such a development helped to keep women "rapable."

In the remainder of this essay I will do three things. First, I will briefly outline the significant shifts of rape law which occurred from the twelfth century forward. Second, I will examine the thematic of rape in women's mystical literature and explore how this discourse encodes rape as a spiritual act linking erotic ecstasy with the suffering of rape. Finally, I will expand on Teresa de Lauretis's notion of male- and female-gendered violence and suggest how this mystical discourse, while admitting the subjectivity of women, ultimately constructs this subjectivity as one that ultimately desires and consents to eroticized violence. Hence, while women are, from the twelfth century forward, considered legal subjects in rape law, in mystical and spiritual literature of the time, they are increasingly constructed as subjects who actually enjoy rape. Thus, for a woman to argue that she did not enjoy rape and that she did not consent to it becomes increasingly difficult indeed.

## Rape, Rapture, and *Raptus* throughout the Middle Ages

Rape is a slippery concept, and it was a much more ambiguous and elusive a term in the Middle Ages than even today. Hence, we can not assume that when it is used in a medieval context that it necessarily refers to our contemporary common sense understanding of rape as the sexual violation of a person, usually a woman. It is therefore important and interesting to track the trajectories of the Latin term for rape, *raptus,* to see how its use in mystical discourse is akin to the modern notion of rape.

In the Middle Ages, the Latin word for rape evoked three distinct but interrelated concepts. The primary connotation of this word *rapere/raptus* was one of abduction, of seizing and carrying off something by force. As such it took on several different valences. First, since at least the fourth century, the term had been used to describe ecstatic spiritual experiences, understood as the carrying off of the soul to heaven or the like.[1] However, as we shall see, this first spiritual connotation did not become predominant until well into the thirteenth and fourteenth centuries. Earlier, it was in the legal realm in which the term was used most often. Here the term *raptus* referred to the theft, the "carrying off by force," of one man's property by another. While this could refer to the rape of any object, it most often referred to the abduction of a virgin for the purpose of marriage or the abduction of a married woman from her husband's home. At the same time, however—perhaps because of the unstated but obvious correlation between abduction for the purpose of marriage and forced sexual intercourse—this second connotation of abduction was supplemented by the third understanding of *raptus,* that of the sexual violation of a person, usually a woman, against her will, with or without a prior abduction. But because of the term's primary emphasis on carrying off by force, in the ancient law codes through the Middle Ages the focus of the crime remained primarily, though not exclusively, on the acts of theft and abduction, not on the sexual violation perpetrated on the woman. Only gradually, beginning in the twelfth century, did the emphasis begin to shift from that of abduction to that of sexual violation.

With the revival of the Justinian law code, which had been lost to the West for over five centuries, and the simultaneous reform of ecclesiastical laws

[1] For instance, in 2 Corinthians 12:2 the fourth-century Latin Vulgate uses the verb *raptus* in Paul's description of a soul "caught up" in the third heaven, and Augustine, in his discussion of this incident, also uses the verb *raptus.* (See *Super Gen. Ad litt.* XII, 3 & 5, 12. See Migne, Latin Fathers, v. 34, 456, 478.)

concerning marriage and sexuality, in the twelfth century the sexual violation endemic to *raptus* began to be emphasized. Whereas in previous centuries the crime of *raptus* was thought to incorporate two distinct acts with no necessary connection—the acts of abduction and the acts of sexual violation—by this time the practical connection between the two was increasingly recognized. Pope Urban II (1088–99) apparently was the first to recognize that the act of abduction created the presumption that the victim was sexually violated as well. Thus the burden of proof shifted: the victim need not prove that she was violated so much as the rapist had to prove that he did not violate her. Hence, in Gratian's *Decretum* of the mid-twelfth century (ca. 1140) we see the first comprehensive attempt to make legal sense out of the various codes and laws of the day, including the variety of laws and attitudes concerning *raptus*.[2] Gratian continued to maintain the earlier distinction between *raptus* as abduction and *raptus* as sexual violation, as well as the fact that rape could be considered a crime against the woman's father, as in a couple's elopement against her parents' will. Yet he also increasingly emphasized the will of the woman involved, noting that simple rape—that is, sexual assault in which no prior abduction occurred—was not necessarily a crime against her parents but against the woman herself and her sexual autonomy. However, Gratian's code did make a distinction between r*aptus* and seduction, and this distinction was significant for the ensuing development of rape law; if a man could prove he seduced but did not rape a woman—that is, if he could prove she consented at some point—then the charge of rape would not adhere.

The generation of decretists after Gratian sealed this slow transformation of the understanding of *raptus* and its emphasis on consent. This generation focused on two factors to distinguish rape from seduction. The first was the degree of violence necessary to deem an act one of coercion, and the second was the amount of resistance a victim needed to put forth. While opinions on these matters varied a great deal, according to one jurist at least, the victim's protest must at least be audible, for "silence means consent."[3] One more key factor for determining the existence of a crime was the prior relationship between the rapist and his victim. If the parties were married or betrothed to be married, no crime was committed, "no matter how atrocious his attack."[4] However, a man could be held liable for injuries he caused his wife or betrothed.[5] Throughout the thirteenth and fourteenth centuries this shift

2 See James Brundage, *Law, Sex and Christian Society in Medieval Europe* (Chicago: University of Chicago Press, 1987) 229ff for a complete discussion of Gratian's influence on canon law.

3 Brundage, *Law, Sex and Christian Society*, 396.

4 Ibid., 312. However, one penalty did befall the man who raped his betrothed: he no longer had a right to the "marital debt"—sex upon demand—once they were married.

5 The fact that the rape itself is not considered to be an injury, either physical, psychological

in rape law became solidified. A general consensus concerning the degree of force necessary to deem an act rape was beginning to emerge. The general parameters included a show of protest by the victim, an attempt to escape, and a threat to either her life or to the lives of her family. From the fourteenth through sixteenth centuries, little changed in ecclesiastical rape law, although women slowly continued to gain rights over their sexual autonomy. For example, by the end of the thirteenth century, physical abuse became grounds for divorce, and by the end of the fifteenth, prostitutes were beginning to find some legal protection against assault and rape. Correlatively, as women gained more rights over their own sexuality, the amount of resistance a woman needed to wage against her attacker also became increasingly significant in determining the severity of the assault.

Hence, the medieval concept of *raptus*/rape is indeed a complex one, and this complexity allows for some rather disconcerting uses of it in late medieval women's mystical literature. In short, late medieval women's uses of the concept of rapture, understood as an ecstasy of the soul, incorporated within in it not only the spiritual connotation of the "carrying away" of the soul but also the more common and more violent connotations of physical abduction and sexual violation. However, because of the increased stress on the affective spiritual experiences of joy, desire, and pleasure associated with rapture in late medieval literature, the developing rhetoric also served to eroticize the notion of sexual assault, or rape, by depicting it as a pleasurable, if also terrifying and excruciatingly painful, event.

## Rape Imagery in Medieval Women's Mystical Literature

While the late medieval milieu and its emphasis on the spiritual and physical suffering needed for one to practice the *imitatio Christi* certainly has much to do with the unqualified glorification of pain and violence we find in much of this literature, I do not believe we can reduce the notion of rapture to a simple, heightened sense of a person's ability to make Christ incarnate in one's bleeding and bruised flesh. Rather, a more interesting question is to ask if it has anything to do with the shifting legal notions of rape and women's developing status as a person with full legal rights under the law. By the late Middle Ages, the term rapture, used in a religious sense to describe a soul carried off to heaven, suggested a state of spiritual and/or sexual ecstacy. Hence, the *sexual* underpinnings of the original understanding of the legal crime of *raptus* became clear, but the violent aspects were now glossed and elided.

---

or spiritual, reflects the malestream theological bias that all sexual relations result in some semblance of sexual pleasure.

But, as I will attempt to show, in mystical literature the notion of rapture maintains both the connotations of violent abduction and sexual violation as well as the newer nuances of ecstasy and joy. Therefore, in this genre we quite clearly see the feminine soul "being raped" and liking it. Here we see a clear example of violence eroticized, albeit spiritualized and therefore supposedly sanitized.

## *Piercing Penetration*

Medieval women mystics used a wide range of imagery and metaphors to describe their experience of union with the divine. One metaphor, which has been examined at great length, is that of the arrow, or dart, plunging into the depths of the mystic's soul. This image is arguably a highly phallic one, and within this literature it carries connotations of both violence and erotic arousal. For example, in her quite explicitly violent rhetoric, Beatrice of Nazareth elaborates on this specific means by which God assaults her, stating that she often "feels an arrow piercing through her heart all the way to the throat and beyond, even to the brain, as if she would lose her mind." As this suggests, medieval mystics utilized the explicitly sexual imagery of penetration—by arrows, darts, swords and rays of divine love—to characterize this experience of assault. In addition to Beatrice, Angela of Foligno speaks of both the "arrow" and the "sword" of love[6] while Hadewijch anguishes over both the "sharp arrows" and "strange hatred" with which Love "transpierces the depths of [her] heart with storm."[7] Catherine of Siena urges her readers to let themselves be pierced by the same double-edged sword and arrow of love with which Christ and his mother were wounded for our salvation.[8] And Catherine of Genoa believed that the "rays" of God's love encircle humanity at all times, "hungrily seeking to penetrate" it; indeed, if allowed, these rays will penetrate "as deep as hell."[9]

Significantly, the allusion to rape is often explicit in these writings. For example, after one particularly powerful vision, Catherine of Genoa described her experience:

6 *Angela of Foligno: Complete Works*, trans. Paul Lachance, O.F.M. (New York: Paulist, 1993) 226ff.

7 Hadewijch, *Hadewijch: The Complete Works*, trans. Mother Columba Hart, O.S.B. (New York: Paulist, 180) 278, 229, 231.

8 *The Letters of Catherine of Siena,* V. I, trans. Suzanne Noffke, O.P. (Binghamton, N.Y.: Medieval and Renaissance Texts & Studies, 1988) 38–39.

9 *Catherine of Genoa: Purgation and Purgatory and the Spiritual Dialogue*, trans. Serge Hughes (New York: Paulist, 1979) 109.

> [God] sent her a ray of His love so burning and deep that it was an agony to sustain. Issuing from the fountain of Christ that love, wounding the soul, stripped it of all other loves, appetites, delights, and selfishness. The soul cried out, sighed deeply, and in its transformation, was taken out of itself. God deeply impressed upon her the fountains of Christ with their fiery bloody drops of love for [humanity].[10]

What is important to note and ultimately to analyze is that this imagery of sexual assault—of stripping and wounding, of burning and deep agony, of crying out in pain, of fountains full of fiery, bloody drops—is coupled with the erotic rhetoric of love and delight, of sighing and ecstasy. In another instance, Catherine attempted to describe the "signs of God's love that are beyond telling" with these words: "A ray of God's love wounded her heart, making her soul experience a flaming love arising from the divine fount. At that instant, she was outside herself, beyond intellect, tongue or feeling. Fixed in that pure and divine love, henceforth she never ceased to dwell in it."[11] "Wounded" by God, the soul experiences "flaming love" and exquisite ecstasy. Catherine asserts that the pain caused by God's penetration and wounding is of a purifying nature, bringing with it great joy as well as great suffering. Indeed, she admits that in the purifying pain of purgatory, "the action of God in penetrating the soul is so fierce that it seems to set the body on fire and to keep it burning until death. The overwhelming love of God gives it a joy beyond words. Yet this joy does not do away with one bit of the pain."[12] In the writings of Catherine as well as other medieval mystics, the imagery and rhetoric of pain and love, rape and eros, become intricately intertwined, so much so that they appear to become constitutive of each other.

Perhaps the most famous of all these mystical images of the penetrating arrow of love is that of the Teresa of Avila (1515–82). In one particular vision, Teresa explicitly utilizes the rhetoric of eroticized violence in her description of God's penetration and wounding of her soul. She speaks of seeing an angel

> with a large golden dart and at the end of the iron tip there appeared to be a little fire. . . .It seemed the angel plunged the dart several times into my heart and it reached deep inside within me. When he drew it out, I thought he was carrying off with him the deepest part of me; and he left me all on fire with the great love of God. The pain was so great that it made me moan, and the sweetness this greatest pain

10 Ibid., 119.

11 Ibid., 109.

12 Ibid., 81, 82.

> caused me was so superabundant that there is no desire capable of taking it away, nor is the soul content with less than God.[13]

The pain caused by this arrow was so extreme that Teresa believed it could not be exaggerated or even described—but neither did she think she could ever experience anything more pleasurable: "The soul would always want, as I said, to be dying of this sickness. . . . Oh what it is to see a wounded soul!"[14] For Teresa, then, and for many other women mystics, pain and pleasure, violence and eros go hand in hand. However, while this imagery of the penetrating arrow or dart is certainly significant in its erotization of the sexual violence of rape, it is the explicit rhetoric of rape/rapture, which parallels the legal definition of rape, that I find even more compelling, and more problematic.

## *Rhetoric of Rape and Rapture*

In her *vida* and other writings, Teresa of Avila explicitly describes her experience of union with God as one of rapture; what is more, this rapture is but a prelude to the spiritual marriage between God and the soul. Teresa's notion of rapture incorporates all of the components of the medieval legal and experiential notion of rape, including issues of abduction, fear, pain, sexual penetration, consent, and even marriage, but it also unites these aspects with the affective dimensions of joy and delight that adhered to this term in its use in courtly and spiritual genres.

### ABDUCTION

For Teresa, rapture was first and foremost a state of transport, or abduction. She states, "The Lord gathers up the soul . . . in the way the clouds gather up the earthly vapors and raises it completely out of itself. The cloud ascends to heaven and brings the soul along." Indeed, "he carries off the spirit as a giant would a piece of straw."[15] Moreover, this abduction of the soul is so sudden that the soul often tries with all its strength to resist it, but the results are futile. As Teresa testifies,

13 Teresa of Avila, *The Book of Her Life* in *Collected Works,* trans. Kieran Kavanaugh (Washington D. C.: Institute of Carmelite Studies, 1987) 1:252. The seventeenth-century sculpture by Bernini, *Santa Teresa in Estasi*, portrays Teresa enraptured with an angel holding a dart standing by. This sculpture has been instrumental in introducing generations to Teresa and her experience and has been interpreted as both erotic and ethereal, orgasmic and otherworldly throughout the centuries. See Robert T. Peterson, *The Art of Ecstasy: Teresa, Bernini and Crashaw* (New York: Atheneum, 1970).

14 Teresa of Avila, *Life*, 251, 430.

15 Ibid., 173, 198.

> it often happens to me that this recollection and elevation of the spirit comes upon me so suddenly I cannot resist. . . . At other times I receive a very intense, consuming impulse for God that I cannot resist. It seems my life is coming to an end, and so this impulse makes me cry out and call to God; and it comes with a great frenzy.[16]

Teresa argues that, in the end, it is useless to attempt to resist such raptures. In fact, trying to resist only increases their frequency;[17] moreover, resisting only makes these raptures worse, for the soul is then "carried away with a noticeably more impetuous movement."[18] She therefore resigned herself to the fact that "the struggle is a fierce one, and in the end, struggle is of little avail against the Lord's desire; there is no power against his power."[19] The best option for the soul then is to simply "abandon itself into the hand of the One who is all powerful," for "the safest thing to do is to make a virtue of necessity."[20]

## Fear

In her assertion that raptures from God are impossible to resist, or for that matter can not be willfully induced,[21] Teresa is attempting, in part, to delineate criteria by which true raptures can be distinguished from false.[22] Further, while Teresa notes that one reason she tried to resist these raptures was the fact that she was sometimes in the presence of other people and she did not want her raptures to be made public,[23] her primary reason for resisting appears to be the great fear they invoked in her. Teresa even goes so far as to sharply question anyone who would doubt her on this point: "Do you think it is a small disturbance for a person to be very much in his senses and see his soul carried off (and in the case of some, we have read, even the body with the soul) without knowing where that soul is going, what or who does this, or how?" Indeed, this rapture takes one by such surprise that "at the begin-

[16] *Spiritual Testimonies, The Collected Works of Teresa of Avila*, vol. 1, trans. Keiran Kavanaugh (Washington D.C.: ICS Publications, 1987) 372.

[17] Ibid., 249.

[18] Teresa of Avila, *Interior Castle*, 386.

[19] Teresa of Avila, *Life*, 174.

[20] Teresa of Avila, *Interior Castle*, 386.

[21] Teresa of Avila, *Life*, 202.

[22] Teresa was, in fact, instructed by her confessor to resist these raptures for a period of two years, for her confessor was not convinced they were of God.

[23] Teresa of Avila, *Life*, 252.

ning of this swift movement there is not much certitude that the rapture is from God."[24]

Teresa ultimately makes sense out of the fear she feels concerning these raptures by deeming them a tool by which God instructs the soul. She notes that it is through the great fear and force of these raptures that the soul learns the lesson of total humility; it is in the force of these raptures that the soul grows to learn that it is not its own master. In such a process "there is revealed a majesty about the One who can do this that makes a person's hair stand on edge, and there remains a strong fear of offending so awesome a God." Yet, in the process of learning this lesson of humility and total surrender to God, Teresa confesses that these raptures "greatly frightened" her, especially in the beginning. Indeed, noting that "at first the fear is extreme," she admits that "with the great fear I bore I resisted for almost two years—and sometimes now I try to resist, but to do so is of little avail." Indeed, one of the primary reasons for her fear of these raptures was the very fact that she can't resist them. [25] Consequently, even after she became convinced that these raptures came from God and not the devil, she noted that "this favor is something frightening," and that "great courage is necessary" for any soul who is granted them.[26]

## Painful Bodily Effects

Interestingly, it is not only the soul that is affected by these raptures, but the body as well. At times it appears that the body and soul become separated during rapture, such that the soul no longer seems to be animating the body. In this state the soul often becomes oddly detached from the body, becoming almost oblivious to the body and its normal functions. Teresa notes:

> While the soul is seeking God in this way, it feels with the most marvelous and gentlest delight that everything is almost fading away through a kind of swoon in which breathing and the bodily energies gradually fail. This experience comes about in such a way that one cannot even stir the hands without a lot of effort. The eyes close without one's wanting them to close; or if these persons keep them open, they see hardly anything—nor do they read or succeed in pronouncing a letter, nor can they hardly guess what the letter is . . . . They hear but don't understand what they hear. Thus they receive no benefit from the senses.

[24] Teresa of Avila, *Interior Castle*, 386.

[25] Ibid., 175, 174, 175, 215, 253.

[26] Teresa of Avila, *Interior Castle*, 387.

Yet, while outside observers of these raptures may think the body is virtually dead and not an integral part of this experience, the body is actually fully participating the experience of rapture. For instance, the body as well as the soul experiences a state of transport such that "the body was left so light that all its weight was gone, and sometimes this feeling reached such a point that I almost didn't know how to put my feet on the ground." Moreover, while the senses appear to fail completely at times during rapture, Teresa states that this is only for a brief period at the height of rapture, and it is not the norm.

> Now when the body is in rapture it is as though dead, frequently being unable to do anything of itself. It remains in the position it was when seized by the rapture, whether standing or sitting, or whether with the hands opened or closed. Although once in a while the senses fail (sometimes it happened to me that they failed completely), this occurs only rarely and for only a short time.

In this transport, then, "one's body [is] so elevated from the ground that even though the spirit carries it along after itself, and does so very gently if one does not resist, one's feelings are not lost." "At least," she notes, "I was conscious in such a way that I could understand I was being elevated." Thus, even though the soul is disoriented during this state, Teresa notes that "it doesn't fail to understand and hear as though it were listening to something coming from far off." Teresa argues that even though the body would seem unworthy of such attention, it apparently is not in the eyes of God:

> In those to whom this experience happens, the effects are remarkable. First, there is a manifestation of the tremendous power of the Lord and of how we are incapable, when His Majesty desires, of holding back the body any more than the soul, nor are we its master. . . . It doesn't seem He is satisfied in truly bringing the soul to Himself, but it seems He desires the body even though it is mortal and, on account of the many offenses it has committed, made of such foul clay.[27]

While Teresa often describes these bodily manifestations as "gentle," this is not always, if ever, the whole picture. In this bodily rapture Teresa recounts that sometimes only her head would be lifted up, while at others her whole body would be raised from the ground.[28] Sometimes, too, the experience was so extreme that it would invoke vomiting,[29] tightening in the chest and nose bleeds.[30] The body might also become cold "because its natural heat leaves

27 Quotations from Teresa of Avila, *Life*, 161–81.

28 Ibid., 173.

29 Teresa of Avila, *Spiritual Testimonies*, 372.

30 Teresa of Avila, *Interior Castles*, 322, 323.

the body, going I don't know where," and "when rapture is intense . . . the hands are frozen and sometimes stretch out like sticks, and the body remains at it is, either standing or kneeling. . . . if the suspension lasts, the nerves are left aching."[31] Indeed, Teresa remarks that the physical dangers to the body are very real, and death is not an impossibility. In the following description, Teresa describes this full array of bodily affects:

> I saw a person in this condition; truly she thought she was dying, and this was not so surprising because certainly there is great danger of death.[32] And thus, even though the experience lasts a short while, it leaves the body very disjointed, and during that time the heart beat is as slow as it would be if a person were about to render his soul to God. This is no exaggeration, for the natural heart fails, and the fire so burns the soul that with a little more intensity God would have fulfilled the soul's desires [by allowing it to die.]

Yet while the physical pain of the body is great, the pain felt within the soul is deeper still:

> This is true not because a person feels little or much pain in the body; although it is disjointed, as I said, in such a way that for three or four days afterward one feels great suffering and doesn't even have the strength to write. And it even seems to me that the body is left weaker. The reason one doesn't feel the pain must be that the interior feeling of the soul is so much greater that one doesn't pay any attention to the body. When one experiences a very sharp bodily pain, other bodily pains are hardly felt even though there may be many. I have indeed experienced this. With the presence of this spiritual pain, I don't believe that physical pain would be felt, little or much, even if the body were cut in pieces.[33]

Yet, Teresa testifies that despite these physical ailments, which often leave the body in pain "as if the bones were disjointed,"[34] raptures also quite often leave her with a feeling of bodily health and strength, as she is "greatly improved throughout the day."[35] Even so, she remarks that the actual death of body and soul "must be more gentle."[36]

31 Teresa of Avila, *Spiritual Testimonies*, 427.

32 Here Teresa is believed to be speaking of herself.

33 Teresa of Avila, *Interior Castles*, 423.

34 Teresa of Avila, *Life*, 177.

35 Teresa notes that this feeling of bodily health occurs most often after she has received Communion.

36 Teresa of Avila, *Life*, 379, 332.

## Rhetoric of Erotic Suffering

As suggested, this whole experience of rapture is most often one of immense pain and suffering of both body and soul, so much so that it is almost unbearable; yet it is also "of such a kind that the soul would never want to be relieved of it as long as it lived."[37] It is here that Teresa's metaphor of the dart of God's love penetrating her soul is most instructive. In the previous section we examined Teresa's most famous use of this metaphor, but it is one that she used repeatedly. With it she describes rapture as a sudden and painful, but ultimately exquisitely delightful, experience. In one instance she notes

> [A]t times an arrow is thrust into the deepest and most living recesses of the heart in such a way that the soul doesn't know what happened, or what it wants. It well understands that it wants God and that the arrow seems to have been dipped in a poisonous herb so that for the love of this Lord it might despise itself; and it would gladly lose its life for Him. You can't exaggerate or describe the way in which God wounds the soul and the extreme pain this wound produces, for it causes the soul to forget itself. Yet this pain is so delightful that there is no other pleasure in life that gives greater happiness. The soul would always want, as I said, to be dying of this sickness.[38]

In another attempt to describe such an experience, Teresa relies again on the notion of the dart or arrow of God:

> While this soul is going about in this manner, burning up within itself, a blow is felt from somewhere. . . . the soul will feel pierced by a fiery arrow. . . .[and] it causes a sharp wound. And, in my opinion, it isn't felt where earthly sufferings are felt, but in the very deep and intimate part of the soul, where this sudden flash of lightening reduces to dust everything it finds in this early nature of ours.

Again, this wounding causes fierce pain and suffering. Teresa continues:

> His Majesty helps at that time with a vivid knowledge of Himself in such a way that the pain increases to a point that makes the one who experiences it begin to cry aloud. Though she is a person who has suffered and is used to suffering severe pains, she cannot then do otherwise.

Indeed, in such a state,

> The soul sees that it is like a person hanging, who cannot support himself on any earthly thing; nor can it ascend to heaven. On fire with

[37] Teresa of Avila, *Spiritual Testimonies*, 373.

[38] Teresa of Avila, *Life*, 250, 251.

> this thirst, it cannot get to the water; and the thirst is not one that is endurable but already at such a point that nothing can take it away.

In such torment, the soul cries out, "Oh, God, help me! Lord, how You afflict Your Lovers!" But still, the soul proclaims its delight in the midst of such suffering:

> Everything is small in comparison to what You give them afterward. . . . Furthermore, in spite of all this torment and affliction, which cannot be surpassed, I believe, by any earthly afflictions . . . the soul feels that the pain is precious; so precious—it understands very well—that one could not deserve it. . . . But with this knowledge the soul suffers the pain very willingly and would suffer it all its life, if God were to be thereby served; although the soul would not then die once but be always dying, for truly this suffering is no less than death.

Hence, Teresa argues that it is not only the immense pain the soul undergoes that puts it in danger of death; so too does the "overwhelming joy and delight, which reaches so extraordinary a peak that indeed the soul, I think, swoons to the point that it is hardly kept from leaving the body."[39] Contemplating such a state the soul declares, "Oh, what it is to see a wounded soul!"[40]

Perhaps not surprisingly, Teresa notes that this combination of pain and joy left her rather confused, for she "couldn't understand how such a combination was possible." She ultimately determined that it occurs this way "for a very sublime reason" and simply because God wants it that way. It is as if "a spark from the very great love the Lord has for it suddenly fell upon it, making it burn all over," and the soul can do nothing about it.[41] In this state of erotic, somewhat confused suffering, the soul is made to see with a "delicate and penetrating pain" such that the soul feels it is being crucified:

> The experience resembles the death agony with the difference that the suffering bears along with it such great happiness that I don't know what to compare it to. It is an arduous, delightful martyrdom . . . such that the soul would desire to spend the remainder of its life in this suffering, even though the suffering is so excessive a person cannot endure it.[42]

Indeed, it is this very combination of pain and delight that ensures the soul that this experience is of God and not the devil, for as Teresa argues, "the devil never gives delightful pain like this. He can give the savor and delight

39 Teresa of Avila, *Interior Castle*, 442–46.

40 Teresa of Avila, *Life*, 251.

41 Ibid.

42 Ibid., 177.

that seem to be spiritual, but he doesn't have the power to join pain—and so much of it—to the spiritual quiet and delight of the soul."[43] Accordingly, understanding itself as highly favored by God, the soul comes to relish and desire this "exquisite" and "precious" wound, this "delightful and sweet" suffering, so much so that the soul "would never want to be deprived of this pain."[44]

## Rapture as Prelude to Spiritual Marriage

Finally, Teresa argues that, just as in legal treatises and in common, though waning, cultural practice, rapture is but a prelude to marriage, a spiritual marriage that is consummated in the inner chambers of the Bridegroom's castle. In her lengthy description of the stages of the spiritual life found in her work *The Interior Castle*, Teresa equates the experience of rapture with that of the betrothal of the soul to God, a betrothal that ultimately leads to spiritual marriage and total, if impermanent, union between the two. As a result of this experience of rapture—the frightening, painful, yet delightful abduction of the soul—the soul becomes betrothed to God and "becomes fully determined to take no other Spouse." However, God, the Bridegroom, delays this union, for he wants this union "to take place at a cost," demanding that the soul undergo severe trials before entering the seventh, and highest, dwelling place of the castle, that of the bridal chamber.[45] Hence, the betrothal period is one in which the soul repeatedly undergoes joyfully painful raptures—when the soul is united with its Betrothed, but not fully—followed by equally painful periods in which the soul is left bereft of the Bridegroom's presence, seemingly abandoned and therefore all the more desirous of attaining the promised union of spiritual marriage.[46] It is only when the Lord finally deigns to have pity on the soul and to grant the marriage that the soul achingly longs for that He brings her into his own dwelling place, into the heart of his bridal chamber.[47]

And here, in this dwelling, "the feeling is so powerful that sometimes the soul cannot avoid the loving expressions they cause, such as: "O Life of my life! Sustenance that sustains me! And things of this sort." But even so, the pain and suffering found in the experience of rapture is not mitigated; in fact, the soul is burdened with "habitual pain and confusion" and even has

[43] Teresa of Avila, *Interior Castle*, 369.

[44] Ibid., 367.

[45] Ibid., 359.

[46] In this portion of the *Interior Castle*, Teresa explicitly refers to the biblical bride and bridegroom imagery found in the Song of Songs.

[47] *Interior Castle*, 428, 429.

"much greater fear than before," not wanting to offend its Spouse in any way. Yet, on the other hand, this pain and fear is of a different order than that of rapture, for it is now experienced with a deeper "interior joy" and with "more peace" than previously. Indeed, in this state, Teresa concludes that "all the trials endured for the sake of enjoying these touches of His love, so gentle and so penetrating, would well be worthwhile."[48]

Further, just as it was determined that a man could not legally rape his wife or betrothed because she had legally given her consent to sex once and for all, since Teresa was betrothed to God, her consent was not a matter of concern. Teresa argues that even though the soul resists these raptures, God is justified in abducting it for it is already betrothed to God, and in such instances there really is "no need for consent of this soul" anyway. This is so because the soul "has already given itself to God, and it knows that it has willingly surrendered itself into His hands and that it cannot deceive Him, because He is aware of all things." Consequently, in rapture as well as in less ecstatic states of prayer, even though the soul may resist outwardly, inwardly it has already consented. Hence, when faced with rapture Teresa argues that the soul must be "resolute and courageous . . . in order to risk all, come what may, and abandon itself into the hands of God and go willingly wherever it is brought, since, like it or not, one is taken away."[49]

## Rape and the Gendering of Violence

What conclusions, then, can we make concerning the increasing recognition of women's subjectivity in rape law and the simultaneous development of feminine subjectivity as that which finds its ultimate fulfillment in violent, albeit spiritual, rapture and rape? In her article "The Violence of Rhetoric,"[50] Teresa de Lauretis argues that violence comes in two gendered forms, that of male and female. What determines the gender of violence is the status of the object of violence; the subject of violence, by virtue of the fact that it is a subject, is always gendered male.[51] Consequently, if the object of violence is just that—considered an object, not a subject in its own right—then this violence is gendered female. For instance, she argues that violence toward nature is considered feminine, as is revealed by the telling phrase, the rape of nature. In this instance, nature is deemed an inanimate object, neither

[48] Ibid., 435–41.

[49] Teresa of Avila, *Life*, 185, 173.

[50] Teresa de Lauretis, "The Violence of Rhetoric," in *The Violence of Representation: Literature and the History of Violence*, ed. Nancy Armstrong and Leonard Tennenhouse (New York: Routledge, 1989).

[51] Ibid., 250.

resisting nor consenting to its own violation. So, too, in rape law and theory up until the late Middle Ages, we see the actual object of this violence—the woman who is raped—quite often rendered just that: an object. The violence done to her is of significance only to the extent that her violation encroaches upon the rights and possession of another, her male guardian. Moreover, her male guardian has also been regarded as an object by the rapist, as one whose rights and possessions are ignored and overridden as if they did not exist at all. It is this treatment of a male as an object—as a female—that constitutes the basis for the legal violation.

However, while this gendering of violence appears appropriate to classical and early medieval constructions of rape, it does not necessarily ring true for later medieval and modern constructions. First, as is evident from Teresa of Avila's writings, her subjectivity remains whole and active throughout her experience of rapture. While at extreme moments she may appear to lose consciousness and her own subjectivity for an instant or two, Teresa takes pains to assure her readers that this is a rare occurrence, and a fleeting one. Throughout her work, Teresa appears as a strong, self-aware subject in her own right, not one to be easily swayed or to accept her objectification lightly. Teresa's claim to her own subjectivity also has resonance with the changing evaluation of the status of rape in late medieval law. As we have seen, in this law we see the growing acknowledgment of the rape victim's subjectivity and autonomy. While the rapist may still treat her like an object, the law is increasingly recognizing her subjectivity and thus treats her as a subject. So, according to de Lauretis's analysis, Teresa's construction of rapture does not qualify as female-gendered violence.

Yet, it does not appear that this construction of rape neatly fits de Lauretis's conception of male-gendered violence either. According to de Lauretis, the key to male-gendered violence is the equality—and the subjectivity—of the two opponents. The enemy is not dismissed as a mere object of one's control, an object that will meekly succumb to one's blows, but rather is considered to be a subject in his own right, with power to wield and the will to use it. The enemy and his power are respected, but not feared; submissive surrender of either party is not an option. Hence, rather than one subject acting unilaterally on an object as in female-gendered violence, in male-gendered violence two subjects fight, at times to the death.[52]

But Teresa of Avila does not fit in neatly with this depiction of male-gendered violence, just as she did not readily fit de Lauretis's notion of female-gendered violence. While she certainly resists God and his sudden and painful raptures, she does not fight back. Indeed, she does not even consider herself

52 Ibid. Here she is drawing on the theory of reciprocal violence developed by Rene Girard.

to be in a battle of any sort. Rather, she appears to readily accept her position and God's actions with few complaints. Moreover, she expresses great joy and delight in the violence and pain God inflicts upon both her body and soul. What then are we to make of this subject who does not fight back, who recognizes that what is happening to her is violent, erotic and painful, but who also rejoices in it and even finds it erotically pleasurable?

I argue that in Teresa's work we see a third gendering of violence at play, or perhaps better, a second type of female-gendered violence, one which recognizes the subjectivity of the object of violence but which constructs her as actually erotically enjoying this violence. Arguably, Teresa is neither a subject equal to God nor an object wholly devoid of subjectivity. Rather, she is a self-described subordinated subject, fully cognizant of what is happening to her and fully capable of resistance and consent. However, throughout her life she chooses most often to consent; further, what she consents to is not mere violence per se but eroticized, sexualized violence.

What ideological purposes might this serve? In early Christian and classical notions of rapture, or rape, there is no indication that the female as object consents to the violence of rape. Rather, in most cases, her consent, to either sex or violence, is not at issue at all. Moreover, in those instances when her subjectivity and will—her consent—are deemed important, her consent is not constructed as consent to sexual violence. Rather, as in the case of elopement, it is conceived of as her willing participation in the theft of her guardian's property and her consent to the subsequent sexual relations that are assumed to follow. In no way does such a construction suggest that a woman might willingly consent to the violence of a sexual assault. While she certainly may want sex within this construction, this construction does not suggest that she would want violence and degradation along with that sex. But with Teresa, as well as in modern and contemporary constructions of female sexuality, the female is now expected to find her highest pleasure in an act of violent sex. In an act of rape.

## Conclusion

In conclusion, just as women are no longer considered objects within rape law but are rather deemed subjects with the ability to either consent or resist such violence, in mystical literature as in contemporary pornography, we see women actually consenting to the violence of rapture/rape. As law began to use the presence or lack of a woman's consent to determine if a rape had actually been committed, we see a new ideology of rape/rapture taking hold in which women are seen actually to enjoy the violence of rape. The ideological implications of this new conception of rapture seem apparent. In previous law, when the consent of the woman was not at issue, we find no attempt to argue that she may have enjoyed the violence done to her. Now that her consent is becoming increasingly important, not surprisingly, we find a new ideology emerging that argues that women actually gain exquisite erotic pleasure specifically through the violence of a rapturous assault, and hence might very well consent to it.

Patriarchal ideology seems to have adapted well to the changing tide of women's newly acknowledged subjectivity, and has, in effect, kept women rapable. Hence, it is not surprising to me that we continue to see the abuse of women and girls—as well as young boys and adolescent males—in society and church today. The issue of rape and sexual assault can not be deemed simply a result of our contemporary secular and sexualized society. Rather, much of the imagery and rhetoric of rape as an ecstatic spiritual pleasure is derived from the Christian tradition itself. While much progress has been made in the last thirty years in combating the prevalent notion that women actually enjoy rape and violent sex—and thus should not be believed if they claim assault because they really did consent to it—more work still needs to be done. Until we, as a society and a church, recognize and admit this fact, sexual assault will continue to haunt us in both our homes and in our sacristies.

# Of Martyrs and Men

## *Perpetua, Thecla, and the Ambiguity of Female Heroism in Early Christianity*

Gail Corrington Streete

In her introduction to the 1985 volume of essays, *Immaculate and Powerful: The Female in Sacred Image and Social Reality*, Margaret R. Miles wrote a statement that seemed at one and the same time a summary and a challenge:

> The relative activity with which religious ideas and images are critically appropriated or the passivity with which they are intrajected seems to be crucial [for women]. . . . In using the religious ideas and images offered within their culture, women must choose carefully the religious symbols that effectively challenge and empower them rather than those that oppress them and render them passive.[1]

Such statements, written in the heady days of the rise of religious feminism and the possibility of recovering a "usable history" for women, were of course laudable but nevertheless invited further questions: What is the connection between these symbols and the power that produces them? Is there always a clear or careful choice to be made or even the possibility of "choice"? What or who determines whether a symbol is "empowering" or "oppressive" and do such definitions change over time? How are images related to gender and what makes the relationship: those who generate such symbols or those who receive them or a more complex interchange between the two? Miles herself realized that her statement was problematic.[2] That same year in *Image As*

[1] Margaret R. Miles, "Introduction," in *Immaculate and Powerful: The Female in Sacred Image and Social Reality*, ed. Clarissa W. Atkinson, Constance W. Buchanan, and Margaret R. Miles (Boston: Beacon, 1985) 2.

[2] Gail Paterson Corrington, *Her Image of Salvation: Female Saviors and Formative Christianity* (Louisville: Westminster John Knox, 1992) 16, n.7.

*Insight: Visual Understanding in Western Christianity and Secular Culture*, she raised the problem of understanding how religious symbols were approached and appropriated by historical women who left little evidence of their choices:

> How can historical women, only a few of whom left any words about their ideas of self and world, their interests, and their daily lives, be studied? Historians of women's culture can look at historical images of women, the images that historical women themselves used . . . [3]

She noted, however, that such a study contained an "inherent ambiguity," since " . . . Not a single image of any woman . . . was designed or created by a woman."[4]

While recent studies have qualified that last assertion, at least as it pertains to literary images,[5] any historian who seeks to uncover the history of women as subjects rather than as objects of description or idealization hits the hermeneutical wall rather quickly. Complicating the matter, as Miles herself recognizes, is the fact that religion itself is the greatest of all interpretive systems: "Religion is first and foremost a way of managing *this* world . . ." through language, through "seeing," and through feeling, and one might also argue, through being conditioned to speak, to see, and to feel in certain "appropriate" ways.[6] Integral to speaking, seeing, and feeling a religious identity, both corporate and individual, are constructions of gender. As Miles observes about the literature of early Christianity in *Carnal Knowing*, "enormous amounts of time and energy" are spent on discussions and depictions of gender roles and how they define and confine women by measuring them against men: "It is . . . fascinating to follow in the literature . . . a familiar but still-puzzling nexus of women's simultaneous empowerment and subordination."[7]

There are few places in the literature of early Christianity where that nexus is clearer than in the accounts of female martyrs and ascetics. Because

3 Miles, *Image As Insight: Visual Understanding in Western Christianity and Secular Culture* (Boston: Beacon, 1985) 64.

4 Ibid.

5 To cite but two landmark examples pertaining to the history of the early church, Steven L. Davies, *The Revolt of the Widows: The Social World of the Apocryphal Acts* (Carbondale: Southern Illinois University Press, 1980); Dennis R. MacDonald, *The Legend and the Apostle: The Battle for Paul in Story and Canon* (Philadelphia: Westminster, 1983). See also the discussion by Shelly R. Matthews, *Thinking about Thecla: Issues in Feminist Historiography*, *JFSR* 17.2 (2001) 39–55.

6 Miles, *Image As Insight*, 1–3.

7 Miles, *Carnal Knowing: Female Nakedness and Religious Meaning in the Christian West* (Boston: Beacon, 1989) xv.

female embodiment and sexuality—the marks of women's gendered being—were often depicted in early Christian narratives as obstacles to spiritual progress, they could be "overcome" only through heroic—that is to say male—effort. This heroic effort was usually identified as *virtus* or *andreia*, often translated as courage but whose primary meaning is manliness. As Miles notes, "The metaphor most frequently used for women who undertook to live an uncompromising Christian faith (either as martyr or ascetic) was that they had 'become male.'"[8] Yet if women were, even symbolically, encouraged to "become men," what consequences might that have for the relative power and authority of men and women in *this* world? The ambiguous nature of idealized figures like the martyrs Perpetua and Thecla, who represent two modes of women's spiritual empowerment in early Christianity, martyrdom, and asceticism, helped to create conflicts over the values of "maleness" and "femaleness" in their relationship to the place of sexuality, the spirit, and the body in Christian life. In Miles's words, "The problem for traditional Christian thinkers is how to connect the body, with its inflexible life cycle and intimate affiliation with mortality, to life—animation, momentum, and orientation—which by definition is a property of the soul."[9]

*The Martyrdom of Saints Perpetua and Felicitas* recounts the death of two young Christian women in a Roman arena in North Africa in 203. The story is remarkable because it purportedly contains Vibia Perpetua's own account of her visions and reflections during her imprisonment.[10] The apocryphal *Acts of Paul and Thecla* dates from approximately the second or third century C.E. Attached to a cycle of legends about the apostle Paul, the Acts, later supplemented by a mid-fifth century *Life and Miracles of St. Thecla* attributed to Basil of Seleucia, chiefly concern the actions of Thecla, a "noble virgin of Iconium" who converts to encratite Christianity.

In the *Martyrdom of Perpetua and Felicitas*, the rhetoric of virilization and feminization of the female martyrs is as obvious as it is complex. Perpetua's story consists of a first-person narrative that it is nonetheless framed by a third-person introduction that addresses his (presumably) "*fratres et filioli*" and a *passio* that continually emphasizes the female bodies and the feminine

[8] Ibid., 55

[9] Miles, *Fullness of Life: Historical Foundations of a New Asceticism* (Philadelphia: Westminster, 1981) 14.

[10] Åke Fridh, *Le problème de la passion des Saintes Perpétue et Félicité*, Studia Graeca et Latina Gothoburgensia 26 (Göteburg: Almqvist & Wiksell, 1986) asserts that nearly all scholars accept the diary portion as authentic rather than a literary fiction. On the other hand, Ernst Rupprecht, *Bermerkungen zur Passio SS. Perpetuae et Felicitatis* (*Rheinisches Museum*, N.F. 90: 180, cited in Fridh, 8) believes it is "entirely possible" that the claim of authenticity is a literary fiction.

behavior of both Perpetua and Felicitas in order to make his point about their masculine bravery.

Perpetua is one of the very few records we have of a woman's conscious choice of a religious self: she defines herself publicly and unmistakably as "*Christiana*" (6.4; note the feminine ending.) She increasingly defines that religious self nevertheless as male.[11] Despite images of control over men (her father and brother address her as *domina* or mistress, 4.1; 5.5.) and Perpetua's own visionary virilization, the story remains at the end, as Maureen A. Tilley notes, "a story about women and their bodies."[12] In this respect, as Miles observes, the *Martyrdom* is typical of many accounts of women martyrs, in which "respect and concern for [the] women martyrs vies with textual interest in their bodies or concern to establish the inferiority of their sex, disclosing male confusion and conflict over heroic Christian women."[13]

On the day before the prisoners are to fight with the beasts, Perpetua has her last (and perhaps most discussed) vision, that of fighting an Egyptian in the arena. Attended by young men, she describes herself as having her clothes stripped off and becoming a man: "*Et expoliata sum et facta sum masculus.*" (10.7) Thus "she" defeats the Egyptian. But does she really have a man's body? Her trainer acknowledges her victory but not her sex change: he calls her daughter (*filia*).

The narrator's account of Felicitas's imprisonment and martyrdom is almost solely concerned with her as a female body, a condition perhaps emphasized by her slave status. As Felicitas and Perpetua move toward the public spectacle (although we as readers have been seeing them all along), the narrator further underlines their female bodies and feminine behavior, as if to balance, if not undercut, their manliness. In the arena Perpetua is described, not as a gladiator, but as "*matrona Christi, Dei delicata* (18.2)." She and Felicitas are not called *matronae* or *mulieres*, but *puellae* (girls, 20.1), a term further diminishing their status. Clothing—and its lack—also serves to feminize the women. Stripped of their clothing, the women are exposed—not as in Perpetua's dream, as men—but as a "delicate girl" and one "who had recently given birth, with dripping breasts." Even the public, who presumably expected their nudity, recoils at this seeming impropriety.[14] Suitably reclothed, Perpetua seems to put on feminine modesty with her dress. When the mad heifer that is "matched with her sex" tosses her, and her tunic is ripped, ex-

[11] Miles, *Carnal Knowing*, 54–55.

[12] Maureen A. Tilley, "The Passion of Perpetua and Felicity," in *Searching the Scriptures: A Feminist Commentary*, ed. Elisabeth Schüssler Fiorenza, 2 vols. (New York: Crossroad, 1994) 2:829.

[13] Miles, *Carnal Knowing*, 57.

[14] Ibid., 56–57.

posing her thigh, the martyrologist rhymingly comments that she is "*pudoris potius memor quam doloris*"—"more mindful of shame than of pain" (20.4). Modestly also, she puts up her hair, as it would not be fitting for a female martyr to suffer with loosened locks (20.5). Perpetua's final words urge her brother and the rest to be brave: "Don't shame us in our suffering" (20.10), but she still screams when the trembling young gladiator strikes her on the bone. She nevertheless guides his wavering hand to her throat, in a classic gesture of chosen—but feminine—death.[15] Concludes the narrator admiringly, "*Tanta femina*," ("Such a woman!") Miles notes of *The Martyrdom*:

> Although, in the bonding of her body to religious subjectivity, Perpetua has 'become male,' her body remains spectacle to the observer . . . . In the editor's portrayal of Perpetua's martyrdom, her body is a textual device, a useful figure on which to advocate modesty for future female readers . . .[16]

As if to prove her point, the Carthaginian church leader Tertullian, Perpetua's contemporary and long assumed to be author of the preface to her diary and of the final account of her death, praised Perpetua as one who could re-enter the Paradise closed to the first woman, Eve, and provide a way for others to enter, albeit at the cost of "their own heart's blood"(*De anima* 51.6). Tertullian's admiration for the spiritual authority of those who had already entered heaven as martyrs[17] did not however translate into immediate approval of living women's charismatic leadership in the North African churches. His notorious rantings, as Miles calls them, in *De cultu feminarum* and *De virginibus velandis*, about women's shame being literally covered by their modest dress, echo the concern of Perpetua in the *Martyrdom*, and result, in Miles's opinion, from "acute discomfort" in third-century North Africa over a perceived "confusion of gender roles [that] threatened the power of a fragile male episcopate."[18]

Augustine, bishop of the North African Hippo Regius, preached three sermons for the feast day of Perpetua and Felicity. Using a traditional male mind/ female body dualism, he emphasized the "manliness of mind" in those who were "women in body," a spirit that routed the devil who deceived the

15 Nicole Loraux, *Tragic Ways of Killing a Woman,* trans. Anthony Forster (Cambridge: Harvard University Press, 1987).

16 Miles, *Carnal Knowing*, 61.

17 He also encourages Christian holy women to become martyrs by proving worthy even of pagan examples like those of Lucretia and Cleopatra (*Ad martyras* 4).

18 Miles, "Patriarchy as Political Theology: The Establishment of North African Christianity," in *Civil Religion and Political Theology,* ed. Leroy S. Rouner (Notre Dame: Notre Dame University Press, 1986) 173–75.

first woman and through her, the first man. (*Serm.* 281.1.1-2) In contrast, Perpetua's story also was used as a model of "dying in persecution . . . [and] living under stress" by the North African Donatists whom Augustine and other Catholic Christians strenuously—and ultimately successfully—opposed.[19] Perpetua's story may have served as inspiration for voluntary martyrdom and for the charismatic authority of women in the New Prophecy,[20] although we have no direct evidence that it did so. Nor, despite the detachment from family advocated as a later alternative to martyrdom and practiced by ascetic women like Paula and the two Melanias, do these women cite Perpetua as their inspiration.[21]

The second story—that of a woman both martyr and ascetic—belongs to the apocryphal *Acts of Paul and Thecla*, later supplemented by Pseudo-Basil's *Life and Miracles of St. Thecla*. Thecla's choice for a severely ascetic Christianity is construed, against the dominant cultural norms, as gender transgression.[22] While the narrative as we have it apparently approves and indeed praises this transgression as gender transcendence, the narrative as we have it also underscores Thecla's gender, a dynamic that persists in multiple interpretations of her story.

Strictly speaking, the *APTh* is not even a martyrdom but a series of near misses, as Thecla does not die in the arena but is miraculously saved and in the end "falls asleep with a beautiful sleep." Nevertheless, Thecla's "virtual martyrdoms" serve to get her out of the house where she is expected to be as virgin daughter and betrothed wife and into the public eye. In both the Iconian and Antiochene episodes of the *APTh*, her physical beauty is spotlighted, and in both parts also, as Gilbert Dagron has wryly observed, she "is depicted naked more often than usual."[23] As counterpart to this naked-

19 Maureen A. Tilley, "Harnessing the Martyrs: Social Control of Hagiography in Roman North Africa," North American Patristics Society, Chicago, May 30, 1998, n.p. [cited 23 September 2003] Online: http://divinity.library.vanderbilt.edu/burns/chroma/saints/martilley.html.

20 Frederick C. Klawiter, "The Role of Martyrdom and Persecution in Developing the Priestly Authority of Women in Early Christianity," *CH* 49 (1980) 251–61.

21 Gillian Cloke, *This Female Man of God: Women and Spiritual Power in the Patristic Age, AD 350–450* (London: Routledge, 1995) 35–37. Cloke claims that this detachment was "advocated as right and necessary for the woman pursuing the ascetic life, very much as earlier female martyrs" abandoned husbands, fathers, and even infants.

22 Miles, *Carnal Knowing*, 55.

23 Gilbert Dagron, *Vie et miracles de sainte Thècle* (Brussels: Société des Bollandistes, 1978) 26, translated and cited by Allison Goddard Elliott, *Roads to Paradise: Reading the Lives of the Early Saints* (Hanover: New England Press for Brown University, 1987) 50. A study of depictions of Thecla in early Christian art by Claudia Nauerth and Rüdiger Warns, *Thekla: Ihre Bilder in der frühchristlichen Kunst*, Göttinger Orientforschungen II. Reihe: Studien zur

ness, part of her exposure in the arenas of Iconium and Antioch, is Thecla's appearance in male guise: she vows to cut her hair short in order to follow the recalcitrant Paul (25) en route from Iconium, and she adopts *schemati andriko* (man's dress) when she finally runs him down in Myra (40). Both this nakedness and the transvestite motif, as Brock and Harvey have termed it,[24] illustrate what Miles has shown to be the "inseparability of women's bodies from their religious commitment," and the double, often conflicting meanings of this message for Christian men and women.[25]

In the Iconian section of the narrative, Thecla, like Perpetua, deliberately loses household and familial relationships when she becomes entranced (*thaumazein*) by hearing Paul preach about the celibate life. To her mother Theocleia, Thecla's transformation means that her maidenly sense of "shame" (*aidōs*) (8) has been "mastered" by "a new (strange) desire and a terrible passion (9)," and she orders the transgressor, the "lawless one" and "unbride" (*anymphon*) to be burned as a spectacle and a lesson to terrify other women who have listened to the word taught by Paul. Thecla is brought in naked and exposed to the crowd. As she silently makes the sign of the cross, God causes a hailstorm to put out the fire, and she is saved. Only later, according to the narrative, do we find out the rescue is a response not to Thecla's action but to Paul's prayer at a (safe) distance (24). Paul, however, will not allow Thecla to follow him, even when she suggests she cut her hair (25), because he fears *she* will be tempted and will act "like a cowardly man (*deilandreses*)." This action of Paul's, according to Miles, is typical of the message of the apocryphal Acts that "the physical beauty of the heroine was not an unambiguous sign of spiritual beauty; it was also a temptation for celibate men."[26]

In Antioch, the gender roles switch with the scene. When Paul denies Thecla and thus exposes her to attack from Alexander, "a very powerful man" who tries to embrace this "loose" woman on the open street, Thecla boldly stands up to him. In turn, she exposes *Alexander* to public shame by pulling the wreath off his head and ripping his cloak. Brought before the governor of Antioch, Thecla (no longer the mute sufferer of Iconium) confesses her deeds, and again is sentenced to death. The women of the city all cry out

spätantiken und frühchristlichen Kunst, vol. 3 (Wiesbaden: Harrassowitz, 1981) show that of the thirty-five genuine representations of Thecla listed on pp. 93–99 and shown in Tables I-XVI, seven represent Thecla as nude or partially nude. Nearly all, clothed or naked, make her breasts distinct, with one notable exception, a relief that represents her in "boyish" attire (*Tafel* II.4).

24 Sebastian Brock and Susan Ashbrook Harvey, *Holy Women of the Syrian Orient*, 2d ed. (Berkeley: University of California Press, 1998) 24–25.

25 Miles, *Carnal Knowing*, 70–75.

26 Ibid., 70.

against this "evil" and "unholy" judgment (32), and when Thecla is led to the beasts, they cry out against the "spectacle". Thecla is once more stripped (her second time naked) and thrown into the stadium. As in the case of Perpetua and Felicitas, the beast is again matched with the martyr's sex, but in Thecla's case the "fierce lioness" does not harm her but defends her to the death.[27] As Thecla faces the next lot of beasts she decides not to wait for the recalcitrant Paul but leaps into the pit of seals, saying, "In the name of Jesus Christ, I baptize myself on the last day!" (34). Apparently approving her decision, God not only destroys the seals with a lightning bolt but also surrounds Thecla with a "cloud of fire" so that none can see her naked, once more preserving her modesty even in martyrdom, as Perpetua did hers. When all attempts to kill Thecla fail, the governor offers to put her clothing back on her, but she retorts, "He who clothed me when naked among the beasts will clothe me with salvation on the last day" (37). Thecla's substitute mother Tryphaena and the maids of her household are converted, thus reversing the earlier situation in Iconium. Thecla's triumph over the powerful men in Antioch is complete, made possible by an all-female cast, including the lioness.

The story, however, does not end there. Adopting male garb, Thecla once more goes in search of Paul, upon whom the tables are turned when he is "amazed" to see her, as she was at first by him. Still trying to avoid her in case of "some other temptation" in her (this time it is clear *he* is tempted, not she), she retorts that she has "taken the bath" he earlier refused her, and therefore is presumably immune either to be tempted or a source of temptation. He sends her away again, but with the words, "Go and teach the word of God."(42) Thecla has had to submit to Paul's feeble authority for the last time.

What does all this switching of male/female roles, silent physically passive witness, and bold speech and action in the *Acts of Paul and Thecla* indicate about constructions and subversions of social ideals of "femininity" and "masculinity"? Margaret P. Aymer's view, that two separate folktales about Paul and Thecla, the male and female apostles, were put together and "harmonized" by an early Christian redactor,[28] is confirmed in part by Daniel Boyarin, who claims that earlier Christian texts, like the *APTh*, that depicted the "virilization" of women were transformed in later centuries to those that

[27] Ambrose, *De virginibus* II.1.19, claims that Thecla overcame a lion by exposing her private parts, a detail not found in the *APTh*.

[28] Margaret P. Aymer, "Hailstorms and Fireballs: Redaction, World Creation, and Resistance in the *Acts of Paul and Thecla*," in *Rhetorics of Resistance: A Colloquy on Early Christianity as Rhetorical Formation*, Vincent Wimbush, guest editor, *Semeia* 79 (1997) 45–48.

"feminized" men by exalting the "passive female virtue" of withdrawal, silence, and virginity.[29]

The earliest clear reference to women's interpreting the story of Thecla as their authority for teaching and baptism is that of Tertullian in the early third century. In *De baptismo aversus Quintillam* 17 he fulminates against "the impudence" of women who appropriate for themselves the authority to teach and even to baptize, using "the example of Thecla for the license," as well as practices "falsely ascribed" to Paul, in writings that Tertullian claims have been forged. We also have the evidence of the travel diary of a fourth-century religious and pilgrim, Egeria. On her way to Tarsus from Antioch, the indefatigable Egeria visits the *martyrium* of Thecla (*Itinerarium* 22.1—23.6).[30] There she finds, in addition to a "very beautiful church" a great number of cells for men and women, and one of her "dearest friends," the deaconess Marthana, who is in charge of cells of *apotactitae*; whether male or female virgins or both is unclear from the context (23.3; cf. 23.6). What is clear is that Thecla provides the inspiration for the ascetic life of both men and women, and for Egeria herself, who reads, in the company of others, "the whole Acts of holy Thecla" and gives "thanks to God who deigned to fulfill all my desires (23.5)."[31]

As Stephen J. Davis shows in his meticulously detailed work on the cult of Thecla, such centers, found as here in Asia Minor, in North Africa, Syria, Egypt, and even Rome attest to the power of Thecla as ascetic, confessor, martyr, and miracle-worker, not only among "communities of ascetic women, female pilgrims, and resident nuns," who may have originated and spread her story but also in the literary productions of church fathers like Pseudo-Basil and Gregory of Nyssa, who "domesticated" Thecla as a model for virginity within the household, whether natal household or church.[32] The density of references to the story of Thecla in the church fathers[33] make Thecla the archetype of female virginity: for example, she becomes the leading spokes-

29 Daniel Boyarin, *Dying for God: Martyrdom and the Making of Christianity and Judaism* (Oxford: Oxford University Press, 2001).

30 Numbering of chapters and sections and English translation from John Wilkinson, *Egeria's Travels* (London: SPCK, 1971).

31 Gregory of Nazianzus also found inspiration at "holy Thecla's" in his retreat there in 374 (*De vita sua* 545-49).

32 Stephen J. Davis, *The Cult of St. Thecla: A Tradition of Women's Piety in Late Antiquity*, Oxford Early Christian Studies (Oxford: Oxford University Press, 2001) 190–91, 61–62.

33 Dennis R. MacDonald and Andrew D. Scrimgeour, "Pseudo-Chrysostom's Panegyric to Thecla: The Heroine of the *Acts of Paul* in Homily and Art," *Semeia* 38 (1986) 151. See also Léonie Hayne, "Thecla and the Church Fathers," *VC* 48 (1994) 209–18; and Monika Pesthy, "Thecla among the Fathers," in *The Apocryphal Acts of Paul and Thecla*, ed. Jan Bremmer (Kampen: Pharos, 1996) 164–78.

woman for the virgin life in Methodius' *Symposium*. Women are not, however, encouraged to follow her example other than her stubborn persistence in chastity. Jerome's famous letter to Eustochium assures her that her fellow virgin Thecla will greet her in heaven (*Ep.* 22.41), but decries those virgins who otherwise act like men by cutting their hair and wearing men's clothes as though they are ashamed to look like women, but not ashamed to look like eunuchs (22.27), a description Jerome proudly claims for himself (22.19). For Jerome, then, as for Tertullian, it was fine to imitate Thecla imitating Paul but only up to a point. As a model of renunciation, especially of the physical and mental frailties of her gender, Thecla is approved, but not as a model of appropriation of privileges reserved for the male leadership. If as Monika Pesthy claims, Thecla became for the fathers the "model of church,"[34] a virgin eternally betrothed to Christ, that meant Thecla became the body of the church, under the leadership of those men who stood for Christ as its head.

Like Perpetua and the North African Montanists and Donatists who looked to her as a model for charismatic authority for women, Thecla and those women who claimed her authority to become itinerants, to teach, and to baptize presented a problem for male ecclesiastical leaders.[35] The solution to this problem lay in the advocacy by church leaders of the women's male virtues—primarily courage and endurance—as achievable by women who denied the presumed frailty of their sex. Pairing them with more traditionally female virtues like chastity and fidelity, however, circumscribed these virtues. Ironically, it is Perpetua's *virtus*, her masculine courage, that leads to her death and to the simultaneous beginning of her exaltation in the church as a martyr and intercessor and the end of her career as a confessor.[36] Just as the narrative of her martyrdom suggests, while living she is a woman and therefore limited; dead, the flesh is of no account and to be fleshless (and sexless) is powerful.[37] Thecla, who dies peacefully at the end of the *Acts of Paul and Thecla*, is revived in the *Life and Miracles* only to have her virginity miraculously preserved forever by God's enclosing her in a cave that later became her miracle-working shrine (*Life* 11:12). Thecla's static virginity is likewise pressed into the service of orthodoxy as a model for virgins within the church; it is not approved as a mandate for challenges to that church.

To return to the question with which we began, how can modern readers see, hear, and respond to such stories within their own tradition, especially

34 Pesthy, "Thecla," 167, 177.

35 Miles, "Patriarchy," 171–72.

36 Klawiter, "Role," 254.

37 In Saturus's vision in the *Martyrdom*, he meets Perpetua in heaven after they have both "put off the flesh" and Perpetua, who says she is "happier like this" helps him mediate a dispute between bishop Optatus and the presbyter Aspasius (12–13).

when they seek evidence of women's historical empowerment? Are we to treat these stories as normative, to deconstruct and dismiss them, or to reconstruct them as part of a "usable (and therefore desirable) past"? Is the latter project simply "feminist fantasy"?[38] To quote Miles once again:

> One can—and must—evaluate, judge, and reject some aspects of Christian tradition. . . . A closer examination of historical Christianity, however, will make us aware that all that is genuinely nontraditional about the task of sorting useful from peripheral or even dangerous ideas, images, and practices is the explicit acknowledgment that we are doing so. Religious leaders of the past found, focused, and emphasized aspects of Christian faith that they found useful and useable; then, instead of critiquing and rejecting other aspects, they simply ignored them. But they adjusted the weight, the central focus, and the emotional intensity of Christian faith in radically new ways that responded to the religious needs of their contemporaries.[39]

To explore and to interpret the stories of Perpetua and Thecla, therefore, as sites where Christian attitudes toward women's authority and power, positive and negative, come into complex play, is to participate in an enduring historical conversation whose center must be acknowledged to be always shifting.

[38] Kate Cooper, *The Virgin and the Bride: Idealized Womanhood in Late Antiquity* (Cambridge: Harvard University Press, 1996) 4, points out that in ancient narratives "the symbolic nature of gender would not have been internalized in a way a modern reader might expect." Elizabeth A. Clark, "Holy Women, Holy Words: Early Christian Women, Social History, and the 'Linguistic Turn,'" *JECS* 6 (1998) 418, also comments on the frustration of the feminist historian's desire to "uncover 'real women'" in these texts that are "nothing if not literary productions." Arguably the most influential of the reconstructionist feminist positions on Christian origins is that of Elisabeth Schüssler Fiorenza, *In Memory of Her: A Feminist Theological Reconstruction of Christian Origins* (New York: Crossroad, 1983). Lynne C. Boughton, "From Pious Legend to Feminist Fantasy: Distinguishing Hagiographical License from Apostolic Practice in the Acts of Paul/Acts of Thecla," *JR* 71 (1991) 362–83, is highly critical of this reconstructionist position.

[39] Miles, *Practicing Christianity*, 11–12.

# Interlude

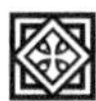

# My Life in Pictures

Jane Daggett Dillenberger

I grew up in Milwaukee, a city, which as far as I know, produced only two notable citizens: Golda Meir and Liberace. My parents and grandparents were lenient and loving. Mine was a middle-class upbringing in the midst of a family whose interests lay in business, politics, and sports. How my brother and I became bookworms at an early age is undocumented; nevertheless, the smell, feel, and look of the dark, rough, fabric bindings of public library books are among my earliest memories.

In the public library, Dimitri Merecjovski's *Romance of Leonardo da Vinci* came to hand. The story—much of it I later discovered to be untrue—was then engrossing but the *event* itself was the encounter with the strange artist and genius. Reproduced in the book were those archetypal keystones of western art–the *Mona Lisa* and the *Last Supper*. Other plates presented the mysterious mother goddesses, *St. Anne and the Virgin*, and the suggestively erotic and even demonic *St. John the Baptist*. Some of Leonardo's extraordinary drawings with their springing contours and clustered shadows were also included. It was Leonardo's work that initiated this twelve-year-old into a new seeing and into a confused and incomplete knowing of things outside the family ken.

As for religious background, we were proper Episcopalians. That is, we three children were faithfully sent off to church on Sundays. I had six years of perfect attendance at weekly Lenten services, while our parents attended more spottily. Whatever was then taught in Sunday School is not part of my background as I was in the choir for the eleven o'clock service. I did, however, get to know the Book of Common Prayer and its readings for the church year almost by rote—a knowing that has influenced my writing style and much of my theology.

My first transfixing experience of a work of art was Pablo Picasso's early etching, *The Bath*. Coming by boat to Chicago to see the 1933 World's Fair, I went first to The Art Institute of Chicago. It was my initial encounter with a great art museum and the awesome experience of seeing original works of art. This seeing must have prepared my eyes and my spirit. The tiny, delicate, domestic character of this etching seems an unlikely source of ecstasy, but that is what happened. Everything I knew and was melted away as I lived within this fragile world of a circus harlequin watching his wife bathe their small son.

The following year I entered Art School at the University of Wisconsin, Milwaukee. Although I did not think of myself as an artist, I was nevertheless convinced that there must be a place for me somewhere in the art world. The first session of our Life Drawing class brought my next revelation. I went promptly to the class so that I could get an artist's bench, called a "horse," near the model. Already seated quietly on her dais, the model was wearing a lovely loose silk, many-colored garment. I readied myself, tacking large sheets of paper to my drawing board, sharpening my charcoal.

When I looked up again, the model sat before me opulently nude—her silk garment a pool of color at her shapely feet. The sight of that voluptuous body, redolent with life and love, was a shock to the thin, self-conscious, and virginal eighteen-year-old who sat transfixed in her presence. Our moonlighting model had a regular job as a fan-dancer at a local nightclub.

While I lived in the world of my studies, my family's situation became increasingly precarious. The election that swept Franklin D. Roosevelt into office swept the Stalwarts, as the Republicans in Wisconsin were known, out, including my grandfather who had been their leader in the state senate. My father lost his business, our house, and eventually his good health, because of the Depression. As a result, I was shipped to Iowa City to go to the university and live with my uncle who was ROTC Commandant at the University of Iowa.

There was a big plus in this arrangement for Grant Wood had just begun teaching there; I was in his first classes in anatomy and mural painting. I was the only woman in a class of seven, all of whom were Wood's studio assistants. It was an oddly appropriate training for me, though I did not pre-vision it at the time. Wood was working on a fresco commission, and the class acted as his apprentices. Using renaissance artists' techniques, we assisted in preliminary studies, the transferring of cartoons, and the preparation of pigments. The twelve hours per week of highly disciplined anatomical studies, working from medical textbooks, were to become immensely important in my training.

On returning home for the summer, I found a job with the WPA, much to the chagrin of my soundly Republican family. Nevertheless, the money was needed. The government had started a project to train women in the crafts to help get them off the dole and in receipt of a salary. A group of young and talented graduates from the Milwaukee Art School were employed as designers of rugs, draperies, children's toys, and books. In turn, they trained women in these crafts and the products were ordered by state hospitals, schools, and institutions. I was hired by the art director, a friend and graduate of the Art School who had fine design sensitivities and extraordinary administrative ability. This was my first job and it proved to be more administrative than actively creative.

As the Depression continued, I remained for three years in order to save money, so that I could attend the University of Chicago, where I had earned a fellowship. My first interview with the eminent Renaissance art historian, Ulrich Middledorf, then head of the art history department, was pivotal. He surveyed my academic record, asked a few questions, and then suggested that I enroll in art history—a field I had never heard of before. He urged me to try it and admitted me to his graduate seminar, which met in the galleries of the Art Institute of Chicago. The first class meeting in the Flemish galleries was unforgettable. This was my first seminar and in it were bright, articulate, advanced students who spoke a tongue foreign to me—"art-history-ese." I struggled between despair born of intellectual insecurity and the emotions awakened by the beautiful paintings around us. Somehow through the unfamiliar vocabulary of the class, I sensed a way of grasping history itself. The paintings were not only radiant objects, they also came to us saturated with past cultures. That day an art historian was born.

The University of Chicago was a vibrant place to be in the late 1930s and early 1940s. Middledorf was a superb teacher, who skillfully used Woefflinian stylistic categories, and taught us to see. The lives of the artists, social or economic factors, wars and famines, gender and race—none of these modern obsessions entered the classroom. All emphasis was upon the single, unique object—the work of art. Similarly in English literature, the largest number of my other courses, a disciplined reading of the total output of one author was the substance of our studies. I learned to read as never before. Two years later I received my B.A. from the hand of Robert Maynard Hutchins, whose presence and philosophy we felt in all courses in the humanities at the University of Chicago.

I had met and married a South African student who was a Commonwealth Fellow earning a Ph.D. in the psychology of hearing. After completing my degree, I got a job at the Art Institute of Chicago as Assistant to the Curator of Prints and Drawings. I then saw again, but now could hold in my hands, Picasso's *The Bath*. The daily physical closeness to the prints and drawings of Rembrandt, Raphael, Picasso, and Degas created a lifelong hunger for this kind of high. In prints and drawings one sees the artist thinking through a problem. The spontaneity of each single line tracks artistic thoughts and feelings with an immediacy seldom present in a painting.

The latter part of my year at the AIC was spent preparing the collection for evacuation. Since the AIC is built over a railroad track, it was feared that enemy bombers might mistake it for a railroad station. Thus, the entire holdings of the print and drawing department were inventoried and given a red, blue, or green designation. I sat next to Carl Schniewind, the brilliant curator and collector who was then head of the Print and Drawing Department, as he evaluated each work by Albrecht Dürer, Rembrandt, Eugene Delacroix, Edward Manet, and Edouard Degas. All red works of art were sent to desert caves in Arizona; blue works were stored in floors five to ten of skyscrapers;[1] and the green works were kept in the museum and used for exhibition and study.

My husband completed his doctorate and was invited to Harvard University to join the research team of the Underwater Sound Laboratory, where submarine testing was conducted. It was my first trip to the East Coast, so I explored Cambridge and Boston, especially the Museum of Fine Arts and its Department of Prints and Drawings. During my days at the Art Institute of Chicago, one of Gauguin's original wood blocks had been purchased. The curator had impressions of that block pulled for the trustees, and one of these fine prints on Japanese paper was given to me at that time.[2] In Boston, I had intercourse with one of his last and most important works, *Where Do We Come From, What Are We, Where Are We Going*? This is a Garden of Eden story set in Tahiti in which Gauguin queried the meaning of life and offered no answer except for the beauty of the asking. Adam and Eve, the tree and the fruit, an image of a Polynesian god, and childhood and old age confront the viewer enigmatically but also poetically.

We lived only a few blocks from the Fogg Art Museum, which was *the* institution in our country for the training of museum curators, so it was not long before I enrolled in the M.A. at Radcliffe. The war had reduced the size of the classes, and simultaneously expanded the wealth of professorial expertise as the exodus of German scholars had enriched the Fogg.[3] Inasmuch as

1 It had been discovered that bombs falling in the street tear out the lower floors and that strafing gets the upper floors, but the middle floors usually remained intact.

2 Lest any of the recipients of the prints might try to pass them off as having been printed by Gauguin himself, they are all impressed with the Art Institute stamp and the date of the pulling of the print (1940). So, though more beautiful in quality of printing than those spoon-printed by Gauguin himself, mine is worth only a portion of Gauguin's handiwork..

3 Germany was the country that had given birth to art history as an academic discipline and a profession.

I had more than one year's work under a distinguished curator at Chicago, I was freed from the required museological training courses. I went directly into seminars and was able to buttonhole particular professors for reading courses in areas of my own interest. With Kenneth John Conant I worked on Venetian prints and paintings with Jakob Rosenberg, and on the history of the Constantinian St. Peter's and its evolution into Michelangelo's, Carlo Maderna's, and Gian Lorenzo Bernini's edifice. I also studied medieval art in a small seminar with Harvard's great Carolingian scholar, Wilhelm Koehler. It was a heady time!

During this time, two formative things happened to me. First, I encountered Italian baroque art for the first time. The Fogg owned a group of wondrous, small terracotta *bozzetti* by Bernini, which literally bore the sculptor's fingerprints—you could see the pattern of his thumb as he urged the wet clay into the swirling movement that the angel's garment made as the angel kneels suddenly before us. Whereas the arts of the High Renaissance present the quintessential movement stilled and held before us forever, in the art of the Baroque the moments before and those that will follow are embodied in the passionate movements of the angels, saints, and holy persons. As spectators we feel a quickened heart beat, a larger living.

My second discovery was how naturally I took to art historical research. I found that I was part-detective by nature and had the knack of holding many disparate pieces of information in mind until the key that would suddenly illumine them was discovered. A good visual memory is required, as is the virtue of patience and a love of dusty archives and remote museum storage areas. One must be able to follow hunches persistently, but start off on another tack when they dead-end.

I completed my M.A. with a thesis on Rembrandt's etchings. I was immediately interviewed for a job with a high-flown title, Art Director, and a miserable salary, $100 per month, at that ancient and honorable private library, the Boston Athenaeum. The job encompassed high and low: the patrons were Boston bluebloods for whom I did bibliographical work. I also inventoried the Athenaeum's collection of American paintings and sculpture, including the well-known portraits of George and Martha Washington by Gilbert Stuart. However, I also shelved books and filed the exquisite catalogue cards, which were still hand-lettered in black and red inks. The Boston Athenaeum building is very beautiful: in the entryway stands a sculpture of *Adam and Eve* by the American Thomas Crawford. It was always remarked that Adam and Eve—who were placed outside the elegant but exclusive library—were mourning because they were not allowed in the Athenaeum, which was open only to members.

The interlude at the Boston Athenaeum was a strange one. The war was at its height and I felt marooned at the sidelines. From my desk, I looked out upon the ancient graveyard of the old Park Street Church. During bad weather I encountered no one but Jacques Barzun, who daily was quietly working in his alcove on one of his books, and the jolly Irish elevator man who delivered books to be shelved. Yet I left one small imprint upon that staid institution, but it was accomplished unknowingly on my part. For years the first thing I put on in the morning were earrings. After working at the Boston Athenaeum for several weeks, the head cataloguer came to me and showed off her new earrings. I complimented her, but she laughed and said I didn't get the point: no one on their almost completely female staff had ever worn earrings to work. When I did, they all watched with bated breath for the moment when the Librarian, a kind of Gertrude Stein-like mannish woman who was a dragon for protocol, protecting New England propriety, would dress me down. When that did not happen, the chief cataloguer sprouted earrings, and subsequently many others followed suit, even unto the ninety-year-old head of the history collection, who daily appeared and fussed about amid piles and piles of books and fly-away papers.

With the end of the war, my experience at the Athenaeum came to an abrupt end: we moved to New Jersey, for my husband had accepted a new research job at Bell Laboratories. Having been city-born and bred, Morristown and Madison were my first experiences of suburbia. I found it stifling. The golden lining was having New York City two hours away by train and ferry. I prowled the museums and used the J. Pierpont Morgan Library, where I studied a set of William Blake's original drawings for the *Book of Job*.

In time, I got a job at the Newark Museum, which was a jolting experience after the Art Institute of Chicago and the Fogg Art Museum. Beatrice Windsor, the director, interrogated me, asking me what would be my ideal museum job. Without a moment's hesitation, I said to be curator of a fine collection of seventeenth-century drawings. She laughed heartily and said they owned only American art and were especially strong in local pottery—did I still want a job? Since I needed it, I took a position in the Registrar's Office. This is the nerve center of every museum for no object enters or leaves a museum without being examined and reported upon by the registrar.

I left the museum in 1946 when my first child, Bonnie, was born. Since I did not drive, we were marooned on the attic floor of an old Morristown house. Our lives consisted of walks to the park, gardening, and the reading of children's poetry and stories. Eventually I discovered that it was the sound of my voice and my full attention that pleased her most. I began to read her art history and show her the plates of art books, including those paintings I later took her to see in the Metropolitan Museum of Art. The fact that in her late thirties she became an art historian makes one believe in subliminal learning.

Occasionally, I saw my former professor, Wilhelm Koehler, the Carolingian scholar, and we corresponded regularly. He intermittently gave me a research chore such as his request that I study, in strong sunlight, Rembrandt's *The Auctioneer* in the Metropolitan Museum. He wanted a detailed report on the background of this compelling portrait for an essay he was writing. Otherwise art history research was on hold.

My son, Christopher, was born in 1950. Quickly I discovered that two little children add up to more than one plus one and we never had the long periods of togetherness that Bonnie and I enjoyed. He was the prototype for all those spirited, fleshly radiant Christ-child images of renaissance art. I watched him grow, awaiting the time when his body would conform with that of the Christ Child in Michelangelo's *Bruges Madonna*—only to discover that American boy children are leaner than their renaissance counterparts, but no less beautiful.

I began scouting for a job. Since museum work is inflexibly nine-to-five with only a one-month vacation, that was out. Teaching was my next option. Drew University was nearby and I studied their catalogue and decided to propose a course in the history of religious art for Drew Theological Seminary. President Fred Holloway sent me to the new dean, Clarence T. Craig, who saw my suggestion as an offering that might attract students as Tom Driver's courses in drama did at Union Theological Seminary in New York, Drew's competitor. I got the job and the hard work of gathering slides for lectures and a bibliography for the library began. I called this course, my first venture into teaching, "From the Catacombs to Guernica in Religious Art." My preparation and class time could be accomplished around the nursery school, household duties, and being a mother.

Once I got my sea legs in teaching, my twelve years at Drew were marvelously rewarding intellectually, though again miserable in terms of salary, security, rank, and perquisites. My colleagues were genuinely interested in my field and I was soon lecturing in their courses as well as doing my own teaching. Barney Anderson had me talk on the "Creation in Art" for his course on the "Doctrine of Creation." I also presented a series of lectures for Franz Hildebrandt's church history courses and a lecture on "Mysticism in Art" for Carl Michalson's seminar on "Mysticism."

Then Stanley Romaine Hopper suggested that we do a seminar together entitled "Man's Self-Interpretation in Modern Art and Poetry." I spoke on Eugene Delacroix and Romanticism, while he discoursed on Baudelaire. My lecture on Odilon Redon was complemented by his on Edgar Allan Poe and

Gustave Flaubert, my Pablo Picasso with his on Wallace Stevens. It was such fun that we did it a second year.

I started teaching at Drew innocent of theology. Relating my own lectures to those of my colleagues called for study and strategy. One Sunday, the Arts Page of the *New York Times* had a brief description of an exhibition of religious art at Union Theological Seminary inspired by Professor Paul Tillich's so-called four categories of relationship of art and religion. I went to see the exhibition, which had some splendid paintings in it; I found that the categories made no sense from an art historical perspective.

I telephoned Paul Tillich, whose name was totally unknown to me, and found that he was soon to speak at Drew. I pressed my colleagues to ask Tillich to lecture on his four categories. So it was that I met Paul Tillich for the first time, on a cold blustery day at the depot of the Lackawanna Railroad Station in Madison. We immediately worked together to choose the slides for his lecture, which, in the form that he gave it at Drew, was eventually published.[4] Tillich became a friend, and in 1958, his former student, editor, and colleague arrived at Drew—one John Dillenberger.

During those years, it became clear that teaching rather than museum work would be best until the children were grown. Since a teaching career required the Ph.D. credential, I began investigations with Columbia University, New York University, and Drew, with the intention of getting a joint degree in art history and theology. I enrolled in doctoral seminars at Drew, passed my language exams, and lined up an auspicious doctoral committee including Tillich and Erwin Panofsky, who was at the Princeton Center for Advanced Studies.

At the very outset my thesis subject was much in mind, "The Image of Evil in Art."[5] It was a subject that interested both Tillich and Panofsky. When I talked with Panofsky, he looked at me with a twinkle in his eye and asked, "Why do you think it is, that it is always women who are interested in evil in art?" Tillich had been scheduled to lecture again at Drew, and I persuaded him and the Drew Committee that his lecture be on the demonic in art.[6]

[4] Carl Michalson, ed., *Christianity and the Existentialists* (New York: Charles Scribner's Sons, 1956), 128–47. This essay was reprinted in Paul Tillich, *On Art and Architecture*, Jane and John Dillenberger, eds. (New York: Crossroad Publishing, 1987) 89–101.

[5] Jane Daggett Karlin, "The Image of Evil in Nineteenth and Twentieth Century Art," *Drew Gateway* 28.3 (1958): 152-67. This essay was reprinted in Jane Dillenberger, *Image and Spirit in Sacred and Secular Art*, ed. Diane Apostolos-Cappadona (New York: Crossroad Publishing, 1990).

[6] "The Demonic in Art" was republished in its entirety in Tillich, *On Art and Architecture*, 102–18.

Tillich asked me about my thesis subject: "Are you sure you can live with evil as much as the thesis will require?" I had no doubt then, but later had bouts of being inhabited by the images I was studying. In particular, Martin Schongauer's *Temptation of St. Anthony* invaded dreams and reality. The consequences, however, came somewhat later. By the end of the first year's studies, it became apparent that I was involved in two degrees, one in art history and one in theology. Neither institution was willing to let me shape a program involving the two together. Thus, I turned instead to writing my first book, *Style and Content in Christian Art*, with the hope that it would establish my credentials and also serve as a text for my own teaching.

I had recently been through a disturbing, indeed frightening experience, which my friend Henry James would have called a "vastation." Again a defining moment in my life was related to a work of art, but this time demonically. The painting that triggered the terror was an eighteenth-century boudoir painting, Francois Drouais's, *Family Portrait*, which hangs in the National Gallery of Art. An unlikely candidate for a vastation, this painting was one that I had never before looked at with care. Eighteenth-century French art was little known or prized by me at the time. It took me years to understand why this particular work set off a reaction that verged on madness. As I stood transfixed before it, the dapper spouse, rosy wife, and strangely mature child suddenly became reality—an intense reality—*my reality*. The people in the gallery to whom I turned for reassurance had flipped into unreality and were like persons in a painting.

This deep confusion between art and life occurred several other times. My marriage, which had become increasingly difficult, was, I knew, part of the problem. I needed help and turned to the only professional I knew, Esther Harding, the Jungian analyst, whom I had heard lecture on "Bunyan's *Pilgrim's Progress* as Paradigm of the Inner Journey of the Spirit." It was a brief encounter, but sufficient in helping me ground myself with regard to reality versus nightmare. Somewhat later it helped me in dealing with a decision that was to tear asunder the fabric of my life.

I received a Rockefeller Grant for summer travel to see and photograph the notable works of modern church art and architecture in Italy, France, and England. The award of that grant, as I look back in time, was a different experience from today's dreary procedures. I wrote a letter stating what I dreamed of doing, but aside from that, my only preparation was to buy a bunch of fresh violets to wear on my suit the day I lunched with the chairman of the Grants Committee in the Rainbow Room of Rockefeller Center. The serious part came afterwards, when I was introduced to four of his colleagues who quizzed me about my teaching and my objectives. Only later did I realize that I had been under examination. However, it was clear that I had passed muster when I received the grant. That summer I saw Venice, Assy, Coventry, and Northampton for the first time. I visited Paul Cèzanne's studio at Aix-en-Provence and the Romanesque abbey churches at Arles, Conques, and Vezelay. I lived for a time at Pro Civitate Christian in Assisi, the center for the worker-priest movement in Italy, a community devoted to the arts as well as the church's mission.

It was upon my return from this trip that I decided to end my difficult and destructive marriage in order to be with John Dillenberger, my colleague at Drew. Together we both decided to leave New Jersey, to go where, we did not yet know. Providentially, there was a glimmer of hope in the form of a telephone call from Ted Gill, then President of San Francisco Theological Seminary, asking John if he would consider a position as Dean of the Faculty, Professor, and SFTS representative to the emerging Graduate Theological Union. Subsequently, Ted came to New York, listened to John's account of our plans, met me, and then returned to discuss the complexities with his Board and faculty. We waited six anxious weeks with no word from Ted, but finally, and quite nonchalantly, he telephoned and said, "Come."

Once the children, our cat, John, and I had settled in at San Anselmo, I again scouted for a job. The San Francisco Museum of Modern Art hired me as a part-time supervisor of the inventory of their entire collection and the preparation for their first catalogue, a job much to my liking with its physical involvement with the works of art. The Museum owned a part of Gertrude Stein's collection, as she was originally an Oakland resident. One of the first Americans to recognize the genius of Matisse and Picasso, Stein's ravishing, small, early works by both these artists eventually came to the museum. On my desk I had a small sculpture of Matisse's supple *Madeleine* and one of his radiant still-life paintings hung on my office wall. I also gave a course jointly sponsored by the Museum and the University of California, Berkeley, Extension Program on the development of modern art. I used the museum's collection as the core and added slides of masterpieces from other museum collections.

Eventually, SFTS hired me to teach courses, too. As at Drew, I had full faculty voice, vote, and committee assignments. I managed one adroit maneuver while still a staff member of the SFMA: it was possible in the interregnum between directors to arrange for some thirty first-rate works of art to be exhibited on the campus in Alexander Hall. For two hallowed weeks, we had paintings by Paul Klee, Diego Rivera, Georges Rouault, Matisse, and Picasso at San Anselmo. Willing students acted as security guards by day and also slept in the room at night. Museum insurance and security requirements have so escalated since that time that any such exhibition would be impossible now. Even then it took sleight of hand to accomplish. How lovely for students and faculty—and for me—to be able daily to rub noses with these great artists' works!

At that time I had begun amassing photographs and data on American religious art, first with an interest in what and how ancient Christian themes were appropriated in the new land. I was interested in how Thomas Eakins's home-grown *Crucifixion* was similar to, or different from, the received tradition as one sees it in Diego Velasquez's *Crucifixion.* Soon my collection of photographs began to assume a shape, a coherence that suggested this was a fascinating and unknown aspect of American art. I talked with Alfred Frankenstein, then art critic for the *San Francisco Chronicle* and known to me through his books on American art. Since I had been bred as an art historian on Leonardo and Rembrandt, American art was a new field for me. Alfred discouraged me, saying, "There is no such thing as American religious art." Six months later I went to him with my piles of photographs. He not only capitulated, but was also excited by my discovery. Later he wrote a long and glowing review of the exhibition that would evolve from my study.

In my research I had written the acknowledged dean of American art historians, Joshua Taylor, to get information about the present location of paintings by William Page, an artist about whom Taylor had written the definitive book. I noted in my letter that I was working on an exhibition of American religious art. His reply gave me the data I had requested, but also asked if I would be willing to work with him jointly on the exhibition. So it was that the exhibition planned for the University of California, Berkeley, and sponsored by the GTU, became tripartite when the National Collection of Fine Arts, of which Taylor was Director, became a partner in this enterprise.

I met Josh Taylor for the first time at the San Francisco airport and brought him to see my then-enormous cache of photographs of American religious art. So, too, began a wonderful friendship, which continued until his untimely death. Known to be a person of prodigious knowledge and with a fine and discriminating eye—that most prized possession for an art historian—he was yet famed as difficult, contentious, and impossible to work with. I never found him so. Josh baptized our exhibition, *The Hand and the Spirit in American Religious Art, 1700–1900.*[7]

In this exhibition were my earlier friends from the Boston Athenaeum, *Adam and Eve.* As a trustee, Walter Whitehill had earlier voted against allowing masterpieces from the Boston Museum of Fine Arts to be sent to the

7 *The Hand and the Spirit in American Religious Art, 1700–1900* opened at the University Art Museum, University of California, Berkeley and then traveled to the National Collection of Fine Arts, Washington, D.C.; the Indianapolis Museum of Fine Arts, Indianapolis; and the Museum of Fine Arts, Dallas.

Metropolitan Museum of Art on the grounds that people should travel, not works of art. This time, given the importance of the theme, he gave his blessing to having the six-ton sculpture join our exhibition in its peregrinations. So it was that *Adam and Eve*, who could never enter the sacred precincts of the Boston Athenaeum, did indeed enter museums in Berkeley, Dallas, Indianapolis, and Washington, D.C.

While working on *The Hand and the Spirit*, the definition of the boundary in time had remained in question. Should twentieth-century art be included? The research material itself answered the question. Since the twentieth century initiated new styles and new contents, in this instance such art should not be exhibited with eighteenth- and nineteenth-century art. I knew, however, that I would do a sequel to the first exhibition, and I began work on what would be the exhibition entitled, *Perceptions of the Spirit in Twentieth-Century American Art*. My husband had been involved in the research for *The Hand and the Spirit* and together we had a grant from the National Endowment for the Arts to follow up the research from that exhibition. We spent fifteen months in Washington as Fellows at the National Collection of Fine Arts. The fruit of that research was John's book on Benjamin West and my study of Elihu Vedder, which formed the basis of an exhibition I later curated of his work.

Here chronology eludes me as we lived through a succession of shattering events in our personal lives. My son, Christopher, was killed in an automobile accident in 1968. A year later, I had surgery for cancer, which was followed by a second surgical episode.

In 1977, John was invited to accept the Presidency of Hartford Seminary in Hartford, Connecticut. We had lived through the 1960s in Berkeley, John dealing with sit-ins and protests and I teaching a new kind of student. My first classes at Drew had many returning GIs who had been stationed in Europe and had the opportunity to see Chartres Cathedral and the Vatican Museums. They eagerly, even passionately, appropriated all they could learn of the art of the past and the present. In the 1960s the flower children who inhabited my classes were of a different character and style. There was a terrible pathos to their slightly stoned, tender spirits, focused more on themselves than on the great illuminating works of art of our common past.

Thus in 1977, John and I were ready for a change of milieu, though the worst had past. So it was that following the opening of our exhibition, *Perceptions of the Spirit in Twentieth-Century American Art* at the University Art Museum, we left Berkeley in January. We departed just ahead of a gigantic snowstorm, which only caught up with us in our last day's journeying.

When we arrived at our destination, a beautiful and historic eighteenth-century mansion in Farmington, Connecticut, the house was an island in three feet of the purest, whitest snow, and festooned with icicles, many of which were three-feet long. The car could not drive up the last stretch of Apple Hill on which the house sat. So our new life began by toting suitcases, pillows, and blankets up the driveway. It had been many years since I had experienced the four seasons and that first cycle in Farmington seemed magically beautiful. I had forgotten how exquisite and various frost upon the window pane is and how brilliant the New England autumn is.

The focus in Hartford for me was not Hartford Seminary, for which my role was restricted to that of the President's wife, but the Wadsworth Athenaeum. One of the oldest museums in the country, with a splendid collection that I had studied on previous trips, the Athenaeum became my new home. I was soon appointed to the Trustees' Acquisition Committee, which put me at the very heart of museum policy, for this committee determined all purchases of works of art for the collection. I also taught courses in the American Studies Program at Trinity College. Coming from Berkeley, it was a pleasant shock to have students who arrived early for the class and who read and diligently viewed works of art. Time seemed to be rolled back to the pre-1960s, but not in this respect alone.

Social life in Hartford was like a scene in one of Henry James's novels. I had recently reread *Portrait of a Lady* and the Hartford social structures and graces, even the conversations at dinner and tea parties, seemed to reecho this earlier era. Through a San Francisco friend who wrote to a socially prominent Hartford friend, we were at once introduced and welcomed into so-called "Old Hartford" society. I was asked to join the Saturday Morning Club, a prestigious club, which had been established by Mark Twain for the benefit of the young Hartford wives whose intellectual faculties were supposed to be stimulated by the scholarly papers—on carefully chosen themes—that they prepared and read to one another. It was true blue-stocking stuff, with the entire meeting taken up by papers and discussion. Tea and coffee were available thereafter, but offered unaccompanied by any goodies or purely social chatter. With true New England inconsequence, the Saturday Morning Club met on Friday mornings.

I should have felt at home in New England. My father's forebears settled first on Martha's Vineyard, originally ceded by the English crown to a certain John Daggett, a distant relation of mine, and a Thomas Mayhew. My mother's ancestors lie buried in an old cemetery in the charming Connecticut town of Woodstock. These places should have exercised a kind of atavism, a sense of belonging for me. In addition, I had for some six years been deeply immersed in research on American art, and in Hartford, we lived at the heart of this past history.

Yet somehow the New England consciousness never became part of my being. I remained outside of it, having it as an object of study, but never with that surge of feeling of identity in which all you are is confirmed, and riches added there unto, as happened and continues to happen to me on every return to Rome. Like my friend. Henry James, I had seen and experienced too deeply a larger world before this visit to my own ancestors.

Now, looking back at my five-and-a-half years in Hartford, it was a productive time for me, despite my loneliness for colleagues and heavier entertaining responsibilities for the Seminary than I had ever had at the GTU. In our second year, we moved from Farmington into Hartford to a big house that was directly across from what would be the new Seminary building. We fed and housed visitors and faculty, had faculty and committee meetings in our living room, and lived generally more publicly than I enjoy.

During the next year in Hartford, I evaded some of this by working on another exhibition for the National Collection of Fine Arts, once again, with its director, Joshua Taylor. Both of us had been interested in Elihu Vedder for some time. During our year in Washington, I had read all of the Vedder documents in the Archives of American Art. Thus I came to know Vedder not only as an artist, but also as a man, as perhaps few of his own contemporaries or family did.

His hundreds of letters written from Rome to his parents, to his wife's family, to his wife when they were separated, and to his own children, brought me into the life and passions of this large-hearted, richly human artist. His letters to his parents described his bride-to-be, later letters told of the death of a beloved son; and his letters to a San Franciscan who had commissioned him to paint *The Three Fates* were fascinating, as were his letters to his Boston publishers about his illustrations, for the then-recently translated *Rubaiyat of Omar Khayyam*. I worked on the Vedder papers, traced lost works of art, and identified the subject matter of particular paintings for which the Vedder drawings were made. With Taylor, I selected what was to be in the exhibition and how we would shape it. The catalogue for the exhibition, *Perceptions and Evocations: The Art of Elihu Vedder*, remains the most comprehensive work on the artist.[8]

My speaking engagements during my Hartford period were used for further opportunities to explore new ground. For the Trinity College Department of Religion, I lectured on "Northern and Southern Sensibilities at the Time of the Reformation." I endeavored to delineate accurately the contrasts between Michelangelo's classical, idealized, and epic style and con-

[8] Joshua C. Taylor, Jane Dillenberger, and Richard Murray, *Perceptions and Evocations, The Art of Elihu Vedder*, Introduction by Regina Soria (Washington, D.C.: Smithsonian Institution Press, 1979) 115–65.

tent in the Sistine ceiling frescoes, and Mathias Grunewald's northern style and content in the *Isenheim Altarpiece* with its particularity and emphasis on intense emotion and finitude.[9] This study was followed by two papers, "Lucas Cranach: Picture-Maker of the Reformation" and "Women in American Art, 1770–1970," for the Saturday Morning Club.[10]

The big Hartford experience, however, was being part of the creation of a great work of architecture. One of John's tasks was to complete the sale of the Seminary's neo-Gothic residential campus and to be the person responsible for exploring a new location. Additionally, he was to hire and work with the architect on the program of the Seminary, which by now was not a resident, degree- granting institution, but oriented toward a research and continuing education program.

I was put on the search committee for an architect. Immediately I sought recommendations from the Curator of Architecture at the Museum of Modern Art; from the Dean of the School of Architecture, Yale University; and from the Dean of the School of Architecture at Rensselaer Polytechnic Institute. Of course, local architects were on the list also. In the final winnowing, there were two local and eight nationally known architects. Yet, Richard Meier was my first choice. I had known him from the world of art, but was not familiar with his architecture. Looking at his work convinced me of the beauty and elegance of proportion in his architecture, which captured and held light, radiating a sense of joy. By skillful leadership of the committee, Richard Meier was selected.

Watching over the design process and the actual building of Hartford Seminary was a wonderful experience. It is said that commissioners and architects are as symbiotic as psychiatrist and patient. It is true; I became and remain a devoted friend of this marvelous architect.

John had decided in his fifties that he would retire at sixty-five in order to do what he thought important for himself; he resisted the siren call by the Seminary to stay and enjoy the beautiful building and programs he had helped bring to birth. We had come East, not certain that we wanted to return to California. However, at Bonnie's pleading, we had kept our house, renting it to the curator at the University Art Museum. Just before we felt we needed to make some decisions, Doug Adams invited me to give the Dillenberger Lecture, a series of his devising with the purpose of bringing special lectures on the visual arts to the GTU. I was hesitant to accept, but later I was glad that I did. Seeing so many of our former colleagues in Berkeley, and witnessing the GTU in its increasing strength and security touched both of us.

9 These essays are included in Dillenberger, *Image and Spirit in Sacred and Secular Art.*

10 Ibid.

We began to think of returning to California, but with the decision that we would continue to travel. A few bitterly cold and endless winters of ice and snow dampened the initial enthusiasm of our first year in Hartford. We returned to Berkeley in 1983.

Since then, Michelangelo, about whom I did not lecture in my early years at Drew because I felt that I needed more time for thought, study, and looking at his work, finally became central to my experience as my life unfolded. In those early years his art seemed peopled by too-heroic figures, too remote from our quotidian life. Physically the figures seemed too awesome and impossibly at variance with my small-boned body. Psychically they dwelt in a realm of exalted myth. The birth of my children and the death of a son in my own life, the tragedy of one marriage's death, and the rebirth in a second marriage brought me to a new seeing of this unfathomable, illimitable genius' art. Subsequently the second marriage was abruptly terminated.

What I know of history, my scaffold for history, is through the signposts provided by art. Thus, the time of Charles V is signaled by Titian's magnificent portrait of the canny ruler painted in 1548. Charlemagne's era is known through his chapel at Aachen and Dante's dates are known because he was at the University of Padua when Giotto was painting his frescoes for the Arena Chapel. The date 1527 is emblazoned in the consciousness of art historians more firmly than 1066 or 1492. It was a shock to me that this significant date had no meaning for church historians or theologians. For 1527 signals the Sack of Rome: the destruction of art and disposal of objects that ended the great surge of creativity known as the High Renaissance. The fact that the Renaissance hardly exists in theological and church history studies has always perplexed and dismayed me. How can a time that produced the art of Leonardo, Michelangelo, and Raphael be ignored by those interested in religious history?

Much of my research centered in these earlier masters, but I was eagerly engaged in the art world of my own day and constantly searching out artists whose work showed a religious dimension, whether it be through iconography or style. I sought out the prominent Abstract Expressionist artists, visiting them in their studios and interviewing them. When Barnett Newman's *Stations of the Cross* (now in the National Gallery in Washington) were first exhibited at the Guggenheim Museum in 1966, I studied these austere, large, black and white canvases and wrote an essay on them for my second book.

I got in touch with Newman, asking him if he would be willing to read my essay before publication. I was concerned that I, a Christian, should not violate his intention in painting the *Stations,* since he was a Jew. He read the essay and gave it his blessing. And so began a lifelong friendship.

I visited Mark Rothko's studio and interviewed him several times while he was working on the velvety dark paintings for the Menil family chapel in Houston. The large unframed canvases of Rothko and Newman resonated with the "Sublime."

My experience of the Abstract Expressionists' large vibrant canvases and their intention as set forth in their writings and in conversation ill-prepared me for Andy Warhol's *Campbell's Soup Cans.* I followed the advent and antics of the Pop artists with increasing anxiety. Their banal subjects and mechanical methods seemed to me the end of art.

In 1970 the Pasadena Museum held the first large survey of the work of Andy Warhol. I went expecting to confirm this opinion, but on entering a large gallery surrounded by his wildly colorful *Flower* paintings, I felt exultant. And a wall of paintings of the *Electric Chair,* in their breath-taking quietude, suggested both death and resurrection. It was clear that Warhol was a creator of stunning images and a great colorist. I was converted—he was admitted to my Pantheon of great artists.

After Warhol's death in 1987, *Vanity Fair* published an article about him by his friend, the art historian John Richardson, with a photograph of Warhol's studio at the time of his death. On the back wall of his studio was a wall-sized Warhol painting of Leonardo da Vinci's *Last Supper.* Excitement! I knew there must be other paintings. I immersed myself in research immediately tracking down the other paintings in this series. This research required intensive sleuthing, fitting together clues, and watching auctions, as well as working with colleagues at the Warhol Foundation and, after its opening, the Andy Warhol Museum. I found that Warhol had painted at least twenty large paintings measuring from twenty-one to thirty-seven feet in width, all based on Leonardo's *Last Supper* and in addition a smaller series, as well as a large group of drawings and prints on paper, certainly totaling more than one hundred works of art in all.The *Last Supper* paintings appear to be Warhol's last series and perhaps his largest. It is also, as Lynne Cooke remarked, arguably Warhol's greatest series. Further, his *Last Supper* paintings are the largest series of religious art by any American artist. John Singer Sargent's murals for the Boston Public Library on the theme of the history of religious thought from paganism to Christianity are the only cycle of works that rivals Warhol's series in size. I discovered that beneath Warhol's public persona was a private Andy—shy, reclusive, religious. And the *Last Supper* paintings, when studied searchingly, yield up their burden of meaning and disclose their religious content. I delved into research on these paintings and five years later, after digging in archives, traveling to see individual paintings, and interviewing family members, studio assistants and friends, my book *The Religious Art of Andy Warhol* (1998) came into being. My strangest and most transforming encounter with a picture was on May 3, 2002. Strange because of the intricacy of the web of coincidences that produced the moment when I first stood transfixed before Oskar Kokoschka's portrait drawing of Wilhelm Koehler.

I was in New York for the first time in quite a few years, to speak about my association with Alfred Barr for the Society for Art Religion and Culture, an organization founded by Barr and Paul Tillich. Of course, being in New York was the occasion for revisiting my beloved paintings in the Met, the Frick, and the Museum of Modern Art and my chance to check out New York's newest museum, the Neue Gallerie. It was in the Neue Gallerie exhibition of Kokoschka's portraits that I suddenly encountered his beautiful drawing of Wilhelm Koehler: the drawing shows an arresting face—acute, fastidious, wholly inward—a soul portrait.

The drawing enchanted me. I had known this man as teacher, scholar, mentor, colleague, and beloved friend. But we met thirty years after Kokoschka drew this haunting portrait of the 28-year-old Viennese art history professor. When I knew him, Koehler was Harvard's famous Carolingian scholar and teacher.

Our friendship began when, by chance, we sat next to each other at a concert in 1943 of Brahms music conducted by Koussevitszky, in Sanders Theater at Harvard. Music was, from that moment till his death in 1959, a strong bond between us. As I mentioned earlier, I took his graduate seminar in Medieval Art and attended electrifying lectures for undergraduates on Michelangelo and Rubens. After leaving Harvard, we met as our lives permitted and we corresponded regularly.

As with my other pivotal encounters with works of art, the Kokoschka drawing redirected the pattern of my life and my inner consciousness. I returned home and located and reread all of his letters. After so many years it was astonishing to find so much of my own life mirrored in them: the births of my two children, my beginning teaching, and then my doctoral studies and my research problems. Subsequently, I gave copies of many of his letters to the Harvard Archives, and found there among his papers, many of my letters to him. Becoming acquainted with the young woman I was, has been a strange experience. In my letters to him, my passion for art and my sense of the organic structure of art history of the Western world is expressed: the primacy of the picture as a work of art above all theories and all academic rhetoric, and with it the power and preciousness of art and our sense of the privilege of teaching art history radiate from his letters and from mine. It was my dialogue with Wilhelm Koehler that focused my passion for art and research. And it was he who brought the experience of sensual beauty into "the conscious embrace of the mind"—Hegel's felicitous phrase. What a rich gift!

In writing this account, I have realized how much of my life at all levels is lived in art. More importantly, it has been art that has startled and perplexed me and ultimately redirected my life. Art provided emblems of suffering when my son was killed, giving a larger context for a sudden, random, pitiful death. Art provided assurance of the power of love when my choice for love caused so much pain to others.

In my years, art has again and again sustained me, summoning me to my true self and grounding me in the common past of our humanity and our faith. Art has given a cohesion and a pattern to what otherwise might be seen as a succession of random occurrences in the flux of illimitable time. It is not that art is my religion, but rather that I experience my faith so deeply in art. Art incarnates, makes visible to our sensibilities, the deeper reality that undergirds our lives, our very being.

## Psyche

She lifts a candle and night, covering its wounds, slips away.
The room contains itself like folded arms:
the lacquer bowl, hair-combs, a camphor smell, gloves
turned in upon themselves, small fists
emptying on air, on this–her grammar of loss
a *body English* spoken by no one else living,
her *terra infirma*, quaking ground.

She stuffs a sack, solitary, with his shirts
in air still sibilant with disapproval, stacks his shoes,
his shaving tackle in a back cupboard under the stairs,
mustering no defense. There never were photographs,
but now the tintype of his face is etched behind her eyelids.
So in time she will resign to follow,
seek him past the fires and the final river,
down through the ground's mouth, undertake unheroic labors,
earn him back with accolades, toddle off with goddesses and gods,
immortal.

But that was her real glimpse of glory: her own hand trembling
over the fall of wax. It is not acceptable not to know,
not to see for oneself, to subsist on a diet of rumors
and promises, gouge out love's eyes for love's sake.
Psyche has shorn her hair, left her golden sandals,
gone out wearing the skin of goats,
but carrying the currency of equals in her purse.

—Jennifer M. Phillips

# Religion and the Visual Arts

# To Touch or Not to Touch

## *Perceiving in Art the Intertextuality of a Faithful and Wise Mary Magdalene with a Doubtful Thomas and a Faithful Miriam*

Douglas G. Adams

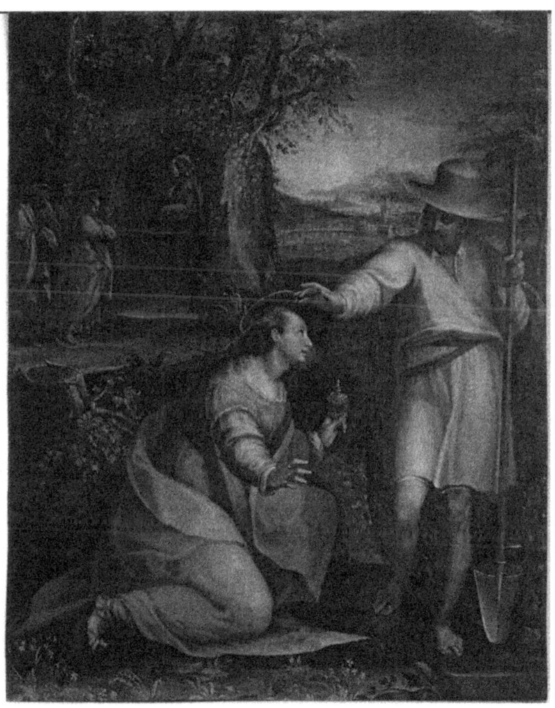

Lavina Fontana. *Jesus Appears to Mary Magdalene.* 1581. (Oil on canvas 80 x 65.5 cm.). Uffizi Gallery, Florence, Italy. Photo by Douglas G. Adams.

Focusing on *Jesus Appears to Mary Magdalene* (1581) by Lavinia Fontana (1552–1614), this essay illumines the intertextuality in art of a faithful and wise Mary Magdalene with a doubtful Thomas and a faithful Miriam. It shows how this and other examples of the *Noli Me Tangere* affirm the Magdalene as evangelist, whom Jesus blesses or commissions—and sometimes subtly touches—while indicating she is not to play a subordinate role. Lavinia Fontana was the first woman painter to be recognized and included in the Uffizi Gallery in Florence, which displays this painting of oil on canvas, 80 x 65.5 cm. The ambiguity of Jesus' gesture in the art may be understood by seeing intertextuality of the Magdalene as the new Miriam to Jesus as the new Moses, and of the Magdalene as the new Wisdom to Jesus as the new Adam.

We read that at the tomb after his resurrection Jesus tells a faithful Mary Magdalene, "Do not touch me, for I have not yet ascended to the Father" (John 20:17). While at first we may think that Jesus is being unkind to Mary Magdalene in telling her not to touch him, later we understand that he honors her faithfulness in that way. A week later at a gathering of the disciples indoors, Jesus is portrayed as inviting an unbelieving Thomas to touch him, "Reach your finger here and see my hands; reach and thrust your hand into my side; do not be faithless, but believe" (John 20:27). The account does not say whether Thomas touched Jesus; and some artists show Thomas touching the wounds while other artists do not. Thomas had said he would not believe unless he touched Christ's wounds: "Unless I put my finger into the place where the nails were, and my hand into his side, I will not believe it" (John 20:25). In contrast, Mary Magdalene believes without touching. While she first thought him to be a gardener, the moment he calls out "Mary," she responds "Rabbouni!," which the Gospel says means "My Master" (John 20:16-17).

In rendering the scene of Jesus and Mary Magdalene near the tomb, many artists show her kneeling and reaching out toward Jesus. (In John's gospel there is no mention of her kneeling, but in Matthew 28:8-10, both Mary Magdalene and the other Mary fall prostrate at the feet of Jesus when he appears on a path some distance from where they had seen an angel roll away the stone that sealed the tomb.) At the center of the foreground, Lavinia Fontana's "Jesus Appears to Mary Magdalene" places the Magdalene kneeling near Jesus, who stands in the foreground at the viewer's far right. In the background is the scriptural scene from Luke 24:1-2 where Mary Magdalene leads a procession of other women (identified in Luke 24:10 as Joanna and Mary the mother or wife or daughter of James, but in Mark 16:1 as Salome and Mary the mother of James and in Matthew 28:1-2 as only "the other Mary").

The women approach the tomb, which is empty except for two angels (John 20:11-12) or for a youth wearing a white robe (Mark 16:5). That procession of women may remind us of another procession of women, which Miriam led in dance at the Exodus; and so Mary Magdalene is cast as the new Miriam to Jesus as the new Moses. Within this understanding, we may see his moving away from Mary Magdalene and saying "Do not touch me" as a parallel to Moses' rejection of Miriam, who went into the desert as a leper, not to be touched by anyone. In Jesus' gesture of blessing or touching the Magdalene, we may remember the intervention of the people who interceded for Miriam and who asked Moses to provide care for her near them, just outside the camp. As Miriam was the one who was always faithful to Moses for whom she cared, so Mary Magdalene is recognized as always faithful to Jesus for whom she cared.

Such art therefore parallels the intertextuality employed by the gospels of Mark and Matthew, which present Jesus as the new Moses and tell the stories of Jesus in terms of the stories of Moses from Exodus and Deuteronomy. At the birth of each, rulers order the death of Hebrew male children, for they fear their reigns will be overthrown by a newborn who might be a king or a leader. Both Moses and Jesus spend time in Egypt; both later experience the wilderness before undertaking their missions. As Moses parts the waters of the Reed Sea so people safely reach the other shore, Jesus stills the waters so the boats reach the other side of the Sea of Galilee. As the sea drowns Pharaoh's army, so the sea drowns the pigs into which the demon called "Legion" enters with Jesus' permission. As Moses feeds the people in the wilderness, Jesus feeds the people in the wilderness. As Moses receives the Ten Commandments on the mountain, Jesus gives the Sermon on the Mount. Moses leads the twelve tribes, as Jesus leads the twelve disciples. Moses is associated with the establishment of the Passover Seder meal, as Jesus is associated with the institution of communion. Moses strikes the rock, while Jesus curses the fig tree. As there are parallels of Moses and Jesus, so also are there parallels with Miriam and Mary Magdalene. Miriam heralds the triumph of Moses in leading the dance of women after the exodus from Egypt, as Mary Magdalene leads the procession of women to the tomb and heralds the resurrection of Jesus.[1]

In the foreground of Fontana's painting, the kneeling Mary Magdalene holds a jar in her left hand. This reminds us of an earlier scriptural story of a Mary who broke open the jar of costly nard to anoint Jesus' feet and to wipe them with her hair (John 12:3). Judas criticized her for such extravagance, but Jesus told Judas not to criticize her: "Let her alone. Let her keep it for the

1 For many more parallels, see Edward Hobbs, "The Gospel of Mark and the Exodus" (Ph.D. dissertation, University of Chicago, 1958).

day of my burial" (John 12:7). Kneeling before another person and washing his or her feet was also an act of a servant as Jesus emphasizes in washing the disciples' feet in John 13:1-17. In this post-resurrection scene near the tomb, when Jesus tells Mary Magdalene not to touch him, he is honoring her by telling her not to play the role of his servant. She looks ready to wash his feet, but he has a more elevated role for her as the text details his words to her. The text continues with his words to her: "Go to my brothers and tell them that I am going to ascend to my Father and your Father, to my God and your God" (John 20:17). She immediately responds by bringing the news to the disciples: "I have seen the Lord and he has told me this" (John 20:18). In so doing, she becomes the first evangelist.

In Lavinia Fontana's painting, Jesus' right hand reaches out in an ambiguous gesture toward Mary Magdalene. His hand could be indicating for her to stay back or it could be blessing her. One of his fingers touches her halo, so while he is telling her not to touch him, he comes close to touching her. His left hand holds a shovel reminding us that she had thought he was the gardener; the shovel pointed into the earth also reminds us of death. In the last judgment scenes, the left hand of Jesus often is pointed in the direction of the unfaithful damned who go to hell, and his right hand is toward the faithful saved who go to heaven. This art, and the scripture upon which it is based, designate Mary Magdalene as an evangelist who is blessed in the company of the one who saves.

In his touching her halo and calling attention to it, several other meanings may be communicated. The halo is an abbreviated form of the mandorla, the oval shape that surrounds the seated Christ in majesty, as on the facade of Chartres Cathedral. It also suggests the entrance way to the womb or to the mother church. As the church is Notre Dame, to be within the halo or the mandorla indicates that one is in the body of Mary or within the body of the church. In art, the halo is usually reserved for those who have died, while the square mortar board is the acknowledgment of inclusion for those who are still alive.[2]

In some other sixteenth-century Italian examples of the *Noli Me Tangere*, Jesus touches Mary Magdalene. At the Uffizi, there is a painting by Federico Barocci (1535–1612) wherein the left foot of Jesus touches the hem of Mary Magdalene's dress. Nearby in the Bargello, the hand of Jesus subtly reaches around behind Mary Magdalene's head to touch her hair in the large *Noli Me Tangere* ceramic (ca.1520) by Benedetto e Santi Buglioni. While one could say that Italians find not touching unthinkable, I am inclined to see such

[2] For more about the halo and mandorla shape in art, see Doug Adams, *Transcendence with the Human Body in Art: Segal, De Staebler, Johns, and Christo* (New York: Crossroad, 1991) 77–78.

subtle touching as softening the words "Do not touch me," as affirming and blessing Mary Magdalene, or even as commissioning her in an evangelical mission to tell the disciples of the resurrection.

The many artists' portrayals of Mary Magdalene as kneeling close to the resurrected Christ in the garden remind the viewer of her faithfulness in another earlier biblical story. She is often portrayed as the one closest to Christ on the cross: she kneels at the feet of Christ being crucified even when the disciples have fled, except for John who sometimes is portrayed as present with Mary the Mother.[3] In some art, Mary Magdalene is the only person anywhere near the crucified Christ.[4] Other art may help us see Mary Magdalene either as Miriam or even more as the new wisdom (or serpent) to Jesus as the new Adam and Mary the Mother as the new Eve. The Magdalene is shown along with Mary the Mother and the baby Jesus in works such as El Greco's *The Holy Family with Mary Magdalene* (seventeenth century) in the Cleveland Museum of Art. The Magdalene seems to be counseling or encouraging Mary, whose right hand shares two figs with the baby Jesus. The Magdalene's head touches Mary's head as the Magdalene's right arm encircles Mary's back, and the Magdalene's hand rests on Mary's shoulder, seemingly animating Mary's sharing of the figs with Jesus. Miriam would be present with the mother when the baby Moses is being nurtured and so could be seen in the Magdalene in such art, but even stronger is the intertextuality with the Magdalene as the new wisdom (serpent) urging Mary (as the new Eve) to share the fruit with Jesus (the new Adam). For El Greco as well for Michelangelo, the fig was the tempting fruit of the tree of knowledge. In such an art work, the imagery tacitly reminds us that Mary and Jesus and Mary Magdalene reverse the fall and all have a role in making possible the good news of resurrection.

Another artistic parallel reminds us of the wisdom of Lavinia Fontana's red-robed kneeling Magdalene with her jar held in her left hand. In some renderings of the *Adoration of the Wisemen*, one of the wise men is shown dressed in a red robe, kneeling before the Christ child, and holding a jar in his left hand.[5] That jar of myrrh in the hand of the wise man reminds us of the jar in the hand of Mary Magdalene, who brought spices and perfumes to the tomb (Luke 24:1-2). And so we may understand her as the wise woman as well as the faithful evangelist.

3 See for example Giotto's *The Crucifixion*, 1303–05, The Scrovegni (Arena) Chapel, Padua.

4 See Luca Signorelli's *Crucifix with Mary Magdalene*, 1502–05, Uffizi, Florence.

5 See Filippino Lippi's *Adoration of the Magi*, 1496, Uffizi, Florence.

# Pictures and Popular Religion in Early Christianity

## *Art as the Bible of the Illiterate?*

Robin M. Jensen

A well-known aphorism, that art functions as the "Bible of the illiterate," generally comes up in any discussion of the value of visual art in religious contexts. Usually meant by the one who cites it to be an endorsement of art's functional value, the adage also (and sometimes unconsciously) implies that art's principal beneficiaries are children, the uneducated, or those with little sophistication or intellect. People of learning or those who are spiritually advanced have left such things behind. Like middle-school children who have advanced beyond picture books to chapter books, art is for the sake of those who can't yet read and so need visual aids in the meantime.

Scholars usually attribute the original assertion to Gregory the Great (ca. 600 C.E.), whose classic formulation of the argument occurs in two epistles, written to his brother Bishop Serenus of Marseilles, documenting one of the first known instances of iconoclasm directed against Christian images. In the first of these letters, Gregory tells Serenus that it has come to his attention that, after having discovered that certain members of his flock were adorers of images (*imaginum adoratores*), Serenus broke and tossed out (*confregit atque proiecit*) the offending objects. While praising him for his zeal against idolatry, Gregory tells Serenus that he should not have destroyed the images and asks him to consider the positive function these images also serve, "that such as are ignorant of letters (*hi qui litteras nesciunt*) may at least read by looking at the walls what they cannot read inbooks."[1] In other words, Gregory tells

[1] Gregory I, *Letters* 9.105, NPNF 13, 23, CCSL 140A, 768.

Serenus to stop his iconoclastic actions, but supports his overarching stance against idolatry.

In Gregory's second letter to Serenus, a year or so later, he takes a more severe tone and tries to assert some authority over him. Evidently Serenus paid little heed to Gregory's first admonition (using the excuse that he assumed Gregory's letter had been forged) and began again to break images and throw them out of churches. Gregory, upset that his urgings had been ignored and appalled at the consequences, again admonishes Serenus to stop the destruction, and once more demonstrates his (Gregory's) pastoral concern for the edification of the unlearned:

> For to adore a picture is one thing, but to learn through the story of a picture what is to be adored is another. For what writing presents to readers, this a picture presents to the unlearned who behold (*hoc idiotis preaestat pictura cernentibus*), since in it even the ignorant (*ignorantes*) see what they ought to follow; in it the illiterate (*litteras nesciunt*) read. Hence, and chiefly to the [foreign] nations (*gentibus*), a picture is instead of reading.[2]

However, instead of instructing them in the right use of visual art, Serenus's actions prevented his flock from availing themselves of a useful instrument for their inspiration and instruction—an aid to a "pious dispensation." Even worse, it turns out that the Bishop of Marseille's campaign has led to a split within the community and caused general scandal and trauma for the church. Gregory therefore exhorts Serenus to announce sweetly to his flock: "If for this instruction for which images were anciently made you wish to have them in the church, I permit them by all means both to be made and to be had."[3]

Gregory's lines were echoed throughout the subsequent history of Western Christianity and show up in any number of western medieval writers, from Bede to Bonaventure to Aquinas. In most of these cases the idea was simply reiterated, that pictures served as aids to the unlearned and were part of a general defense of the usefulness of visual art.[4] Bonaventure, for example,

[2] Gregory I, *Letters* 11.13, NPNF 13:53–54, CCSL 140A, 873–76.

[3] Ibid., trans. 54. I am indebted to the excellent article by C. M. Chazelle, "Pictures, Books, and the Illiterate: Pope Gregory I's letters to Serenus of Marseilles," *Word and Image* 6.2 (1990) 138–53. This article provides a close reading of the relevant texts and some contemporary parallels, and argues that Gregory did not mean to suggest that such images could function apart from knowledge of the texts.

[4] See the survey of Gregory's possible influences, as well as his own influence on later (medieval and western) theologians, by L. Duggan, "Was Art Really the 'Book of the Illiterate'?" *Word and Image* 5.3 (1989) 227–51. See also H. Kessler, "Pictorial Narrative and Church Mission in Sixth-Century Gaul," and "Diction in the Bibles of the Illiterate," in *Studies in Pictorial*

claims that images were made for the sake of "the simplicity of the ignorant, so that the uneducated who are unable to read scripture can, through statues and paintings of this kind read about the sacraments of our faith in, as it were, more open scriptures." However, Bonaventure also expands on the value of images for the sake of stimulating and maintaining piety, adding that images also were introduced because seeing with the eye is more effective than hearing with the ear for arousing devotion and because images are better aids to memory than words.[5]

By contrast, the sixteenth-century Protestant reformers challenged the power or effectiveness of images, even for the unlearned, and many of them even advocated the kind of iconoclasm that Gregory had condemned. Although John Calvin himself did not promote the destruction of images, he actually refers to Gregory by name—not in order to reinforce or praise his defense of visual art for the church, but rather to disparage images and to privilege the word. According to Calvin, anyone who deems images useful for instructing the faithful is doing them more harm than good: "I know it is pretty much an old saw that images are the books of the uneducated. Gregory said this: yet the Spirit of God declares far otherwise; we have learned from the prophets that whatever we learn of God from images is futile, indeed false."[6]

In any case, as Gregory claims to support his position, he was not the first church official who saw some value in visual art. According to him, the church used pictorial representations in this way since ancient times. Such an appeal to venerable tradition provides him good cover for his defense of images. And, in fact, at least one earlier Latin author, Paulinus of Nola, had claimed a similarly positive function for visual art, its ostensible aim being to reach the unlearned through their appreciation of pictures. Paulinus defended his almost obvious appreciation of the visual art that he placed in his church as a means of "enlivening" the church that he founded in honor of St. Felix, and as an effective way to lure "country folk unskilled in reading" away from their rowdy feasts at martyrs' graves and into the church for more solemn celebrations. According to him, however, the paintings not only educated but also inspired "rustics" to more lofty pursuits than holding picnics at a saint's shrine. Having thus provided a more salutary tourist attraction, Paulinus claims that his decorated walls have been a success: "Notice in what

---

*Narrative* (London: Pindar, 1994) 2–40.

5 Bonaventure, *Commentary on the Sentences of Peter Lombard*, lib. 3. sent. 9, art. 1. q. 2. An English translation of this text, as well as a brief discussion of its sources and influence, may be found in C. Garside, *Zwingli and the Arts* (New Haven: Yale University Press, 1966) 90–93.

6 Calvin, *Institutes* 1.11.5.

numbers they assemble from all the country districts, and how they roam around, their unsophisticated minds beguiled in devotion."[7]

By contrast, to the east, and a few decades earlier, the Cappadocian fathers had discussed the usefulness of art, without disparaging its values or presuming pictures were primarily made for the sake of the unlearned. Unlike Paulinus, they offered no excuses for visual art; in their opinion, rather than creating competition between paintings of the saints and their relics, visual representations of saints' heroic deeds were appropriately near their relics and equated with inspirational oral narratives that described their valiant acts and sacrificial deaths. The Cappadocians' perspective challenges a too-simple conclusion that early church intellectuals or authorities typically valued words more than images or thought that pictures were for the uneducated.

Basil of Caesarea, for example, delivered a feast-day homily in the church housing the relics of the Forty Martyrs. In this homily he proclaimed that the words of orators, like the images of visual artists, are equally able to make dead heroes vividly present, exciting courage and commitment in listeners and observers alike. He says, "Those parts of the story that a sermon presents through the hearing, the silent picture sets before the eyes for the sake of imitation."[8] We can assume that Basil's sermon was addressed to an audience that was comprised of both readers and nonreaders, whose sentiments were aroused as much by the rhetoric of the speaker as the work of the visual artist. Basil certainly could have argued that a well-preached sermon is also a "book of the illiterate."

In a similar fashion Basil's brother, Gregory of Nyssa praised the paintings in a martyrium dedicated to St. Theodore near Amaseia in Pontus. Admiring the beauty of the building and its elaborate interior space with its beautiful mosaics, wood carving, and masonry, Gregory specifically commends the paintings depicting the saint's heroism, adding: "all of these he [the painter] wrought by means of colors as if it were a book that uttered speech . . . for painting, even if it is silent, is capable of speaking from the wall and being of the greatest benefit."[9] Very much like Basil, Gregory here identifies painting as a silent, but highly effective form of storytelling, and makes no claim that such pictures were intended specifically for the illiterate members of the flock.

7 Paulinus, *Carm.* 27.

8 Basil, *Hom.* 19, in PG 31:507–10. The Forty Martyrs were executed by Licinius in ca. 316, frozen to death on a lake near Sebaste.

9 Gregory of Nyssa, *St. Theod. Mart.* PG 46:739–40, trans. C. Mango, *The Art of the Byzantine Empire 312–1453, Sources and Documents* (Toronto: University of Toronto Press, 1986) 36–37. Mango notes some doubt about Gregory's authorship of this letter.

Lest this evidence lead to a conclusion that Greek-speaking church authorities were more pro-art than those in the Latin-speaking West, we should note that the late fourth-century Latin poet Prudentius wrote highly literate verses containing detailed descriptions of paintings of martyrs, as well as scenes from the Old and New Testaments. Prudentius was clearly an art-enthusiast, and never gives the impression that visual art was in any way controversial or only for the illiterate.[10] Moreover, two examples from the East offer closer parallels to Gregory's view of the value of pictures for the unlettered. The first is credited to the ascetic St. Nilus of Ancyra, a younger contemporary of Paulinus. In a letter responding to the Eparch Olympiodorus concerning a church that he (Olympiodorus) was about to build in honor of the holy martyrs, Nilus confirms that while some church art is merely distracting decoration, other art has a salutary and edifying purpose. Olympiodorus had asked whether it would be appropriate to set up images of the saints in the sanctuary in order to show forth their labors and sufferings, as well as elaborate paintings of exotic animals, birds and reptiles, hunts, and fishing scenes on the side walls, in order to delight the eye of the visitor. Nilus responds that the merely decorative natural images are infantile and distracting to the eyes of the faithful and that it would be better simply to place a single cross in the sanctuary. On the other hand, he encourages Olympiodorus to have a skilled painter cover the adjacent walls on both sides with illustrated stories from the Old and New Testaments, so that those who are unable to read or understand the Holy Scriptures may, "by gazing at the pictures, become mindful of the heroic deeds of those who have genuinely served the true God, and may be roused to emulate those glorious and celebrated feats."[11]

The second example comes from the early sixth-century Bishop of Ephesus, Hypatius, who (like Gregory) took a fellow bishop to task for destroying pictures in his church for the same reason that Serenus allegedly had: because they were mistaken for objects of worship. Writing to Julian of Atramytium, Hypatius offers a two-level view of art: "We ordain that the unspeakable and incomprehensible love of God for us and the sacred patterns set by the saints be celebrated in holy writings since so far as we are concerned, we take no pleasure at all in sculpture or painting. But we permit

[10] Prudentius, *Peristephanon* (Martyrs' Crowns) and *Dittochaeon* (Twofold Nourishment). See M. Roberts, *Poetry and the Cult of the Martyrs: The Liber Peristephanon of Prudentius* (Ann Arbor: University of Michigan Press, 1993). On the eastern side, compare Aterius of Amaseia, *On Dives and Lazarus*; and *In Praise of Euphemia*, both texts describing visual representations of martyrs, as well as John Chrysostom, *Homily in Praise of Melitius*; all three documents can be found in English translation in Mango, *Art of the Byzantine Empire*, 37–40.

[11] Nilus, *Ep.* 4, 61 (Olympiodoro Eparcho), PG 79:577–80, trans. Mango, *Art of the Byzantine Empire*, 32 (slightly adapted).

simpler people, as they are less perfect, to learn by way of initiation about such things by [the sense of] sight, which is more appropriate to their natural development, especially as we find that, often and in many respects, even old and new divine commandments lower themselves to the level of weaker people and their souls for the sake of their salvation."[12] Hypatius continues, however, with a somewhat contrasting argument, making a comparison between images and the use of analogies in language or the use of metaphors or familiar stories. He believes that many of faithful can be guided and lifted up toward the divine beauty and immaterial light through the inspiration of the intelligible beauty and light found in the sanctuaries that are adorned with the work of fine artisans.[13]

Thus, from the fourth century forward, certain Christian teachers assumed that art along with oral storytelling or sermonic exposition might be very useful as an aid to the faithful, both illiterate and literate, for their inspiration, discipline, and devotion. Conversely, visual art also was seen as potentially problematic, if a line was not firmly established against inappropriate adoration of images or neglect of the written word in favor of pictures. A canon from a local church council held in Elvira, Spain, in 305 demonstrates a concern similar to that of the Bishop of Marseille, but it comes nearly three hundred years earlier. The Latin of the canon reads, "*Placuit picturas in ecclesia esse non debere, ne quod colitur et adoratur in parietibus depingatur*" and may be translated: "There shall be no pictures in churches, lest what is reverenced and adored be depicted on the walls." An alternative translation reverses the verb and pronoun modifiers and reads instead: "lest what is depicted on the walls be reverenced and adored." Both versions prohibit art in the churches, but for slightly different reasons. The first suggests that certain holy things might be wrongly portrayed if visual art is allowed at all, the second raises concern about the possible misuse of any religious art.[14]

In any case, almost no extant ancient writing suggests that since pictures were primarily designed for the less educated or adept members of the

12 Text and trans., P. J. Alexander, *Religious and Political History and Thought in the Byzantine Empire: Collected Studies* (London: Variorum Reprints, 1978) 6:117–84. See also S. Gero, "Hypatius of Ephesus on the Cult of Images," in *Christianity, Judaism and Other Greco-Roman Cults: Studies for Morton Smith at Sixty*, ed. Jacob Neusner (Leiden: Brill, 1975) 2:208–16. Whether Hypatius's letter had any influence on Gregory (and whether Gregory read Greek) is a subject raised by several scholars and discussed by Chazelle, "Pictures, Books, and the Illiterate," 145–46.

13 See Alexander, "Hypatius," 180 for the translation (slightly adapted by this author).

14 Council of Elvira, Latin text and translation in C. J. Hefele, *History of the Christian Councils*, trans. W. Clark (London: T. & T. Clark, 1894) 151. A discussion of the alternative readings was summarized by M. C. Murray, "Art and the Early Church," *JTS* 18 (1977) 229 and n.2.

community, it would be sign of true progress and universal enlightenment if the church could eventually dispense with such aids altogether and worship God in "spirit and in truth."[15] This point of view really only emerged during the periods of iconoclasm, in the eighth century in the East and during the Protestant Reformation in the West, when visual art was generally associated with idolatry and efforts were made to expunge it from the church. Prior to that, concerns were raised in certain places about the proper use and value of particular kinds of art and the need to understand art's benefits as well as possible abuse, but visual art itself was never generally condemned. Nevertheless, later historians and theologians, especially those coming from those reformed traditions that are wary or even condemnatory of visual art in the church, often portray early Christians as universally aniconic and resistant to the idolatrous materialism of the pagan culture, which would have included all kinds of pictorial art.[16]

These perceptions, combined with the lack of extant evidence for Christian visual art prior to the late second century, led such scholars not only to argue that the earliest, "original" Christians were anti-art because they were also consciously obedient to the requirements of the second commandment. According to this view, these true believers fashioned no graven images because, like good Jews, they wanted to avoid the idolatry inherent in the manufacture and use of art objects.[17] Eventually, the prohibition was gradually loosened by the next generations of church officials who, while they remained opposed to images, realized that some concessions were necessary because of the influx of half-hearted pagan converts who were not fully indoctrinated into, nor rigorously committed to, the strictures of their new religion. Thus, art is perceived to be something that challenged the sensibilities and values of the theologically aware, but yet was tolerated for the sake of newer members of the flock, who didn't understand that their adopted

[15] Here I distinguish between idols or cult statues (which were repudiated by many early writers) and visual art in general, and especially narrative images depicting biblical stories or deeds of the saints.

[16] See for example, Adolf von Harnack's *Lehrbuch der Dogmengeschichte*, 3 vols., 4th ed. (Tübingen: Mohr, 1909) 2:467–79. Here Harnack argues that an original anti-material, "spiritual" Christianity became gradually Hellenized through the era of pagan conversion.

[17] T. Klauser's serially published essays, "Studien zur Entstehungsgeschichte der christlichen Kunst," *JAC* 1 (1958) 20–51 through 10 (1967) 82–120, used archaeological evidence to argue that early Christians were essentially aniconic. More recently, M. Frazier made this same claim, *Age of Spirituality*, ed. K. Weitzmann (New York: Metropolitan Museum of Art, 1979) 513. See M. Charles Murray's excellent challenge to this classic position, "Art and the Early Church," 302–45; and P. C. Finney's subsequent work, *The Invisible God: The Earliest Christians on Art* (New York: Oxford University Press, 1994).

religion asked them to worship God in spirit and in truth and to renounce the mediation of crass material objects made by human hands.[18]

More recently, however, some historians studying the cultural context or social matrix of the early church have presented a different perspective of the situation, but one that still maintains a marked distinction between readers and nonreaders in early Christianity and presents those two groups representing the "official" tradition on one hand and those who practiced "popular" religion on the other.[19] The second group, "the common folk" in this view, might further be linked to certain marginalized groups or the lower classes, who are portrayed as more likely than to incorporate visual art into their devotional lives than the more educated and powerful members of the community and either to resist or be unaware of the judgment of elitist church officials who comprised the ecclesial establishment and believed that pictures could be dangerous and lead people astray into idolatry.

The difference between these two scholarly views is more one of sympathy than of substance, however, since both positions maintain that early Christian art was primarily made for or even by the unsophisticated, underprivileged, or common folk, as opposed to those in authority. In the first instance this "disadvantaged" group is assumed to have been comprised of pagan converts who continued in familiar idolatrous habits, either unaware of, or resistant to, the urgings of officials, while in the second instance, the art users are identified with the economically disadvantaged or socially marginalized nonreaders of the society, including those coming from the lower social classes, foreigners, and women. Moreover, while the first view tends to portray the art users in a negative light, as only half-baked Christians, the second view casts them more sympathetically, and sometimes as resistant to

18 For instance consider H. Chadwick's claim that early Christian teachers regarded the prohibition of images as absolutely binding on Christians and that images and cult statues belonged exclusively to the pagans, or (in the second century) to Gnostic heretics. See Chadwick, *The Early Church* (London: Penguin, 1967) 277. Augustine similarly discredited the cult of the martyrs and their feasts, by claiming that they were vestiges of a pagan past, but at the same time tolerated them in private spaces, for practical and pastoral reasons, offering some consideration for the weaker members of the congregation, *Ep*. 22, 29.

19 This is a very rough view of the position of Graydon Snyder, as elucidated in the first edition of his much-used handbook, *Ante Pacem: The Archaeological Evidence of Church Life before Constantine* (Macon, Ga.: Mercer University Press, 1985) 3–7. Snyder credits the German scholars, Hans Leitzmann, Franz Joseph Dölger, and Theodor Klauser as founders of a more scientific, "non-dogmatic, archaeological" approach to the study of early Christian art. Snyder further cites the work of those who have studied the social context of early Christianity, including Wayne Meeks and Gerd Theissen.

dogmatically narrow authorities, and the art they used as a subtle but potentially subversive medium of expression.[20]

A related controversy is over the relative value of ancient texts for the interpretation of early Christian art and the complexity that different interpreters credit to the artworks themselves. For example, some scholars have treated most images as merely illustrative of ideas expressed in texts—as straightforward pictorial signs or referents to stories found in scripture, or rather simplistic didactic images on the order of those found in illustrated Bibles for children. For others the images contain cryptic or encoded messages of hope or deliverance, or even having a wide range of possible meanings or profound significance, revealing much more about the culture than they might at first appear to do.[21]

Older historians who viewed the emergence of visual art as a sign of insipient decadence or lack of theological sophistication, ironically also tended to interpret the images themselves through a doctrinal or dogmatic lens, referring to normative teaching and traditions as if the ideas in iconography and texts presented a unified or coherent theology. For example, when Walter Lowrie, first wrote his *Christian Art and Archaeology* at the turn of the last century, he depended on the groundbreaking work of members of the Roman school, including Giovanni De Rossi and Joseph Wilpert. In this work, as in his later edition in the mid-1940s, he asserts that Christian theologians were almost universally opposed to art.[22] At the same time, he claims that Christian art was subservient to its content, "an abstract theological content," and that subject matter was derived from early Christian literature and biblical exegesis. He agrees with Wilpert's view that although the artisans who first made Christian images were likely pagans, they were directed by Christian patrons, who received theological assistance that prescribed themes and influenced

[20] Snyder, for example, identifies two distinct social groups within the church; the rural "cemetery party," which was theologically simple and identified with the common folk, and the urban group, which was more focused on dogma and sympathetic to secular authorities, 163–64. I note that in his second edition of this book (Mercer University Press, 2003), he takes a more subtle and nuanced position on this point. See also the early work of Margaret R. Miles, *Image as Insight* (Boston: Beacon, 1985) 36–38, where she asserts that visual images in general "are primarily addressed to comprehending physical existence," and "provide a history of the ways by which the non-privileged understood and coped with physical existence" against the "antagonism of a few theologians to visual images and their injunctions to 'spiritual'—that is, verbal—worship of God." She adds that it would be mistaken to exaggerate a "few men's antagonism to image," however, and says that typically they only urged "critical appropriation of images" rather than their exclusive use.

[21] See Ernst Kitzinger, *Byzantine Art in the Making* (Cambridge: Harvard University Press, 1980) 20, where he describes early Christian images as "ciphers conveying an idea," which he identifies as "a message of deliverance and security through divine intervention."

[22] Walter Lowrie, *Art in the Early Church* (New York: Norton, 1969) 9–13.

the forms.[23] Simply stated, his view is that art, even if grudgingly allowed by church authorities, was nonetheless under their supervision. Interpreters of this art should then refer to the writings of early learned theologians as their primary source.

Contrary to this position is a more modern suspicion of using literary evidence as the primary tool for interpreting visual art and a consequent perceived value in analyzing the iconography of the early church apart from reference to written documents, which may impose certain interpretations or viewpoints, rather than letting the art "speak for itself."[24] By avoiding the "textism" of merely hunting down clues in ancient documents in order to explain art objects, these scholars hope to have a more unprejudiced analysis of the imagery free from the unfortunate skewing of its meaning toward conformity with one or another orthodox portrayal of the church. Instead, they argue art should be examined within the context of the socio-cultural context and compared with the remains of contemporary religions and other evidence of popular culture. Taken together with the view that art reveals the religious values or beliefs of those "from below," this approach arguably offers some glimpse of the religious sentiments and values of those overlooked and/or ignored groups of nonreaders for whom we have little other evidence and for whom the art may have been made in any case (if we subscribe to the "Bible of the illiterate" proposition).

In addition, according to this view, art has its own mode of communication and should not be presumed simplistically subservient to an idea expressed in the writings of intellectuals or church officials. According to Brendan Cassidy: "Only at some times, in some places, and in particular cultural milieux, were images created to convey philosophical propositions or subtleties of Christian doctrine"[25] Furthermore, images are more open to multiple meanings than texts and potentially provoke an almost infinite number of different responses in viewers. As Margaret Miles argues in *Image as Insight*: "Surely visual religious images are susceptible to an even more bewildering

23 Ibid., 4–7.

24 Snyder cites V. Schultz who argued in the late nineteenth century "that a painting should be understood in terms of its immediate context rather than according to patristic or dogmatic norms," *Ante Pacem*, 6. Snyder later praises scholars who have sought to avoid literary evidence in their analysis of archaeological remains, 10. See the important summary article of B. Cassidy, "Introduction: Iconography, Texts and Audiences," *Iconography at the Crossroads*, Index of Christian Art 2 (Princeton: Princeton University Press, 1993), 1-15; as well as R. Jensen, "Giving Texts Vision and Images Voice," and D. Cartlidge, "Which Path at the Crossroads: Early Christian Art as a Hermeneutical and Theological Challenge," in *Common Life in the Early Church: Essays Honoring Graydon F. Snyder*, ed. Julian V. Hills (Harrisburg, Pa.: Trinity, 1998) 344–56 and 357–72.

25 Cassidy, *Iconography*, 8.

range of understandings and misunderstandings than are written theological formulations." A little further on Miles adds: "The use of images in worship modifies the tendency of words to exclude people who cannot subscribe to a precisely defined concept. Images also challenge the tendency to confine ourselves religiously to intellectualizing activity."[26] This argument sends a strong signal that historians ought to pay more attention to the messages conveyed by and with images and to seek to discover the original meaning or import of religious art in more than theological texts or treatises. Instead, those who wish to understand visual art must take a wider view of the cultural context and circumstances in which the work was made and used.

Hence, the argument that Gregory the Great made more than thirteen hundred years ago still seems very relevant to the way historians view and analyze the evidence of visual art and returns us to the basic question of whether early Christian art was in some sense folk art, specifically intended as an aid for the unlearned, or some kind of especially revealing entrée into the world of nonlanguage users over against language users, to use Roland Barthes' distinction between the majority in a culture whose use of language is unselfconscious and the minority who are skilled in the use of language and who leave a legacy that historians more easily access.[27] A related problem is who Gregory's illiterate nonreaders were and whether they can be equated with a distinct underprivileged class or some group excluded from, or perhaps in opposition to, religious authority. A final question is whether the meaning or message of visual art shares in or diverges from official religious teachings (the great tradition), as they are discerned from chronologically contemporaneous documents.

If we return to a careful examination of Gregory's two letters, we can see that his concern is essentially pastoral. The images he wants Serenus to stop destroying were not made *only* for the illiterate and non-Latin speaking members of the community, although they were certainly displayed in the church for the sake of their edification and as an aid to developing a pious attitude (*adiuuetur in studio piae dispensationis*), which would have been beneficial for anyone, literate or not. Gregory suggests that the very sight of these depictions of heroic and holy deeds will inspire (all) viewers to bow down, not to the images, but solely to the omnipotent Holy Trinity. Determining whom Gregory means when he refers to the foreigners (*gentes*) or the illiterate or ignorant (*illiteratus*, *nescians litteras*, *ignorans*, *idiota*) ones—and whether

[26] Miles, *Image as Insight*, 32–33. Here, citing Roland Barthes's *Image–Music–Text* (New York: Hill and Wang, 1977) 199, Miles clarifies that she does not wish to assert that "intellectualizing" is the exclusive prerogative of the educationally privileged, but might be a sign of "siding with the power of language."

[27] Miles discusses this distinction, referring to Barthes, in *Image as Insight,* 18–22.

these are all the same persons—is more problematic, however. It is possible that this group is merely an abstract type for the purpose of his argument. If, however, he has a specific group in mind, perhaps those persons who were unable to read and write in Latin (*nescians litteras*), or even the non-Roman native population in and around Marseilles (*gentes*), the group would likely be rather large. But if he only means those who were unable to understand some spoken Latin, or had no understanding of the church's teachings and tradition even through orally delivered sermons or catechism, the group would be comparably small.[28]

To make matters worse, Serenus's tempestuous actions, most certainly reported to Gregory by some of those most scandalized or infuriated, caused a schism in the church. And this schismatic group was not a small minority either, since the letter states that the greatest part of the membership withdrew from communion with their bishop—a dangerous situation at a time when unity was seen as a paramount value. It is worth noting that Gregory must have received word of Serenus's continuing iconoclasm by means of a letter written by a representative of the pro-image group who were in open rebellion against their bishop. Moreover, that letter must have been sent by courier to Rome, a costly undertaking. Gregory's response urges Serenus to be solicitous and "make haste to recall" those wandering sheep, and also to make it clear that what displeased him was not their possession of the images, nor the contents of them, but that adoration had been mistakenly shown. He instructs Serenus to remind his flock that images were made for instruction even in antiquity. Gregory suggests that Serenus will in this way soothe their minds and bring them back into harmony with him.

Carefully read, the letter seems to suggest that religious pictures may actually have at least two valuable functions, first to instruct the illiterate and/or non-Latin speakers, by seeing the story, and second, to inspire the faithful in general to a pious attitude. The second function is comparable to the value and function of narrative or biblical images as described by Basil and Gregory of Nyssa and may apply to the majority of Serenus's flock, while the unlettered users of art were a smaller subgroup. Also, if Basil's, Gregory's or Nilus's descriptions of the iconography as found in the martyria are at all comparable, these works of art were not made for or by the lower classes or the uneducated, no matter how edifying they may have been for those groups. Rather they seem to be rather extensive and complex images that must have been made at great expense—most likely paid for by a patron of some financial means.

28 See Chazan, 142, and H. L. Kessler, "Pictorial Narrative and Church Mission," 21–22; and M. Camille "Seeing and Reading: Some Visual Implications of Medieval Literacy and Illiteracy," *Art History* 8 (1985) 26–49.

The fact that these paintings were commissioned for and placed in cathedrals and other official ecclesial spaces also seriously challenges the theory that the imagery informed or reflected the particular faith or values of marginalized members of the society or projected the theological positions of an oppositional group. Moreover, neither Serenus nor Gregory refer to the paintings' content as an issue, but only to their problematic misuse versus their potential value. Gregory's statements imply that the images were perfectly acceptable as such and, properly understood, could inspire an appropriate and pious response on the part of the viewer. Nor do we see any concessions to or concerns about art especially promoting a theology "from below" in the relevant writings of Basil, Gregory of Nyssa, Nilus, or even the elitist Paulinus, who explicitly commissioned pictorial art for the sake of attracting the lower classes into the church.

The only early, clear example of a theological objection to the content of an art object comes to us from Tertullian at the end of the second century, when he reveals his particular distaste for images of the Good Shepherd because they may indicate a general support for a laxist position in regard to sin after baptism, as contained in the text of the Shepherd of Hermas.[29] The ubiquity of Good Shepherd images in the third and early fourth centuries, however, hardly indicates the presence of a widespread sectarian group that was soft on fornicators. No doubt the art made for church walls, saints' tombs, or liturgical objects and furniture and was seen by all members of the community, wealthy as well as poor, educated as well as illiterate. Although different groups might well see different meanings in the artwork on the walls, in most cases it was equally available to everyone and likely paid for by the wealthy minority (including clergy) who patronized the church in this way.

In addition to the matter of authorization and patronage of art in public ecclesial spaces is the problem of how viewers who were uneducated or illiterate would have understood the images they saw without the benefit of some kind of explanation. Despite the so-called Chinese proverb that a single picture is worth ten thousand words, narrative art alone cannot tell a whole story or function entirely without the interpretive aid of words. Picture books, even those without words, are still read to children. In a sense this is exactly what Basil of Caesarea was doing when he preached in the martyrium—he interpreted the silent pictures as his audience listened and looked at the same time.

Clearly, Gregory and all those others who believe that art has a value for nonreaders also presume that the link between verbal narrative and visual

[29] Tertullian, *Pud.*, 7.12.

imagery is made one way or another, whether through a sermon, oral reading of scripture in the daily and weekly liturgy, or catechetical lessons. In addition, a large number of church images in both wall and apse frescoes, as well as mosaics, are supplemented with text messages, clearly to assist the literate viewer in correctly identifying the characters or story. For example, most portraits of saints from the sixth century onwards helpfully provide the names of their subjects somewhere near their faces. Sometimes even the scenes themselves are identified. Stained glass windows in many more modern churches similarly supply identifying captions. Interpretation is a necessary aspect of narrative art, even after the primary document has disappeared or the original story has been long forgotten. To the extent that visual art is used to impart a particular lesson or present an edifying or inspiring example of heroism or steadfast faithfulness, it must be associated with a spoken or written explanation, even if that explanation still exists only in the memory or imagination of the viewer.

Nevertheless, as Margaret Miles would remind us, this simple truth does not reduce the function of art to being merely didactic or slavishly tied to the task of illustrating verbal narratives in a literalistic way. Nor is there only one kind of text that is best employed for the task of interpretation. Chronologically contemporary prayers, poems, liturgies, and homilies are perhaps more suited to interpretation of visual art in the church than more abstract theological treatises. Readers of literature also realize that stories have many layers of meaning and signification and can be interpreted in an almost infinite variety of ways, having different import or meaning for different readers and in different contexts. Visual art is no less complex and multivalent and no more socially constructed than texts are.

Visual art communicates in a different mode than written text and its function is not limited to pictorially portraying the details of a prose narrative. Visual images that are linked in one way or another with sacred stories do more than serve as aids to the nonreaders, but also may amplify, expand, and deepen the power and impact of those stories in the imagination of viewers. They also serve as memory aids, not just because a picture is more easily recalled than a page of writing (or stored in a different part of the brain), but also because they impart a vivid and even concrete reality to the words and ideas found in oral or written communication. Images, of course, are made by the imagination of readers, but when a text is enriched by the work of a skilled artist, the added dimension of vision, not to mention color, form, and beauty, illuminates the experience of reading or hearing. Finally, narrative images, unlike portraits, are unlikely to attract prayer or devotion. Different kinds of images engender different kinds of responses in viewers.

In Gregory's second letter to Serenus, he claimed that images were in churches from ancient times for the sake of instruction. Although we cannot know exactly which examples he had in mind, he could have been thinking of the great churches in Rome and their rich decoration. One possible, very prominent example is the Basilica of Sta. Maria Maggiore, which one can still see today. Far from being decorated merely for the edification of the ignorant or illiterate, or reflecting the religious views of the marginalized, the program of Bible-based narrative images on the walls of the nave and covering the triumphal arch are wonderfully complex and sophisticated, and reflect the values and theology of the church hierarchy (even including the Pope's own name in the dedication at the apex of the arch).

Although interpreting the possible messages of these images of scenes from the Hebrew scriptures, as well as the advent, birth, and adoration of Christ, may vary from being a rich but subtle interplay of typology and fulfillment or one of supercessionist claims for Christianity over Judaism, the meaning was clearly mediated to viewers by means of preaching, catechesis, liturgical actions, hymns, and prayers, as well as theological treatises and scripture commentaries.[30] As Margaret Miles asserted with justification: "The building and decoration of Santa Maria Maggiore played an important role in the consolidation and public announcement of papal power."[31] And, according to her analysis, in this case art was used as a tool to support the marginalization of an unpopular and disenfranchised group—the Jews. Based on this, we can only conclude that art in the early church had a wide range of purposes or roles, from the entertainment of the masses, to the edification of the unlettered, to the inspiration of the devout, and even the assertion of ideology. Visual art is neither the special possession of the privileged or primarily for sake of the underprivileged. We cannot assume that it was keyed to official teachings on one hand, or that it diverges from or challenges them on the other. Seeing images, as early writers demonstrate, was a way of gaining knowledge, arousing devotion, and inspiring the imagination apart from reading or hearing, which had advantages for those who were unable to read, but was equally effective for the literate. Accordingly, a century or so after Gregory, John of Damascus also affirmed that art is the "book of the illiterate," but at the same time insisted that when artists produce worthy images, they sanctify the noblest of the senses (vision), and claiming that just

[30] See for example, S. Spain, "The Promised Blessing: The Iconography of the Mosaics of S. Maria Maggiore," *Art Bulletin* 61 (1979) 518–40; and Miles, "Santa Maria Maggiore's Fifth-Century Mosaics: Triumphal Christianity and the Jews," *HTR* 86 (1993) 155–221.

[31] Miles, "Santa Maria Maggiore," 155.

as words instruct through the ear, the image teaches through sight and thus brings understanding.[32]

[32] John of Damascus, *On Holy Images* 1.17.

# Blessed Irreverence

## *What Black Theology Can Learn from the Visual Arts*

Anthony B. Pinn

The February 28, 2003 issue of the *Minneapolis Star Tribune* contained a story titled "Modern & Muslim" describing the "Sheherazade: Risking the Passage" Show in which Muslim women used their artistic creativity to explore the intersections between personal faith, culture, and world developments. Of particular interest, because of its controversial nature, was the photo exhibit by Lalla Essaydi.

The context for one of Essaydi's photographs is a "'House of Obedience' belonging to Essaydi's family in Morocco." It is the place in which women are imprisoned for "extended periods, apparently to compel repentance after they've broken an Islamic custom." Essaydi "persuaded Moroccan women friends to pose for her in that beautiful prison. Naked, their bodies are painted." This presentation would be interesting but less confrontational if it involved an arrangement of colors and designs, but instead the artists clothed the bodies in "lacy calligraphy that includes floral designs and quotations from the Qur'an." This was considered an outrage in that calligraphy "is a sacred Islamic art forbidden to women," and "by literally robing themselves in the words of the Qur'an, the women are both submitting to and violating Muslim strictures."[1]

I find the content of Essaydi's artistic statement intriguing. In part it is appealing because of my interest in the formation of a constructive black theology concerned with issues of justice. But it is also appealing because of the theological paradigm implied by the form of expression used. In a word, Essaydi affirms irreverence as an important source of transformation because it serves to reconfigure societal margins or boundaries, using the despised to

1 Mary Abbe, "Modern & Muslim," *Minneapolis Star Tribune* (February 28, 2003) E20.

reshape the language and grammar of beauty in terms of both body and soul. By irreverence in this context I mean modalities of subversion, attitudes, and sensibilities that run contrary to the norm and are therefore considered indecent because they question what discourses of power are meant to enforce.[2]

What is so brilliant about this photo and its underlying paradigm of irreverence is the manner in which holy pronouncements of a disembodied deity placed on the supple curves and sensuous places of the human body provoke in the viewer a reaction: Is this permissible? If it is not, what does it say about the creation of this God—the female body—through its inability to house or display the sacred? Ultimately, I imagine, what lurks behind such questions is an unspoken discomfort with embodiment and an effort to apologize for it in the presence of the transcendent. But this is an odd dilemma in that both the words of the Qur'an and human body speak, yet in different ways, to the presence of the divine in history. Both the body and words have a materiality, a firm presence, a realness, that in turns speaks to the realness and ultimate intentions of the divine, according to theists. Even so, there is a tension here in that the words of the divine elicit a striving for more, a push through history, a type of embrace and conquering of ourselves and our socioeconomic, cultural, psychological, and historical environment; while the body, the flesh, elicits a discomfort, a sense of being that runs contrary to the objectives of the sacred text. The sacred text, in this case the Qur'an, pushed beyond history, and the human form embodies history.

In this essay I seek to explore the implications of Essaydi's work for black theology through an examination of the manner in which theological studies might gain a sense of irreverence as an important religious value through attention to the visual arts, particularly Abstract Expressionism and Pop Art.[3] I suggest attention to this point may help theologians recognize the manner in which theology (perhaps recognized as a artistic process itself) might force new understandings of reality—the relationships and interactions that mark the formation of life's meaning.[4] That is to say, theology might become an irreverent, thereby more useful, enterprise.

[2] I am indebted to the work of Marcella Althasu-Reid's *Indecent Theology: Theological Perversions in Sex, Gender and Politics* (New York: Routledge, 2000). Her work has provided me with a framework and vocabulary for thinking through this alternate perspective on black theology as an art of irreverence.

[3] See Anthony J. Pinn, *Terror and Triumph: The Nature of Black Religion* (Minneapolis: Fortress, 2003), chapters 7 and 8. As a note of clarification my goal here does not involve the presentation of art criticism, an articulation of the "good" and "bad" of various styles of artistic production or particular artists or pieces. Such designations are certainly possible, but they are unnecessary and rather burdensome with respect to the intent of this essay.

[4] Arthur C. Danto, *The Philosophical Disenfranchisement of Art* (New York: Columbia University Press, 1986) 103.

By making this argument I want to suggest that creativity in the realm of religious experience and theological discourse along the lines of the "liberation" certain theologians and religious communities promote requires an irreverent stance toward oppressive social regulations and norms. Such a stance must involve a bold questioning of what is "real" about the reality offered us by existing social structures and the social order. Irreverence as a theological paradigm is positive in that it entails an uncovering and bringing into question modalities of interaction and relationship that gave "meanings that we have come to attach to our bodily life."[5] It involves a rejection of metanarratives—the framing or scripting of life in rigid ways that encourage us to exist happily in the houses of obedience exposed in Essaydi's art.

## Post-World War II Art: Flipping the Script

Prior to the advent of the twentieth century much of what was done within the visual arts entailed a mimicking of historical reality, the presentation of what *is* exactly as it meets the eye, in accordance with the established rules of aesthetics and practice. With the creation of cinematography, the ability to capture reality was perfected, and the artist was free to impose his or her own sensibilities on art, giving the world captured a new quality of presentation and meaning. Within this new artistic freedom, imagination, a creative "what if," was applied to the artistic representation of the world. What I mean to say is that the visual arts after cinematography, for the purposes of this essay, painting, did not simply copy moments and structures of life. Rather the arts were used to raise questions concerning sociopolitical, religious, cultural, or economic matters, but this was done within the context of accepted rules governing the world of art and the social sensibilities that informed the art world's regulations. Artists, then, were free only to a degree.

Even Picasso's cubism paintings, with their uniqueness, maintain something of the familiar: the existing language and grammar of the social system and the art world still apply, although filtered at times through his attention to the sensibilities of the outsider—the African. Or, think in terms of the settings presented by Henry Ossawa Tanner, the African-American artist who captured perfectly the tender moments of life within the context of a larger society seething with ill will. There is something comforting in Tanner's presentation of reality in that it is, although nuanced, familiar or recognizable and using the accepted tools of social interaction. More recently, the sensibilities and positioning of what is referred to as Outsider Art called into question aspects of arts production, presentation, and refinement, but this style still works within the confines of the established system. It, like Picasso's cubism

[5] James B. Nelson, *Body Theology* (Louisville: Westminster John Knox, 1992) 43.

or Henry Ossawa Tanner's life settings, involves an imaginative presentation of social realities in such a way as to signify or veil them without a fundamental frustration of said realities. The work of such artists seeks to create additional space, to reconceive the geography of life, but without fundamental challenge to the basic structures used to describe life. In a sense, their work is an acceptable rebellion.

With the emergence of Abstract Expressionism in the 1940s, the relationship between the artist and the expression of reality changed. Imagination as the aesthetic practice of recreating the historically real was questioned and problematized, although never fully conquered. Transcendental reality and surrealism were combined in this new art form in ways that brought into question basic structures of reality and the ways in which it might be depicted or captured. Artistic representation took on a new meaning, new possibilities. As shepherded by Jackson Pollock, Abstract Expressionism did not simply present historical reality in creative ways. Instead, in the words of B. H. Friedman, it marked a vision inscribed by freedom because, "for Pollock the acceptance of freedom, the striving for fluidity, is and has been the supreme discipline."[6]

This form of painting sought to demonstrate that the only reality was found within the "hidden consciousness" and this was projected onto the canvas. In Pollack's words: "The source of my painting is the unconscious. I approach painting the same way I approach drawing. That is direct—with no preliminary studies. The drawings I do are relative to my painting but not for it.[7] This practice brought into question the established framework of artistic production, its language and grammar. Pollock remarks concerning his style that

> My painting does not come from the easel. I hardly ever stretch my canvas before painting. I prefer to tack the unstretched canvas to the hard wall or the floor. I need the resistance of a hard surface. On the floor I am more at ease. I feel nearer, more a part of the painting, since this way I can walk around it, work from the four sides and literally be *in* the painting. I continue to get further away from the usual painter's tools such as easel, palette, brushes, etc. I prefer sticks, trowels, knives and dripping fluid paint or a heavy impasto with sand, broken glasss and other foreign matter added.[8]

This sentiment was echoed by Bruno Alfieri who wrote: "It is easy to detect the following things in all of his paintings: chaos, absolute lack of harmony,

6 Francis V. O'Connor, *Jackson Pollock* (New York: The Museum of Modern Art, 1967) 73.

7 Ibid., 40.

8 Ibid.

complete lack of structural organization, total absence of technique, however rudimentary, once again, chaos. . . . Pollock has broken all barriers between his picture and himself."[9]

Pollock was in a sense absorbed by the process of painting, while he also absorbed it. Because it required attention not to particularly recognizable entities, it became necessary to work with this art in terms of "objectless feelings: joy, depression, generalized excitement, etc." This required "a totally different structure" for understanding the history of art as something other than a "a progressive history," as Arthur Danto remarks. I am not suggesting Abstract Expressionism entails an escape from the influence of others, from attention to existing structures of production. To the contrary, the artist, as Jonathan Weinberg notes, does not work in a vacuum, completely independent of others, "generat[ing] art from nothing."[10] But Abstract Expressionism involves a recognition of regulations on production as interference as opposed to necessary influence. Perhaps this is the meaning behind Pollock's eventual rejection of two traditional tools of painting: brushes and easel. It is through his effort to dismiss standards by "negating the practice of his precursor [Picasso], Pollock seeks to negate all precursors, as if endeavoring to be the first artist to paint a picture entirely from within himself."[11] By this process, the nature of relationship (in this case between artists and product) is changed, radically reinvented. In this way Pollock's work teaches irreverence.

How well this reinventing took place is uncertain when one considers that the emergence of Pop Art, during the 1960s, demonstrates the degree to which even Abstract Expressionism involves a masking of realities.[12] That is to say, there are ways in which dimensions of Abstract Expressionism are viewable as a mistake, as being a misunderstanding or an abuse of artistic language and symbols rather than a rejection of this language and these symbols.[13] Hence, even Abstract Expressionism's critique of the art form implies a recognition of the traditional structures, but distorted, deformed. It leaves damaged but intact the metanarrative of art's meaning and modalities. The degree to which this is true about Abstract Expressions is expressed by its advocates who subtly affirm social tradition by proclaiming Pop Art a blemish—a bad and indecent move. But as I hope is already evident, the truly irreverent teaches it's good to be bad.

[9] Ibid., 55.

[10] Jonathan Weinberg, *Ambition and Love in Modern American Art* (New Haven: Yale University Press, 2001) 31.

[11] Ibid., 49.

[12] I was fortunate to experience prime examples of both styles of art at the National Museum of Modern Art, Georges Pompidou Center, Paris, and the Tate Modern, London, England.

[13] Weinberg, *Ambition and Love*, 215.

Training its attention on commercial developments and symbols of commercial acquisition, Pop Art challenged the substance of human life and the ways in which the meaning of life is constructed. In so doing it fostered sensitivity to previously ignored or even despised relational qualities of life. This, for example, entailed an appreciation for the erotic qualities of life to the extent such realities focus on the expression of beauty through relationship, particularly those often ignored. This was troubling for some, and Warhol is said to have been a killer of art, "a killer of beauty."[14] But perhaps Pop Art as produced by Warhol really entailed a recognition of beauty within the traditionally ignored items and relationships that mark typical moments of life. Perhaps this is one of the challenges posed by his installation of the Brillo boxes.

In either case, Abstract Expressionism or Pop Art, the relationship between "things" is broken and exposed to new possibilities and it is this development that interests me. Both suggest new possibilities of meaning. For the former, Abstract Expressionism, this involves diving deep into the inner self and for Pop Art, the external world of images and objects says a great deal. It, as did Abstract Expressionism to a certain extent, critiqued stilted depictions of humans in relationship with other humans and materials. Each form of artistic presentation dislodged the beautiful from traditional structures and thereby allowed for the formation of new modalities of relationship with ideas, objects, and other persons. In this sense both raise questions concerning the manner in which social structures create icons of life that prohibit other ways of being and doing. While different in numerous ways, both Abstract Expressionism and Pop Art share an attitude of disruption with respect to the typical manner in which content and form relate. Thereby both, to varying degrees, teach irreverence.

## Art as Challenge to the Perception of Meaning

Raising the question of 'what is beautiful' phrased in terms of 'what is the nature of art'—whether intended or not—allowed for a disregard of established norms. It considered what can be approached as interesting and worthy of attention, what is the proper subject of relationship or connection. According to Andy Warhol, "Pop art is a way of liking things."[15]

Liberation theologies, such as black theology, raise similar questions concerning the likability of despised bodies (e.g., "Black is beautiful!"), but

[14] Arthur C. Danto, *Philosophizing Art: Selected Essays* (Berkeley: University of California Press, 1999) 68.

[15] Kyneston McShine, ed., *Andy Warhol: A Retrospective*, 441, quoted in Danto, *Philosophizing Art*, 74.

without going so far as to question the fundamental nature and meaning of beauty. This being the case, theological discourse has much to learn from artistic developments of the twentieth century. The irreverent questioning of art's nature, source, and meaning holds useful implications for theological discourse's struggle over narratives of life's meaning and purpose.

Both forms of art briefly noted here require viewers to surrender the safety of visual comprehension. One cannot fully understand such art using the eye because the eye allows distance, disconnection. Abstract Expressionism and Pop Art challenge basic assumptions, established sensibilities, in ways requiring different relationships to the work of art. For some, this process begins by an altered relationship to the artist through a rather crude but common questions: couldn't I make this? (This is in part a question of quality—the true artist produces what I cannot—vs. quantity—anyone can make this.) What was so offensive about Pop Art was the manner in which it boldly presented established, commercialized realities—Brillo boxes and soup cans—and through them raised questions concerning the meaning and context for art. For those who disliked Pop Art such a display lacked necessary sophistication—the veiling or presenting as interference of established schemes and structures.

From my perspective one of the great appeals of Pop Art, and the center of its importance for this essay's work, is the manner in which it calls into question the nature and meaning of relationships—the artists to the art; the art to the public and the meaning and nature of art over against traditional perceptions of the "real." "What is art? Does it really come out of you or is it a product?"[16] Does integrity—the self as a self in relationship to other selves—exist only within the geography of the established order and its standard of acceptable behavior, or does it exist only through the destruction of this established order? Is the latter the actual nature of embodiment?

As an interesting aside, there are ways in which some of this art and these questions bring the sexual into play in both overt and subtle ways, and by so doing make visible various dimensions of bodily pleasuring. I provide this aside because the sensual nature of human interaction expressed in Warhol's work, for example, holds great promise in that it can be used to push for a more inclusive presentation of black theological embodiment through an embrace of the erotic as important modalities of meaning and relationship.[17] Take, for example, Warhol's work post-1960s, such as "piss paintings"

[16] Andy Warhol's *Diaries*, 8 October 1984, 606, quoted in Weinberg, *Ambition and Love*, 238.

[17] I have in mind Paul Tillich's understanding of the erotic. As I have described it elsewhere, Tillich understands eros as a force that gives shape to human ingenuity and expression on a variety of fronts and in a variety of forms. It is libidinal and as a result concerned with physical pleasure, but it is more than this because it is also concerned with the "beautiful" in far-

named because of the technique involved. The following statement outlines this process of blending the sex(ual) body and the visual arts within Warhol's depiction of young artist Jean-Michel Basquiat:

> In this extraordinary picture, a screen print based on a Polaroid photo of Basquiat's face has been layered onto the field of one of Warhol's *Oxidation Paintings*. The result combines Warhol's standard portrait format of celebrities and socialites with the oxidation technique in which a male urinates on a copper field, producing a so-called "piss painting." The urine stains now take the place of the typical multicolored brush strokes that were applied to the ground of Warhol's society portraits by his assistants. Warhol's usual oxidation process provides only the trace of a performance in which young men put their genitals to work for Warhol. The *Oxidation Paintings* are like the stained sheets of an erotic encounter.[18]

Warhol is not the only one to make use of the body in ways that emphasize its functions—its often despised or segregated functions. But by so doing, in Warhol's work, the body gains importance as a multidimensional reality—the basis of art and the tool for its construction. One might say, this is another example of the irreverent as the ability not to find "beauty in the banal" as much "as to find the banal as beautiful" and in the process to find "the ordinary extraordinary."[19]

Pop Art raised questions concerning the content and location of reality as well as the source of pleasure associated with visual images. This, I believe, is the basic assertion made by Nicholas Davey when saying "art works do not merely reinterpret and represent subject matters but extend and alter their being. . . . It is in the notion of subject-matter . . . [that we gain] insight into how an art work can transcend the temporal restrictions of its historical origin and affect the contemporary world . . . and it can only do so if it successfully enables us to understand that there is something more to be seen in it than what is immediately before the eyes."[20] Pop Art moves close to captur-

reaching terms and the desire to create relationships saturated with this beauty. See Alexander C. Irwin: *E.R.O.S Toward the World: Paul Tillich and the Theology of the Erotic* (Minneapolis: Fortress, 1991) 1, 5, 6. Also see Paul Tillich: *Love, Power, and Justice: Ontological Analyses and Ethical Applications* (New York: Oxford University Press, 1954).

18 Weinberg, *Ambition and Love*, 212.

19 Danto, *Philosophizing Art*, 73, 74. While intriguing, I must emphasize that what I propose here is not reducible to the playfulness with sex and sexuality evident in Andy Warhol's work such as *Jean-Michel Basquiat, 1984,* or the images of Marilyn Monroe. Or, one might consider the images in *A Rake's Progress* series developed by David Hockney during the 1960s modeled after William Hogarth's *A Rake's Progress* of the 1700s.

20 Nicholas Davey, "The Hermeneutics of Seeing," in *Interpreting Visual Culture: Explorations in the Hermeneutics of the Visual*, ed. Ian Heywood and Barry Sandywell (New York: Routledge,

ing in the world of art what body theology seeks to accomplish within the religious realm—uncover deep meanings through the obvious. For Pop Art, the obvious means common items, and for body theology, the obvious is the body. But there is even a relationship here if one pushes Arthur Danto's labelling of artwork as being "embodied meanings."[21]

This changing of reality's substance points to the tension between imagination and the irreverent. One also gets a sense of this tension between established and possible realities and more indecent possibilities in the collage style of Romare Bearden. According to Bearden, his work presents and surfaces the hidden possibilities of life in that it acknowledges the various "roads out of the secret places within us along which we all must move as we go to touch others."[22] Through his art, revelation becomes a type of existential encounter, one that raises questions concerning acceptable presentations of life by taking objects and making them serve new purposes—a irreverent act to be sure.

Bearden constructs the Conjure Woman collages, for example, out of bits and pieces of other "bodies" or realities—pieces of paper and so on. There is something sensual about this process and its outcome. There is an interchange/ability at work that calls into question the nature and shape of realness. Bearden accomplishes through the collage what black theology attempts through various mediums—to take bits and pieces of fragile cultural and historical memory and express a reality that counters the dominant perception of the world and its content. Such a move raises important questions: What is a subject? Are there set ways in which a subject must occupy space, or define space, even be distinguishable from space? On one level, the Conjure Woman is the realness of social sensibility as it relates to long-standing folk community and culture; but she is also unreal in that she is an odd configuration of pieces that taken alone hold little meaning.

## In Conclusion . . . from Art to Theology

Black theology, like the art discussed above, should push beyond imagination through acts of irreverence, by which I mean acts that show disregard for existing social structures and symbols—not in an effort to jettison them, but to make use of them.

---

1999) 4, 8.

21 Arthur C. Danto, *After the End of Art: Contemporary Art and the Pale of History* (Princeton: Princeton University Press, 1997) 98.

22 Sharon F. Patton, "Memory and Metaphor: The Art of Romare Bearden, 1940–1987," The Studio Museum in Harlem, *Memory and Metaphor: The Art of Romare Bearden, 1940–1987* (New York: Oxford University Press, 1991) 70.

Ultimately, Abstract Expressionism and Pop Art damage narratives of art and artistic production in the same way theology should question narratives of certain life interactions and relationships. It is a provocative type of embodiment. In this case, true embodiment as a theological concept must involve fully approaching the body in all its possible relationships. Black theology should, like these art forms, rebel against history. The work of art demands a different perception of the history of an object or subject, an intense inspection of its contours. That is to say, "by bringing to fruition potentialities for meaning hidden within ourselves and actuality, art, far from distorting reality, brings it to an even greater fullness of being."[23]

There is much for black theology to learn from the visual arts: whereas the social system seeks to project the world as complete—things are forever as they are—the visual arts remind us that the world is in process, meaning remains to be made. Art can involve imagination to the extent the artist seeks to give new dimension to reality as encountered by the observer, but it is not content with this process: it also pushes the boundaries of what is real about reality, and what is the nature and meaning of relationship between humans and the world. This is an irreverent act. Even when the art is figurative, there is a quality to the work that seeks to create new spaces of interaction, of connectedness to the world, done through erotic realities as pleasurable. Some of this involved an appreciation for homosexuality over against the social norm opposing it.[24] Such a stance would allow black theology more consistently to critique the homophobia that plagues many black religious institutions and communions. From Abstract Expressionism to some degree, but certainly from Pop Art, I find value in reconceiving black theological discourse so as to better address erotic realities or what Arthur Danto termed an "aesthetic of meaning."[25] Attention to the manner in which these two forms of artistic production raise questions concerning the nature of art and the nature and meaning of relationship to art may help black theology push beyond the boundaries of morality, which prevent proper recognition of a much fuller range of relationships represented by the erotic. Pop Art suggests that in the realm of art anything is possible because the traditional indicators of a work of art have been disregarded.[26] In the same way, application of this sensibil-

23 Davey, "The Hermeneutics of Seeing," 22.

24 Yet, as Jonathan Weinberg remarks concerning the early work of visual artist David Hockney, "we need to remember that a new honesty about homosexuality does not add up to new power structures and social relationships." Weinberg, *Ambition and Love*, 163.

25 Danto, *After the End of Art*, 77.

26 As readers have probably deciphered at this point, I find Arthur Danto's philosophy of art convincing on this point. In addition to the books listed in previous notes, also see Danto, *The Philosophical Disenfranchisement of Art* (New York: Columbia University Press, 1986);

ity in the work of black theology could stimulate an openness to an embrace of relationship and interactions that extend beyond those traditionally embraced. It might provide the groundwork for celebrating those that were once considered inappropriate and socially unacceptable.

There is a sense in which the forms of artistic expression briefly depicted here, from the perspective of a theologian, push us toward an irreverent process—an indecent depiction of life in tune with the truth of our complex relational possibilities. Abstract Expressionism and Pop Art encourage suspicion concerning the current arrangement and structure of reality.

Guided by this sensibility, the task for black theological discourse is simple: Look deep. See the alternate possibilities. Challenge the norms of interaction and celebrate the emerging possibilities as we, to borrow from Frantz Fanon, "restructure the world." So conceived, black theology becomes equipped to challenge both historical conditions and the assumed proper "attitudes toward these conditions."[27] This ultimately means celebrating the irreverent and the indecent for the new ways of being and the new levels of meaning provided. In the words of the old song, "I once was lost, but now I'm found."[28]

---

and idem, *The Transfiguration of the Commonplace: A Philosophy of Art* (Cambridge: Harvard University Press, 1981).

27 Frantz Fanon, *Black Skin, White Masks* (New York: Grove, 1967) 82, 84.

28 John Newton (1725–1807), *Amazing Grace.*

# Answering the Call of Goya's Dog

## *Seeing with Vision, Seeing with Responsibility*

S. Brent Plate

As much as I want to resist a preface and plunge right in, the following presentation demands some context. This is a study on the relation between words and images. I am not concerned simply with the differences between various media; rather, I wish to display how the word/image relation may also straddle the divide between aesthetics and ethics. To put it in other words, this presentation is an attempt at "Becoming Answerable for What We See," as Margaret Miles phrased her 1999 Presidential Address to the American Academy of Religion.[1] To be truly responsible for what we see is demanding work, for words and images do not always congeal very well, especially when we are faced with an upsetting image of suffering. I am interested in the verbal ability to respond (response-ability) to an image, as well as the inability to respond, particularly when the response to the image becomes overwhelming and leaves one without voice. As Elaine Scarry suggests in *The Body in Pain,* "Whatever pain achieves, it achieves in part through its unsharability, and it ensures this unsharability through its resistance to language."[2] To become answerable for what we see is thus to struggle with what images can do where words fail and how to respond nonetheless. And since responsibility depends on its ability to be shared, to become an act of communication, a conversation ensues herein between a handful of thinkers on the possibilities and impossibilities of response.

So there I was, in Madrid, a hot summer's day at Museo del Prado, seeking out the Goyas. I secretly wanted to get to the so-called Black Paintings but first I somehow patiently waded through the miles of grotesque portrai-

1 Published in *JAAR* 68 (2000) 471–85.

2 Elaine Scarry, *The Body in Pain* (New York: Oxford University Press, 1985) 4.

tures whose baroque extravagance left me queasy. And then I found the hidden room. It was easy enough to find, for that's where everyone wanted to go, to crane their necks at *Saturn Devouring his Children,* perhaps just to say how terrible it is. But the room was hidden nonetheless, not because it revealed the secrets—the deep, dark, terrible secrets—of Goya, but because it revealed what was concealed in us, the viewers, about *our* deep, dark, terrible lives.

And there, even there among the other Black Paintings was the unexpected, the *canis familiaris* in a very unfamiliar setting, the familiar turned wild and mysterious. It was a mystery that administered, but *what* was it that was administered? Grace? What strange messenger was this dog? What has the dog to show us? And what disaster is becoming the dog and viewer? What mystical revelations might we find in an encounter with this dog? And how can words relate the experience this image carries with it?

> Wittgenstein's "mysticism," aside from his faith in unity, must come from his believing that one can *show* when one cannot *speak.* But without language, nothing can be shown. And to be silent is still to speak. Silence is impossible. That is why we desire it. Writing precedes every phenomenon, every manifestation or show: all appearing.[3]

---

> After the Fall, however, when God's word curses the ground, the appearance of nature is deeply changed. Now begins its other muteness, which is what we mean by the "deep sadness of nature." It is a metaphysical truth that all nature would begin to lament if it were endowed with language.[4]

Oh, this dog! Eyes upturned, helpless beyond belief, appearing at the moment of its disappearing, a fragment remaining. The painting demanded numerous viewings that day in el Prado, looking, searching, questioning, going away for stimulants and/or intoxicants, coming again to the site of the drowning animal, I could not take my eyes off it, and yet, was helpless myself to do anything to save it. Or to save myself.

> Save me O God! For the waters have come up to my neck. I sink in deep mire, where there is no foothold; I have come into deep waters, and the flood sweeps over me. I am weary with my crying; my throat

[3] Maurice Blanchot, *The Writing of the Disaster,* trans. Ann Smock (Lincoln: Nebraska University Press, 1966) 10–11.

[4] Walter Benjamin. "On Language as Such and the Language of Man," in *Walter Benjamin: Selected Writing, Volume One, 1913–1926,* trans. Harry Zohn (Cambridge, Mass.: Belknap, 1996) 72.

> is parched. My eyes grow dim with waiting for my God. . . . Hide not thy face from thy servant. (Psalm 69:1-4, 17)

Do I protest? Mourn? Cry? Sing a song of lament? Do I leave the museum with the dog still drowning? Do I search for something to say, to break the silence? Or are my questions already breaking?

> There is a question and yet no doubt; there is a question, but no desire for an answer; there is a question, and nothing that can be said, but just this nothing, to say. This is a query, a probe that surpasses the very possibility of questions.[5]

---

> "Knowledge means questioning."
>
> "What will we get out of these questions? What will we get out of all the answers which only lead to more questions, since questions are born of unsatisfactory answers?"
>
> "The promise of a new question."
>
> "There will be a moment when we have to stop interrogating. Either because there will be no answer possible, or because we will not be able to formulate any further questions. So why should we begin?"
>
> "You see, at the end of an argument, there is always a decisive question unsettled."[6]

If I were to question the painting, I might begin in the space of art history, a thoroughly disciplined knowledge. But art history speaks silence on this work of Goya. In the huge host of catalogs, biographies, and art books devoted to that most famous of Spanish painters, barely more than a few sentences are spoken on it. The fragments of sentences here and there do little more than express how such a work is difficult to comment on, and even how odd it is in spite of its inclusion with the other Black Paintings of this period in Goya's life. Even those studies that take on the Black Paintings refrain from the dog, as if a huge "Beware of . . ." sign were posted there. Here, let me reveal some of the silences uttered by historians and critics:

> "It is one of the strangest works of all in Spanish painting." (Gudial)
>
> "A dog is being buried in quicksand. Still alive—but for how long?—in a frame completely naked and abstract. The theme challenges any analysis . . ." (Gassier and Wilson)
>
> "It is perhaps the strangest of all the [black] paintings. . . leaving the

5 Blanchot, *Writing of the Disaster*, 9.

6 Edmond Jabès, *The Book of Questions*, in *From the Book to the Book: An Jabès Reader*, trans. Rosmarie Waldrop (Hanover, N.H.: University Press of New England, 1991) 47.

imagination of the spectator to fly freely, without a possible answer to the question about the true intention of the artist." (Gassier and Wilson)

"A dog's head, ghostly and appealing, rises suppliant from the cloudy void of eternity. . . . It may be the shadow of a dead master. It may be the head of another dog, or the god of all dogs." (Poore)

"The figure of a dog (Abandoned? Witness of something he should not have seen?) is the most mysterious of all the "Black paintings." All manner of interpretations have been put forward, all seeing the dog as an incarnation of suffering." (Perez Sanchez)

"Only one picture remains mysterious, that of a dog buried in the sand, the most worn of all, the least attractive, and the most disturbing." (Descargues)

"It is the strangest and most incomprehensible of the [Black Paintings]." (Gibson)

"[I]t represents nothing. . . . It is the frustration and defeat of painting." (Vallentin)

"This work is without doubt the most enigmatic of the black paintings." (Luna and Moreno)

"The dog is a tragic emblem of meaninglessness. The pathetic hope of the beast is not betrayed by an unseen master. There *is* no master, and consequently there is no justification for the dog's upward glance. But even such a bare interpretation is probably off the mark just because it *is* an interpretation. *The Dog* may very well be an undecipherable signal emitted by some mechanism that is either beyond or below the human intellect and intuition." (Licht)

What we do know is that Goya in his old age painted his dog around 1820, along with the other Black Paintings, directly onto the plaster walls of his house. Recent radiographs reveal the deeper secret that the Black Paintings were painted over decorative "joyful" (as one commentator put it) pictures. The house in which the images were created came to be known as *quinta del sordo,* "House of the Deaf Man." Goya, you see, was deaf by the time this piece was painted, by the time of its showing. Wandering in silence in this interior space, he surrounded himself with images of monsters, myths, and mysteries. He died only a few years later.

> Keep silence. Silence cannot be kept; it is indifferent with respect to the work of art which would claim to respect it—it demands a wait which has nothing to await, a language which, presupposing itself as the totality of discourse, would spend itself all at once, disjoin and fragment endlessly.[7]

[7] Blanchot. *The Writing of the Disaster.* 29.

Death cultivates visibility.

There is no silent image.

There is a silence we lock it in.

Attracted by all of them, we can scrutinize only one image at a time. For all the words of the language, we accompany only one word into death.

Our image of the cold is our own image out in the cold; anonymous sketch of a body shivering.

The image does not reflect reality, but, rather, shows the spectacular end of all reality.

To see, means to die; to watch, dying.

Wind and sand revel in worsting the eye, making it cry.

Yellowed with age, the image yields only nostalgia: image of a lost image.[8]

Even the name of the dog or the name of the painting is silent. What name shall we give the painting? And the dog? And, to what name might the dog respond? Is it, as el Prado has it, *Perro semihundido* (half-buried dog)? Or, as a British catalog stated, simply *the dog*? Or, stranger still, on the back of a postcard reproduction, *Dog on a leash*? One prominent scholar (Yriarte) considered it unfinished and called it *Dog struggling against the current.* "I have come into deep waters and the flood sweeps over me."

> The name: What does one call thus? What does one understand under the name of name? And what occurs when one gives a name? What does one give then? One does not offer a thing, one delivers nothing, and still something comes to be, which comes down to giving that which one does not have, as Plotinus said of the Good. What happens, above all, when it is necessary to sur-name, re-naming there where, precisely, the name comes to be found lacking? What makes the proper name into a sort of sur-name, pseudonym, or cryptonym at once singular and singularly untranslatable?[9]

---

> To be named—even when the namer is godlike and blissful—perhaps always remains an intimation of mourning. But how much more melancholy it is to be named not from the one blessed paradisiacal language of names, but from the hundred languages of man, in which name has already withered, yet which, according to God's pronouncement, have knowledge of things. In the language of men, however, they are overnamed.[10]

8 Jabès. *The Journey,* in *From the Book to the Book,* 202.

9 Jacques Derrida, *On the Name* (Stanford: Stanford University Press, 1955) xiv.

10 Walter Benjamin, *The Arcades Project,* trans. Howard Eiland and Kevin McLaughlin

> The moment I came into life, I trembled: from the fear of separation, the dread of death. I saw death at work and guessed its constancy, the jealousy that wouldn't let anything escape it alive. I watched it wound, disfigure, paralyze, and massacre from the moment my eyes opened to seeing, I discovered that the Face was mortal, and that I would have to snatch it back at every moment from Nothingness. I didn't adore that-which-is-going-to-disappear; love isn't bound up for me in the condition of mortality. No. I loved. I was afraid. I am afraid. Because of my fear I reinforced love, I alerted all the forces of life, I armed love, with soul and words, to keep death from winning. Loving: keeping alive: naming.[11]

---

> Great seas cannot drown love,
> no river can sweep it away. (Song of Songs 8:7)

Loving is keeping alive, naming. But perhaps fragmented and failed words vis-à-vis an image (the art of criticism itself) is all we can muster in the face of the nameless and in the name of love.

And then again, perhaps it is not for me to give the name. Perhaps it is for me to be named, to be called. In an Adamic reversal, the animal names the human.

> [Melancholy] is the most genuinely creaturely of the contemplative impulses, and it has always been noticed that its power need be no less in the gaze of a dog than in the attitude of a pensive genius. "Sir, sorrow was not ordained for beasts but men, yet if men do exceed in it they become beasts," says Sancho Paza to Don Quixote.[12]

---

> There were seventy of us in a forestry commando unit for Jewish prisoners of war in Nazi Germany. . . . We were beings entrapped in their species; despite all their vocabulary, beings without language. . . . How to deliver a message about one's humanity which, from behind the bars of quotation marks, will come across as anything else than the language of primates.

(Cambridge, Mass.: Belknap, 1999) 73.

11 Hélène Cixous, "Coming to Writing," in *"Coming to Writing" and Other Essays,* ed. Deborah Jenson (Cambridge: Harvard University Press. 1991) 2.

12 Walter Benjamin, *The Origin of German Tragic Drama,* trans. John Osborn (London: Verso, 1977) 146.

> And then, about halfway through our long captivity, for a few short weeks, before the sentinels chased him away, a wandering dog entered our lives. One day he came to meet this rabble as we returned under guard from work. He survived in some wild patch in the region of the camp. . . . He would appear at morning assembly and was waiting for us as we returned, jumping up and barking in delight. For him, there was no doubt that we were [human].
>
> Perhaps the dog recognized that Ulysses beneath his disguise on his return from the Odyssey was a forebear of our own. But no! There, it concerned Ithaca and the fatherland. Here, the place was nowhere. Last Kantian of Nazi Germany, not having the brains needed to universalize maxims out of one's drives, this dog descended from the dogs in Egypt. And his friendly growling—the faith of an animal—was born from the silence of his forefathers on the banks of the Nile.[13]

Through the surface of the walls of the House of the Deaf Man, the dog we are faced with calls us, names us, tells us we are human—for better or worse. We are con-fronted, faced with, the dog, just as we must bring about a necessary resur-facing of the dog, keeping it from complete burial. The only thing that remains of the dog that might allow it to be saved is the face.

> There is first the very uprightness of the face, its upright exposure, without defense. The skin of the face is that which stays most naked, most destitute. . . . [T]here is an essential poverty in the face; the proof of this is that one tries to mask this poverty by putting on poses, by taking on a countenance. The face is exposed, menaced, as if inviting us to an act of violence. At the same time, the face is what forbids us to kill. . . . [T]he face is meaning all by itself. You are you. In this sense one can say that the face is not "seen." It is what cannot become a content, which your thought would embrace; it is uncontainable, it leads you beyond. It is in this that the signification of the face makes its escape from being, as a correlate of knowing. . . .
>
> Face and discourse are tied. The face speaks. It speaks, it is in this that it renders possible and beings all discourse. . . . The first word of the face is the "Thou shalt not kill." It is an order. There is a commandment in the appearance of the face, as if a master spoke to me. However, at the same time, the face of the Other is destitute; it is the poor for whom I can do all and to whom I owe all. And me, whoever I may be, but as a "first person," I am he who finds the resources to respond to the call.[14]

[13] Emmanuel Levinas, "The Name of a Dog, or Natural Rights," in *Difficult Freedom,* trans. Seán Hand (Baltimore: Johns Hopkins University Press. 1990) 152–53.

[14] Levinas. *Ethics and Infinity* (Pittsburgh: Duquesne University Press, 1985) 86–87, 89

I must respond, be responsible, but I cannot set out from a stance of knowledge, from a secure position. I am instead exposed, and I turn to undertake a search for the resources to pull myself together to respond. At the same time I cannot narrativize this other, fill in the gaps, make silence speak, or the deaf hear. I remain suspended, fragmented, without knowledge, unnamed, sinking in questions.

> Don't shatter me, don't fragment me.
>
> This is not merely the effect of a will to self-protection, no more than the *Noli me tangere* of the Scriptures is. Don't touch me, says Christ arisen, because you couldn't, because you wouldn't know what you were touching, and because you would think you knew. You can't know anything or will anything about what is called a glorious body.
>
> Above all, we must not believe that we could know how to fragment, that we could know ourselves in fragments, that we actually could fragment. No one fragments, unless perhaps it is that *Noli me frangere* that all writing utters: don't fragment me, don't wish to fragment me—fragmentation goes on, and I'm fragmented enough; anyway, it's not up to you.[15]

---

> Fragments of a vessel that are to be glued together must match one another in the smallest details, although they need not be like one another. In the same way a translation, instead of imitating the sense of the original, must lovingly and in detail incorporate the original's way of meaning, thus making both the original and the translation recognizable as fragments of a greater language, just as fragments are part of a vessel.[16]

I left el Prado that day fragmented, dissected by many voices, speaking through the walls of the House of the Deaf Man. Wanting to protest *Noli me tangere,* or better, *Noli me frangere,* Don't fragment me. But I am always already fragmented. This is the struggle that leaves me suspended *between* aesthetics and ethics, between the fragmenting experience and the collection needed to respond to the face of the other, the call of the animal that names me and demands a response.

[15] Jean-Luc Nancy, with Philippe Lacoue-Labarthe. *"Noli me Frangere."* in *The Birth to Presence,* trans. Brian Holmes (Stanford: Stanford University Press. 1993) 267.

[16] Walter Benjamin, "The Task of the Translator," in *Walter Benjamin: Selected Writings, Volume One: 1913–1926,* 260.

# Critical Generosity

## *The Significance of Mary's Presentation to the Temple for Medieval Women Surviving Plague*

Kimberly Vrudny

In her book *Image as Insight*, Margaret R. Miles develops a method for image analysis she elsewhere calls "critical generosity."[1] Miles argues with generosity that, though many of the medieval images historians examine were made by men and therefore express the worldview from a male perspective, these images nonetheless convey aspects of experience not always accessible to historians in texts; they are, therefore, rich sources for historical inquiry. Even so, she argues that it is the responsibility of the historian to critique these visual sources for ways in which they diminished the humanity of those men and women whose lives were both reflected in and shaped by their existence. After constructing her method, she turns to its application by analyzing images from the fourth, fourteenth, and sixteenth centuries.

In this essay, written with appreciation for the integrity with which Miles has proven that images can serve as historical evidence and with respect for the manner in which Miles has exemplified her critical and generous methodology, I would like to develop a point Miles makes briefly in her essay on "Images of Women in Fourteenth-Century Tuscan Painting" in her book *Image as Insight*.[2] Miles argues with generosity that Italian women could identify with Mary at each stage of their lives, for surrounding them were numerous paintings of Mary's conception, childhood, betrothal, child-

[1] Margaret R. Miles, *Image as Insight: Visual Understanding in Western Christianity and Secular Culture* (Boston: Beacon, 1985). The methodology of "critical generosity" is specifically articulated in her book *Reading for Life: Beauty, Pluralism, and Responsibility* (New York: Continuum, 1997).

[2] Miles, *Image as Insight*, 63–93.

birth, and death. But with criticism, Miles goes on to assert that these images deny the very experiences of fourteenth-century women, for in nearly every circumstance, Mary's experiences were otherworldly and were, therefore, set apart from their own.

Certainly I do not dispute that Mary's experiences, including her own conception in the womb of Anna without the stain of sin as well as her virginal conception of Jesus and assumption into heaven, were extraordinary and unable to be replicated in the lives of medieval women. However, Mary was accessible to women especially in one experience that became all too familiar in the latter half of the fourteenth century: grief over the loss of a child. Mary's anguish over her brutalized son, and her grief over his subsequent death, made her accessible to a population whose infant mortality rates were high in regular circumstances, but who were particularly confronted with the death of children when plague revisited Europe in 1361, and roughly once a decade for the next century, killing infants, toddlers, and children at an overall death rate of three times the average.[3] Whereas Miles emphasizes how Mary was unlike the medieval women who were devoted to her, it is my contention that the experience of grief, with which the medieval population in the latter half of the fourteenth century could readily empathize, pervaded each stage of Mary's life, making her more accessible to the public despite the otherworldly nature of much of her experience.

This context of plague is important to keep in mind when considering fourteenth-century Marian piety, for Mary's experience of Christ's death extended beyond the year of his passion. In medieval understanding, his death overshadowed her entire life. She was born without the stain of sin—a feat made possible by the application of Christ's redemptive merits to Mary while she was still in Anna's womb. She was presented to the Temple, an exemplification of her own sacrifice, in order to prepare for his sacrificial atonement on the cross. And her sorrow was predicted in the first weeks of his life, when Simeon proclaimed at Christ's presentation that a sword would pierce Mary's own heart (Luke 2:35). Though Mary would not experience Christ's actual death until, tradition maintains, thirty-some years later, Simeon's prophecy cast its shadow. She knew of his death at least from the moment of his circumcision and experienced the intensity of her grief at the cross. But medieval Christians understood the experience of loss to color the years leading to her

[3] A fuller treatment of the impact of plague and religious response in the midst of plague appears in Kimberly Vrudny, "Scribes, Corpses, and Friars: Devotion to the Genetrix, Mediatrix, and Redemptrix through Dominican Didactic Use of the *Speculum humanae salvationis* in Late Medieval Europe" (Ph.D. diss., Luther Seminary, 2001) 34–73; see especially 54–55 for a discussion of the 1361 outbreak. See also Rosemary Horrox, ed. and trans., *The Black Death* (Manchester: Manchester University Press, 1994) 11–12, 85–98.

own death as well, for legends say that, despite the joy she experienced upon Christ's resurrection, she spent the two decades after his ascension yearning for her son, visiting the sites where he preached and performed miracles.[4] Upon her assumption, medieval Christians understood Mary to care for the souls of the blessed in heaven. Thus, the crucifixion of Christ overshadowed the entirety of Mary's life. Less than diminishing her accessibility to the medieval populace, the pervasive sense of sorrow throughout her life made her existence, despite the otherworldly nature of her experience, an advantage for those medieval Christians who hoped their deceased and beloved children were in this nanny's care in paradise.

In asserting that Mary's experiences were extraordinary, Miles admits that Mary becomes most accessible to women in the experience of the loss of their own children. "Only in motherhood, in her human pain over the death of her son, does Mary become a "typical' woman."[5] Miles goes on, despite this admission, to emphasize how Mary was unlike medieval women:

> A bewilderingly vast spectrum of images of women existed in fourteenth-century Italy. Among them, as we have seen, were idealized images of Mary, the "perfect" woman at each biological stage of her life. Thus a series of images was available with which a medieval woman might identify and in which she might find articulated the interests and values peculiar to her stage of life. Yet the clear message of these images, both verbal and visual, is the freedom of the Virgin from biological necessity at every stage of her life. She was conceived in a "special" way and was physically and religiously precocious in childhood. Her betrothal was attended with supernatural signs. She conceived without sexual intercourse and experienced childbirth without discomfort or loss of virginity. . . . Even her death was not a real human death; from the twelfth century on, she is shown ascending bodily on clouds into heaven. Mary, the Virgin/Mother, has a characteristic female life cycle but does not experience the biological life of human women. . . . On the one hand, women's experience and life cycle are articulated in a sequence of nuanced and profound images. On the other hand, women's sexuality and biological experience are pointedly rejected.[6]

[4] The poet discusses the places the Virgin visited after Christ's ascension in Chapter 35 of the *Speculum*. His source is Jacobus de Voragine. See Jacobus de Voragine, "The Assumption of the Blessed Virgin Mary," in *The Golden Legend: Readings on the Saints*, trans. William Granger Ryan II (Princeton: Princeton University Press, 1993) 77–78.

[5] Miles, *Image as Insight*, 83.

[6] Ibid., 82–83.

Miles goes on to argue critically and convincingly that these idealized images of Mary were destructive to medieval women, who could not compare with the standard for the spiritual life set by Mary.

> Male anxiety concerning the physicality and sexuality of real women, in addition to the threat of women's changing social roles, was translated into fantasies of women as purely spiritual and purely visual. These images did not, however, promote a transfer of esteem, affection, and acceptance by men from the images to actual women but emphasized the inferiority of women in comparison with the images.[7]

Even so, Miles acknowledges with generosity that these images, while devoid of inspiration for some present-day men and women, may have been admired nonetheless by medieval women for legitimate social reasons.

> An image that to many modern women has come to carry a repressive content may have meant something very different to medieval women. The idealization of the virginal woman, for example, may have symbolized to medieval women freedom from the burden of frequent childbearing and nursing in an age in which these natural processes were highly dangerous.[8]

In making these generous and critical observations, Miles downplays the example of Mary's sorrow. I propose the context of the loss of children during the second and subsequent outbreaks of plague in the fourteenth and subsequent centuries is a critical consideration in assessing the impact of images on fourteenth-century men and women. The experience of the loss of a child, which overshadowed every stage of Mary's life just as it profoundly impacted the lives of men and women in the fourteenth century, made Mary less the idealized image Miles characterizes her to be and more a figure of hope for a grieving population confronting the horrors of contagious disease. Instead of damaging women's self-image, depictions of Mary—even in stages considered biologically fantastic—may have served to give life and hope to men and women whose children did not survive to adulthood.

By focusing on images of the Presentation of the Virgin from the medieval epic poem *Speculum humanae salvationis* (*The Mirror of Human Salvation*), images representing loss in Mary's life long before her experience of Christ's passion, we can gain insight into the medieval practice of Marian piety, which understood the Presentation of Mary as an initiation of salvation history. Mary's sacrifice of her own aspirations made salvation, even the salvation of children, possible in the Middle Ages. Such a reality surely made more bio-

[7] Ibid., 87.

[8] Ibid., 88.

logically feasible representations of Mary undesirable for women experiencing loss in the fourteenth century, even if twenty-first-century women yearn for a sacred feminine more attuned to life cycles of modern-day women.[9]

In the last decades of the thirteenth century, or perhaps in the first years of the fourteenth, the *Speculum humanae salvationis*, whose author still remains anonymous to us, began to circulate in Europe.[10] Originally a Dominican preaching aid, the *Speculum* emphasized the role of Mary in redemption by placing Christ's life and passion in the wider context of Mary's life, from conception through dormition.[11] Though the *Speculum* itself was written decades before 1347, the first outbreak of plague, the book maintained its popularity throughout this first and most virulent outbreak despite the loss of a scribal force that could be devoted to its copying. Statistics about the book's production and distribution attest that there was a demand for this title both during and after the first outbreak, perhaps precisely because the poet is emphatic about Mary's role in redemption.[12] The ongoing popularity of the book indicates a hungering in the culture for more information about this mother, Mary, whose experience of sorrow over her suffering son

[9] For basic introductions to the *Speculum humanae salvationis*, see Vrudny, *Scribes*, 1–34; Albert C. Labriola and John W. Sneltz, *The Mirror of Salvation: Speculum humanae salvationis: an edition of British Library Blockbook G.11784* (Duquesne, Pa.: Duquesne University Press, 2002); Adrian Wilson and Joyce Lancaster Wilson, *A Medieval Mirror: Speculum humanae salvationis 1324–1500* (Berkeley: The University of California Press, 1984); and Avril Henry, *The Mirour of Mans Saluacioune: A Middle English Translation of Speculum humanae salvationis* (Philadelphia:: University of Pennsylvania Press, 1987).

[10] Dating of the *Speculum humanae salvationis* has long been debated. See Vrudny, *Scribes*, 1–34; see also Evelyn Ann Silber, "The Early Iconography of the *Speculum humanae salvationis*: The Italian Connection in the Fourteenth Century" (Ph.D. diss., Cambridge University, 1982).

[11] Though Dominican authorship was questioned for a time, almost all scholars now agree that the manuscript is Dominican. Most recently, the prolific scholar of the *Speculum,* Bert Cardon, has written, "It seems from what has been cited above that the author should be sought in Dominican circles. . . . If the identity of the author cannot yet be determined, one can at least state with a high degree of certainty that he was a Dominican." See Bert Cardon, *Manuscripts of the Speculum humanae salvationis in the Southern Netherlands (ca. 1410–ca. 1470): A Contribution to the Study of the Fifteenth Century Book Illumination and of the Function and Meaning of Historical Symbolism* (Leuven: Peeters, 1996) 41.

[12] For a discussion of distribution, see Vrudny, *Scribes*, 58–60, esp. n. 168. It should be noted that all computations are based on surviving manuscripts resulting in statistics that might be skewed, as there is no way to tell how many manuscripts were made and what random forces enabled 394 of them to survive. Of the 106 copies that can be dated from the 1300s, 10 are believed to have been copied before 1350. Of the remaining 96 copies, 38 are simply designated "14th century," 32 are dated 1350 or later, and 26 are late fourteenth century. The numbers point to sustained popularity after 1348.

so closely paralleled the lives of grief-stricken women in the latter half of the fourteenth century.

The *Speculum* described God's plan to save humankind from the impact of sin. By situating the history of the world within the context of the life of the Virgin Mary, the poet insisted that salvation history began when Mary was conceived in the womb of her mother, Anna, and would be concluded in the age after her Assumption into paradise and coronation as Queen of Heaven. Using a typological method of biblical interpretation, the poet understood certain events in the history of the world prior to the coming of Christ, events told in the Old Testament and in some carefully selected extra-biblical texts, to foreshadow events in Mary's life. Therefore, figures such as Eve and Esther were understood to prefigure moments in the life of Mary. Just as Eve brought sin into the world, so would Mary play a role in removing its consequences.[13] Just as Esther went to the king on behalf of the Jews who relied on her intervention to prevent their annihilation, so would Mary go to Christ on behalf of those Christians who prayed for her intercession to prevent their eternal damnation.[14] Because the poem is believed to have been a source book for Dominican preaching, portions of the populace may, indeed, have had access to its teachings in their churches and confraternities.[15] In this way, Christians who gained access to the poem's insights either directly or through sermons and artistic programs it inspired were prepared to understand with greater clarity God's intention for their eternal destiny generally and Mary's role in their redemption specifically.[16] In his fifth chapter, the poet

[13] For a discussion of the Mary/Eve typology, see Vrudny, "Scribes," 166–77.

[14] For a discussion of the Mary/Esther typology, see Vrudny, "Scribes," 200–15; see also Kimberly Vrudny, "Medieval Fascination with the Queen: Esther as Queen of Heaven and Host of the Messianic Banquet," *ARTS: The Arts in Religious and Theological Studies* 11.2 (1999) 36–43.

[15] For a discussion of the possible authorship of Dominican Friar Nicola da Milano, see Vrudny, "Scribes," 6–34 and 274–325.

[16] The *Speculum* was used as a model for iconographical sequences in other media. Its influence on the stained glass in Stephanskirche, Mulhouse, is indisputed. Studies have also been conducted on the sequences in Colmar, Rouffach, Wissembourg, St. Alban's Abbey, Bern Minster, King's College Chapel, Vic-le-Comte (Puy de Dôm) and Ste. Chapelle. Wall paintings in Le Monêtier (Hautes Alpes) and Brixen Cloister are related to *Speculum* panels, as are tapestries at Kloster Wienhausen, St. Bertin, La Chaise-Dieu (Auvergne), and Rheims. Archivolts at St. Maurice in Venice also seem to depend on the *Speculum*. Jan van Eyck is believed to have worked from a *Speculum* in the triptych for the church of Saint-Martin in Ypres, and the atelier of Roger van der Weyden shows dependence, too, on the *Speculum* in its Bladelin triptych. Likewise, its influence on the Duc de Berry and Konrad Witz has been treated. A relationship has also been shown in the mystery cycles. For discussion and bibliographic references of the *Speculum*'s spread to other media, see Silber, 28–29; Wilson, 28–29; and Henry, 12.

describes Mary's presentation to the Temple. Traditionally understood to take place at the age of three, when Anna weaned Mary from her breast, Mary was dedicated to a life of service to God in the Temple so that nothing sinister would be expected of her when she much later would conceive a child out of wedlock. As was the poet's pattern, three accompanying panels were selected from biblical and extra-biblical historical chronicles to elaborate theological understanding of the meaning of Mary's life in pure service to the Lord. The first was an episode recorded in Valerius's historical chronicle where a golden table in the sand was offered to the temple of the sun.[17] The second and third are of particular interest here for their interpretations of women. The second was from the book of Judges and recorded the sacrifice of Jephthah's daughter (Judg. 11:30-39). The third recounted the Assyrian Queen Semiramis surveying the city she had built from atop a palatial tower.[18]

The author of the *Speculum* drew upon Jacobus de Voragine's *Legenda Aurea*, or *The Golden Legend*, to recount Mary's presentation to the Temple, though the Infancy Gospel of James likewise recorded the early traditions regarding Mary's infancy and childhood. According to Jacobus, Mary was weaned from Anna's breast at the age of three. Upon reaching that milestone, Mary's parents were true to their vow to dedicate their daughter to the service of the Temple. On the day of the ceremony, Mary was placed at the bottom of fifteen steps leading to the Temple's door. She mounted these steps without assistance, as if fully grown.[19] And, the Infancy Gospel of James tells us, "The priest welcomed her, kissed her, and blessed her. . . . And he sat her down on the third step of the altar, and the Lord showered favor on her. And she danced, and the whole house of Israel loved her." Mary did not look back at Joachim and Anna upon entering the Temple, something that pleased her parents greatly.[20] In service to the Temple, Jacobus resumes, Mary advanced steadily in holiness, enjoying the vision of God daily within a regimen of

[17] Valerius Maximus, *Valerii Maximi Dictorvm factorvmq memorabilivm exempla: Adiecto indice Propriorum nominum, Rerumq; memoria dignarum locupletissimo* (Lvgdvni: Apvd Ioan. Tornaesivm et Gvl. Gazeivm, 1558) iv.i.7. Microfilm, University of Minnesota Wilson Library. See also Plutarch, *Plutarch: The Lives of the Noble Grecians and Romans, The Dryden Translation*, ed. Mortimer J. Adler, Great Books of the Western World 14 (Chicago: Encyclopaedia Britannica, 1952) 65.

[18] Comestor, *Historia Scholastica*, 1453.

[19] Voragine, *Golden Legend*, 152.

[20] Ronald F. Hock, editor, *The Infancy Gospels of James and Thomas*, Scholars Bible (Santa Rosa, Calif.: Polebridge, 1995) 47.

praying and weaving.[21] The Infancy Gospel simply adds that, in the Temple, Mary received "her food from the hand of a heavenly messenger."[22]

The poet of the *Speculum* is terse in his comments on this scene. Of the presentation of Mary to the Temple, he simply writes,

> In the preceding chapter we heard how the Virgin Mary was born;
> Consequently, let us hear how she was offered in the Temple to the Lord.
> When she was three, her parents brought her to the Temple
> And handed her over to the priest, so that she might serve the Lord and learn her letters.[23]

Medieval artists who illustrated the poet's text established Mary firmly within a Christian context. The copy owned now by the Kremsmünster monastery in Austria attests and will serve as an exemplar here. Mary, though three years of age and thus smaller than the adults, is depicted as a young woman, thereby emphasizing her spiritual maturity. She kneels on the altar of the Temple, which has been transformed into a church. The priest, Abiathar, holds his Bible in his left hand, and places his right hand on Mary's shoulder, a position reflected by Anna who stabilizes the depiction on the left. Joachim stands behind his wife, his hands folded prayerfully. Mary receives the church's blessing, which she then passes on to all of Christendom. In her work as Genetrix, Mary provided a gate of access to the holy of holies. She opened the world to the life of Christ himself. By sacrificing her life by devoting it wholly to the will of God, the poet understood Christians to gain access to God's own essence through the birth, crucifixion, and resurrection of Christ. The drama of Christ's later life is already palpable here, though he has not yet been conceived. The purpose of Mary's presentation was to prepare her to give birth to the incarnate Son of God, who would open the doors to paradise.

The second copy used as an exemplar here, currently housed at the Staatsbibliothek in Berlin, dates from the fourteenth or fifteenth century. According to a fifteenth-century colophon statement, it was owned by the Heiligengeist Hospital in Münich. Though faded, a nimbused Anna can be discerned presenting her child, Mary, to the altar. This time, Mary appears more like a child than a woman, but she already wears the crown of heavenly royalty. Mary seems to approach the altar gingerly, behind which two priests conduct the ceremony. The presence of this manuscript in a hospital in the fifteenth century, which undoubtedly housed plague victims in addi-

[21] Jacobus, *Golden Legend*, 152–53.

[22] Ronald F. Hock, editor, *The Infancy Gospels of James and Thomas*, Scholars Bible (Santa Rosa, Calif.: Polebridge, 1995) 47.

[23] *SHS* 5.1–4.

tion to others who were equally concerned about issues of human salvation, strengthens the argument that the *Speculum* was used for pastoral purposes and, moreover, that its lessons were thought to be of some comfort to the dying. Whether or not the hospital was served by a mendicant friar or even a priest who actually showed the book to patients, or personally consulted the book in preparation for conversations with the ill and dying, is a question that unfortunately cannot be answered on existing evidence, although such a prospect is certainly not impossible. Mendicants were known, and not only during times of plague, for their involvement with the ill.[24]

If the poem was written for Dominican friars, especially those in the service of Marian confraternities, as is generally believed, the poet's pattern of discussing three types for each antitypical scene from the New Testament is quite logical. The friars consulting the *Speculum* would have been able to weave the poet's typological interpretations into their own sermons easily, without requiring a great investment of resources to identify and research each New Testament topic and its Old Testament prefigurements. The theme of Mary's sacrifice brought to the poet's mind another story of sacrifice in the Bible, a story which he thought would illuminate the nature of those sacrifices required of Mary in her life of dedication to God. The story of Jephthah's daughter occupies the second panel relating to the presentation of Mary to the Temple.[25] Her story is told in the eleventh chapter of Judges.

[24] See Carlo M. Cipolla, "A Plague Doctor," in *The Medieval City*, Harry A. Miskimin, David Herlihy, A. L. Udovitch, eds. (New Haven, Conn.: Yale University Press, 1977) 65–72. Dominican confraternities in Italy, especially, were affiliated with hospitals. For a discussion, see Fra Nicola da Milano, *Collationes De Beata Virgine*, M. Michele Mulchahey, ed. (Toronto: Pontifical Institute of Mediaeval Studies, 1998) 7, 9–12. See also M. Michele Mulchahey, *First the Bow Is Bent in Study…: Dominican Education Before 1350*, Pontifical Institute of Mediaeval Studies 132 (Toronto: Pontifical Institute of Mediaeval Studies, 1999); and Barbara Wisch and Diane Cole Ahl, "Introduction," and Louise Marshall, "Confraternity and Community: Mobilizing the Sacred in Times of Plague," both in *Confraternities and the Visual Arts in Renaissance Italy: Ritual, Spectacle, Image* (Cambridge: Cambridge University Press, 2000) 1–19, 20–45.

[25] Patristic and medieval exegetical works on the book of the Judges include: Jerome, *Commentarius in Liber Judicum*, PL 28:507; Augustine, *Quaestiones et locutiones*, PL 34:545, 790; Paterius, *Liber de testimoniis*, PL 79:785; Isidore of Seville, *Quaestiones*, PL 83:379, 412; Bede, *Quaestiones super Librum Judicum*, PL 93:423; Rabanus Maurus, *Commentaria in Librum Judicum*, PL 108:1107; Walafrid Strabo, *Glossa ordinaria*, PL 113.521; Peter Damian, *Collectanea Vetus Vestamentum*, PL 145:1077; Rupert, *Commentaria*, PL 167:1023; Hugh of St. Victor, *Adnotationes elucidatoriae*, PL 175:87 and *De filia Jephte, in Append. ad Hugonem*, PL 177:323. See also E. Dinkler and V. Schubert, "Jephte," in *Lexicon der Christlichen Ikonographie*, 8 vols., ed. E. Kirschbaum (Rome: Herder, 1968–1976) 2:384–87, who adds John Chrystostum, *Hom. 14*, PG 49:147; Augustine, *Quaestionum in Heptateucham, CSEL* 28.2:481–501; Theodoret, *Quaestionum ad iud.*, PG 80:508; Anastasius, *Hexaem.*, PG 89:580–81. See also Peggy L. Day, "From the Child is Born the Woman: The Story of Jephthah's

Jephthah was "a most valiant man," (Judges 11:1) who was born the son of a harlot. His half-brothers resented the idea that a man of such poor birth should share their inheritance, so they "thrust [him] out" (Judg 11:2). Jephthah left his Israelite homeland and entered the land of Tob. He gathered around him an army of men even as Ammon made war against Israel. Becoming fearful of defeat at the hands of their enemies, the elders of Gilead humbled themselves, approached Jephthah, and asked him to be their leader. Jephthah agreed given the stipulation that if he should lead them to victory, he would become their "prince" (Judg 11:9). After sending correspondence to Ammon in which Jephthah justified the impending attack on the grounds that Ammon ought not to have disturbed a land that Yahweh had won from the Amorite god, with confidence the Israelite warrior "pass[ed] over . . . to the children of Ammon" (Judg 11:29). Then, without explanation, Jephthah began to doubt the presence of the Spirit of the Lord. Fatefully, Jephthah prayed to Yahweh. He vowed that he would offer as a burnt offering or holocaust "whosoever shall first come forth out of the doors of my house, and shall meet me when I return in peace from the children of Ammon" (Judg 11:31). When Yahweh granted Israel victory, Jephthah returned home only to be defeated. His daughter—his only child—rushed to greet her beloved father. When she saw that her father began to mourn her greeting, she accepted her fate with dignity (Judg 11:36). She requested sixty days to "bewail [her] virginity" (Judg 11:37). Then, after a two-month stay of execution, Jephthah "did to her as he had vowed" (Judg 11:39). This verse adds, "and she knew no man" (Judg 11:39).

The association of Jephthah's daughter with the Virgin Mary is, initially, perplexing. Though both were obedient daughters, what does this unwitting daughter, the victim of her father's egregious faithlessness, have to do with the Virgin Mary, who surrendered to her exceedingly faithful "Father"? The work of medieval exegete Rabanus Maurus does enable us to understand, at least in part,[26] the tradition of Jephthah's daughter as a type of the Virgin

Daughter," in *Gender and Difference in Ancient Israel*, ed. Peggy L. Day (Minneapolis: Fortress, 1989) 58–74; and Gertrud van Loon, "The Sacrifice by Abraham and the Sacrifice by Jephthah in Coptic Art," in *Coptic Art and Culture,* ed. H. Hondelink (Cairo: Shouhdy, 1990).

26 Phyllis Trible counts the story of Jephthah's daughter as a text of terror; see *Texts of Terror: Literary-Feminist Readings of Biblical Narratives,* Overtures to Biblical Theology (Philadelphia: Fortress, 1984) 93–116. Although one might guess that Jephthah perishes in the *Inferno* for his hateful act, Dante never says so explicitly. Rather, Jephthah is mentioned in the *Paradiso* in Beatrice's exposition on the sanctity of the vow and the perils of evil vows. "Let no man make his vow a sporting thing. / Be true and do not make a squint-eyed choice / as Jephthah did in his first offering. / He had better have cried, "I had no right to speak!' / than, keeping his vow, do worse." See Dante Alighieri, *The Divine Comedy: The Paradiso,* trans. John Ciardi (New York: Penguin, 1970) 5.64–68. See also Thomas Aquinas, *Summa Theologiae*, ii. 2, q.

Mary.[27] In his *Commentaria in Librum Judicum et Ruth*, Rabanus retells the story of Jephthah's daughter in some detail, making frequent reference to the story of Abraham and Isaac in the book of Genesis, emphasizing the differences in character between Abraham, the faithful one, and Jephthah, the weaker in faith. Rabanus reasoned that Jephthah clearly believed that his daughter would not be the first to greet him upon his return. It was not with malicious forethought that Jephthah murdered his daughter, Rabanus reasoned. He expected someone else to greet him first. Nonetheless, in so bartering, Jephthah exhibited great lack of faith. In a tropological vein, Rabanus wrote that Jephthah needed to carry out the vow in order to underscore that such faithlessness would be punished with great severity. The wrenching pain one experienced upon hearing of his sacrifice would act as a preventative measure, Rabanus hoped; surely no one else would make the same fateful mistake.[28]

But Rabanus could not avoid the horrifying nature of Jephthah's act. He took an almost scolding tone when he asked: "But whom did he think would meet him first—he who did not have any sons?"[29] He answered his own question, saying that Jephthah, perhaps, thought his wife would greet him first upon his return from battle. This is still offensive—why would the sacrifice of Jephthah's wife be any less horrifying than the sacrifice of his daughter? But Rabanus's move is a strategic one. He moves skillfully to explain why, in the allegorical scheme of things, Jephthah could not have sacrificed his wife. This episode, to Rabanus, was a prefigurement of the presentation of Mary to the temple. Thus, just as Jephthah and, presumably, his wife, sacrificed their daughter, so did Joachim and Anna give up their daughter on an altar to the Lord. If the characters were changed to accommodate the sacrificial slaughter of Jephthah's wife rather than his daughter, Rabanus reasoned, the parallel could not have been drawn. Such an allegory would have required the sacrificial slaughter of Anna, rather than of her daughter. Thus, the allegorical scheme rehearsed in God's mind from the beginning of time required the death of Jephthah's daughter, not the death of his wife.

In Rabanus's mind, just as Jephthah was victorious due, in some measure, to a vow he had made to God to sacrifice his daughter so, too, was the church victorious over death through the sacrifices of Mary. Rabanus believed

---

lxxxviii, a. 2 ad 2.

27 As in the case of Balaam and his ass, Jephthah's daughter was a type of Christ in the early church. Again, a change from a Christological to a Mariological interpretation has taken place in the exegetical tradition, but precisely when and how the transition was made remains unclear.

28 Rabanus Maurus, *Commentaria in Librum Judicum et Ruth,* PL 108:1186–90.

29 Ibid., 1189.

that God, from the beginning of time, had orchestrated the events of the Old Testament and that, in time, their allegorical meanings would be revealed. God needed, or so thought Rabanus, to coordinate a similarly wrenching sacrifice in the Old Testament in order for humans to comprehend God's offering to humanity in the New. In order to keep the parallel rigid, the sacrifice needed to encompass purity. Clearly, Rabanus reasoned, Jephthah's wife was no longer a virgin and so God could not allow the sacrifice of such a character who would prove, in time, to be an inappropriate and impure allegorical parallel for the Christian church. His daughter alone was equal to the task of representing such purity: she alone was worthy to be an allegory of the most blessed Virgin Mary. So it was that in Jephthah's act, Rabanus sees the glorious rising of a new age—an age which would be revealed in Christ.[30]

The daughter's unselfish sacrifice of her own life to the service of God is what enables the parallel to Mary, and is what makes the typological interpretation useful in the poet's book on the theme of salvation. The sacrifice represents, finally, the resurrection of the dead. This association is made clear in Rabanus's commentary on the daughter's request for a sixty-day stay of execution. In this section, the exegete speaks more directly of the association between the two women. He interprets that, allegorically, his fellow human beings in the ninth century still experience the stay of execution of Jephthah's daughter through his division of temporal time into six ages: the first from Adam to the flood, the second from the flood to Abraham, the third from Abraham to David, the fourth from David to the exile, the fifth from the exile to the birth of the Virgin, and the sixth from the birth of the Virgin to the end of this age. Clearly, he conceives himself and his fellow Christians to be experiencing the sixth age, a time that ought to be spent in repentance and preparation for living in a perpetually redeemed state. He writes, "Throughout these six ages, as if throughout sixty days, the church of the blessed Virgin mourned its virginity since even virginal things should be mourned like sins had been mourned."[31] In this in-between time in which believers wait for the second coming of the Lord, Rabanus encouraged the penitent to mourn their sins, which prevent them from enjoying a full life, just as the request for sixty days enabled Jephthah's daughter to mourn her own life, which would not be lived in its fullness. Furthermore, before she perished, Rabanus understood Jephthah's daughter to mourn the deaths of those for whom there would be no eternity. She mourned for those whose sins would go unrepented, whose stubbornness prevented them from seeing God face-to-face. The stay of execution would be lifted, he believed, when

30 Ibid.

31 Ibid.

the sixth age came to a close—when the day of judgment passed on to the timeless and glorious age of the Kingdom of God.[32]

The poet of the *Speculum* borrowed the association between Jephthah's daughter and Mary, although much less enthusiastically than did Rabanus. The poet's reflections illuminate the differences between the sacrifice of Jephthah's daughter and the sacrifices required of Mary. While Jephthah sacrificed his daughter "inappropriately and wrongly" because afterwards she could not serve God, "Joachim and Anna offered their daughter properly and perfectly . . . so that living she might serve the Lord." While Jephthah's vow must be "censured by holy doctors," Mary's vow was praised "as much by God as by His angels." Jephthah's daughter mourned her virginity while Mary approved gladly of her own. Jephthah's daughter "was offered after a victory, to give thanks" while Mary "was offered before victory so that victory could be gathered." Finally, and perhaps most importantly, while Jephthah's daughter "was offered for the sake of victory over worldly foes," Mary "won victory over infernal enemies."[33]

Those who consulted the Kremsmünster manuscript saw an unhappy Jephthah, clothed in full armor. His sword had been removed from its sheath with, one can surmise, some level of reservation. It was then plunged through the daughter's abdomen, stained with blood as it protruded from her back. The daughter, kneeling before her father on top of a brick altar draped with cloth and decorated with one burning candle, extended her hands to her father, whose own hands bound her wrists. The deranged father, with obligatory reluctance, drove his sword through his daughter's body, finishing the act with a final thrust, his sword piercing his daughter's very heart in an early prefigurement of the sword that would pierce Mary's heart also.[34] The sacrifice was accomplished. And yet, for the medieval audience, there was consolation. The story pointed beyond itself, foreshadowing sacrifices Mary would make, first, in the dedication of her life to God just as the life of Jephthah's daughter was offered to God and second, in the sacrifice of the fruit of her womb, represented by the knife piercing the daughter's abdomen.

The panel from Berlin eliminates the reference to the sword. Indeed, whereas the Kremsmünster copy captures the climactic moment just as the sword strikes, this panel captures the somber atmosphere that doubtlessly filled

32 Ibid., 1189–90.

33 *SHS* 5.37–53.

34 Some believed the sword of Simeon's prophecy predicted Mary's failure in faith on Calvary, while others interpreted the prophecy as proof of Mary's simultaneous passion. For a discussion of the various interpretations surrounding Simeon's pronouncement, see Michael O'Carroll, *Theotokos: A Theological Encyclopedia of the Blessed Virgin Mary* (Wilmington, Del.: Glazier, 1986) 143–44, 387.

the sanctuary. Three figures are depicted, their reverence palpable. Jephthah, crowned and robed, stands beside a priest, also crowned and robed. Both men's hands are folded in front of their hearts. With sober facial expressions, they look at Jephthah's daughter who bows on top of the altar, as though quietly accepting her fate. The act is left unconsummated. The act itself is replaced in this panel with a pervading sense of holiness that relates it much more readily to the medieval interpretation accompanying it. The dedication of Jephthah's daughter to the will of God signifies Mary's presentation to the altar and the sacrifice of her womanhood to the will of God.

Just as Jephthah sacrificed his daughter to Yahweh after promising to offer the firstfruits, so to speak, of his victorious homecoming, so too did Joachim sacrifice his daughter to God after promising to dedicate his offspring to the Lord's service should he be blessed with progeny. Surely, their sacrifices entailed different losses, but the association of the two stories held significance for lives of faith in the Middle Ages. In Jephthah's commitment to the law of God, medieval Christians were to remember how the Virgin Mary's parents, Joachim and Anna, were committed to the service of the Lord in the act of offering their daughter to the church. In the announcement that the beloved daughter would be killed, the Christian devotee was to meditate on the Virgin's sacrifice. She dedicated her will and her dignity to the service of her God who, in time, asked for the sacrifice of her Son, Jesus the Christ. In the daughter's request for a stay of execution, the believer was likewise to repent, confess one's sin, and await redemption. Finally, in the daughter's joyful submission, the devout medieval Christian was to reflect on one's own joyful submission to the church of all believers, which would be victorious over sin, death, and the power of the devil on the day of the Last Judgment (Luke 2). By the penetration of a sword through her womb, the sacrifice of Jephthah's daughter became an image of glory, her death an image of victory. It called to mind the like sacrifice of Mary, a sword piercing her soul (Luke 2:35) even as it guaranteed Christ's death, an act, though brutal, deemed necessary by God for the redemption of the world.[35] Jephthah's sacrifice of his daughter was an act with which Joachim and Anna could empathize, for they had made a like offering. Through Mary's sacrifice, medieval Christians knew they, and their baptized children, were absolved and could stand before God free from the guilt of their sins. It was a rich tradition, which inspired Christians to greater faith when encountered, interwoven into text and picture, in the *Speculum humanae salvationis*.

At the same time, however, the method of historical inquiry encouraged by Margaret Miles is that we take a critical appraisal of the texts and images

[35] See Thomas Aquinas, *Summa Theologiae*, III.1.2.

that may have proven harmful to the men and women whose spiritual lives had been shaped by interaction with them. Left almost unexplored in the previous examination of the medieval understanding of the story of Jephthah's daughter is the textual horror of Jephthah's fateful carelessness and faithlessness, which led to the brutality shown to his own daughter in the name of religious devotion. Rabanus recognized the offensive nature of the text, but was compelled to find theological meaning in relation to Mary, which left unquestioned the cruelty shown to the unnamed daughter. Such devotion prevented a serious questioning of the value of the allegorical relation. If the story of Jephthah demonstrates the lack of faith in the one who oversees the sacrifice, theological questions are raised. Though Joachim is parallel to Jephthah, God, finally, is the one calling for the sacrifice in both situations: Jephthah must carry out his vow to please God in the same way that Joachim and Anna must carry out their vow to ensure that God's plan for the salvation of humankind is carried out. God is true to both sacrifices by granting Jephthah victory in battle and by granting Joachim and Anna the conception of a child. But the nature of a God who demands such sacrifices is left unquestioned. Also left unexplored in the medieval treatment of these themes is the theological dimension of a God who would intervene to preserve the life of a beloved son, Isaac, when shown the faithfulness of Abraham, but who would neglect to intervene to preserve the life of an unnamed girl, when shown the faithlessness of Jephthah.[36] Left unexplored is the experience of the unnamed daughter in the face of the terror befallen her by her father's lack of faith, as is the experience of the Virgin Mary whose very life was threatened in an ancient culture intolerant of conceptions outside of marriage, and whose economic status was dependent on those men who would be alienated by her announcement of a babe now present in her womb. Left unexplored is the impact of such interpretations on those women who encountered these understandings in churches and confraternities where such exegesis was preached. Noting the void is, in itself, significant, though judgment of the impact of the lapse perilous, for Miles's own generous appraisal insists that "[a]n image that to many modern women has come to carry a repressive content may have meant something very different to medieval women."[37] We stand, then, in awe of the complexity, and look to clues for understanding medieval perceptions in more expansive interpretive frameworks. Offered here is the context of plague as a consideration in assessing the power of the typology of Jephthah's daughter for Mary, whose sacrifice enabled the redemption of the baptized infants and children who succumbed to the plague's ferocity.

36 Day, *From the Child Born*, 58–74.

37 Miles, *Image*, 89.

The third and final *Speculum* panel to elaborate the theological meaning of the presentation of Mary to the Temple involved another woman who acquired a position of allegorical significance in the church. The source for this parallel, however, comes not from Hebrew scriptures but from secular accounts of history.[38] This figure lived some eight hundred years before Christ and was renowned in secular circles for the expansion of Assyria. Her name was Semiramis.[39]

That Semiramis's identity is known to us is to the credit of Diodorus Siculus, a Greek historian from the first century BCE.[40] Diodorus wrote a "universal" history entitled *Bibliotheca Historica*, which in forty books told the mythic history of the non-Hellenic and Hellenic tribes to the destruction of Troy, from the destruction of Troy to the death of Alexander, and from the death of Alexander to the beginning of Caesar's Gallic War. The latest event he mentions occurred in 21 BCE; it is likely that he died shortly thereafter.[41]

Having completed an account of the beginnings of civilization in Egypt, Diodorus turns to the history of the Assyrian Empire. He begins with the military exploits of King Ninus, who conquered the territories of Babylon, Media, Egypt, and Persia. Upon acquiring these vast territories, Ninus concentrated his efforts on building a great city in Syria. He named it Nineveh after himself, then "marched with an army against the Bactrians."[42] It was in this confrontation that he met and subsequently married Semiramis. Of her, Diodorus writes, "being so famous above any of her sex, (as in history it is related), we cannot but say something of her here in this place, being one

38 The author of the *Speculum* found reference to the story in Peter Comestor, *Historia Scholastica–Liber Danielis*, PL 198:1453. Perhaps the most thorough record of Semiramis is found in Diodorus the Sicilian, *The Historical Library of Diodorus the Sicilian, in Fifteen Books, to which are added The Fragments of Diodorus, and those published by H. Valesius, I. Rhodomannus, and F. Ursinus*, ed. G. Booth (London: McDowall, 1814) 1:99–117. See also J. W. McCrindle, ed., *The Invasion of India by Alexander the Great as Described by Arrian, Q. Curtius, Diodoros, Plutarch, and Justin, Being Translations of such portions of the Works of these and other Classical Authors as describe Alexander's Campaigns in Afghanistan the Panjab, Sindh, Gedrosia and Karmania*, 2d ed. (Westminster: Constable, 1896) 170, 173, 246, 358.

39 It is significant that, unlike Jephthah's daughter, Semiramis is named. Historically, Semiramis probably refers to Queen Sammuramat, the wife of Assyrian King Shamshi-Adad V, and queen-regent 810–805 BCE for her son, Adad-Niram III.

40 Diodoros, *Historical Library*, 99–117.

41 The *Bibliotheca* is a valuable resource. It preserves to some extent the works of Ephorus (for 480–340 BCE) and Hieronymus of Cardia (for 323–302 BCE), whose works have not survived but which were compiled into Diodorus' work. Additionally, he mentions Ctesias's history in the text. Diodorus's other sources are unknown.

42 Diodorus, *Historical Library*, 102.

advanced from so low a fortune, to such a state and degree of honour and worldly glory."[43]

Diodorus explains that Semiramis had been born to the goddess Derceto. When Venus became angry with Derceto for an unknown transgression, Venus arranged for her to fall in love with a young man. Burning with passion for the handsome bachelor, Derceto became pregnant and bore a daughter. Ashamed then of her actions, she killed the young man, "exposed the child among rocks in the desert," and then, in great sorrow, cast herself into the lake where she was promptly transformed into a fish-goddess.[44]

Although the daughter was exposed to the elements, the gods looked upon her with favor. She was cared for by a flock of pigeons, which nestled near her and kept her warm. In order to feed her they took milk from nearby farms and then, returning to the nest, poured the milk from their beaks into the baby's mouth. When she was a year old and in need of stronger nourishment, the pigeons stole cheese from nearby shepherds. One day the shepherds followed the pigeons in order to learn why pigeons needed cheese. They were surprised to find that the chase led them to a baby girl. The shepherds took the young lady to Simma, the king's highest ranking herdsman, who reared the girl as his own and named her Semiramis, the Syrian word for pigeon.[45] She grew to be a woman who exceeded "all others of her sex for the charms of her beauty."[46]

The first to fall in love with Semiramis was Menon, one of the king's officers who was enamored with her from first sight. He obtained permission from Simma to marry her, although there was "much entreaty" regarding this transfer of property.[47] They moved to Nineveh where Semiramis bore two sons. Diodorus, noting that Semiramis was also a woman of surpassing intelligence, indicated that Menon would do nothing without her advice and, because of her charmed mind, was always successful. She was successful, that is, until Ninus completed his building projects in Nineveh, at which time he attacked the strongly fortified nation of Bactria. Menon, who took part in the siege, grew lonely for his beloved Semiramis when he realized how long the battle might last. He called for her to join him on the front line. She readily accepted the invitation but, knowing the danger that awaited her, dressed like

43 Ibid.

44 Ibid. Diodorus notes that "at this very day the Syrians eat no fish, but adore them as gods."

45 Diodorus notes that the Syrians ever after worshipped pigeons as goddesses.

46 Diodorus, *Historical Library*, 103.

47 The details regarding the exchange of property are lacking.

a man for her journey. In that way, Diodorus notes, she was "more nimble" if forced to retreat.[48]

Semiramis joined her husband and carefully observed the ensuing battles. She noticed that the castle was protected only on the lower level. She thought of a way for her husband's army to triumph over its enemies; she climbed one of the unmonitored walls with some Assyrian warriors, surprised the Bactrians from behind, took the castle, and claimed victory. King Ninus took notice of Semiramis due to her unprecedented combination of wit, bravery, and beauty. He asked for her hand in marriage and threatened Menon with death should his request be denied. In rage and madness, Menon hanged himself. Ninus then married the widowed Semiramis and named her the Queen of Assyria. Shortly thereafter, they had a son together. Ninus did not live to see his son a man; when he died he left Semiramis queen regent of Assyria.

Semiramis was "ambitious to excel all her predecessors in glorious actions" and therefore decided to build a city second to none in the province of Babylon. She planned the city so that the Euphrates would run right through it and so that the city walls would be wide enough for "six chariots abreast . . . [to] be driven together upon them." Diodorus describes the city in some detail, commenting especially on the extravagant city walls, palaces, and towers. On one tower, for example, artists painted a colorful picture of Semiramis as a huntress. She was depicted on horseback, killing a leopard with a dart while her husband killed a lion with a lance. It was said that Semiramis stood atop these towers to "have a prospect over the whole city."[49]

When she had finished the construction of Babylon, which, Diodorus notes with a hint of pride, took only one year, Semiramis traveled to places such as Mount Bagistan and Chaone in Media, where she planted gardens wherein she could give "herself [up] to all kinds of pleasures and delights."[50] She refused to marry, for she intended to keep her place of honor in the government, and she contented herself by enjoying the company of the most handsome commanders. Without passing judgment, Diodorus writes that "after they had lain with her she cut off their heads."[51] She continued her construction projects throughout Persia and Egypt, but somehow became bored with it all. Her thoughts turned to her own death. In Libya, she consulted an

48 Diodorus gushes with praise for Semiramis. He says that she wished to show "the world her own natural valour and resolution." Furthermore, when Semiramis decided to dress like a man, Diodorus notes that it became fashionable throughout the world (Diodorus, *Historical Library,* 104).

49 Diodorus, *Historical Library*, 105–6.

50 Ibid., 110.

51 Ibid.

oracle to learn how much longer she would live. The oracle responded that her death was near, for her son Ninyas was plotting against her.

Apparently unalarmed by this threat to her well-being, Semiramis began a plot of her own to acquire the rich country of India, which had escaped even her husband's exploits. Semiramis was confident that she would have ample numbers of men to defeat the Indians, but she was concerned by the number of elephants the Indians possessed in their arsenal. In answer to this significant challenge, she hired a number of mechanics and cobblers to design fake elephants that, from a distance, would fool the Indians and fill them with terror. When Stabrobates, the Indian king, learned of Semiramis's impending invasion, he readied his people to defend their country. In addition, he sent ambassadors to Semiramis to complain about her instigation of war without provocation. He concluded the letter with an expression of disgust for her "whorish course of life."[52]

Initially, Semiramis was victorious in battle. Her army, complete with fake elephants, sieged the Indians, who retreated over the river. But, alas, Semiramis's "cheat could not be long concealed."[53] Fallen Indians, getting a closer look at the Assyrian elephants, saw that they were merely disguised men. They sent word throughout the ranks. Hearing that they had been tricked, Stabrobates turned his troops to face the advancing Assyrians led by Semiramis herself. At first, Semiramis gained the advantage, for the Indians lost control of their horses, which feared the mock elephants. The wheel of fortune would turn against Semiramis, however, for the Indian elephants "easily bore down and destroyed all that opposed them, so that there was a great slaughter; for some they trampled under foot, others they rent in pieces with their teeth, and tossed up others with their trunks into the air."[54] The Assyrians fled. Semiramis was hit in the arm by an arrow shot by the Indian king and in the shoulder by an unidentified soldier's dart. Many were trampled in the retreat, but Semiramis's wounds were not mortal. After most of her men had crossed the bridge, she cut the bridge's cords, sending the pursuing Indians into the strong currents of the river. Multitudes, reports Diodorus, were drowned. Only one-third of Semiramis's own army survived.

Perhaps humbled by the narrow escape, perhaps tired of war and building projects, or perhaps wiser with age, Semiramis readied herself to resign. Remembering the oracle about the plot against her life, she passed the crown to her son without struggle. Afterwards, she disappeared. Some said she was "translated to the gods." Others said she was "metamorphosed into a pigeon."

52 Ibid., 114.

53 Ibid., 115.

54 Ibid.

The reign of Semiramis was ended, at any rate, and her kingdom was now in the hands of her son.[55]

The *Speculum* poet looked to Semiramis's military conquests and building projects as a way to extol the figure as a type of the Virgin Mary. The poet found his entry point in the gardens Semiramis was said to plant atop her palatial towers. The poet of the *Speculum* explains the association in this way:

> After her consecration Mary continuously served the Lord.
> But how she served God and what life she embraced
> Were prefigured in that famous garden, said to be suspended.
> The king of Persia planted it for his wife on lofty supports,
> And from it she strove to gaze upon her distant homeland.
> By this is designated Mary's contemplative life
> That pressed always to contemplate the heavenly home.[56]

Given the understanding of the garden as the dwelling place of the Virgin Mary,[57] whose womb produced great fruit, modern readers may begin to see the poet's attraction to Semiramis, who was said to own many of these sanctuaries throughout Babylon, from the heights of which she was able both to meditate upon and survey her city's activities. This was the scene borrowed by the artists of the Kremsmünster *Speculum* manuscript under examination here. The crowned queen surveys the countryside, the *civitas mundi,* from atop a stone tower. The left side of the image represents Semiramis, symbolized by the pigeon held in the woman's left hand. A flowerless vine grows, indicating she is Queen over the sinful *civitas mundi*. Yet the woman is also the Virgin Mary, on whose right grows a flowering vine indicating she is Queen over the righteous *civitas dei*. The tower, from the tops of which this Virgin devotes her life to contemplation of things godly, is locked. Based on Ezekiel 44:2, the lock was a motif used to emphasize Mary's virginity, suggesting Mary's womb was the doorway through which no man trespassed: "And the Lord said to me: This gate shall be shut, it shall not be opened, and no man shall pass through it: because the Lord the God of Israel hath entered in by it, and it shall be shut." Differentiating Mary from Semiramis, the poet writes,

> The other virgins would return to their own concerns;
> She tried to remain always in the temple of the Lord;
> She stayed and always would study;
> By reading and reading again she advanced.[58]

55 Ibid.

56 *SHS* 5.54–60.

57 See Vrudny, "Scribes," 91–106.

58 *SHS* 5.71–74

While Semiramis was said to have contemplated the countryside from the gardens the poet says her husband had planted for her atop palatial towers, Mary, crowned Queen of Heaven, devoted her existence to the righteous contemplation of God. It is noteworthy that, in the Berlin copy, Semiramis is joined by a male—her husband, one hopes, rather than the other men with whom she is said to have kept company on these towers, considering she is here representative of the most Blessed Virgin Mary. If the man depicted is, in fact, her bridegroom, surely he represents Christ, to whom Mary was married in a mystical marriage.

Left unexamined in this medieval treatment of Semiramis, however, is the independence, inner resolve, and even cunning nature of the Queen Regent—qualities that enabled her to conquer the throne, foreign nations, and even her own consorts. Ignoring these qualities, the poet elevated those aspects of Semiramis, and thereby of the Virgin Mary, men found most desirable in women: her serene and contemplative nature made visible by those hours spent in gardens. Miles explains, "Simplified thus, the strong and sometimes threatening women of fourteenth-century culture became manageable for men, and not just manageable but inspirational; a danger and threat had been converted to an advantage."[59]

Certainly, some of Semiramis's characteristics required sublimation in order to make the parallel to Mary possible for medieval exegetes. The earthly queen's sexual escapades, for one, certainly were contrary to the purity of the Virgin Mary and were necessarily put aside for doctrinal reasons. Whereas the poet found aspects of Semiramis's life compelling in drawing a parallel to Mary, other Christian authors addressed the obvious interpretive problems directly. Augustine, in *The City of God*, argued that there are two opposing civilizations: the city of God, founded by Abraham (*civitas dei*), and the city of humankind, rejuvenated by Semiramis (*civitas mundi*).[60] Much later, Dante likewise interpreted Semiramis to be the motivating force behind the degenerate society that opposes God's divine order. She perishes in the second circle of hell among the lustful whose eternal punishment consists of being forever whirled about in a dark, stormy wind:

> And just like cranes in flight, chanting their lays,
> stretching an endless line in their formation,
> I saw approaching, crying their laments,
> spirits carried along by the battling winds.
> And so I asked, "Teacher, tell me, what souls

[59] Miles, *Image*, 64.

[60] Augustine, *Concerning the City of God against the Pagans*, trans. Henry Bettenson (New York: Penguin, 1972, 1984) 764–65.

are these punished in the sweep of the black wind?"
"The first of those whose story you should know,"
my master wasted no time answering,
"was empress over lands of many tongues;
her vicious tastes had so corrupted her
she licensed every form of lust with laws
to cleanse the stain of scandal she had spread;
she is Semiramis, who, legend says,
was Ninus' wife as well as his successor;
she governed all the land the Sultan rules. . . ."[61]

Augustine and Dante emphasized Semiramis's desire for lustful pleasure, leaving unexamined her political savvy. The poet, by drawing only on her more contemplative moments in those hanging gardens and by ignoring the sexual prowess and even violent potential witnessed therein, left unexamined the theological and anthropological significance of the presence of a female overseeing the kingdoms of both God and of humankind. Left unexamined, too, is the transformative impact that such interpretations could have served the men and women who encountered them. Even so, the story's placement in a chapter about Mary's Presentation to the Temple assured the medieval interpreter of Mary's presence overseeing both kingdoms from her heavenly station. For men and women of the fourteenth century, her presence there promised consolation; they could be sure their deceased children were in Mary's care.

The *Speculum humanae salvationis* captures in poem and picture the medieval fascination with the Virgin Mary through biblical typological interpretation. The fifth chapter examines the sacrifices required of Mary through its discussion of Joachim and Anna's presentation of Mary to the Temple and especially its two types: Jephthah's daughter and the Queen Semiramis. These episodes express in visual terms the belief that, by God's design, Mary was chosen to inaugurate the redemption of the world. The medieval poet recorded how one milestone on the journey to redemption was achieved when Mary accepted willingly her role and sacrificed her will to God, as was exemplified in her Presentation to the Temple. The generous and critical methodology developed by Margaret Miles has enabled us to appreciate the medieval understanding of Mary's role in redemptive history generously without forcing us to dismiss the critical reality that the author's selective interpretation of Jephthah's daughter and Semiramis as types for Mary's presentation served simultaneously to limit human potential in medieval culture. By keeping the context of plague in the background of our discussion, moreover, we have

[61] Dante Alighieri, *The Divine Comedy: Vol. I: Inferno*, trans. Mark Musa (New York: Penguin, 1984) 3.46–60.

been able to understand the medieval impulse to find similarity with Mary despite the otherworldly nature of much of her experience. Seeing in the story of Jephthah's daughter a prefigurement of Mary's role in redemption, and in the story of Semiramis a prefigurement of Mary's role in caring for souls in the afterlife, the *Speculum* poet allows us to gain access to fourteenth-century piety. We can imagine how these events in Mary's admittedly extraordinary life were significant for fourteenth-century women despite their fantastic and irreplicable nature. Though Miles is undoubtedly right, that these images had destructive effects for women who were not able to achieve the spiritual perfection of Mary, it is my contention that the poet's interpretations, accessible to medieval men and women who encountered the poet's understandings in the *Speculum* and in the sermons of preachers who were inspired by it, surely consoled men and women who, unlike Mary in many ways, nevertheless resonated with Mary's experience of loss, and were comforted by the knowledge of her care-giving presence in paradise.

## Shamhat

Hair of the dog, un-
sympathetic magic, broke
pony yoked to a wild
stallion—so I was sent
to Enkidu, the wooly genius of the woods
and grasslands, ibex-familiar,
who winters torpid with the bear, insatiable
slinker with ocelot and lynx,
single, simple-seeing savage
innocent.

So I displayed my body
temple-painted, ibis-slender,
(red-rump paid goods)
for his domestication.
The exotic musky child,
unfrightened by the swarm,
tongued my honey,
took my scent.

At the oasis the tiger
startles from him,
foxes skitter back to the brush.
The deer's sly language fumbles
on his tongue, tasting of
treason. Now he is alone
in his diminishment.

Lonely at first for me, as I
led him love-muzzled down
to Uruk to play gladiator
to the whoring, sotted boar
Gilgamesh, unprincely
prince Chellish, hell-bent.

All night they wrestled, sweat to sweat
breast to breast, breath spent,
then lazed in one another's arms and rose
friends inseparable, blood-let
tempered twins, complete.
So I was sent

packing to the shrine where sisters turned away,
where Anu withdrew his confidences, where
the cats spit, the finches flee my hand, and even
Ishtar is silent.

At what cost, Uruk, this peace
for which Shamhat was spent?

—Jennifer M. Phillips

# Bibliography of Margaret R. Miles

## Books


*A Complex Delight: The Secularization of the Breast, 1350–1750.* Chicago: University of Chicago Press, forthcoming.

*The Word Made Flesh: A History of Christian Thought.* Includes CD-ROM. Oxford and Malden, Mass.: Blackwell, 2005.

*Plotinus on Body and Beauty: Society, Philosophy, and Religion in the Third-Century Rome.* Oxford and Malden, Mass.: Blackwell, 1999.

*Reading for Life: Beauty, Pluralism, and Responsibility.* New York: Continuum, 1997.

*Seeing and Believing: Religion and Values in the Movies.* Boston: Beacon, 1996.

*Desire and Delight: A New Reading of Augustine's Confessions.* New York: Continuum, 1992; Italian ed., *Agostino "Le Confessioni."* Turin, Italy: Lindau, 1991.

*Carnal Knowing: Female Nakedness and Religious Meaning in the Christian West.* Boston: Beacon, 1989. British ed., Tunbridge Wells: Burns & Oates, 1990. Paperback ed., New York: Vintage, 1991.

*Practicing Christianity: Critical Perspectives for an Embodied Spirituality.* New York: Crossroad, 1988. British ed.: *The Image and Practice of Holiness: A Critique of the Classic Manuals of Devotion.* London: SCM, 1988.

*Shaping New Vision: Gender and Values in American Culture,* edited by Clarissa W. Atkinson, Constance H. Buchanan and Margaret R. Miles. Harvard Women's Studies in Religion Series. Ann Arbor and London: UMI Research Press, 1987.

*Immaculate and Powerful: The Female in Sacred Image and Social Reality,* edited by Clarissa W. Atkinson, Constance H. Buchanan, and Margaret R. Miles. "Introduction" by Margaret R. Miles. Boston: Beacon, 1985; British ed., Wellingborough: Crucible, 1987.

*Image as Insight: Visual Understanding in Western Christianity and Secular Culture.* Boston: Beacon, 1985.

*Fullness of Life: Historical Foundations for a New Asceticism.* Philadelphia: Westminster, 1981.

*Augustine on the Body.* American Academy of Religion Dissertation Series 31. Missoula, Mont.: Scholars, 1979.


## Chapters in Books


"Not Nameless but Unnamed: The Woman Torn from Augustine's Side." In *Feminist Interpretations of Augustine,* edited by Judith Stark. Rereading the Canon. University Park: Pennsylvania State University Press, 2005.

"Passion for Social Justice and *The Passion of the Christ.*" In *The Passion of the Christ: Biblical and Theological Perspectives,* edited by Timothy K. Beal and Tod Linafelt. Chicago: University of Chicago Press, 2005.

"North African Christianity in the Roman Period." In *African Spirituality: Forms, Meanings, and Expressions*, edited by Jacob K. Olupona. World Spirituality 3. New York: Crossroad, 2000.

"Disney Spirituality: An Oxymoron?" In *Riding on Faith: Essays on Religion, Culture, and the World of Disney*, edited by Laurie Zoloth and Simon Harek. American Academy of Religion: Religion and Culture Series, 1999. Reprinted from *Christian Spirituality Bulletin* (Spring, 1999).

"Image." In *Critical Terms for Religious Studies*, edited by Mark C. Taylor, 160–72. Chicago: University of Chicago Press, 1997.

"Carnal Abominations: The Female Body as Grotesque." In *The Grotesque in Art and Literature*, edited by James Luther Adams and Wilson Yates, 149–68. Grand Rapids: Eerdmans, 1997.

"What You See Is What You Get: Religion on Primetime Fiction Television." In *Religion and Primetime Television*, edited by Michael Suman. Westport, Conn.: Praeger, 1997.

"Happiness in Motion: Desire and Delight." In *In Pursuit of Happiness*, edited by Leroy S. Rouner, 38–56. Boston University Studies in Philosophy and Religion 16. Notre Dame: University of Notre Dame Press, 1995.

"Introduction." In *Sex, Priests, and Power: Anatomy of a Crisis*, by A. W. Richard Sipe. New York: Brunner/Mazel, 1995.

"'*Jesus patabilis*': Augustine's Debate with the Manichaeans." In *Faithful Imagining: Essays in Honor of Richard R. Niebuhr*, edited by Sang Lee, Wayne Proudfoot, and Albert Blackwell. Scholars Press Homage Series 19. Atlanta: Scholars, 1995.

"Textual Harassment: Desire and the Female Body." In *The Good Body: Asceticism in Contemporary Culture*, edited by Mary G. Winkler and Letha B. Cole. New Haven: Yale University Press, 1994.

"The Virgin's One Bare Breast: Female Nudity and Religious Meaning in Renaissance Culture." In *The Expanding Discourse: Feminism and Art History*, edited by Norma Broude and Mary D. Garrard. New York: IconEditions, 1992.

"Theory, Theology, and Episcopal Church Women." In *Episcopal Women: Gender, Spirituality, and Commitment*, edited by Catherine M. Prelinger. Religion in America Series. New York: Oxford University Press, 1992.

"Infancy, Parenting and Nourishment in Augustine's *Confessions*." In *The Hunger of the Heart: Reflections on the Confessions of Augustine*, edited by Donald Capps and James E. Dittes. Society for the Scientific Study of Religion Monograph Series 8. West Lafayette, Ind.: Society for the Scientific Study of Religion, 1990.

"The Body and Human Values in Augustine of Hippo." In *Grace, Politics, and Desire: Essays on Augustine*, edited by H. A. Meynell. Calgary: University of Calgary Press, 1990.

"Violence against Women in the Historical Christian West and in North American Secular Culture: The Visual and Textual Evidence." In *Shaping New Vision: Gender and Values in American Culture*, edited by Clarissa W. Atkinson, Constance H. Buchanan and Margaret R. Miles, 11–29. Harvard Women's Studies in Religion Series. Ann Arbor: UMI Research Press, 1987.

"Nudity, Gender, and Religious Meaning in the Italian Renaissance." In *Art as Religious Studies*, edited by Diane Apostolos-Cappadona and Doug Adams. New York: Crossroad 1987.

"Patriarchy as Political Theology: The Establishment of North African Christianity." In *Civil Religion and Political Theology*, edited by Leroy S. Rounder, 169–86. Boston University Studies in Philosophy and Religion 8. Notre Dame: University of Notre Dame Press, 1986.

"The Virgin's One Bare Breast: Female Nudity and Religious Meaning in Renaissance Culture." In *The Female Body in Western Culture: Contemporary Perspectives,* edited by Susan Rubin Suleiman, 193–208. Cambridge: Harvard University Press, 1986.

"The Courage to be Alone, In and Out of Marriage." In *The Feminist Mystic and Other Essays on Women and Spirituality,* edited by Mary E. Giles. New York: Crossroad, 1982.

## Articles

"Mapping Feminist Histories of Religious Traditions." *JFSR* 22.1 (2006).

"Sex and the City (of God): Is Sex Forfeited or Fulfilled in Augustine's Resurrection of Body?" *JAAR* 73 (2005) 307–27.

"Becoming Answerable for What We See." *JAAR* 68 (2000) 471–85. [1999 AAR Presidential Address]

"Disney Spirituality: An Oxymoron?" *Christian Spirituality Bulletin* 7 (Spring, 1999) 13–18.

"Reading For Life: Hermeneutics of Generosity and Suspicion." *STR* 41 (Christmas, 1997) 19–58.

"On Reading Augustine and Augustine's Reading." *Christian Century* 114.17 (May, 1997) 510–14.

"Larry Flynt in Real Life—Social Effects of the Motion Picture 'The People vs. Larry Flynt.'" *Christian Century* 114.14 (April, 1997).

"Religion and Food: The Case of Eating Disorders." *JAAR* 67 (1995) 549–64.

"Fashioning the Self." *Christian Century* 112.8 (March, 1995) 273–75.

"The Revelatory Body: Signorelli's *Resurrection of the Flesh* at Orvieto." *ThEd* 31.1 (1994) 75–90.

"Santa Maria Maggiore's Fifth-Century Mosaics: Triumphal Christianity and the Jews." *HTR* 86 (1993) 155–75.

"A Sea of Love: Marguerite Porete's *A Mirror for Simple Souls.*" *Christian Century* 110.4 (February, 1993).

"Imitation of Christ: Is it Possible in the Twentieth Century?" *Princeton Seminary Bulletin* 10.1 (1989) 7–22.

"Pilgrimage as Metaphor in a Nuclear Age." *ThTo* 40 (1988) 166–79.

Contributor: "A Vision of Feminist Religious Scholarship." *JFSR* 3 (1987) 91–111.

Contributor: "Favorite Books and How They Influence." *Christian Century* 104.17 (May, 1987) 490–95.

"The Body and Human Values in Augustine of Hippo." *Augustinian Heritage* 33.1 (1987) 57–70.

"Hermeneutics of Generosity and Suspicion: Theological Education in a Pluralistic Setting." *ThEd* 13 (Supplement 1987) 34–52.

"Art and Liturgy: Cooperation or Competition?" *Faith and Form* 19 (Spring, 1986) 10–12.

"'The Rope Breaks When It Is Tightest': Luther on the Body, Consciousness, and the Word." *HTR* 77 (1984) 239–58.

"The Pursuit of Lifefulness; In Search of a Method." *Studia Mystica* 7.4 (Winter, 1984) 63–69.

"Voyeurism and Visual Images of Violence." *Christian Century* 101.10 (March, 1984) 305–6.

"El redescubrimiento del asceticismo," *Criterio* 56.1906 (28 July 1983).

"Vision: The Eye of the Body and the Eye of the Mind in St. Augustine's *De trinitate* and the *Confessions.*" *JR* 63 (1983) 125–42.

"The Recovery of Asceticism," *Commonweal* (28 January 1983) 40–43.

"Infancy, Parenting, and Nourishment in Augustine's *Confessions.*" *JAAR* 50 (1982) 349–64.
"The Mystical Method of Meister Eckhart." *Studia Mystica* 4.4 (1981) 57–69.
"Toward a New Asceticism." *Christian Century* 98 (October, 1981) 1097–98.
"Temor y amor en san Augustin," *Augustinus* 26 (July-December, 1981).
"Theology, Anthropology, and the Human Body in Calvin's *Institutes of the Christian Religion.*" *HTR* 74 (1981) 303–23.

www.ingramcontent.com/pod-product-compliance
Lightning Source LLC
LaVergne TN
LVHW020525100826
845148LV00010B/1337